The Complete Round-the-World
Meat Cookbook

The Complete
Round-the-World

MEAT
COOKBOOK

Myra Waldo

Garden City, New York

DOUBLEDAY & COMPANY, INC.

Library of Congress Catalog Card Number 67–11158
Copyright © 1967 by Myra Waldo Schwartz
All Rights Reserved. Printed in the United States of America

Contents

Recipe for ingredients marked with an asterisk (*) may be found by consulting the Index.

Introduction

Meat was prehistoric man's most desired food—when he could get it. He settled for nuts and berries and greenery when he couldn't, but meat was what he always wanted and we haven't changed very much. In fact, the French word for meat, *viande,* and the English word *viand* are both derived from the Latin *vivanda,* which comes from *vivere,* to live, to maintain life. Today, however, eating meat has become a status symbol over almost the entire world, representing the ultimate in quality food.

At first, meat was eaten raw, after being crudely hacked from freshly killed animals. Brains and liver, in particular, were thought to have magical powers, supposedly transmitted to those who ate them. In the course of time, meat became associated with religion. Butchers in ancient times were usually priests, and they made a religious ceremony out of the act of slaughtering cattle. Peculiar customs regarding the consumption of meat arose. For example, about 350 B.C., it became the practice in Greece for whole roasted animals to be served at feasts, regardless of size, one to a person, whether it was a boar or a kid. In Homer's time, anything other than meat was not considered a proper food to serve a gentleman.

Darius, King of Persia, had hundreds of animals served in his palace every day, including camels, oxen, and many varieties of deer. Smoked meats were quite popular then, particularly camel's hump, which was regarded as a great delicacy. It was in Persia too, although some years later, that *kebab* cooking began, the delicious method of roasting cubes of meat on a skewer. This style of cookery spread to most of the countries surrounding Persia, as far as India, and most of Southeast Asia.

The Tartars, those savage invaders from Central Asia who harassed Western Europe, ate raw meat almost exclusively, and perhaps are responsible for our present day steak Tartare. The Tartars traveled on horseback, and usually kept the meat under their saddles. This, unknowingly, was a method of tenderizing the meat, the constant friction breaking down the fibers, a process now accomplished with the flat side of a meat cleaver.

In many countries even today, a man's wealth is judged by the number of cattle he owns. This was true as far back as the early ninth century, when Charlemagne reigned over most of Western Europe, and it is especially true in Africa today. The Massai, a nomadic people of Central Africa, own no land, but travel with their cattle constantly to find food. They have no possessions other than their wandering meat supply.

In Argentina, the gauchos spend months on the fertile pampas allowing enormous herds of cattle to graze. Here, on the pampas, huge barbecues take place, because eating is one of the few pleasures these lonesome men have during the long months away from civilization. Argentina boasts of having the best meat in the world. I do not agree with this. As an over-all statement, I would say that the United States has the best meat of any country. Certain small exceptions come to mind: very young lamb in Italy, baby veal in France, and a small amount of really superior beef produced in Japan. In the Kobe and Matsuzaka regions of Japan, there are cattle raisers who keep only one or two animals at a time, feeding them a beer mash, and massaging them daily to distribute the fat as evenly as possible. This is superb beef of premium quality, but it is hardly typical of the vast majority of Japanese beef.

Man's capacity for meat varies considerably. I remember vividly being in Africa on a safari, hunting for eland, a huge variety of deer. Our native bearers had not eaten meat in several days and were ravenous. The White Hunter shot a superb specimen; upon our return to camp, the natives quickly skinned and cut up the animal, then sat up all night eating, each man consuming about ten pounds. I found this fact almost incredible, but our White Hunter assured me that it was a commonplace occurrence.

On trips to countries all over the world, as food consultant to Pan American World Airways, I am constantly amazed by the national differences in the preparation of meat. Whereas we, in the United States, tend to limit ourselves to broiled or roasted meat, foreign cookery is much more varied. Herbs, spices, and marinades are regularly used to enhance the flavor of meat, particularly in Europe and Asia. Thin pieces of meat, prepared in the Japanese, Korean, or Genghis Khan style (that is, cooked on skewers over an open fire), are delicious as well as economical. Indian spices can be used with inexpensive cuts, quickly turning them into exotic company dishes. In Chinese preparations, tiny slivers of meat are used to garnish and flavor dishes, rather than to form the main ingredient. The *haute cuisine* of France offers literally hundreds of meat recipes. Foreign cooks use the same meats we do in the United States, but with far more imagination. They also make extensive use of the *abats,* or organs, of the animal, such as sweetbreads, liver, and kidneys. New dishes of this type will assist greatly in menu planning.

Recently I did a survey on the foods served at state dinners in ninety foreign countries; invariably the main course was meat, the single most popular being fillet of beef. Although the method of preparation differs from country to country, meat is the most popular of all foods.

In purchasing meat, a trustworthy butcher or reliable meat packer is more than half the battle. But the homemaker should learn to recognize good meat. What satisfies the knowledgable eye will undoubtedly satisfy the palate; rich red beef with streaky marblings of creamy fat is sure to taste as good as it looks.

Beyond this, however, the U. S. Department of Agriculture supervises the distribution of meat, inspects it, and grades it according to factors which determine the flavor, tenderness, and eating qualities. The government grades are identified by a stamp on the cut of meat. Beef, lamb, and veal are graded into prime, choice, good, standard, commercial and utility. Pork is graded too, but because of more uniformity in age of the hogs when they are slaughtered, pork shows fewer differences in quality and there are therefore fewer grades.

The meat packer too may grade his cuts to indicate differences in quality, but since a knowledge of each individual packer's grading scale is necessary for the homemaker to make a decision, she is best advised to follow the U. S. Government's purple stamping (which, incidentally, is made with an edible food coloring and need not be removed before cooking the meat).

Whether to shop at the butcher store or buy your meat at the supermarket in packages is a question of personal preference. Each has its advantages. From the point of timesaving, the butcher can on occasion be more advantageous. He will cut and slice the meat to your specifications, whereas at the supermarket, to get the cut you want, you may have to take it prepacked. Keep your knives sharp, and you can slice, dice, and cube with the best of them. (I would suggest a good professional sharpening from time to time, as the butchers themselves advise.) And as for pounding the fillets and cutlets "paper-thin," as is sometimes required, this is easily done by placing the slices between two sheets of waxed paper and pounding away with the side of your meat cleaver.

There is a grade of meat for every purpose and a cut to fit every budget. The rating of the government or the packer should not necessarily be the guide. Higher grades contain more fat and are usually more tender. They also cost more. But all grades contain the same valuable proteins, minerals, and vitamins, and there is a palatable method of cooking each one of them.

Whether the homemaker has an accommodating butcher or shops in the supermarket, she will be wise to consider the following factors:

1. Choose a dealer who handles high-quality meat.

2. Take advantage of lower prices resulting from heavy seasonal supplies or "specials" of a particular cut.

3. Use the less tender cuts, which, by proper cooking, can be as tasty and flavorful as higher grades.

The following general suggestions will be an aid to getting the most out of your meat purchases.

Oven Roasting. For large tender cuts.

1. Place the meat, fat side up, in a shallow roasting pan. Use a rack under boneless cuts. Season with salt and pepper. Insert a meat thermometer into the thickest part of the roast, being careful that the tip does not touch the bone or rest in fat.

2. Do not add water. Do not cover. Place the roast in a 325° oven and roast to desired degree of doneness as registered on the thermometer, or follow the Timetables for Cooking Meat, given below, for approximate cooking time. Fat melts and bastes the roast as it cooks.

3. Take the roast from the oven and allow to stand for 15 to 20 minutes for easier carving.

Broiling. For small tender cuts such as steaks and chops and for ground meat patties.

1. Place the meat on a rack in the broiler pan.

2. Place the rack so that the surface of the meat is 2½ to 3 inches from the source of heat (farther for thicker cuts). Broil for about half of the time allowed in the tables below. Season, turn, and finish broiling.

3. Except with pork, which should always be well done, the degree of doneness depends upon individual preference, but avoid overcooking. The degree of doneness of steak, however, can get you into an argument with anyone at any time. In any case always serve sizzling hot.

Pan Broiling and Pan Frying. These two methods of cooking are variations of broiling in which the meat is cooked by direct contact with the hot pan instead of the direct heat itself. In pan broiling no fat is added to the pan. In pan frying, a little fat is added. This latter method is used for breaded or floured meats, and for meats low in fat, such as liver or cubed steaks.

Braising. For less tender cuts, and for pork and veal chops, steaks and cutlets, and pork liver.

1. Coat with seasoned flour and brown slowly in a little fat in a heavy preheated pan.

2. Add seasoning and about 1 cup water, broth, cider, tomato juice, wine, etc., and simmer 35 to 40 minutes, depending on thickness.

Stewing. For small pieces of economical, less tender cuts of beef, veal, and lamb.

1. Have meat cut in uniform cubes. Shake in seasoned flour in a paper bag.

2. Brown slowly and evenly in about 2 tablespoons hot fat in a heavy skillet or casserole.

3. Add hot water, broth or other liquid to cover meat, about 2 cups.

4. Cover skillet or casserole tightly and simmer until meat is tender. Do not boil. Slow cooking makes the meat tender and brings out the flavor. Add more liquid if necessary, but don't make a "soup" of it.

5. Add vegetables the last part of cooking time. Do not overcook the vegetables.

6. Remove meat and vegetables and thicken the liquid for gravy. Serve in the container in which it was cooked or in in-

dividual ramekins. Or top with pastry or biscuit dough for a meat pie.

Cooking Meats in Water. For large, less tender cuts and as a step in making soup.

1. Cover the meat with hot water. The meat may first be browned, if you wish.

2. Add seasonings and your choice of herbs, spices, or "seasoning" vegetables such as onion, celery, and leeks.

3. Cover tightly and simmer until meat is tender. Do not overcook.

4. If the meat is to be served cold, cool in the stock in which it was cooked and then store the stock in the refrigerator.

5. For "boiled dinners," add vegetables the last part of the cooking time. Do not overcook the vegetables.

Frozen meats may be cooked from the frozen state or after partial or complete thawing. If the meat is completely frozen, additional time is necessary for cooking. If the meat is partially thawed, cooking time will be only slightly longer; and if completely thawed, no longer than for fresh meat. In preparing commercially frozen meat, follow the package directions.

In general, large frozen roasts will require half again the time; steaks and chops one-fourth to once again the time (to broil, place 4 inches from the source of heat). Pan broiling requires one-fourth to one-half again the time, and the skillet should be very hot. Lower the heat after browning.

Frozen round steak and cubed boneless meat to be braised should be at least partially thawed to facilitate dredging in flour. Frozen ground meat should be thawed in order that it may be shaped.

The seasonings to use for meats vary with individual taste buds. I much prefer freshly ground black pepper, freshly squeezed lemon juice, and freshly ground Parmesan cheese and bread crumbs, which require just a whir of the blender (if these are not available, however, the packaged varieties are an adequate substitute).

The above general suggestions are applicable to all cuts of meat. Specific directions, however, are given in the recipes that follow.

Where it seemed appropriate, I have suggested trimming off the fat. There are two schools of thought about this and you may leave it on if you think it enhances the flavor. Personally I do not.

Most meats have enough invisible fat for proper nourishment, and I prefer to remove the excess. This procedure too I feel will find favor with our generally sedentary society, many of whom are calorie or cholesterol conscious.

In this book, I have attempted to make menu planning easier, and the menus themselves more interesting, by bringing together the classic as well as the lesser known meat dishes from countries around the world.

MYRA WALDO

TIMETABLE FOR ROASTING PORK

	Weight	Oven Temperature Constant	Interior Temperature on Thermometer	Approximate Minutes per Pound
HAM, FRESH:	10–12 pounds	350°	185°	30–35
LOIN:				
Center	3–5 pounds	350°	185°	35–40
Half	5–7 pounds	350°	185°	40–45
SHOULDER:				
Boned and rolled	4–6 pounds	350°	185°	40–45
Cushion	3–5 pounds	350°	185°	35–40

TIMETABLE FOR BROILING MEAT WITH BROILER PREHEATED

	Thickness	TOTAL BROILING TIMES IN MINUTES Rare	Medium	Well done
STEAK:	1 inch	12	15	20
	1½ inches	15	20	25
	2 inches	25	30	35
FLANK STEAK:				
(London broil)		7	9	12
LAMB CHOPS:	1 inch	8	10	12
	1½ inches	12	15	18

Broil meats about 3 inches under source of heat. Preheat the broiler at high heat, then reduce the heat a little.

TIMETABLE FOR ROASTING LAMB

	Weight	Oven Temperature Constant	Interior Temperature on Thermometer	Approximate Minutes per Pound
LEG:	5–8 pounds			
Medium rare		325°	140°–150°	15–20
Well done		325°	175°–180°	25–30
BONED ROLLED ROAST:	3–5 pounds			
Medium rare		325°	140°–150°	20–25
Well done		325°	175°–180°	30–35
SHOULDER:	4–6 pounds			
Medium rare		325°	140°–150°	15–20
Well done		325°	175°–180°	25–30

TIMETABLE FOR ROASTING VEAL

	Weight	Oven Temperature Constant	Interior Temperature on Thermometer	Approximate Minutes per Pound
LEG:	5–8 pounds	325°	170°	20–25
BONED AND ROLLED:	4–6 pounds	325°	170°	35–40
LOIN:	4–6 pounds	325°	170°	25–30
RIBS:	3–5 pounds	325°	170°	25–30
SHOULDER:	5–8 pounds	325°	170°	20–25

TIMETABLE FOR ROASTING BEEF

	Weight	Oven Temperature Constant	Interior Temperature on Thermometer	Approximate Minutes per Pound
STANDING RIB ROAST:	6–8 pounds	325°		
Rare			130°	15–18
Medium			140°–150°	20–22
Well done			160°–170°	25–27
ROLLED ROAST:	6–8 pounds	325°		
Rare			130°	25–30
Medium			140°–150°	33–35
Well done			160°–170°	40–45

The above method produces little shrinkage but does not have a crisp brown exterior. The two-temperature method, that is, searing the meat at a higher heat, then reducing the oven temperature, will result in a brown exterior and a juicy center.

	Weight	Oven Temperature	Interior Temperature on Thermometer	Approximate Total Minutes per Pound
STANDING RIB ROAST:	6–8 pounds	450° for 15 minutes 325° for balance of roasting time		
Rare			130°	15–18
Medium			140°–150°	20–22
Well done			160°–170°	25–27

Beef

The luxury meat of the world deserves respect and care in selection and buying. Look for the U. S. Department of Agriculture purple stamp to be sure you are getting the best grade for your purpose. The cattle range from one to three years old and from 900 to 1300 pounds each when slaughtered. The grades are determined by the aging of the beef and the quality, quantity, and distribution of fat.

"Prime" beef, the top grade, is a cherry red with many tiny streaks of creamy white fat, called marbling, and the more abundant the marbling the more tender and juicy the beef. However, only a small percentage of prime is found in the retail markets. Since there is a high amount of fat loss, most prime goes to restaurants and hotels which are prepared to absorb the expense of the loss in weight.

"Choice" beef, just one step below prime, can be almost as good as prime. It is a little less expensive, and also a little less marbled, which makes it slightly lower in calories. For steaks, fillets, and roast beef, buy prime or choice.

"Good" beef is next, and excellent for stews, pot roasts, and marinated meats.

"Standard" has only a thin covering of fat; and "commercial" and "utility" grades identify meat from older cattle. These grades should be cooked by moist heat and usually for longer periods in order to render them tender and tasteful.

It is economical to take advantage of any bargains your store offers. A large pot roast can serve several purposes: one-third for the pot roast, one-third sliced for dishes such as "Swiss steak," and one-third cubed for stews. A large rib roast can be cut to suit your needs: roast a portion of it, cut some ribs into steaks, braise the short ribs or use them for boiled beef, make stock from the bones, and grind the meat scraps for hash or hamburgers.

BEEF CUTS[1]

Short Loin (7) – The section from which the best steaks are cut, including the porterhouse, containing a fairly large fillet; T-bone, similar to porterhouse but with a smaller fillet; club, Delmonico, shell, all of these are the same cut (but with different names) and are from the small end of the short loin, containing no fillet; fillet, or tenderloin, is the whole fillet removed from the short loin, which can be left in one piece for roasting, or cut into individual steaks. Although fillet is expensive by the pound, there is absolutely no waste.

Sirloin (8) – The section just behind the short loin from which pinbone and sirloin steaks are cut.

Rib (2) – The section which provides standing rib roasts. (There are usually seven ribs from which the butcher cuts your roast.) The first four ribs are best, and if more is needed, it is advisable to buy two three-rib roasts, rather than one five- or six-rib piece. Have the rib bones, called short ribs, cut down short, and use them for braising, boiled beef, or stews. It is impractical to roast less than a two-rib roast. One rib may be broiled or roasted and then cut like a steak.

Flank (6) – An oval-shaped thin boneless cut of meat, usually weighing ¾ to 1½ pounds. Prime or choice flanks are used for London broil. The meat should be scored and then broiled or sautéed very quickly to the rare state. Carve into very thin diagonal slices. Less expensive grades should be braised or used in stews.

Short Plate (5) – The section includes the plate and short ribs and is used for braising, for soups, or in stews. The meat has small bones.

Brisket (4) – A fairly flat cut of meat containing layers of meat, fat, and bones, but the meat is usually sold boned. The first cut is much leaner than the other cuts. Use for pot roast, in soup, or stews. Brisket is the cut most often used for corned beef.

Round and Rump (9, 10) – These sections include round steak, eye round, top round, standing rump, rolled rump, and sirloin tip. All these cuts are excellent for braising, pot roasts, and stews.

[1] The numbers in parentheses refer to the Beef Chart.

Chuck (1, 3) – Includes the arm, blade, shank, and boneless chuck. Good for braising, pot roast and ground beef.

Ground Beef – Preground ground beef or hamburger usually contains a high percentage of fat. It is advisable to buy the meat you want, have it trimmed and then ground to order, or do it yourself. A combination of chuck and sirloin provides a superior type of ground meat, but chuck, top round, shank, neck meat, or flank may all be used. Always keep ground beef refrigerated until time to cook, and use the meat within twenty-four hours. Frozen ground beef should be used within one month.

Marinated Broiled Steak

Sirloin, porterhouse, or
   individual club steaks, cut
   1 inch thick
½ cup olive oil
¼ cup lemon juice
1½ teaspoons salt
½ teaspoon freshly ground
   black pepper
1 clove garlic, minced
1 tablespoon minced parsley
2 tablespoons butter

Trim the fat from the steak. Mix together the oil, lemon juice, salt, pepper, garlic, and parsley. Marinate the steak in the mixture for 3 hours at room temperature, turning frequently. Drain the meat. Broil to desired degree of rareness. Spread the butter over the steak.

Angkor Wat Marinated Steak

4 club steaks, cut 1 inch
   thick
2 cloves garlic, minced
1 teaspoon salt
½ teaspoon freshly ground
   black pepper
Dash Tabasco
2 tablespoons sugar
½ cup soy sauce
1 tablespoon anchovy paste
2 tablespoons dry sherry
½ cup crushed toasted
   peanuts

Trim the fat from the steaks and reserve a piece. Mix together the garlic, salt, pepper, Tabasco, sugar, soy sauce, anchovy paste, and sherry. Marinate the steaks in the mixture for 1 hour at room temperature, turning frequently. Drain the steaks, reserving the marinade.

Rub the reserved fat on a hot broiling pan, and place the steaks on it. Broil 6 minutes on each side, or to desired degree of rareness. While the steaks are broiling, heat the marinade. Add the pan juices and peanuts and pour over the steaks.

Serves 4.

Australian Beef Collops with Bread Sauce

3 pounds top round of
  beef, cut in thin slices
  and pounded flat
2 cups beef broth
1½ teaspoons salt
¼ teaspoon freshly ground
  black pepper
⅛ teaspoon thyme
⅛ teaspoon marjoram

1 cup chopped onions
6 anchovies, coarsely
  chopped
½ cup dried bread cubes
1 tablespoon butter
Sautéed French bread slices
1 lemon, thinly sliced
1 tablespoon capers

Combine the meat in a heavy saucepan with the broth, salt, pepper, thyme, marjoram, and onions. Cover and cook over low heat 1¼ hours.

Transfer the meat to a warm platter and keep hot. Strain the pan juices and return to pan; mix in the anchovies and bread cubes. Cook until slightly thickened. Stir in the butter. Pour the sauce over the meat and surround with sautéed bread. Garnish with lemon slices dotted with capers.

Serves 6.

Esterházy Rostelyos

AUSTRIAN STEAK IN SOUR CREAM SAUCE

6 rib steaks, cut 1 inch
  thick and boned
¼ cup flour
2 teaspoons salt
½ teaspoon freshly ground
  black pepper
4 tablespoons butter
¾ cup chopped onions

1 carrot, grated
¼ pound mushrooms, sliced
2 tablespoons minced
  parsley
1 bay leaf
½ cup water
1 cup sour cream
2 tablespoons capers

Trim the fat from the steaks. Dip the steaks in a mixture of the flour, salt, and pepper. Melt the butter in a large skillet; brown the steaks quickly on both sides. Add the onions, carrot, mushrooms, and parsley; let brown 5 minutes. Add the bay leaf and water. Cover and cook over low heat 15 minutes. Transfer steaks to a heated platter and keep warm.

Discard the bay leaf and purée the gravy in an electric blender or force through a sieve. Return to skillet, blend in the sour cream and capers. Taste for seasoning, heat, and pour over the steaks. *Serves 6.*

Opar Daging

BALI STEAK IN COCONUT CREAM

1½ pounds sirloin steak,
  cut ½ inch thick
½ teaspoon ground cumin
½ teaspoon dried ground
  chili peppers
¼ teaspoon ground
  coriander

3 tablespoons vegetable oil
2 cloves garlic, minced
1½ cups chopped onions
1 teaspoon salt
¾ cup heavy cream
¼ cup flaked coconut

Cut meat in strips 1 inch wide by 2 inches long. Toss with the cumin, chili peppers, and coriander. Heat the oil in a skillet; brown the steak, garlic, and onions in it. Add the salt, cream, and coconut; cook over low heat 10 minutes.

Serves 4–6.

Butterfly Steak

2 tablespoons olive oil	1½ pounds fillet of beef,
1 tablespoon butter	split lengthwise and
⅛ teaspoon sage	pounded lightly
¼ teaspoon rosemary	¾ teaspoon salt
½ teaspoon finely crushed	¼ teaspoon freshly ground
bay leaf	black pepper
	3 tablespoons warm cognac

Heat the oil and butter in a skillet; mix in the sage, rosemary, and bay leaf, then add the meat. Cook over high heat 2 minutes on each side, or to desired degree of rareness. Season the meat with the salt and pepper, pour the cognac over it, and set aflame. Turn the fillet over for a few seconds, then serve.

Serves 4–6.

Chinese Steak and Onions

1½ pounds sirloin steak,	½ teaspoon sugar
cut ¼ inch thick	2 tablespoons soy sauce
5 tablespoons vegetable oil	2 tablespoons dry sherry
4 cups sliced onions	2 tablespoons cornstarch

Cut the steak into narrow slices. Heat half the oil in a skillet and sauté the onions 3 minutes. Add the sugar, 1 tablespoon soy sauce, and 1 tablespoon sherry. Cook a few seconds. Remove onion mixture.

Toss the steak with the cornstarch, remaining soy sauce, and sherry. Heat the remaining oil in a skillet and brown the steak in it. Return the onion mixture to pan and cook 2 minutes.

Serves 6–8.

Pra Ram Long Song

BANGKOK BEEF IN COCONUT MILK

2½ pounds sirloin steak,
  cut ¼ inch thick
2 cups milk
1 cup packaged shredded
  coconut
2 tablespoons oil
1 tablespoon anchovy paste
1 teaspoon sugar
¾ teaspoon dried ground
  chili peppers

¾ cup ground peanuts
4 cloves garlic, minced
½ cup chopped shallots or
  onions
2 teaspoons grated lemon
  rind
2 tablespoons cornstarch
¼ cup heavy cream
1 8-ounce can water
  chestnuts

Cut the meat into 3-inch squares. Combine the milk and coconut in a saucepan. Bring to a boil, remove from the heat, and let stand 30 minutes. Blend in an electric blender or strain, pressing through all the liquid.

Heat the oil in a saucepan; lightly brown the meat in it. Add the coconut milk and anchovy paste. Cover and cook over low heat 30 minutes.

Pound or chop to a paste the sugar, chili peppers, peanuts, garlic, shallots or onions, and lemon rind. Stir into the saucepan. Mix together the cornstarch and cream; add, and bring to the boiling point, stirring steadily. Cook over low heat 5 minutes.

Slice the water chestnuts and cook in their own liquid for 5 minutes. Drain and place on a hot platter. Pour the meat mixture over them. *Serves 6–8.*

Mørbradsteg Bøf København

DANISH STEAK WITH BLUE CHEESE

4-pound sirloin steak,
  cut 1½ inches thick
¼ pound blue cheese
¼ pound (1 stick) butter

2 teaspoons salt
½ teaspoon freshly ground
  black pepper
Thinly sliced radishes

Trim the fat from the steak. Mash blue cheese and butter together until smooth. Broil the steak 8 minutes on each side, or to desired degree of rareness. Sprinkle with the salt and pepper when turning. When steak is done, immediately spread it with the cheese mixture, so that it melts slightly. Garnish with the radish slices. *Serves 6–8.*

Steak Diane

2 boneless club steaks, cut
½ inch thick
4 tablespoons butter
¼ cup green onions
(scallions)
2 tablespoons chopped
chives

1 tablespoon minced parsley
1 tablespoon Worcestershire
sauce
1 tablespoon meat glaze
1 teaspoon salt
⅛ teaspoon freshly ground
black pepper

Cut the steaks horizontally through the middle, leaving them connected at one side. Open the steaks like a book and pound lightly to flatten the connected sides.

Melt 2 tablespoons butter in a large skillet; sauté the green onions 5 minutes. Add the steaks and sear quickly on both sides. Add the chives, parsley, Worcestershire sauce, meat glaze, and remaining butter. Stir well and turn steaks; sprinkle with the salt and pepper. *Serves 2.*

Boeuf à la Flamande

FLEMISH BEEF SLICES

2 tablespoons butter
4 pounds rump or round
of beef, cut in ½-inch
slices
2 cups sliced onions
1 cup sliced carrots

2 teaspoons salt
½ teaspoon freshly ground
black pepper
2 cups beer
1 tablespoon sugar
¼ teaspoon thyme

Melt the butter in a Dutch oven or heavy skillet and brown the beef. Add the onions; cook until browned. Pour off the fat. Add the carrots, salt, pepper, beer, and sugar. Cover and cook over low heat 1½ hours. Add the thyme, re-cover, and cook 15 minutes longer, or until the meat is tender. *Serves 8–10.*

Biftek Sauté

FRENCH SKILLET STEAK

2-pound club or rib steak, cut 1 inch thick
2 tablespoons vegetable oil
3 tablespoons butter
1½ teaspoons salt
½ teaspoon freshly ground black pepper
½ cup beef broth, dry red wine, or water

Cut slits in the fatty edges of the steak to keep it from curling. Be sure the meat is dry.

Heat the oil and 1 tablespoon butter in a heavy skillet until it bubbles but doesn't brown. Add the steak and cook over medium heat 4 minutes on each side or to desired degree of rareness.

Transfer to a hot platter, season with salt and pepper, and keep hot. Immediately pour the fat out of the skillet. To the skillet add the liquid. Cook over high heat, scraping the bottom of browned particles, until liquid is reduced to one-third. Remove from heat and mix in the remaining butter until melted and amalgamated with the pan juices. Pour over the steak.

Serves 2–3.

Hong Kong Fried Beef with Snow Pea Pods

1½ pounds sirloin steak, cut ⅛ inch thick
3 tablespoons dry sherry
½ cup soy sauce
2 tablespoons cornstarch
1 pound snow pea pods
¾ cup vegetable oil
2 cloves garlic, minced
1 teaspoon sugar

Cut the meat into matchlike strips. Toss the beef with the sherry, 3 tablespoons of the soy sauce, and the cornstarch. Let stand 20 minutes.

Remove strings from snow peas and cook in boiling water 3 minutes or until tender but still crisp. Heat ½ cup oil in a skillet and sauté the beef until browned.

Heat the remaining oil in another skillet and sauté the snow peas 2 minutes. Stir in the beef, garlic, sugar, and remaining soy sauce. Mix well.

Serves 4–6.

Vindaloo

EAST INDIAN SPICED BEEF

2 pounds chuck steak	4 cloves garlic, minced
1 tablespoon crushed coriander	1½ teaspoons salt
1 tablespoon turmeric	1 cup minced onions
1 teaspoon crushed cuminseed	½ cup cider vinegar
2 teaspoons powdered ginger	3 tablespoons butter
	2 bay leaves

Cut the meat in narrow strips about 3 inches long. Pound to a paste the coriander, turmeric, cumin, ginger, garlic, salt, and onions. Blend in the vinegar. Add the meat and toss until pieces are covered with the spice mixture. Cover and refrigerate 24 hours.

Melt the butter in a skillet; add the undrained meat and the bay leaves. Cover and cook over low heat 45 minutes, or until the meat is tender. Stir frequently, and remove the cover for the last 5 minutes.

Serves 4–6.

Bistecca Cacciatora

BEEFSTEAK, ITALIAN HUNTER'S STYLE

4 rib steaks, cut 1 inch
thick
1 tablespoon olive oil
1½ teaspoons salt
½ teaspoon freshly ground
black pepper

3 tablespoons Marsala or
sherry wine
¾ cup dry red wine
2 tablespoons water
1 clove garlic, minced
½ teaspoon fennel seeds
1 teaspoon tomato paste

Trim the fat from the steaks. Heat the oil in a skillet; sauté the steaks 5 minutes on each side or to desired degree of rareness. Season with the salt and pepper. Transfer the steaks to a heated platter and keep warm. Add the wines to the skillet and cook over high heat, scraping bottom of pan, until reduced to ⅓ the original quantity. Blend in the water, garlic, fennel seeds, and tomato paste; cook 1 minute longer. Pour over the steaks and serve.
Serves 4.

Bife à la Madère

BEEF SLICES IN MADEIRA WINE

4 pounds eye round or
rump of beef, cut in 1-
inch slices
2 teaspoons salt
½ teaspoon freshly ground
black pepper
2 cloves garlic, minced
3 slices bacon, half cooked
2 cups thinly sliced onions

12 small carrots, scraped
1 pound mushrooms, sliced
2 teaspoons finely chopped
bay leaf
¼ cup minced parsley
¼ pound cooked ham,
chopped
1½ cups Madeira wine
¼ cup cognac

Trim the fat from the beef. Rub meat with a mixture of the salt, pepper, and garlic. Arrange the sliced bacon on the bottom of a Dutch oven or heavy casserole. Spread ⅓ of the onions, carrots, mushrooms, bay leaf, parsley, and chopped ham over the bacon. Arrange some slices of beef over it, then repeat the layers of vegetables and meat twice more. Add the Madeira. Heat the cognac in a ladle, set aflame, and pour into the pan. When flames die, cover, bring to a boil, and then cook over low heat 2½ hours, shaking the pan occasionally.

Serves 8–10.

Bistecca alla Pizzaiola

NEAPOLITAN STEAK

2 rib steaks, cut 1 inch
   thick
2 tablespoons butter
1 tablespoon olive oil
1 clove garlic, minced
¾ cup peeled chopped
   tomatoes

1¼ teaspoons salt
¼ teaspoon freshly ground
   black pepper
¼ teaspoon orégano
2 tablespoons chopped
   parsley

Trim most of the fat from the steaks. Heat the butter and oil in a skillet. Brown the steaks in it over high heat 3 minutes on each side. Add the garlic, tomatoes, salt, pepper, and orégano. Cook over low heat, turning the steaks a few times, 10 minutes, or to desired degree of rareness. Sprinkle with the parsley.

Serves 2–4.

Banke Oksekjøtt

NORWEGIAN BEEF RAGOUT

3 pounds eye round, sliced
   1 inch thick
2 teaspoons salt
½ teaspoon freshly ground
   black pepper
¼ cup flour

2 slices bacon, diced
2 tablespoons butter
1 cup thinly sliced onions
2 cups hot beef broth
1 bay leaf

Dip the meat slices in a mixture of the salt, pepper, and flour. In a Dutch oven or heavy casserole, lightly brown the bacon. Pour off the fat. Add the butter and onions; sauté 5 minutes. Add the meat; cook over medium heat until browned on both sides. Stir in the broth and bay leaf; cover and cook over low heat 1½ hours. Taste for seasoning, and discard bay leaf.

Serves 6–8.

Bistecca Parmigiana

PARMA BREADED STEAK

6 club steaks, cut ½ inch thick and boned
2 eggs, beaten
⅓ cup grated Parmesan cheese
⅓ cup dry bread crumbs
⅓ cup vegetable oil
¾ cup chopped onions
1 teaspoon salt
¼ teaspoon freshly ground black pepper
½ teaspoon orégano
2 8-ounce cans tomato sauce
¼ cup water
½ pound mozzarella cheese, sliced thin

Trim the fat from the steaks. Dip the steaks in the eggs, then in a mixture of the cheese and bread crumbs. Let stand while preparing the sauce.

Heat 2 tablespoons of the oil in a skillet; sauté the onions 5 minutes. Mix in the salt, pepper, orégano, tomato sauce, and water. Bring to a boil and cook over low heat 10 minutes. Taste for seasoning.

Heat the remaining oil in a skillet; quickly brown the steaks in it on both sides over high heat. Arrange the steaks in a single layer in a shallow baking dish. Pour ¾ of the sauce over the steaks and arrange the mozzarella cheese over the sauce. Pour the remaining sauce on top.

Bake in a 425° oven 10 minutes, or until the cheese is melted.
Serves 6.

Steak au Poivre

PEPPER STEAK

1 tablespoon black
  peppercorns, coarsely
  crushed
2 boneless shell steaks, cut
  1 inch thick
1 tablespoon olive oil
2 tablespoons sweet butter

1 tablespoon chopped
  shallots or onions
1 cup dry red wine
1 teaspoon prepared French-
  style mustard
1 teaspoon Worcestershire
  sauce

With the heel of the hand, press the crushed peppercorns heavily into both sides of the steaks.

Heat the oil in a skillet; brown the steaks in it on both sides, then cook 4 minutes longer, or to desired degree of rareness. While the steaks are browning, melt 1 tablespoon butter in a skillet; sauté the shallots 2 minutes. Add the wine to the shallots; cook over high heat until reduced to ¼ the original quantity. Remove from the heat and immediately stir in the mustard, Worcestershire sauce, and the remaining butter, broken into small pieces. Transfer the steaks to a heated serving dish and pour the sauce over them. *Serves 2–4.*

Chinese Pepper Steak

1½ pounds sirloin steak
3 tablespoons vegetable oil
¾ teaspoon salt
¼ teaspoon pepper
1 cup thinly sliced green
  onions (scallions)

1 clove garlic, minced
2 cups sliced green peppers
2 cups sliced celery
½ cup beef broth
2 teaspoons cornstarch
2 tablespoons soy sauce

Cut the steak in pencil-thin strips 2 inches long. Heat the oil in a heavy skillet; brown the meat in it. Mix in the salt, pepper, green onions, garlic, green peppers, and celery; cook 2 minutes, stirring almost continuously. Stir in the broth; cook over low heat 5 minutes. Mix together the cornstarch and soy sauce until smooth; add to the meat mixture, and bring to the boiling point, stirring steadily. Cook 3 minutes longer. Serve with rice or noodles. *Serves 4–6.*

Australian Pepper Steak

4 tablespoons vegetable oil
2 pounds round steak,
  sliced ⅛ inch thick
2 cups chopped onions
2 cloves garlic, minced
1½ teaspoons salt
½ teaspoon freshly ground
  black pepper

2 cups diced green peppers
1½ cups beef broth
1½ cups drained canned
  tomatoes
1½ tablespoons cornstarch
1 tablespoon Worcestershire
  sauce
¼ cup water

Heat the oil in a large skillet; add the steak, onions, and garlic and cook over high heat until the meat is browned. Add the salt, pepper, green peppers, broth, and tomatoes; cover and cook over low heat 15 minutes.

Mix together the cornstarch, Worcestershire sauce, and water and stir into the meat mixture. Cook, stirring steadily until thickened. Serve with mashed potatoes. *Serves 6–8.*

Lot Ju Kair Ngow

HANGCHOW PEPPER STEAK

3 pounds top sirloin
1 tablespoon cornstarch
¼ cup water
3 cloves garlic, minced
1 teaspoon powdered ginger
¾ cup peanut or vegetable
  oil
1½ cups chopped onions

2 green peppers, cut
  julienne
2 tomatoes, cut into small
  wedges
1 teaspoon sugar
1 teaspoon salt
¼ teaspoon freshly ground
  black pepper
1 cup chicken broth
4 tablespoons dry sherry

Cut the meat into pencil-thin strips 2 inches long. Mix the cornstarch with the water until smooth; add the garlic, ginger, and beef. Heat the oil in a heavy skillet and cook the meat mixture in it over high heat 5 minutes, stirring constantly. Remove the meat. Add the onions, green peppers, and tomatoes. Cook over medium heat, stirring frequently, 2 minutes. Stir in the sugar, salt, pepper, broth, and sherry. Cook 3 minutes. Add the meat and cook 2 minutes longer, stirring. Serve immediately with boiled rice.
Serves 6–8.

Swiss Steak

3 pounds round steak, cut in 1 piece 1½ inches thick	1 cup chopped onions
	1 20-ounce can tomatoes, drained
¼ cup flour	¾ cup sliced carrots
3 teaspoons salt	¾ cup sliced celery
½ teaspoon pepper	1 bay leaf
3 tablespoons vegetable oil	

Dip the meat in a mixture of the flour, salt, and pepper, pounding it in with the side of a knife or edge of a plate. Heat the oil in a Dutch oven or deep skillet; add the steak and brown well on both sides. Mix in the onions, tomatoes, carrots, celery, and bay leaf; cover and cook over low heat 1½ hours or until tender. Transfer the meat to a warm platter and keep hot. Strain the gravy and skim the fat from the surface. Pour over the meat.
Serves 6–8.

Taipei Sliced Sautéed Beef

1½ pounds sirloin steak, cut ⅛ inch thick	⅛ teaspoon Tabasco
	⅓ cup soy sauce
½ cup chopped green onions (scallions)	2 tablespoons sugar
1 clove garlic, minced	2 tablespoons sesame or vegetable oil

Cut the steak into narrow slices. Mix together the green onions, garlic, Tabasco, soy sauce, sugar, and oil and pour over the meat. Marinate 15 minutes. Drain the beef and sauté in an ungreased skillet over high heat until lightly browned.
Serves 4–6.

Beef Stroganoff

2 pounds round steak, cut
   ½ inch thick and
   pounded lightly
3 tablespoons butter
½ cup minced onions
½ pound mushrooms, sliced
1¼ teaspoons salt

¼ teaspoon freshly ground
   black pepper
1 clove garlic, minced
1 teaspoon Worcestershire
   sauce
4 tablespoons tomato sauce
2 cups sour cream

Cut the steak into strips 1½ inches long by ¼ inch wide. Melt the butter in a skillet; sauté the onions 5 minutes. Add the meat and let brown. Mix in the mushrooms, salt, pepper, garlic, Worcestershire sauce, and tomato sauce. Cover and cook over low heat 30 minutes or until the meat is tender. Just before serving, mix in the sour cream. Heat but do not let boil. Serve with rice or noodles.
Serves 4–6.

Szechuan Shredded Beef with Chili Peppers

1½ pounds sirloin steak,
   cut ⅛ inch thick
3 tablespoons dry sherry
3 tablespoons soy sauce
1 teaspoon minced garlic

1 teaspoon minced ginger
1 cup vegetable oil
1 cup grated carrots
½ teaspoon dried ground
   chili peppers

Cut the steak into matchlike pieces. Mix together the sherry, soy sauce, garlic, and ginger; marinate the beef in the mixture 30 minutes. Heat the oil in a skillet; add the undrained beef, the carrots, and chili peppers and cook over high heat, stirring constantly, 3 minutes. Drain off all the oil and cook 3 minutes longer. *Serves 4–6.*

Taiwan Shredded Beef with Onions

1½ pounds sirloin steak, cut ⅛ inch thick	¾ cup vegetable oil
1 tablespoon cornstarch	2 cups chopped onions
4 tablespoons soy sauce	1½ teaspoons salt
	¼ teaspoon freshly ground black pepper

Cut the steak into matchlike pieces; toss with the cornstarch and 2 tablespoons soy sauce. Heat 4 tablespoons oil in a skillet; add the onions and salt and sauté 3 minutes. Remove the onions. Heat the remaining oil in the skillet. Sauté the meat until lightly browned. Mix in the onions, remaining soy sauce, and the pepper, stirring well for 1 minute.
Serves 4–6.

Bistecca alla Fiorentina

TUSCAN BEEFSTEAK

2 club steaks, cut 2 inches thick	2 tablespoons minced parsley
4 tablespoons olive oil	½ teaspoon salt
2 tablespoons lemon juice	⅛ teaspoon freshly ground black pepper
1 clove garlic, minced	3 tablespoons butter

Trim the fat from the steaks and rub them with a mixture of the oil, lemon juice, garlic, and parsley. Let stand 1 hour at room temperature. Broil the steaks 6 minutes on each side or to desired degree of rareness. Sprinkle with salt and pepper and put dots of the butter on it before slicing.
Serves 2.

Émincé de Boeuf Bourgeoise

BEEF FILLETS WITH CHICKEN LIVER SAUCE

8 fillets of beef, cut ¼
  inch thick
4 tablespoons butter
½ pound chicken livers
1 teaspoon salt
¼ teaspoon freshly ground
  black pepper

1 bay leaf
¼ teaspoon thyme
¼ cup dry sherry
¼ cup beef broth
2 tablespoons cognac

Trim the fat from the meat, and cut the fillets in very narrow strips. Melt 2 tablespoons of the butter in a skillet; sauté the livers over high heat 3 minutes. Add the salt, pepper, bay leaf, and thyme; sauté 2 minutes. Discard the bay leaf; place the livers, sherry, and broth in an electric blender and purée until smooth. Return to skillet and keep warm while preparing the meat.

Melt the remaining butter in a skillet; sauté the meat over high heat 2 minutes, shaking the pan frequently. Heat the cognac and pour over the meat; set aflame. Transfer the meat to a heated serving dish and pour the liver sauce over it. *Serves 6–8.*

Tournedos Rossini

FILLET OF BEEF WITH FOIE GRAS

6 fillets of beef, cut 1 inch
  thick
1 small can truffles
⅓ cup Madeira or sweet
  sherry
3 tablespoons butter

1¼ teaspoons salt
¼ teaspoon freshly ground
  black pepper
6 slices sautéed French
  bread
6 slices pâté de foie gras

Have the fillets trimmed of fat and tied up in a nice shape. Drain and slice the truffles, reserving the liquid.

In a small saucepan, combine the Madeira or sweet sherry, truffles and their liquid, and 1 tablespoon of the butter; cook over very low heat while preparing the fillets.

Melt the remaining butter in a skillet until it begins to brown. Sauté the fillets in it 3 minutes on each side or to desired degree of rareness. Season with the salt and pepper. Cut off the strings. Put a fillet on each slice of sautéed bread, over it a slice of *foie gras,* and then pour the truffle sauce over it.

Serves 6.

Tournedos Lyonnaise

SAUTÉED BEEF FILLETS WITH ONIONS

6 fillets of beef, cut ½ inch thick	¼ teaspoon freshly ground black pepper
6 tablespoons butter	1 teaspoon wine vinegar
1½ cups thinly sliced onions	1 tablespoon minced parsley
1½ teaspoons salt	

Trim the fat from the fillets and pound them lightly. Melt 3 table-spoons of the butter in a skillet; sauté the onions until delicately browned. Remove the onions. Melt the remaining butter in the skillet and brown the beef on both sides. Return the onions and season with the salt and pepper. Cook over low heat 5 minutes, turning the fillets once. Sprinkle with the vinegar and parsley.

Serves 6.

Filet à la Souillac

FILLET OF BEEF WITH PÂTÉ SAUCE

6 fillets of beef, cut 1½ inches thick	2 tablespoons butter
1½ teaspoons salt	⅓ cup Marsala or sweet sherry
½ teaspoon freshly ground black pepper	4-ounce can pâté de foie gras, mashed
2 tablespoons olive oil	¼ cup warmed cognac

Trim the fat from the meat. Season the fillets with the salt and pepper and rub with the oil. Let stand at room temperature 1 hour.

Melt the butter in a skillet; cook the fillets over high heat until well browned on both sides. Remove the fillets and keep warm. Add the wine and *pâté* to the skillet; cook over low heat, stirring constantly until smooth. Return the fillets; cook 3 minutes, turning the fillets once. Pour the cognac over the fillets and set aflame; shake the pan until flames die. Transfer steaks to a serving dish and pour the pan juices over them.

Serves 6.

Filetto Ripieno

ITALIAN STUFFED BEEF FILLETS

4 fillets of beef, cut 1 inch thick	**¼ teaspoon freshly ground black pepper**
4 slices prosciutto (ham)	**⅓ cup flour**
4 thin slices mozzarella cheese	**2 eggs, beaten**
1 teaspoon salt	**½ cup dry bread crumbs**
	6 tablespoons butter

Trim the fat from the fillets and cut the steaks horizontally through the middle, leaving 1 side attached. Open like a book and pound each side lightly to flatten. Put a slice of ham and a slice of cheese on each, then close up, pressing the edges together firmly. Season with the salt and pepper, dip in the flour, then in the eggs, and finally in the bread crumbs.

Melt the butter in a skillet; sauté the steaks 4 minutes on each side, or to desired degree of rareness.

Serves 4.

Tournedos Dauphinoise

FILLETS OF BEEF WITH PORT WINE SAUCE

6 tablespoons butter
¾ pound mushrooms, sliced
1½ teaspoons salt
½ teaspoon freshly ground
 black pepper
2 teaspoons flour

1 cup heavy cream
6 beef fillets, cut ¾ inch
 thick
6 slices sautéed French
 bread, cut ½ inch thick
½ cup port

Melt 3 tablespoons of the butter in a saucepan; sauté the mushrooms 5 minutes. Blend in the salt, pepper, and flour, then stir in the cream until thickened. Keep hot while preparing the fillets.

Melt the remaining butter in a skillet. Trim the fat from the fillets. Place the fillets in the skillet and sauté 3 minutes on each side, or to desired degree of rareness. Put a fillet on each slice of sautéed bread and arrange the slices in a ring on a hot platter. Put the mushroom mixture in the center. Stir the port into the pan juices, and, scraping the bottom of browned particles, bring to a boil. Pour over each fillet.
Serves 6.

Filetto alla Noce

BEEF FILLETS WITH RAISIN-NUT SAUCE

12 fillets of beef, cut 1 inch
 thick
¼ pound (1 stick) butter
3 slices prosciutto (ham),
 diced
¾ cup chopped mushrooms
2 tablespoons Marsala or
 sweet sherry
2 tablespoons flour

1 cup beef broth
¼ cup pine nuts or slivered
 almonds
1 tablespoon seedless
 raisins
½ cup flour
1½ teaspoons salt
½ teaspoon freshly ground
 black pepper

Trim the fat from the meat. Melt 2 tablespoons butter in a skillet; sauté the ham 3 minutes, remove the ham. Add 3 tablespoons butter to the skillet; sauté the mushrooms 3 minutes. Return the ham and add the wine; cook over medium heat 3 minutes. Mix the flour and broth, add to the skillet and bring to the boiling point, stirring steadily. Mix in the nuts and raisins and cook over low heat 10 minutes. Prepare the steaks meanwhile.

Dip the beef slices in a mixture of the flour, salt, and pepper. Melt the remaining butter in a skillet; quickly brown the meat on both sides. Add to the sauce, scraping the meat glaze from the bottom. Cook 2 minutes longer. Transfer to a heated serving dish.

Serves 6–8.

Filetto alla Siciliana

SICILIAN SAUTÉED FILLETS OF BEEF

6 fillets of beef, cut 1 inch thick	**½ teaspoon freshly ground black pepper**
4 tablespoons butter	**½ cup Marsala or sherry**
2 tablespoons olive oil	**¼ cup water**
1 cup sliced onions	**1 tablespoon minced parsley**
1¾ teaspoons salt	

Have a narrow strip of fat tied around each fillet. Heat 2 tablespoons of the butter and the oil in a skillet; sauté the onions 10 minutes. Remove the onions. In the fat remaining, cook the fillets over high heat 2 minutes on each side. Stir in the remaining butter, the salt, pepper, wine, water, parsley, and sautéed onions. Cook 4 minutes longer, or to desired degree of rareness. Turn the meat once.

Serves 6.

Singapore Barbecued Filet Mignon

4 tablespoons soy sauce
2 tablespoons dry sherry
1 teaspoon powdered ginger
1 teaspoon sugar
⅛ teaspoon freshly ground
  black pepper

1 pound fillet of beef,
  sliced and pounded
  thin
½ cup vegetable oil
2 pounds spinach, washed,
  drained, and shredded
1 teaspoon salt

Mix together the soy sauce, sherry, ginger, sugar, and pepper. Marinate the beef in it 2 hours. Drain.

Heat 3 tablespoons oil in a skillet and fry the spinach 3 minutes, stirring frequently. Mix in the salt.

In a separate skillet heat the remaining oil. Sauté the beef over high heat 2 minutes, turning the slices once. Arrange spinach on a hot serving dish, arrange beef on top and pour juices from sautéed beef over all. *Serves 4–6.*

Filet à la Lucullus

FILLET OF BEEF WITH SWEETBREADS

¼ cup olive oil
¾ cup chopped onions
1 clove garlic, minced
¾ cup grated carrots
2 slices bacon, half
  cooked and drained
2 tablespoons flour
2 cups beef broth
¼ cup dry white wine
2 tablespoons tomato paste
1 bay leaf

3 tablespoons chopped
  parsley
2 pairs Parboiled Calfs'
  Sweetbreads*
⅓ cup bread crumbs
2 teaspoons salt
½ teaspoon freshly ground
  black pepper
6 tablespoons butter
2 egg yolks
6 beef fillets, cut 1 inch
  thick

Heat the olive oil in a saucepan. Add the onions, garlic, carrots, and bacon. Sauté 10 minutes. Sprinkle with the flour, stirring until smooth. Add the broth and bring to the boiling point, stirring constantly. Add the wine, tomato paste, and bay leaf. Cover and cook over very low heat 1 hour. Taste for seasoning. Discard the bay leaf and stir in parsley.

Cut each sweetbread in half. Mix the bread crumbs with 1 teaspoon of the salt and ¼ teaspoon of the pepper. Dip 6 pieces of sweetbread in it. Heat half the butter in a skillet. Brown the breaded sweetbreads in it. Keep warm. Dice the remaining sweetbreads.

Beat the egg yolks. Gradually add the wine sauce, stirring constantly to prevent curdling. Return to heat and cook until thickened, stirring constantly. Do not allow to boil. Add the diced sweetbreads.

Heat the remaining butter in a skillet. Trim the fat from the fillets. Place the fillets in the skillet and cook over high heat 4 minutes on each side. Sprinkle with remaining salt and pepper. Arrange the fillets on a heated serving dish with a sweetbread over each. Pour the sauce over them. *Serves 6.*

Churrasco Rebosado

URUGUAY BEEF FILLETS IN BATTER

6 fillets of beef, cut ¾ inch thick	1½ teaspoons salt
3 eggs, separated	½ teaspoon freshly ground black pepper
1 cup sifted flour	½ teaspoon marjoram
¼ cup milk	1 cup vegetable oil
1 clove garlic, minced	

Trim the fat from the meat. Beat the egg yolks in a bowl, add the flour, and beat until smooth. Beat in the milk, garlic, salt, pepper, and marjoram until smooth. Beat the egg whites until stiff, and fold into the flour mixture. Dip the steaks in the batter, coating them well. Heat the oil in a skillet until it smokes; fry the steaks in it for 2 minutes on each side. Serve with sautéed potatoes and a green salad. *Serves 6.*

Filetti al Vermouth

ITALIAN BEEF FILLETS WITH VERMOUTH

4 fillets of beef, cut 1 inch
   thick
4 tablespoons butter
½ cup sliced green olives
1 teaspoon salt

¼ teaspoon freshly ground
   black pepper
¼ cup dry vermouth
¼ cup heavy cream

Trim the fat from the fillets. Melt the butter in a skillet; add the fillets and olives. Cook over high heat 2 minutes on each side, shaking the pan a few times. Sprinkle the meat with the salt and pepper. Add the vermouth and cream. Cook over low heat 2 minutes longer on each side for rare meat, or to desired degree of rareness.

Arrange the fillets on a hot serving dish and pour the sauce over them.

Serves 4.

Tariyaki

JAPANESE SKEWERED STEAK

2 pounds sirloin steak, cut
   ½ inch thick
1 16-ounce can pineapple
   chunks
1 cup soy sauce
⅓ cup dry sherry

1½ teaspoons powdered
   ginger
4 tablespoons brown sugar
2 teaspoons grated onion
1 clove garlic, minced
18 mushroom caps
1 tablespoon cornstarch

Cut the steak into 1-inch squares. Drain the pineapple and reserve the juice. Mix together the soy sauce, sherry, ginger, brown sugar, onion, and garlic. Marinate the steak in the mixture 3 hours at room temperature. Drain, reserving the marinade. Alternating the steak, pineapple, and mushrooms, thread on 6 skewers, starting and ending with steak. Broil 4 minutes, or to desired degree of rareness, turning the skewers to brown all sides.

Mix together the cornstarch, marinade, and 3 tablespoons of the reserved pineapple juice. Cook over low heat until thickened, stirring steadily. Serve with the meat. *Serves 6.*

Anticuchos

PERUVIAN SKEWERED STEAK

2 pounds sirloin steak, cut in 1-inch cubes
1½ teaspoons salt
½ teaspoon dried ground chili peppers
6 peppercorns

¼ teaspoon saffron
3 cloves garlic, minced
1 cup wine vinegar
½ cup water
¼ cup olive oil

Trim the fat from the meat. In a bowl, mix together the salt, chili peppers, peppercorns, saffron, garlic, vinegar, and water. Add the meat and marinate overnight in the refrigerator.

Drain the meat; reserve the marinade. Thread the meat on 4–6 skewers; brush with the olive oil. Broil as close to the heat as possible 6 minutes, or to desired degree of rareness, turning and basting frequently with the marinade. *Serves 4–6.*

California Skewered Steak

2 pounds boneless sirloin tip, cut in 1½-inch cubes
½ cup orange juice
2 tablespoons lemon juice
¼ cup olive oil
2 tablespoons wine vinegar
½ cup chopped onions
1 tablespoon Worcestershire sauce

¾ teaspoon salt
¼ teaspoon freshly ground black pepper
¼ teaspoon dry mustard
¾ teaspoon thyme
12 small white onions
2 small zucchini
2 green peppers
6 cherry tomatoes

Trim the fat from the meat. Mix together the orange juice, lemon juice, olive oil, wine vinegar, chopped onions, Worcestershire sauce, salt, pepper, mustard, and thyme. Place the meat in the mixture and marinate overnight in the refrigerator.

Peel the white onions and cook in boiling salted water 10 minutes. Drain. Cut the zucchini in 1-inch lengths. Cut each pepper into 6 pieces.

About 1½ hours before serving time, drain the meat, reserving the marinade. Thread 6 skewers, alternating the meat and vegetables. Broil over charcoal or under a hot broiler 10 minutes, turning the skewers and basting frequently with the reserved marinade.

Serves 6.

Rib Roast of Beef

To roast beef accurately, use a thermometer. Insert a heavy skewer in the fleshy part of the meat, making sure it does not touch the bone or rest in fat, then withdraw the skewer and insert the thermometer. When the thermometer registers 130° the beef is very rare, 140° is medium rare, 160° medium well done, and 170° indicates very well done. The trimmed weight will, of course, give you an approximate time, but the shape of the roast and the amount of bone and fat will all affect the cooking time. There are two methods of roasting beef, and you can choose the one you prefer.

When the beef is seared in a 450° oven for 25 minutes, then roasted at 325° for the remaining time, it will be brown and crisp outside and juicy inside, but there will be some shrinkage of the meat. For this method (if you do not have a meat thermometer), allow 15 minutes per pound for rare, 18–20 for medium, and 25 for well done.

If the beef is roasted in a one-temperature moderate oven, 325°, there will be minimum shrinkage but the outside will not be crisp or very brown. For this method, allow 20 minutes per pound for rare, 25 for medium, 30 for well done. For cosmopolitan restaurant-style rare, try 15 minutes per pound. The slices will look beautiful, but they may occasionally moo at you.

Experienced cooks can judge the doneness of meat by pressing it with a finger. The firmer the meat is, the more well done it is.

Place the ribs in a shallow roasting pan, fat side up—a rack is not needed, for the bones make their own rack—and proceed according to the preferred method—it is not necessary to season or baste the meat. Transfer the meat to a hot platter and let stand at room temperature for 20 minutes before carving.

Rotisserie Roast Beef

It is not advisable to roast more than 2 to 3 ribs on a rotisserie. Have the rib bones cut down very short and the meat tied securely. Insert the spit diagonally so that it balances the meat. Insert the meat thermometer as close to the center as possible, being sure it doesn't touch the spit or bones or rest in fat. Roast until thermometer registers 130° for very rare, 140° for medium rare, 160° for medium well done, and 170° for very well done. Or if you haven't a thermometer, allow 15 minutes a pound for rare, 18 for medium, and 22 for well done.

Australian Rib Roast in Wine

5-pound boned rib roast
¼ cup flour
4 tablespoons butter
1 cup chopped onions
½ cup chopped carrots
1 clove garlic, minced
2 tablespoons warm cognac

2 cups dry red wine
2 teaspoons salt
½ teaspoon freshly ground
   black pepper
1 bay leaf
½ teaspoon thyme

Rub the meat with the flour. Heat the butter in a Dutch oven or heavy skillet and brown the meat on all sides. Add the onions, carrots, and garlic and cook until browned. Set the cognac aflame and pour it over the meat. Mix in the wine, salt, pepper, bay leaf, and thyme. Cover and bake in a 325° oven 1¼ hours, or to desired degree of rareness.

Transfer the meat to a hot platter. Taste the gravy for seasoning, strain, and serve in a gravy boat.
Serves 8–10.

Lendenbraten

BAVARIAN ROAST BEEF WITH SOUR CREAM GRAVY

3 tablespoons butter	**½ cup peeled, diced**
5-pound boned rib roast	**tomatoes**
1 cup sliced onions	**½ cup water**
2½ teaspoons salt	**2 tablespoons flour**
½ teaspoon freshly ground	**½ cup dry white wine**
black pepper	**1 cup sour cream**

Melt the butter in a Dutch oven or heavy skillet and brown the meat on all sides. Add the onions and let brown. Pour off the fat; sprinkle with the salt and pepper; add the tomatoes and water, and roast in a 400° oven 1 hour and 10 minutes, or to desired degree of rareness. Baste frequently. Transfer the meat to a hot platter.

Mix the flour with the wine and add to the pan juices. Bring to the boiling point, stirring steadily. Blend in the sour cream. Taste for seasoning. Heat and serve in a sauceboat.
Serves 8–10.

Filet de Boeuf Braisé

BRAISED FILLET OF BEEF

4-pound fillet of beef	**1½ cups thinly sliced**
2 teaspoons salt	**onions**
½ teaspoon freshly ground	**1 cup thinly sliced carrots**
black pepper	**1 bay leaf**
2 tablespoons olive oil	

Have the fillet completely covered with a thin layer of beef fat. Rub with the salt and pepper.

Heat the oil in a Dutch oven or heavy skillet. Spread the onions, carrots, and bay leaf on the bottom and place the fillet on top. Cover and cook over medium heat 30 minutes (for rare), or to desired degree of rareness. Turn the meat frequently. Serve with sautéed mushrooms.

Serves 6–8.

Selkäliha-Paisti

FINNISH ROAST FILLET OF BEEF WITH SOUR CREAM SAUCE

4-pound fillet of beef	½ cup grated carrots
2 teaspoons salt	2 tablespoons chopped
½ teaspoon freshly ground	parsley
black pepper	1 tablespoon flour
1 tablespoon olive oil	1 cup sour cream
½ cup chopped onions	

Trim the fat from the meat. Rub the meat with the salt and pepper. Rub a shallow roasting pan with the oil and in it place the meat, onions, carrots, and parsley. Roast in a 400° oven 40 minutes, or to desired degree of rareness. Transfer meat to a heated serving dish.

Pour off all but 2 tablespoons of fat from the pan. Place the pan over direct low heat and blend in the flour until browned. Add the sour cream, stirring steadily until thickened, but do not let boil. Strain over the meat.

Serves 8–10.

Filet de Boeuf Farci

FRENCH PROVINCIAL STUFFED FILLET OF BEEF

4-pound fillet of beef	3 tablespoons minced
2½ teaspoons salt	parsley
¾ teaspoon freshly ground	⅛ teaspoon thyme
black pepper	⅛ teaspoon finely chopped
Truffles	bay leaf
1 cup Madeira or sweet	4-ounce can pâté de foie
sherry	gras
6 tablespoons butter	1 tablespoon cognac
¾ cup chopped onions	1 long piece beef fat
¾ cup chopped carrots	1 tablespoon vegetable oil
½ cup chopped celery	2 cups beef broth
¼ cup chopped cooked ham	1 tablespoon cornstarch

Cut a deep slit lengthwise on the flat side of the fillet, leaving both ends intact. Season the slit with a little of the salt and pepper.

Slice the truffles (as many as you like or can afford) and marinate in ⅓ cup of the wine in a covered cup for 30 minutes.

Melt 3 tablespoons of the butter in a small saucepan; add the onions, carrots, celery, ham, parsley, thyme, bay leaf, ½ teaspoon of the salt, and ⅛ teaspoon of the pepper. Cover and cook over low heat 10 minutes, but do not let brown. Add ⅓ cup of the wine; cook over high heat until wine is almost evaporated.

Mash the *pâté,* and beat in the cognac and 1 tablespoon of remaining wine. Spread in the slit of the fillet. Drain the truffles (reserve marinade) and arrange in a row on the *pâté* mixture. Close the slit and cover with the fat; tie securely with thread at close intervals.

In a heavy pan, heat the oil and 2 tablespoons of the butter. Brown the fillet in it lightly on all sides. Pour off the fat. Sprinkle the meat with the remaining salt and pepper. Spread the cooked vegetables over the meat and add the broth. Bring to a boil, cover and bake in a 350° oven 35 minutes (for rare), or to desired degree of rareness. Baste a few times. Remove the meat, cut the strings, and discard the fat. Place slit side down on a hot serving platter.

Pour the pan juices into a saucepan. Skim the fat. Add the truffle marinade. Cook over high heat 5 minutes. Mix the cornstarch with the remaining wine, stir into the sauce with the remaining butter until thickened, then cook 3 minutes longer. Taste for seasoning.

Cut the fillet into ¾-inch slices, pour a little sauce over it and serve the rest in a sauceboat.

Serves 8.

Filet de Boeuf en Chemise

FILLET OF BEEF IN PASTRY I

MEAT:

4-pound fillet of beef
2 tablespoons butter
1 onion, sliced
2 carrots, sliced
2 sprigs parsley
1 bay leaf
⅛ teaspoon sage
¼ teaspoon thyme
⅛ teaspoon nutmeg
1½ cups dry white wine
½ pound mushrooms, chopped and sautéed

¼ pound ham, chopped and sautéed
2 slices bacon, browned and chopped
¼ pound chicken livers, chopped and sautéed
¾ teaspoon salt
¼ teaspoon freshly ground black pepper
1 egg, beaten
1 tablespoon cognac
1 to 2 tablespoons Madeira

Trim the fat from the meat. Melt the butter in a Dutch oven or heavy skillet. Add the onion, carrots, parsley, bay leaf, sage, thyme, and nutmeg and sauté 5 minutes. Combine the sautéed mixture with the white wine in a bowl; add the fillet and marinate 24 hours in the refrigerator, turning from time to time.

Mix together the sautéed mushrooms, ham, bacon, and chicken livers and season with the salt and pepper. Mix in the beaten egg and 2 tablespoons of the marinade. Add the cognac. Drain the meat, pat dry with paper towels, and cover the meat completely with the chicken-liver mixture. Wrap in the pastry.

PASTRY:

2 cups sifted flour   **½ pound (2 sticks) butter**
¾ teaspoon salt   **⅓ cup ice water**

Sift the flour and salt into a bowl. Cut in 1½ sticks of the butter. Add the water, tossing with a fork until the particles adhere. Form into a ball, wrap, and chill 20 minutes. Roll out the dough on a lightly floured surface, dot with the remaining butter, fold over into thirds, and roll out again. Fold over and roll again. Chill 1 hour before rolling out into a sheet large enough to cover the meat completely.

Place meat in the center of the pastry. Bring edges of dough together, moisten with water, and seal well. Cut 2 or 3 small holes in the top. Place on a baking pan.

Bake in a preheated 425° oven for about 15 minutes per pound for rare beef (20 minutes per pound for medium), pouring the Madeira through the holes in the crust toward the end of the baking time. Turn off oven and allow to stand 15 minutes before slicing.

Serves 8–10.

VARIATION:

Filet de Boeuf Wellington
FILLET OF BEEF IN PASTRY II

Prepare the pastry as directed in the recipe for Fillet of Beef in Pastry I. Roast a 4-pound fillet in a 425° oven 20 minutes. Allow the meat to cool thoroughly. Mash the contents of an 8-ounce can of *pâté de foie gras,* and spread on all sides of the fillet. Roll out the pastry and completely enclose the meat in it, sealing the edges. Place on a baking sheet, flat side down, and bake in a preheated 425° oven 25 minutes, or until the pastry is browned. Let stand 5 minutes before slicing. Serve with *Sauce Périgueux.**

Bife a la Portugaise

FILLET OF BEEF WITH MUSHROOMS

3-pound fillet of beef
3 tablespoons butter
¾ pound mushrooms,
  chopped
¼ pound ham, chopped
2 teaspoons salt

¾ teaspoons freshly ground
  black pepper
6 slices French bread, cut
  ½ inch thick
2 tablespoons olive oil

Place the meat in a shallow roasting pan and roast in a 450° oven 35 minutes (for rare), or to desired degree of rareness, turning the meat to brown on all sides.

Melt the butter in a skillet; sauté the mushrooms 5 minutes. Add the ham; cook 5 minutes. Season with ½ teaspoon of the salt and ¼ teaspoon of the pepper.

Sauté the bread in the hot olive oil until delicately browned on both sides.

Cut the fillet into 6 slices and season with the remaining salt and pepper. Place a slice of meat on each piece of sautéed bread; cover with the mushroom mixture.

Serves 6.

Carne Asado

SOUTH AMERICAN MARINATED ROAST BEEF

6-pound rolled roast of beef
2 teaspoons salt
1 teaspoon freshly ground
  black pepper
2 cloves garlic, minced
1½ cups dry red wine
½ cup wine vinegar

¼ cup olive oil
2 cups chopped onions
1 cup chopped green
  peppers
2 cups peeled, diced
  tomatoes
1 bay leaf

Rub the meat with a mixture of the salt, pepper, and garlic. Marinate the meat in a mixture of the wine and vinegar in the refrigerator 24 hours, turning a few times. Remove from refrigerator 2 hours before roasting.

Drain the meat, reserving the marinade. Heat the oil in a roasting pan over direct heat and brown the meat on all sides. Pour off half the fat. Add the onions, green peppers, tomatoes, bay leaf, and half the marinade. Roast the meat in a 350° oven 1¼ hours (for rare), or to desired degree of rareness, basting frequently with the pan drippings and the remaining marinade. Transfer the meat to a hot platter. Discard the bay leaf, skim off the fat, and purée the gravy in an electric blender or force through a sieve. If too thick, add a little water. Taste for seasoning, heat, and serve in a sauceboat.

Serves 8–10.

Rindfleisch mit Äpfeln

GERMAN BEEF SLICES WITH APPLES

4 tablespoons butter
3 tablespoons flour
½ teaspoon salt
2 cups beef broth
1 tablespoon lemon juice
2 teaspoons sugar

4 tart apples, cored, cut in
　1-inch slices
12 thin slices roast or
　boiled beef
1 dill pickle, sliced thin

Melt the butter in a saucepan, blend in the flour and salt until browned. Gradually add the broth, stirring steadily to the boiling point. Add the lemon juice, sugar, and apple slices. Cook over low heat 10 minutes. Add the beef. Cook 5 minutes. Just before serving, add the sliced pickle.

Serves 4–6.

Roast Beef Slices in Mushroom Sauce

2 tablespoons butter
¾ cup thinly sliced onions
¼ pound mushrooms, sliced
2 tablespoons flour
1 teaspoon salt
¼ teaspoon freshly ground
   black pepper

¼ teaspoon marjoram
⅓ cup dry red wine
¾ cup beef broth
¼ cup ketchup
8 slices roast beef, cut ¼
   inch thick

Melt the butter in a saucepan; sauté the onions 5 minutes. Add the mushrooms; sauté 5 minutes. Blend in the flour, salt, pepper, and marjoram. Add the wine, broth, and ketchup and bring to the boiling point, stirring steadily. Cook over low heat 10 minutes. Add the beef, heat, and taste for seasoning.
Serves 4.

Deviled Short Ribs

3 pounds short ribs of
   beef, cut in serving-sized
   pieces
2 teaspoons salt
½ teaspoon freshly ground
   black pepper
1 teaspoon chili powder
½ teaspoon sugar

2 tablespoons lemon juice
2 tablespoons prepared
   mustard
¼ cup vegetable oil
¼ cup chopped onions
1 clove garlic, minced
1 tablespoon flour
¾ cup beef broth

Trim the fat from the meat. Mix together the salt, pepper, chili powder, sugar, lemon juice, mustard, oil, onions, and garlic; pour over the ribs. Cover and marinate 2 hours at room temperature, turning the meat several times. Drain, reserving the marinade.

Arrange the ribs on a rack in a shallow roasting pan; bake in a 425° oven 30 minutes or until browned. Pour off the fat. Add the reserved marinade, reduce the heat to 350°, cover, and bake 1½ hours longer or until tender. Transfer ribs to a hot platter. Skim the fat from the gravy. Place pan over direct heat. Mix the flour with the broth and stir into the pan juices until thickened. Pour over the ribs. *Serves 4–6.*

Deviled Roast Beef Slices

6 slices roast beef, cut ¼ inch thick	**1 teaspoon dry mustard**
⅓ cup flour	**1 teaspoon chili powder**
½ teaspoon salt	**4 tablespoons butter**

Dip the roast beef slices in a mixture of the flour, salt, mustard, and chili powder, coating both sides well. Melt the butter in a skillet; brown the slices on both sides over high heat.
Serves 3–6.

Sztufada

POLISH SHORT RIBS OF BEEF

4 pounds short ribs of beef, cut in serving-sized pieces	**1½ teaspoons salt**
2 slices bacon, diced	**2 tablespoons caraway seeds**
1½ cups chopped onions	**⅓ cup wine vinegar**
	1 cup boiling water

Trim the fat from the meat. In a Dutch oven or deep skillet, cook the bacon until it begins to brown. Add the onions and short ribs; cook over medium heat 10 minutes, stirring frequently. Mix in the salt, caraway seeds, vinegar, and water. Cover and bake in a 350° oven 2 hours, or until the meat is tender. Baste frequently, adding a little more boiling water if container becomes dry. Skim the fat before serving.
Serves 4–6.

Texas Short Ribs of Beef

4 pounds short ribs of beef,
   cut in serving-sized pieces
¼ cup flour
2 tablespoons vegetable oil
1 cup chopped onions
1½ teaspoons salt
½ teaspoon freshly ground
   black pepper

½ teaspoon thyme
¼ cup boiling water
1½ cups bottled chili sauce
1 bay leaf
¼ cup chopped dill pickles

Trim the fat from the meat. Sprinkle the ribs with the flour. Heat the oil in a Dutch oven or heavy saucepan and brown the meat. Pour off the fat. Add the onions and cook until browned; mix in the salt, pepper, thyme, and water. Cover and cook over low heat 1¼ hours. Add the chili sauce, bay leaf, and pickles. Re-cover and cook 1 hour longer or until meat is very tender.
Serves 6–8.

Vullen Oni Kapp

NETHERLANDS BEEF BIRDS WITH ONIONS

1½ pounds round steak, cut
   in 6 slices and pounded
   thin
2 teaspoons salt
¼ teaspoon freshly ground
   black pepper
¼ teaspoon marjoram

6 small white onions
¼ cup flour
2 tablespoons vegetable oil
1 20-ounce can tomatoes
2 tablespoons prepared
   horseradish

Season the meat with the salt and pepper; sprinkle the top sides with the marjoram. Place an onion on each and roll up; tie with thread or fasten with toothpicks. Roll the birds in the flour.

Heat the oil in a heavy skillet and brown the rolls on all sides. Pour off the fat. Add the tomatoes and horseradish; cover and cook over low heat 1½ hours. Taste for seasoning.
Serves 6.

Roulade à la Suisse

SWISS BEEF BIRDS

12 beef fillets, sliced thin and pounded flat	½ cup grated Swiss cheese
1¼ teaspoons salt	¼ cup chopped parsley
½ teaspoon freshly ground black pepper	3 tablespoons butter
	1 cup peeled, chopped tomatoes
½ teaspoon thyme	¾ cup dry white wine
⅛ teaspoon nutmeg	¼ pound mushrooms, sliced
½ cup chopped ham	1 bay leaf

Trim the fat from the meat. Season 1 side of each fillet with the salt, pepper, thyme, and nutmeg. On the unseasoned side, spread a mixture of the ham, cheese, and parsley. Roll up and fasten with toothpicks or tie with thread.

Melt the butter in a deep skillet; brown the rolls on all sides. Add the tomatoes, wine, mushrooms, and bay leaf. Bring to a boil and cook over low heat 20 minutes. Taste for seasoning. Discard bay leaf. *Serves 6.*

Paupiettes de Boeuf

BEEF ROLLS

1 pound ground pork	½ teaspoon freshly ground black pepper
2 tablespoons sweet sherry	
¼ teaspoon thyme	4 tablespoons butter
¼ teaspoon marjoram	2 cups dry red wine
3 pounds round steak, cut in 12 ½-inch slices and pounded very thin	2 onions, thinly sliced
	1 clove garlic, minced
	1 carrot, thinly sliced
2½ teaspoons salt	1 bay leaf
	1 tablespoon flour

Mix the ground pork with the sherry, thyme, and marjoram; spread a little of the mixture on each slice of beef. Roll up and tie with thread or fasten with toothpicks. Season with salt and pepper. Melt the butter in a skillet and brown the rolls on all sides. Remove the rolls. Add the wine to the skillet and bring to a boil, scraping up the browned particles.

Spread the onions, garlic, carrot, and bay leaf on the bottom of the skillet.

Arrange the beef rolls on top. Sprinkle with the flour. Cover and cook over low heat 1½ hours or until meat is tender, turning the rolls frequently. Taste for seasoning.

Serves 6.

Benløse Fugle

DANISH BEEF ROLLS

¼ pound bacon	2 teaspoons salt
2 pounds top round of beef, cut in thin slices and pounded flat	½ teaspoon freshly ground black pepper
1 cup chopped onions	4 tablespoons butter
½ cup chopped mushrooms	1 cup beef broth
3 gherkins, sliced	¼ teaspoon thyme
¼ cup flour	2 tablespoons chopped parsley

Place a slice of bacon on each slice of meat, then some of a mixture of the onions, mushrooms, and gherkins. Roll up and tie with thread or secure with toothpicks. Roll in a mixture of the flour, salt, and pepper.

Melt the butter in a skillet and brown the rolls on all sides. Add the broth, thyme, and parsley. Cover and cook over low heat 45 minutes, or until tender. Transfer the rolls to a hot platter and remove fastenings. Skim the fat and thicken the gravy if necessary with a little flour and water.

Serves 4–6.

Liharullia

FINNISH BEEF ROLLS

8 fillets of beef, cut ¼ inch thick and pounded very thin	8 slices bacon, half cooked
	3 tablespoons butter
	1½ tablespoons flour
1 teaspoon salt	1 cup boiling beef broth
½ teaspoon freshly ground black pepper	or water
	¼ cup sour cream

Trim the fat from the meat. Sprinkle with salt and pepper, and put a piece of bacon on each slice. Roll up and tie with string or fasten with toothpicks. Melt the butter in a skillet and brown the rolls on all sides. Blend in the flour, then stir in the beef broth. Cover and cook over low heat 25 minutes. Transfer the rolls to a hot platter and remove fastenings. Blend the sour cream into the pan juices. Heat, but do not let boil, and pour over the rolls.
Serves 4.

Manzo Ripieno I

ITALIAN BEEF ROLL

2-pound flank steak, pounded thin	¼ pound cooked tongue, cut julienne
2 slices white bread	1 egg, beaten
½ cup milk	2½ teaspoons salt
¼ pound chicken livers, diced	¾ teaspoon freshly ground black pepper
¾ cup chopped onions	¾ teaspoon orégano
¼ cup chopped celery	3 tablespoons olive oil
¼ cup minced parsley	2 cups beef broth
¼ cup grated Parmesan cheese	

Trim the fat from the meat. Soak the bread in the milk 10 minutes; drain and mash smooth. Combine with the livers, onions, celery, parsley, cheese, tongue, egg, 1 teaspoon of the salt, ¼ teaspoon of the pepper, and ¼ teaspoon of the orégano. Spread on the steak; roll up and tie with string. Heat the oil in a Dutch oven or heavy skillet and brown the roll on all sides. Sprinkle with the remaining salt, pepper, and orégano; add the broth. Cover and cook over low heat 2 hours, or until tender. Let meat stand at room temperature for 20 minutes. Remove the string and slice. *Serves 4–6.*

Manzo Ripieno II

ITALIAN BEEF ROLL WITH CHICKEN LIVER STUFFING

2 pounds top sirloin, cut in 1 piece and pounded thin

2 slices white bread, trimmed

½ cup dry white wine

¼ pound raw chicken livers, diced

¾ cup chopped onions

¼ cup chopped celery

¼ cup minced parsley

¼ cup grated Parmesan cheese

¼ pound cooked ham, cut julienne

1 egg, beaten

2½ teaspoons salt

¾ teaspoon freshly ground black pepper

¾ teaspoon orégano

3 tablespoons olive oil

1½ cups beef broth

Trim the fat from the meat. Soak the bread in the wine 10 minutes; drain and mash smooth. Combine the bread with the livers, onions, celery, parsley, cheese, ham, egg, 1 teaspoon of the salt, ¼ teaspoon of the pepper, and ¼ teaspoon of the orégano. Spread on the steak; roll up and tie with string.

Heat the oil in a Dutch oven or heavy deep skillet and brown the roll on all sides. Sprinkle with the remaining salt, pepper, and orégano; add the broth. Cover and cook over low heat 2 hours or until tender, turning occasionally. Let stand at room temperature 15 minutes before slicing. Remove the string. Serve hot or cold. *Serves 6–8.*

Rinderroulade

GERMAN BEEF ROLLS

12 thin slices top sirloin, pounded thin	6 slices bacon, half cooked and shredded
1½ teaspoons salt	¼ cup flour
¼ teaspoon freshly ground black pepper	½ cup boiling water
6 tablespoons butter	½ cup peeled, chopped tomatoes
1 cup chopped onions	½ cup sour cream
1 cup pumpernickel crumbs	

Trim the fat from the meat. Season with the salt and pepper.
Melt 2 tablespoons of the butter in a skillet; sauté the onions
10 minutes. Mix in the bread crumbs and bacon. Taste for
seasoning. Spread some of the mixture on each piece of meat and
roll up. Tie with thread or fasten with skewers. Roll in the flour.

Melt the remaining butter in a skillet and brown the rolls on all
sides. Add the water and tomatoes. Cover and cook over low heat
1½ hours, or until tender. Transfer the rolls to a hot platter and
remove the fastenings. Stir the sour cream into the gravy and taste
for seasoning.

Serves 6.

Asticciole alla Calabrese

ITALIAN PROVINCIAL BEEF ROLLS

12 fillets of beef, cut ½ inch thick and pounded thin	1½ teaspoons salt
12 thin slices mozzarella cheese	½ teaspoon freshly ground black pepper
4 Italian or other spicy sausages, sliced and sautéed	1 teaspoon crushed bay leaves
	3 tablespoons olive oil

Trim the fat from the meat. On each fillet place a slice of cheese and some sausage slices. Roll up the beef and fasten with toothpicks or tie with thread. Rub the rolls with the salt, pepper, and bay leaves, and brush with the oil. Broil under a hot broiler 15 minutes, turning to brown all sides. Transfer to a hot platter and remove the fastenings. *Serves 6.*

Braciola alla Lucania

ITALIAN BEEF ROLL WITH GIBLET STUFFING

¼ cup seedless raisins
3 tablespoons butter
½ pound chicken giblets, chopped
1 cup fresh fine bread crumbs
½ cup chopped parsley
2 cloves garlic, minced
¼ pound salami, chopped
3 hard-cooked eggs, mashed
1½ teaspoons salt
¾ teaspoon freshly ground black pepper

½ cup coarsely chopped pine nuts or almonds
3 pounds top round, cut in 1 piece and pounded thin
¼ cup olive oil
½ cup chopped onions
1 29-ounce can Italian-style tomatoes
1 cup water
¼ cup tomato paste

Soak the raisins in hot water 10 minutes. Drain. Melt the butter in a skillet; sauté the giblets 10 minutes. Mix together the raisins, giblets, bread crumbs, parsley, garlic, salami, eggs, ½ teaspoon of the salt, ¼ teaspoon of the pepper, and the nuts. Spread on the meat and roll up jelly-roll fashion. Tie with heavy string.

Heat the oil in a Dutch oven or heavy casserole. Brown the meat and onions in it. Add the tomatoes, water, tomato paste, and remaining salt and pepper. Cover and cook over low heat 2½ hours, or until meat is tender. Taste for seasoning. Transfer the meat to a heated platter and remove the string. Cut into slices and serve with the gravy. *Serves 6–8.*

Morcón

MINDANAO BEEF ROLL

2-pound boneless sirloin
  steak, cut ¼ inch thick
  and pounded thin
¼ cup wine vinegar
2 cloves garlic, minced
¾ teaspoon freshly ground
  black pepper
½ pound ham, cut julienne
2 Spanish or other spicy
  sausages, sliced

3 hard-cooked eggs, sliced
½ cup chopped green olives
1 cup vegetable oil
1 cup chopped onions
1 bay leaf
2 cups boiling water
1 8-ounce can tomato sauce
2 tomatoes, diced
2 teaspoons salt

Marinate the meat in a mixture of vinegar, garlic, and pepper 30 minutes. Drain and dry the meat, reserving the marinade.

Put the steak on a flat surface; on it arrange the ham, sausages, and eggs in successive rows. Sprinkle the olives over all. Roll up and tie securely with string. Heat the oil in a deep skillet until it bubbles and brown the meat roll on all sides. Pour off all the oil carefully; add the onions, bay leaf, water, tomato sauce, tomatoes, salt, and reserved marinade. Cover and cook over low heat 1½ hours or until meat is tender. Taste for seasoning. Transfer the meat to a hot platter. Let stand 15 minutes, remove the string, and slice. Arrange on a platter and pour sauce over all.
Serves 6–8.

Oxrulader

SWEDISH BEEF ROLLS

1½ pounds fillet of beef,
  pounded very thin
1¼ teaspoons salt
½ teaspoon freshly ground
  black pepper
⅛ teaspoon nutmeg
¼ pound ham, chopped

¼ cup chopped parsley
3 tablespoons butter
¼ pound mushrooms, sliced
1 bay leaf
1 cup beef broth
¼ cup heavy cream

Trim the fat from the fillets. Sprinkle them with the salt, pepper, and nutmeg. On the unseasoned side, spread a mixture of the ham and parsley. Roll up and fasten with toothpicks or tie with thread.

Melt the butter in a deep skillet; brown the rolls on all sides. Add the mushrooms, bay leaf, and broth. Bring to a boil and cook over low heat 20 minutes. Transfer the rolls to a hot platter and remove the fastenings. Add the cream to the pan. Taste for seasoning, discard the bay leaf, and pour over the rolls.
Serves 8.

Boeuf Rôti à la Bordelaise

BORDEAUX MARINATED BEEF

4-pound rump or eye round of beef	½ teaspoon thyme
½ cup olive oil	2 teaspoons salt
1 cup dry red wine	½ teaspoon freshly ground black pepper
1 cup sliced onions	3 strips bacon, half cooked and drained
¼ cup chopped parsley	
1 bay leaf	1 tablespoon wine vinegar

Trim the fat from the beef. Mix together the oil, wine, onions, parsley, bay leaf, thyme, salt, and pepper. Marinate the meat in the mixture overnight in the refrigerator.

Put the strips of bacon on the bottom of a roasting pan. Drain the meat, strain and reserve the marinade, and spread the vegetables on the bacon. Put the meat on top and add ½ cup of the marinade. Roast in a 350° oven 1¾ hours, or until tender, basting frequently. Transfer meat to a hot serving platter and keep hot.

Strain the pan juices into a saucepan and add the remaining marinade. Cook over high heat 5 minutes; skim off the fat. Mix in the wine vinegar, bring to a boil, and serve separately in a sauceboat.
Serves 8–10.

Boeuf à la Mode

FRENCH POT ROAST

4-pound pot roast of beef
1 cup sliced onions
2 bay leaves
2½ teaspoons salt
½ teaspoon freshly ground
  black pepper
¼ teaspoon thyme
⅛ teaspoon mace
2 tablespoons wine vinegar

4 tablespoons olive oil
4 cups dry red wine
1 veal knuckle
2 cloves garlic, minced
3 tablespoons cognac
12 small white onions
4 carrots, quartered
12 mushroom caps

Have the meat larded, that is, strips of fat inserted in the meat. In a glass or pottery bowl, combine the sliced onions, bay leaves, salt, pepper, thyme, mace, vinegar, 2 tablespoons of the oil, and 1½ cups of the wine. Add the meat, cover, and let marinate in the refrigerator at least 24 hours, turning occasionally. Drain and reserve marinade. Dry the meat.

Heat the remaining oil in a skillet; brown the meat on all sides over high heat. Transfer the meat to a Dutch oven or deep heavy saucepan. Pour the marinade into the skillet and bring to a boil, scraping the brown particles from the bottom of the skillet. Add to the Dutch oven or saucepan, along with the veal knuckle, garlic, and cognac. Cover, bring to a boil over direct heat, then roast in a 350° oven 2½ hours, adding some of half the remaining wine from time to time. Discard the veal knuckle and skim fat from the gravy. Add the white onions, carrots, mushrooms, and remaining wine; re-cover and roast 1 hour longer. Taste for seasoning. Carve the meat and arrange on a hot serving platter. Surround with the vegetables and pour some of the gravy over the meat. Serve the rest of the gravy in a sauceboat.

Serves 6–8.

Boeuf à la Mode en Gelée
COLD BEEF IN ASPIC

Prepare the meat as directed for *Boeuf à la Mode* (above). Arrange the vegetables in an attractive design on the bottom of a mold or casserole. Strips of pimientos, sliced olives, and green peas may be used too.

Slice the cooked beef thinly and arrange slices over the vegetables. Overlap the slices. Strain the gravy and remove all the fat. Soften 1 envelope (1 tablespoon) of gelatin in 2 tablespoons of water and stir into the hot gravy until dissolved. Pour over the meat. Chill until firm. Carefully turn out of mold onto a chilled platter. *Serves 6–8.*

Sauerbraten
GERMAN POT ROAST

4-pound pot roast of beef	2 cloves garlic, minced
2 cups cider vinegar	1 cup sliced onions
1 cup water	2 tablespoons butter
8 peppercorns	1½ cups chopped onions
3 cloves	1 cup grated carrots
2 bay leaves	2 tablespoons sugar
2½ teaspoons salt	1 cup sour cream

Trim the fat from the meat. In a saucepan, combine the vinegar, water, peppercorns, cloves, bay leaves, salt, garlic, and sliced onions. Bring to a boil. Place the meat in a glass or pottery bowl and pour the hot mixture over it. Let marinate 2–3 days in the refrigerator, turning the meat a few times. Drain and dry the meat; strain and reserve 2 cups of the marinade.

Heat the butter in a Dutch oven or heavy skillet and brown the meat on all sides. Add the chopped onions and continue browning. Add the carrots, sugar, and marinade. Cover tightly and cook over low heat 3 hours or until tender. Skim the fat and taste for seasoning. Transfer meat to a hot platter; stir the sour cream into the gravy. *Serves 8–10.*

Lábas-Sült

HUNGARIAN POT ROAST

4-pound pot roast of beef
¼ cup flour
2 teaspoons salt
½ teaspoon freshly ground
   black pepper
2 tablespoons vegetable oil

1½ cups sliced onions
1 tablespoon paprika
2 teaspoons caraway seeds
1 8-ounce can tomato sauce
½ cup water

Trim the fat from the meat. Rub the meat with a mixture of the flour, salt, and pepper. Heat the oil in a Dutch oven or heavy saucepan; brown the meat in it on all sides. Mix in the onions until browned. Add the paprika, caraway seeds, tomato sauce, and water. Cover and cook over low heat 3 hours or until tender. Serve with egg barley.

Serves 8–10.

Pieczén Husarska

POT ROAST, HUSSAR STYLE

3-pound eye round of beef
4 tablespoons butter
1 cup sliced onions
½ cup vodka
2½ teaspoons salt
¾ teaspoon freshly ground
   black pepper

1½ cups chopped onions
½ cup fresh bread crumbs
2 tablespoons minced
   parsley
1 tablespoon flour
½ cup beef broth

Put the meat in a hot skillet and brown it on all sides. Drain. Melt 2 tablespoons of the butter in a Dutch oven; add the meat and sliced onions. Cook until onions brown. Add the vodka, 2 teaspoons of the salt, and ½ teaspoon of the pepper. Cover and cook over low heat 2 hours, turning the meat a few times. Remove the meat from the pan, and cut into thin slices, leaving the bottom uncut.

While the meat is cooking, melt the remaining butter in a skillet; sauté the chopped onions 5 minutes. Mix in the bread crumbs, parsley, and remaining salt and pepper. Put some of the mixture between every second slice. Press meat together into original shape. Return to the pan and sprinkle the top with the flour. Add the broth, re-cover, and cook 30 minutes longer. Cut the meat through to the bottom on the unstuffed slices. There will now be sets of 2 slices, with stuffing between, for serving. Serve the pan juices separately.

Serves 6–8.

Basar Tz Aloouie

ISRAELI SWEET AND SOUR POT ROAST

4-pound pot roast of beef	**⅓ cup lemon juice**
3 cups diced onions	**4 tablespoons brown sugar**
1½ teaspoons salt	**4 gingersnaps, crushed**
3 cups boiling water	

Place meat in a preheated heavy saucepan or Dutch oven, cover, and brown on all sides over medium heat. Add the onions and brown lightly. Pour off the fat. Add the salt and 1 cup of boiling water. Cover and cook over low heat 2 hours, adding the remaining water from time to time. Stir in the lemon juice, sugar, and gingersnaps. Cook 20 minutes longer. Taste for seasoning.

Serves 8–10.

Stufato di Manzo

ITALIAN POT ROAST

3-pound pot roast of beef
2 tablespoons olive oil
2 tablespoons butter
3 cups thinly sliced onions
2 teaspoons salt
½ teaspoon freshly ground
   black pepper
1½ cups dry white wine
1 cup peeled, diced
   tomatoes
¾ cup sliced carrots
¼ cup sliced celery
½ teaspoon basil

Trim the fat from the meat. Heat the oil and butter in a Dutch oven or heavy skillet; sauté the onions until soft and yellow. Add the meat and brown on all sides. Season with the salt and pepper. Add the wine; cook over high heat 5 minutes. Add the tomatoes, carrots, celery, and basil. Bring to a boil, cover and cook over low heat 2½ hours or until the meat is tender. Slice the meat and serve with the gravy. *Serves 6–8.*

Manzo al Forno

BAKED ITALIAN POT ROAST

3-pound pot roast of beef
1 tablespoon olive oil
2 tablespoons butter
½ cup chopped onions
2 cloves garlic, minced
2 teaspoons salt
½ teaspoon freshly ground
   black pepper
½ teaspoon rosemary
1 8-ounce can tomato sauce
½ cup beef broth
2 tablespoons dry vermouth
2 tablespoons minced
   parsley

Trim the fat from the meat. Heat the oil and butter in a skillet; brown the meat, onions, and garlic in it. Season with the salt, pepper, and rosemary, then add the tomato sauce, broth, vermouth, and parsley. Cover and bake in a 350° oven 2½ hours or until meat is tender. Skim the fat off the gravy. *Serves 6–8.*

Jamaican Pot Roast

3-pound pot roast of beef
⅓ cup flour
2½ teaspoons salt
½ teaspoon freshly ground
  black pepper
3 tablespoons vegetable oil

¾ cup chopped onions
1 clove garlic, chopped
1 16-ounce can tomatoes
½ teaspoon marjoram
½ teaspoon powdered ginger
Dash Tabasco

Rub the meat with a mixture of the flour, salt, and pepper. Heat the oil in a Dutch oven or heavy saucepan; add the meat and brown on all sides. Pour off the fat. Add the onions and garlic. Cook until onions begin to brown, stirring frequently. Mix in the tomatoes, marjoram, ginger, and Tabasco. Cover and cook over low heat 2½ hours or until tender. Transfer the meat to a heated platter. Slice and serve with the gravy.

Serves 6–8.

Bue alla Lombardia

LOMBARDY POT ROAST

4-pound pot roast of beef
2 tablespoons butter
1 cup thinly sliced onions
½ cup sliced carrots
2½ teaspoons salt
½ teaspoon freshly ground
  black pepper
1 clove garlic, minced

¼ cup wine vinegar
1½ cups dry white wine
1½ pounds tomatoes, peeled
  and diced
2 bay leaves
¼ teaspoon sugar
¼ cup heavy cream

Trim the fat from the meat. Melt the butter in a Dutch oven or heavy saucepan; add the meat; brown well on all sides. Add the onions, carrots, salt, pepper, and garlic. Cook over medium heat 5 minutes. Add the vinegar, wine, tomatoes, bay leaves, and sugar. Cover and cook over low heat 2½ hours or until meat is tender. Taste for seasoning. Transfer the meat to a hot platter.

Discard the bay leaves and purée the gravy in an electric blender or force through a sieve. Return to the saucepan, stir in the cream, and heat. Slice the beef and pour gravy over it. *Serves 8–10.*

Slöttstek

SWEDISH POT ROAST

4 pounds round steak, cut in 1 piece	1 cup chopped onions
1 tablespoon salt	4 anchovies, minced
1 teaspoon freshly ground black pepper	2 bay leaves
	2 tablespoons vinegar
	1 tablespoon sugar
2 tablespoons butter	½ cup heavy cream
2 cups beef broth	2 tablespoons cognac

Rub the meat with salt and pepper. Melt the butter in a Dutch oven or heavy skillet and brown the meat on all sides. Remove the meat. Stir the broth into the pan and bring to a boil. Mix in the onions, anchovies, bay leaves, vinegar, and sugar; return the meat. Cover and cook over low heat 2 hours. Stir the cream and cognac into the gravy. Taste for seasoning. *Serves 8.*

Grytstek

SWEDISH SWEET AND SOUR POT ROAST

4-pound pot roast of beef	¼ cup cognac
4 tablespoons butter	2 cups boiling water
2½ teaspoons salt	¼ teaspoon allspice
¾ teaspoon freshly ground black pepper	2 bay leaves
	2 teaspoons anchovy paste
1½ cups chopped onions	1 tablespoon cider vinegar
2 carrots, sliced	2 tablespoons flour
¼ cup molasses	1½ cups light cream

Trim the fat from the meat. Melt the butter in a Dutch oven or heavy saucepan and brown the meat on all sides. Sprinkle with the salt and pepper. Add the onions and carrots; cook 10 minutes. Stir in the molasses, cognac, water, allspice, bay leaves, anchovy paste, and vinegar. Cover and cook over low heat 2½ hours or until tender. Transfer the meat to a heated platter. Mix the flour and cream until smooth; blend into the gravy and bring to the boiling point, stirring steadily. Cook 5 minutes. Discard bay leaves, taste for seasoning, and serve gravy separately.
Serves 8–10.

Estouffat Catalán

SPANISH BEEF WITH WHITE BEANS

5-pound pot roast of beef
2 cloves garlic, slivered
4 strips salt pork
¼ cup vinegar
½ cup flour
1½ cups thinly sliced onions
2 carrots, cut in narrow strips
2 small white turnips, peeled and quartered
3 tomatoes, peeled and diced

3 sprigs parsley
1 bay leaf } tied together
½ teaspoon thyme
⅛ teaspoon powdered cloves
2 teaspoons salt
½ teaspoon freshly ground black pepper
4 cups dry red wine
2 cups cooked or canned white beans

Cut a few slits in the beef and insert the garlic slivers, then tie the salt pork over the meat. Brush the meat with the vinegar and roll in the flour. In a Dutch oven or other heavy pan spread the onions, carrots, turnips, tomatoes, parsley, bay leaf, thyme, cloves, salt, and pepper. Put the meat on top. Add the wine, bring to a boil over direct heat, cover pan tightly, and bake in a 275° oven 4 hours. Ten minutes before the beef is done, add the beans and bake 10 minutes longer. Discard the parsley and bay leaf.
Serves 8–10.

Texas Barbecued Pot Roast

4-pound pot roast of beef
2 tablespoons vegetable oil
1½ cups sliced onions
1 clove garlic, minced
2 teaspoons salt
½ teaspoon freshly ground
  black pepper
1 8-ounce can tomato sauce

¼ cup chili sauce
⅓ cup cider vinegar
2 tablespoons brown sugar
2 teaspoons Worcestershire
  sauce
½ cup water
2 teaspoons chili powder

Trim the fat from the meat. Heat the oil in a Dutch oven or heavy skillet and brown the meat on all sides. Add the onions and garlic; cook until browned. Mix in the salt, pepper, and tomato sauce; cover and cook over low heat 1½ hours. Stir in the chili sauce, vinegar, sugar, Worcestershire sauce, water, and chili powder; cover and cook 1 hour longer or until tender. Skim the fat from the gravy.
Serves 8–10.

Gjelle me Zarzavata

ALBANIAN BEEF AND VEGETABLE CASSEROLE

¼ cup olive oil
2 pounds top round of
  beef, cut in ½-inch cubes
4 large potatoes, peeled
  and thinly sliced
2 cups chopped tomatoes
2 carrots, grated
¼ cup chopped celery
1 cup chopped onions

1 green pepper, cut julienne
2 cloves garlic, minced
3 tablespoons chopped
  parsley
2½ teaspoons salt
½ teaspoon freshly ground
  black pepper
2 cups chicken broth

Heat 3 tablespoons of the oil in a skillet and brown the meat on all sides.
Arrange the potatoes in a greased casserole. Spread the meat

over them. Mix together the tomatoes, carrots, celery, onions, green pepper, garlic, parsley, salt, and pepper and spread over the meat. Add the broth. Cover and bake in a 375° oven 45 minutes. Pour the remaining oil over the top and bake uncovered 20 minutes longer.

Serves 6–8.

Fa-Sool-Ya Ib Zeyt

ARABIAN BEEF AND BEAN STEW

3 pounds boneless beef, cut in 2-inch cubes
1 cup dried white beans
1½ cups chopped onions
3 tablespoons vegetable oil
2 teaspoons salt
½ teaspoon freshly ground black pepper
¼ teaspoon cinnamon
1 bay leaf
4 cups hot beef broth
¾ cup raw rice
1½ cups peeled, diced tomatoes

Trim the fat from the meat. Wash the beans. Cover with water, bring to a boil, and let soak 1 hour. Drain. Add fresh water to cover, bring to a boil and cook over low heat 1 hour. Drain. Brown the beef and onions in the hot oil. Add the beans, salt, pepper, cinnamon, bay leaf, and 1 cup of the hot beef broth. Cover and cook over low heat 1½ hours. Stir in the rice, tomatoes, and remaining broth; re-cover and cook 25 minutes longer or until meat and beans are tender.

Serves 6–8.

Australian Marinated Braised Beef

3 pounds cross rib or rump
of beef, cut in 2-inch
cubes
2½ cups beer
2 teaspoons salt
¼ teaspoon freshly ground
black pepper
1 cup minced onions

3 tablespoons butter
⅓ cup grated carrots
1 tablespoon cornstarch
3 tablespoons orange juice
2 tablespoons grated orange
rind
2 tablespoons currant jelly

Trim the fat from the meat. In a glass or pottery bowl, mix together the beer, salt, pepper, and onions. Marinate the beef in the mixture overnight in the refrigerator. Drain, reserving the marinade.

Melt the butter in a Dutch oven or heavy skillet and brown the meat on all sides. Add the carrots and marinade. Cover and cook over low heat 2½ hours. Mix the cornstarch with the orange juice; stir into the gravy with the orange rind and jelly. Cook over low heat 10 minutes. Taste for seasoning.
Serves 6–8.

Australian Steak and Kidney Pie

PASTRY:

1½ cups sifted flour
¾ teaspoon salt
½ cup shortening

1 egg yolk, beaten
3 tablespoons ice water

Sift the flour and salt into a bowl. Cut in the shortening until the mixture looks like coarse corn meal. Add the egg yolk mixed with the water. Toss with a fork until all the particles cling together. Form into a ball, wrap and chill while preparing the filling.

FILLING:

4 veal kidneys
2 pounds top round steak,
cut in 1½-inch cubes
¼ cup flour
3 tablespoons vegetable oil
1 cup thinly sliced onions
½ pound mushrooms, sliced

2 teaspoons salt
¾ teaspoon freshly ground
black pepper
½ teaspoon thyme
1 tablespoon tomato paste
1 cup dry red wine

Wash the kidneys, cut in half, and discard the core. Cover with boiling water, let stand 2 minutes, drain, and cube.

Toss the cubed meat and kidneys with the flour. Heat the oil in a skillet and brown the meat and kidneys.

In a buttered 2-quart casserole, arrange the sautéed meats, onions, and mushrooms in 3 layers. Mix together the salt, pepper, thyme, tomato paste, and wine; pour into the casserole. Cover the casserole and bake in a 350° oven 2½ hours.

Roll out the pastry ¼-inch thick and a little larger than the casserole, and cut a few gashes in the top. Remove the cover of the casserole and taste the mixture for seasoning. Place the pastry over the casserole mixture and press the edges down with a fork. Increase the oven heat to 400° and bake 25 minutes longer or until the pastry is browned. *Serves 6–8.*

Ahme Hnat Hin

BURMESE SPICED BEEF

3 pounds top sirloin, cut
in 1-inch cubes
4 cloves garlic, minced
3 cups finely chopped
onions
1-inch piece fresh
gingerroot, chopped, or 2
teaspoons powdered ginger

½ teaspoon dried ground
chili peppers
2 teaspoons turmeric
2 teaspoons salt
½ cup sesame oil or peanut
oil
2½ cups peeled, chopped
fresh or canned tomatoes
1 cup beef broth

Trim the fat from the meat. Chop or pound to a paste the garlic, onions, ginger, chili peppers, turmeric, and salt. Put the beef in a bowl and toss with the spice mixture until the meat is well coated. Let stand 3 hours, turning frequently.

Heat the oil in a deep saucepan until it bubbles. Add the coated beef cubes and brown well all over. Add the tomatoes and cook over medium heat 10 minutes. Mix in the broth, cover, and cook over low heat 45 minutes or until meat is tender. Serve with fried noodles.

Serves 8–10.

Stifatho

GREEK BEEF STEW

3 pounds eye round or chuck of beef, cut in 1-inch cubes	12 small white onions
	2 cups beef broth
3 teaspoons salt	1 8-ounce can tomato sauce
½ teaspoon freshly ground black pepper	3 cups diced eggplant
	2 green peppers, cut in slivers
1 teaspoon cinnamon	½ cup raw rice
⅓ cup olive oil	

Trim the fat from the meat. Season the meat with 2 teaspoons of the salt, the pepper, and cinnamon. Heat ¼ cup of the oil in a Dutch oven or heavy casserole and brown the meat. Transfer the meat to a platter. In the oil remaining in the Dutch oven or casserole, sauté the onions until golden. Return the meat and add ½ cup of the broth and the tomato sauce. Cover and cook over low heat 1¼ hours.

Heat the remaining oil in a skillet; sauté the eggplant for 10 minutes. Sprinkle with the remaining salt and add to the Dutch oven or casserole with the green peppers, rice, and remaining broth. Re-cover and cook 30 minutes longer. Taste for seasoning.

Serves 6–8.

Cholent

ISRAELI BEEF AND LIMA BEAN CASSEROLE

3 pounds rump or round
of beef, cut in 1-inch
cubes
2 cups dried lima beans
4 tablespoons vegetable oil
1½ cups chopped onions
1 cup peeled, chopped
tomatoes

3 cups beef broth
2 teaspoons salt
½ teaspoon freshly ground
black pepper
2 teaspoons paprika
1 tablespoon flour
4 spicy sausages, cut in 1-
inch pieces

Trim the fat from the meat. Wash the beans, cover with water,
and bring to a boil. Let soak 1 hour. Drain, add fresh water to
cover, and bring to a boil. Cover and cook over low heat 1½ hours.
Drain.

Heat 2 tablespoons oil in a casserole and brown the onions.
Add the remaining oil to the casserole and brown the meat on
all sides. Add the beans, tomatoes, broth, salt, pepper, paprika,
and flour. Mix ingredients lightly with 2 spoons. Cover the casserole and bake in a 325° oven 2½ hours. Watch carefully and
add a little boiling water if casserole becomes dry. Remove cover
and arrange sausages on top. Bake 20 minutes longer.

Serves 6–8.

La Carbonnade

BEEF STEW, LE PUY STYLE

3 pounds rump steak, cut
into ½-inch cubes
3 tablespoons butter
1 cup thinly sliced onions
1 cup peeled, diced
tomatoes
2 teaspoons salt
½ teaspoon freshly ground
black pepper

2 cups cooked rice
1½ cups canned or frozen
corn
½ cup thinly sliced green
peppers
¼ teaspoon saffron
½ teaspoon sugar
Pinch cinnamon
1 cup dry white wine

Trim the fat from the meat. Melt the butter in a deep skillet and brown the meat on all sides. Add the onions, tomatoes, salt, and pepper; cover and cook over medium heat 10 minutes, shaking the pan occasionally. Mix in rice, corn, green peppers, saffron, sugar, cinnamon, and wine. Cover and cook over medium heat 15 minutes. *Serves 6–8.*

Ichdeera

MIDDLE EAST BEEF AND LENTIL STEW

3 pounds rump or chuck of beef, cut in 1-inch cubes	1 clove garlic, minced
	3 cups beef broth or water
1 cup lentils	1½ teaspoons salt
2 tablespoons olive oil	¼ teaspoon freshly ground black pepper
¾ cup chopped onions	¼ teaspoon orégano

Trim the fat from the meat. Wash the lentils thoroughly, cover with boiling water, and let soak while preparing the meat.

Heat the oil in a casserole; brown the meat and onions in it. Add the garlic, broth, salt, and pepper. Cover and cook over low heat 1 hour. Drain the lentils and add to the casserole with the orégano. Re-cover and cook 30 minutes longer or until meat and lentils are tender. Taste for seasoning. *Serves 4–6.*

Finker

BEEF CASSEROLE, SCANDINAVIAN HUNTER'S STYLE

6 tablespoons butter	¾ cup beef broth
1½ cups thinly sliced onions	4 cups seasoned mashed potatoes
1½ pounds top round, cut in 1-inch cubes	2 cups thinly sliced cooking apples
1¼ teaspoons salt	2 tablespoons dry bread crumbs
½ teaspoon freshly ground black pepper	
¼ teaspoon nutmeg	

Melt 3 tablespoons of the butter in a skillet and sauté the onions 10 minutes. Remove the onions. Put the meat in the skillet and brown over high heat, stirring frequently. Mix in the salt, pepper, nutmeg, and broth.

In a greased 2-quart casserole, arrange as many layers as possible of the potatoes, meat, onions, and apples, starting and ending with the potatoes. Sprinkle with the bread crumbs and dot with the remaining butter. Bake in a 375° oven 25 minutes.

Serves 4–6.

Pastel de Choclo

SOUTH AMERICAN BEEF AND CORN PUDDING

1 pound top sirloin, cut in small dice	¾ cup sliced stuffed olives
½ cup seedless raisins	½ teaspoon ground cuminseed
3 tablespoons olive oil	2 tablespoons butter
1 cup thinly sliced onions	½ cup chopped onions
1 tablespoon flour	2 cups canned corn kernels
3 teaspoons salt	2 egg yolks
¼ teaspoon dried ground chili peppers	¼ cup heavy cream
¼ cup beef broth	

Trim the fat from the meat. Soak the raisins in hot water while preparing the meat. Heat the oil in a skillet and sauté the sliced onions 5 minutes. Mix in the meat and brown on all sides. Sprinkle with the flour, 2 teaspoons of the salt, and the chili peppers. Stir in the broth. Cook over low heat 5 minutes, stirring frequently. Remove from heat and mix in the olives, cumin and drained raisins. Turn into a 10-inch buttered pie plate.

Melt the butter in a skillet and sauté the chopped onions 5 minutes. Mix in the corn and remaining salt. Cook 5 minutes. Beat the egg yolks and cream and add to the corn mixture. Spread over the meat and bake in a 350° oven 20 minutes, or until the custard is firm.

Serves 4–6.

Cazuela de Carne y Papas

SPANISH STEAK AND POTATO CASSEROLE

2 pounds top sirloin, cut
  in ½-inch cubes
2 tablespoons butter
3 cups sliced raw potatoes
1½ cups chopped onions
1½ cups chopped green
  peppers

2 teaspoons salt
1 tablespoon chili powder
¾ cup cracker meal
1 cup chicken broth
1 cup light cream

Trim the fat from the meat. Melt the butter in a skillet and brown the meat on all sides. Arrange in 1 layer, on the bottom of a buttered casserole, some of the potatoes, onions, and green peppers. Sprinkle with some salt, chili powder, and cracker meal. Arrange a second layer of some of the meat. Repeat the layers until all ingredients are used up, ending with the salt, chili powder and cracker meal. Mix together the broth and cream; pour into the casserole. Cover and bake in a 350° oven 2 hours, removing the cover for the last 15 minutes. *Serves 6–8.*

Texas Chile Con Carne

1½ pounds boneless beef,
  cut in small dice
3 tablespoons vegetable oil
1½ cups thinly sliced onions
1 cup chopped green
  peppers
1 29-ounce can tomatoes

2 teaspoons salt
½ teaspoon freshly ground
  black pepper
2 tablespoons chili powder
1 clove garlic, minced
1 16-ounce can kidney
  beans

Trim the fat from the meat. Heat the oil in a saucepan; sauté the onions and green peppers 10 minutes. Add the meat and brown over medium heat, stirring frequently. Mix in the tomatoes, salt, pepper, chili powder, and garlic. Cover and cook over low heat 2 hours. Add the beans, taste for seasoning and cook 10 minutes longer. *Serves 6–8.*

Majedra

TURKISH BEEF STEW

2 pounds eye round or
  chuck of beef, cut in 2-inch
  cubes
1 cup lentils
2 tablespoons olive oil
1½ cups chopped onions

2 teaspoons salt
½ teaspoon freshly ground
  black pepper
4 cups boiling water
½ cup raw rice
¾ cup tomatoes

Trim the fat from the meat.
Soak the lentils in cold water 2 hours. Drain.
Heat the oil in a casserole; brown the meat and onions in it.
Add the lentils, salt, pepper, and 3 cups of the boiling water.
Cover and cook over low heat 1½ hours. Stir in the rice, tomatoes,
and remaining water; re-cover and cook 25 minutes longer or
until meat is tender. *Serves 6–8.*

Rindfleisch mit Sauerkraut

TYROLEAN BEEF AND SAUERKRAUT CASSEROLE

3 pounds eye round or
  chuck of beef, cut in 1½-
  inch cubes
2 tablespoons vegetable oil
1½ cups sliced onions
1½ teaspoons salt
½ teaspoon freshly ground
  black pepper

1 teaspoon paprika
1½ pounds sauerkraut,
  drained
1 bay leaf
1½ cups chopped canned
  tomatoes

Trim the fat from the meat. Heat the oil in a casserole and
brown the meat and onions. Sprinkle with the salt, pepper, and
paprika. Cover and cook over low heat 30 minutes. Watch carefully and add a very little water if necessary to keep from burning.
Mix in the sauerkraut. Cook 10 minutes. Add the bay leaf and
tomatoes. Cover and cook 1¼ hours longer or until meat is tender.
Discard the bay leaf. *Serves 6–8.*

Southern Baked Hash

3 cups diced cooked beef
  or corned beef
2 cups diced raw potatoes
1½ cups chopped onions
¾ cup chopped green
  peppers
3 tablespoons minced
  parsley

1½ teaspoons salt
½ teaspoon freshly ground
  black pepper
¼ teaspoon thyme
1 10½-ounce can beef gravy
1 teaspoon Worcestershire
  sauce

Mix all the ingredients together. Turn into a greased 2-quart casserole; cover and bake in a 375° oven 1 hour, removing the cover for the last 15 minutes.
Serves 4–6.

New Zealand Chipped Beef

1 pound dried chipped
  beef
4 tablespoons butter
½ cup grated onion
4 eggs
4 tablespoons cream cheese

½ cup cottage cheese
2 tablespoons chopped
  parsley
¼ teaspoon freshly ground
  black pepper

Shred the beef. Melt the butter in a skillet; sauté the chipped beef and onion 10 minutes, stirring frequently. Transfer the mixture to the top of a large double boiler, and place over hot water.

Beat the eggs in a bowl. Mix together the cream cheese and cottage cheese until smooth and add to the eggs, with the parsley and pepper. Mix well. Taste for seasoning, adding salt if necessary. Add to the chipped beef mixture. Stir constantly until the eggs set.
Serves 4–6.

Rindfleisch, Hamburger Art

BEEF IN ASPIC, GERMAN STYLE

4 pounds eye round of beef
1 cup chopped onions
2 stalks celery
6 peppercorns
2 cloves
1 bay leaf
2 teaspoons salt

⅛ teaspoon cayenne pepper
1 tablespoon molasses
¼ cup white wine vinegar
1 cup beer
1 cup boiling water
2 teaspoons gelatin
¼ cup cold water

Have the meat wrapped in beef fat. Place in a hot Dutch oven or heavy saucepan and brown all over. Add the onions, celery, peppercorns, cloves, bay leaf, salt, cayenne, molasses, vinegar, beer, and boiling water. Bring to a boil, cover, and cook over low heat 2½ hours or until meat is tender.

Remove the meat and cool. Slice thinly and arrange on a deep platter. Strain the gravy. There should be about 2 cups; if there isn't, add a little boiling water. Mix the gelatin with the cold water, then stir into the hot gravy until dissolved. Cool in the refrigerator until the consistency of egg white, then pour over the meat. Chill until set. *Serves 8–10.*

Corned Beef and Cabbage

6 pounds brisket of corned
    beef
1 onion
1 carrot

2 cloves garlic, sliced
2 bay leaves
2 4-pound heads of cabbage

Wash the corned beef, cover with water and add the onion, carrot, garlic, and bay leaves. Bring to a boil, cover, and cook over low heat 3 hours or until tender. Add boiling water from time to time to keep meat covered. At the end of 2¾ hours' cooking time, remove 3 cups of liquid. Cut each cabbage in 8 wedges and cook it in the 3 cups of liquid for 15 minutes or until tender. Drain well. Slice the meat and arrange the cabbage wedges around it. *Serves 10–12.*

California Glazed Corned Beef

5 pounds brisket of corned
beef
1 onion
1 clove garlic, sliced
1 teaspoon mixed pickling
spice

¼ cup brown sugar
1 tablespoon prepared
mustard
½ cup orange juice

Wash the beef, then cover with cold water. Add the onion, garlic, and pickling spice. Bring to a boil, cover, and cook over low heat 3 hours, or until almost tender. Let cool in the liquid 20 minutes, then drain. Place the meat in a shallow roasting pan and score the fat. Cover with a mixture of the brown sugar and mustard. Pour the orange juice into the pan. Bake in a 325° oven 45 minutes, basting frequently. Serve hot or cold.
Serves 10–12.

Pickling Brine

(FOR CORNED BEEF OR PICKLED TONGUE)

1¼ cups salt
2 tablespoons pickling spice
1 teaspoon saltpeter
(available in drugstores)

1 teaspoon sugar
6 bay leaves
12 cloves garlic
1 quart water

Put the meat to be pickled in a large stone crock. Mix the salt, pickling spice, saltpeter, sugar, bay leaves, and garlic with 1 quart of water; bring to a boil and pour over the meat. Add enough additional boiling water to cover the meat completely. Use a heavy bowl or board to weight the meat down. Cover the crock with cheesecloth, tie it in place, then cover the cheesecloth with aluminum foil.

Let stand in a cool place for 10 days. Drain and rinse the meat before cooking.

Sufficient brine for a 5-pound piece of meat which will serve 8–10.

Veal

The French and Italians have taught us a great deal about veal, not only the preparation of it, but the proper age for slaughtering, which is when the young calf is between four and fourteen weeks old. It is usually abundant in late winter and spring. At other times, most of the meat sold as veal is really older calf, from animals fourteen weeks to one year old.

The meat of young milk-fed veal is very pale, almost white with just a faint pink tinge. It darkens with age, and older veal, or baby beef, is red in color. The true delicacy of flavor and texture is gone from such veal, so it is worth the trouble to try to find young veal. This is particularly true for the proper preparation of the thin *scaloppine* so popular in Italian cuisine.

Veal is cut in the same manner as beef, except, of course, the pieces are smaller. The cooking methods, however, are quite different. Veal, having comparatively little exterior fat, and no marbling, is lower in calories than beef. Because of this lack of fat, and its large amount of connective tissue, large pieces of veal require long, slow cooking. Overcooking, on the other hand, results in coarse-textured meat. So don't just "put it in the pot"; give veal the same care as you do your choice beef steaks and roasts and you and your family will share the enthusiasm of the French and Italians for this delicate-flavored addition to your menu.

VEAL CUTS[1]

Leg of Veal (8, 7, 3) – The whole leg includes the rump and shank end. Either half can be roasted or braised. Cutlets and scallops for *scaloppine* are cut from the leg. The hind shanks are

[1] The numbers in parentheses refer to the Veal Chart.

used for *osso bucco,* a traditional Italian dish. Either half of the leg can also be boned and rolled, for roasting or braising.

Saddle (6) – This cut includes both loins. The saddle can be split into two loins, or cut into individual chops. Roast the saddle or whole loins. The chops can be broiled, sautéed, or braised. The tenderest *scaloppine,* used in fine Italian and French restaurants, are cut from the boned loin.

Ribs (5) – The whole rib section is similar to a beef rib roast and can be roasted. Rib chops are cut from this portion. Broil, sauté, or braise the chops. A crown roast is made from both rib sections.

Sirloin (6) – This portion contains the hip- and backbones, and is similar to sirloin of beef. Individual steaks are also cut from this section of the animal.

Blade (1, 2) – Includes the section of shoulder which contains the blade bone. Roast or braise it. Chops cut from this portion have a bone in every other chop; sauté or braise them.

Breast (4) – A thin flat cut containing the rib ends and breastbone. This cut is excellent for stuffing, either with a pocket or boned, and may be roasted, braised, or stewed.

Zrazy W Sosie Pomidorowyn

POLISH LEG OF VEAL IN TOMATO SAUCE

Leg of veal, boned and tied	2 cloves garlic, minced
2½ teaspoons salt	1 29-ounce can tomatoes,
½ teaspoon freshly ground	drained
black pepper	1 teaspoon thyme
2 tablespoons olive oil	3 tablespoons minced
1 cup thinly sliced onions	parsley

Rub the veal with the salt and pepper. Heat the oil in a Dutch oven or heavy saucepan and brown the veal on all sides. Add the onions and garlic; cook until browned. Add the tomatoes and thyme. Cover and cook over low heat 2½ hours or until tender. Skim the fat from the gravy and stir in the parsley. Remove the strings, slice the veal, and serve the gravy in a sauceboat.
Serves 8–10.

Kalbsbraten

SWISS ROAST LEG OF VEAL

Leg of veal, boned, larded,   4 onions, quartered
and tied   4 carrots, diced
2 teaspoons salt   ⅛ teaspoon thyme
½ teaspoon freshly ground   1 bay leaf
black pepper   ½ cup melted butter
1 clove garlic, minced   1 cup dry white wine

Rub the veal with a mixture of the salt, pepper, and garlic. Place the veal in a roasting pan; roast in a 375° oven 20 minutes. Pour off the fat. Add the onions, carrots, thyme, bay leaf, butter, and wine. Reduce heat to 300° and roast 2 hours longer, or until meat is tender (170° on a meat thermometer), basting frequently. Transfer meat to a hot serving platter and remove the strings. Skim the fat from the gravy. Serve with the vegetables around the meat.

Serves 6–8.

Geschmorte Kalbfleisch

MUNICH BRAISED LOIN OF VEAL

2 tablespoons vegetable oil   1 cup chopped onions
Whole loin of veal, boned,   4 carrots, quartered
rolled, and tied   1 cup sliced celery
2½ teaspoons salt   2 tomatoes, quartered
½ teaspoon freshly ground   ½ cup water
black pepper   3 tablespoons minced
¼ teaspoon marjoram   parsley
1 bay leaf

Heat the oil in a Dutch oven or heavy saucepan and brown the veal on all sides. Sprinkle with the salt, pepper, and marjoram; add the bay leaf, onions, carrots, celery, tomatoes, and water.

Cover and cook over low heat 3 hours, adding water from time to time.

Remove the strings, carve the veal, sprinkle with parsley, surround with the vegetables, and pour pan juices over all.

Serves 4–6.

Pieczén Cielęca Zawijana ze Slonina
POLISH ROAST VEAL

4-pound rolled leg or loin of veal	**1 cup sliced onions**
4 slices bacon, cut julienne	**½ cup grated carrots**
	¼ cup sliced celery
2 teaspoons salt	**1 cup dry white wine**
½ teaspoon freshly ground black pepper	**¼ cup light cream**
	2 teaspoons flour
¼ teaspoon marjoram	**¾ cup beef broth**
¼ teaspoon thyme	**1 cup chopped mushrooms**
3 tablespoons soft butter	**2 tablespoons minced parsley**

Use a sharp knife or larding needle and pierce the veal in several places. Cover the bacon with water, bring to a boil and cook 10 minutes. Drain. Press the strips into the pierced places of the veal. Rub with a mixture of the salt, pepper, marjoram, and thyme; spread with the butter. Place in a roasting pan with the onions, carrots, and celery around it.

Roast in a 400° oven 25 minutes. Stir the wine and cream into the pan; baste the meat several times. Reduce the heat to 300° and roast the veal 2 hours longer, basting frequently. Transfer the veal to a heated serving dish and keep warm. Purée the vegetables and gravy in an electric blender or mash smooth.

In a saucepan, combine the flour, broth, mushrooms, and parsley. Bring to a boil, stirring constantly. Add the gravy; cook over low heat 10 minutes. Taste for seasoning. Carve the veal and pour sauce over all.

Serves 6–8.

Pieczén Cielęca na Sposób Sarniej

MOCK VENISON, POLISH STYLE

4-pound shoulder of veal	1 bay leaf
20 juniper berries, crushed	1 cup sliced onions
1 cup wine vinegar	2 tablespoons butter
3 cups water	2 teaspoons salt
3 cloves	1 tablespoon flour
10 peppercorns	1 cup sour cream

Rub the meat with the crushed juniper berries and place in a bowl. In a saucepan, combine the vinegar, water, cloves, peppercorns, bay leaf, and onions. Bring to a boil and cook over low heat 10 minutes. Pour over the meat and place a weight on the meat to keep it submerged. Marinate in the refrigerator 48 hours.

Drain and dry the meat, reserving ½ cup of the marinade. Rub the meat with the salt and place it in a shallow roasting pan, dot with the butter. Roast in a 425° oven 25 minutes, then reduce the heat to 350°. Add the marinade and continue roasting 1¾ hours, basting occasionally. Mix the flour with the sour cream and spread it over the meat, roast 10 minutes longer.

Serves 8–10.

Veau à la Bordelaise

BORDEAUX BRAISED VEAL

3 tablespoons butter	2 teaspoons salt
5-pound boned loin or rump of veal	½ teaspoon freshly ground black pepper
1½ cups sliced onions	½ teaspoon rosemary
¾ cup thinly sliced carrots	½ cup dry white wine

Melt the butter in a Dutch oven or heavy skillet. Add the meat and brown over low heat on all sides. Add the onions and carrots. Cook until browned. Add the salt, pepper, rosemary, and wine. Cover and cook over low heat 2½ hours, or until tender. Turn meat frequently and add a little boiling water if necessary. Serve with sautéed mushrooms and parsley potatoes. *Serves 8–10.*

English Shoulder of Veal with Bread Stuffing

4-pound boned shoulder of veal
2½ teaspoons salt
¾ teaspoon freshly ground black pepper
6 tablespoons butter
¾ cup chopped onion
¼ pound mushrooms, chopped
½ cup chopped celery with leaves
1 clove garlic, minced
¼ cup chopped parsley
½ teaspoon thyme
3 cups fresh bread crumbs
1 carrot, sliced
3 sprigs parsley
1 onion, sliced
1½ cups chicken broth

Rub the veal with 2 teaspoons of the salt and ½ teaspoon of the pepper. Melt 3 tablespoons of the butter in a skillet; sauté the onion, mushrooms, celery, and garlic 10 minutes, stirring frequently. Mix in the parsley, thyme, bread crumbs, and remaining salt and pepper.

Lay the meat flat, skin side down. Spread with the stuffing and roll up. Tie in several places.

Put the carrot, parsley sprigs, and sliced onion in a roasting pan or Dutch oven and place the meat on top. Dot with the remaining butter.

Roast in a 425° oven 25 minutes. Reduce the heat to 350°, add ¾ cup of the broth, cover, and bake 2 hours longer or until tender. Baste frequently and add some of the remaining broth from time to time. Remove cover for the last 15 minutes. Place the meat on a hot platter, strain the gravy, and pour over the veal. *Serves 8–10.*

Mostek Nadziewany Wątróbką

POLISH SHOULDER OF VEAL WITH CHICKEN LIVER STUFFING

4-pound boned shoulder
of veal
2½ teaspoons salt
¾ teaspoon freshly ground
black pepper
1 pound chicken livers,
chopped
½ cup chopped onions

½ cup soft bread crumbs
½ pound mushrooms,
chopped and sautéed
⅛ teaspoon marjoram
1 egg, lightly beaten
¾ cup dry white wine
3 tablespoons butter
1 cup chicken broth

Rub the veal with 2 teaspoons of the salt and ½ teaspoon of the pepper.

Mix together the chopped raw chicken livers, onions, bread crumbs, mushrooms, marjoram, egg, ¼ cup of the wine, and the remaining salt and pepper. Spread the veal flat, skin side down and cover with the liver mixture. Roll up and tie in several places.

Melt the butter in a Dutch oven or heavy saucepan and brown the meat on all sides. Add the chicken broth and remaining wine; cover and cook over low heat 2½ hours or until the veal is tender, turning the meat occasionally. Transfer the meat to a hot platter and keep warm. Strain the gravy and serve in a sauceboat.
Serves 8–10.

Arrosto Semplice di Vitello

ITALIAN POT ROAST OF VEAL

3 dried mushrooms
5-pound rolled rump of
veal
½ cup flour
2 tablespoons olive oil
3 tablespoons butter
¾ cup chopped onions
1 clove garlic, minced

¼ cup chopped celery
1 tablespoon minced parsley
½ teaspoon freshly ground
black pepper
¼ teaspoon thyme
1 teaspoon tomato paste
2 cups beef broth

Wash the mushrooms. Cover with warm water and let soak 15 minutes. Drain and chop. Rub the veal with the flour.

Heat the oil in a roasting pan or Dutch oven. Add the veal; roast in a 450° oven 30 minutes, turning to brown all sides. Pour off the fat and reduce heat to 300°.

Melt the butter in a skillet; sauté the onions, garlic, celery, and parsley 5 minutes; add to the veal with the pepper, thyme, tomato paste, mushrooms, and broth. Cover and bake 3½ hours, turning the meat after 2 hours. Add a little water if necessary to keep the bottom of the pan covered. Strain the gravy and skim off the fat. Serve in a sauceboat.

Serves 8–10.

Falszywy Losós

SPICED COLD VEAL, CENTRAL EUROPEAN STYLE

3-pound boned rolled leg of veal	**2 carrots, sliced**
Veal bones	**2 teaspoons salt**
1 cup wine vinegar	**1 bay leaf**
3 cups water	**10 peppercorns**
1 cup sliced onions	**3 hard-cooked egg yolks**
2 stalks celery	**1 cup olive oil**
1 celery root, sliced	**½ cup lemon juice**
5 sprigs parsley	**1 can anchovies, mashed**
	1 tablespoon capers

Have the veal tied up in a nice shape, and the veal bones cracked.

In a saucepan, combine the bones, vinegar, water, vegetables, and seasonings. Bring to a boil and add the veal. Cover and cook over low heat 3 hours. Cool the meat in the stock, then refrigerate, still in the stock, overnight.

Before serving, mash the egg yolks. Beat in the olive oil very gradually, as for making mayonnaise, then beat in the lemon juice. Blend in the anchovies and capers. Drain the meat thoroughly, and cut in thin slices. Arrange the slices on a platter, and cover with the sauce. *Serves 8–10.*

Poitrine de Veau à l'Etuvée

BRAISED BREAST OF VEAL

3-pound breast of veal, cut
in serving-sized pieces
2 teaspoons salt
½ teaspoon freshly ground
black pepper
4 tablespoons butter

2 tablespoons warm cognac
½ pound sausage meat
12 small white onions
1 clove garlic, minced
½ cup boiling water

Season the veal with the salt and pepper. Melt the butter in a
Dutch oven or heavy skillet and brown the veal on all sides. Set
the cognac aflame, and pour it over the veal. When the flames die,
add the sausage meat, onions, and garlic. Cover and cook over
low heat 30 minutes, shaking the pan frequently. Pour off the fat
and add the boiling water. Cover and cook 1 hour. Skim the fat
again before serving with sautéed potatoes.
Serves 4–6.

Galantine de Veau

ROLLED STUFFED BREAST OF VEAL

Breast of veal, boned and
pounded flat (reserve the
bones)
2½ teaspoons salt
½ teaspoon freshly ground
black pepper
¼ teaspoon nutmeg
1 pound sausage meat
¼ cup minced onions
¼ cup minced parsley
½ cup dry bread crumbs

¼ teaspoon powdered sage
1 egg, beaten
6 slices prosciutto (ham)
3 hard-cooked eggs
3 tablespoons vegetable oil
1 cup sliced onions
1 carrot, sliced
1 clove garlic, minced
2 stalks celery and leaves
Boiling water

Rub the veal with the salt, pepper, and nutmeg.
Mix together the sausage meat, minced onions, parsley, bread

crumbs, sage, and beaten egg. Spread over the veal and arrange the ham on top. Put the hard-cooked eggs at one end, then from that end roll up the veal like a jelly roll. Tie securely in several places with string.

Heat the oil in a Dutch oven or heavy skillet and brown the veal on all sides. Remove the veal, cool slightly, then tie in cheesecloth. Add the sliced onions, carrot, and garlic to the fat in the pan; cook 10 minutes. Return the veal, still in the cheesecloth; add the veal bones, celery and leaves, and enough water to reach halfway up the meat. Bring to a boil, cover, and cook over low heat 3 hours, or until the veal is tender. Let the roll cool in the liquid.

Drain the roll, place in a dish, cover with another dish, and put enough weights on it to press the roll down. Chill overnight. Carefully remove the cheesecloth and strings. Place the veal on a platter and garnish as you like. Serve in half-inch slices.
Serves 8–10.

Telece Grudi Punjene Spanaćem

CROATIAN STUFFED BREAST OF VEAL

Breast of veal, boned and with a pocket	**1 cup milk**
3 teaspoons salt	**¼ pound (1 stick) butter**
¾ teaspoon freshly ground black pepper	**2 slices white bread, crusts trimmed**
2 packages frozen chopped spinach	**½ cup water**
2 tablespoons flour	**⅓ cup sour cream**
	1 egg, beaten
	1 cup sliced onions

Rub the veal with 2 teaspoons of the salt and ½ teaspoon of the pepper.

Cook the spinach as the package directs. Drain thoroughly, and return to the saucepan. Blend in the flour, then gradually add the milk and bring to the boiling point, stirring constantly. Add 2 tablespoons of the butter and the remaining salt and pepper. Cook over low heat 3 minutes. Cool.

Soak the bread in the water, mash, then squeeze dry. Mix the bread into the spinach with the sour cream and egg. Stuff the veal, and sew or skewer the opening.

Melt half the remaining butter in a roasting pan, and put the meat into it. Roast in a 375° oven 45 minutes, basting frequently. Add the onions and remaining butter; reduce heat to 325° and roast 1½ hours longer, basting frequently and adding a little water if necessary. Let stand 15 minutes. Remove fastenings and slice. Serve with parsley potatoes.

Serves 6–8.

Vitello Tonnato I

ITALIAN COLD LEG OF VEAL IN TUNA FISH SAUCE

4-pound rolled leg of veal	1 clove
1 teaspoon salt	4 cups boiling water
½ teaspoon freshly ground black pepper	1 7¾-ounce can tuna fish
	8 anchovy fillets
½ cup sliced onions	¼ cup lemon juice
1 carrot, sliced	¾ cup olive oil
3 sprigs parsley	2 teaspoons capers
1 clove garlic	

Rub the veal with the salt and ¼ teaspoon of the pepper. Place in a Dutch oven or heavy saucepan and brown on all sides over high heat. Pour off the fat. Add the onions, carrot, parsley, garlic, clove, and boiling water. Cover and cook over low heat 1½ hours or until tender. Drain, dry, and cool.

Purée the tuna fish, anchovies, and lemon juice in an electric blender (or mash very smooth). Very gradually beat in the oil, until the consistency of thin mayonnaise. Mix in the capers.

Place the veal in a glass or pottery bowl; pour sauce over it. Marinate in the refrigerator 24 hours before serving. Serve sliced very thin, with the sauce on top. Cold string beans or sliced tomatoes are a good accompaniment.

Serves 8–12 as a first course, 6–8 as a main course.

Vitello Tonnato II

ITALIAN COLD LEG OF VEAL IN TUNA FISH SAUCE

1 orange	2 bay leaves
¼ cup olive oil	½ teaspoon thyme
Leg of veal, boned and tied	2 cups dry white wine
	1 cup chicken broth
1 cup sliced onions	1½ teaspoons salt
1 7¾-ounce can tuna fish	½ teaspoon freshly ground black pepper
1 can anchovy fillets, minced	½ cup mayonnaise
2 cloves garlic	Capers

Wash the orange, cut in quarters and remove the seeds.

Heat the oil in a Dutch oven or heavy saucepan and brown the veal on all sides. Pour off the fat. Add the orange, onions, undrained tuna fish, anchovies, garlic, bay leaves, thyme, wine, broth, salt, and pepper. Cover and cook over low heat 2 hours or until tender. Let the meat cool in the gravy. Remove the veal; discard the orange and bay leaves.

Purée the gravy in an electric blender or force through a sieve; gradually mix in the mayonnaise. Remove the strings, slice the veal and pour the gravy over it. Marinate in the refrigerator at least 4 hours before serving. Garnish with capers.

Serves 10–12 as a first course.

Gevulde Kalfsborst

DUTCH BREAST OF VEAL WITH RICE STUFFING

Breast of veal, boned and with a pocket	½ pound mushrooms, chopped
2½ teaspoons salt	1 cup cooked or canned green peas
¾ teaspoon freshly ground black pepper	1 cup cooked rice
1 clove garlic, minced	1 egg, beaten
¼ pound (1 stick) butter	½ teaspoon thyme
¾ cup chopped onions	1 cup water

Rub the veal with 2 teaspoons of the salt, ½ teaspoon of the pepper, and the garlic.

Melt 3 tablespoons of the butter in a skillet and sauté the onions and mushrooms 5 minutes. Mix in the peas, rice, egg, thyme, and remaining salt and pepper. Stuff the pocket of the veal breast with this mixture and sew or skewer the opening. Melt 2 tablespoons of the remaining butter in a shallow roasting pan. Put the meat in the pan. Dot with the remaining butter and add half the water. Cover with aluminum foil and bake in a 350° oven 1¾ hours. Remove the foil, add remaining water, and bake 45 minutes longer, basting frequently. Transfer to a hot platter and remove the fastenings.

Serves 6–8.

Gefullte Kalbsbrüst

GERMAN STUFFED BREAST OF VEAL

4-pound breast of veal, with a pocket	¼ cup sour cream
4 teaspoons salt	2 eggs, beaten
¾ teaspoon freshly ground black pepper	1 tablespoon minced parsley
4 tablespoons butter	1 cup dry white wine
1 cup chopped onions	1 cup boiling water
¼ pound mushrooms, sliced	2 carrots, sliced
¾ cup fresh bread crumbs	1 onion, sliced
	1 bay leaf
	½ teaspoon thyme

Rub the veal with 2½ teaspoons of the salt and ½ teaspoon of the pepper.

Melt 2 tablespoons of the butter in a skillet and sauté the chopped onions 5 minutes. Add the mushrooms and sauté 5 minutes. Mix in the bread crumbs, sour cream, eggs, parsley, and the remaining salt and pepper. Stuff the pocket of the veal and sew or skewer the opening.

Melt the remaining butter in a Dutch oven or covered roasting pan and brown the veal. Add the wine, water, carrots, onion, bay leaf and thyme. Cover and cook over low heat 2½ hours

or until tender. Turn the meat once or twice. Transfer the meat to a hot platter and remove the fastenings. Discard the bay leaf, and purée the gravy and vegetables in an electric blender or force through a sieve. Taste for seasoning and serve in a gravy boat.
Serves 6–8.

Egel Memoula
ISRAELI STUFFED BREAST OF VEAL

Breast of veal, with a pocket	**½ cup minced onions**
4 teaspoons salt	**¼ cup cracker meal**
¾ teaspoon freshly ground black pepper	**1 egg**
	2 tablespoons vegetable oil
1 teaspoon paprika	**¾ cup sliced onions**
1 clove garlic, minced	**1 cup hot water**
2 cups grated raw potato, drained	

Rub the veal with 2½ teaspoons of the salt, ½ teaspoon of the pepper, the paprika, and garlic.

Mix together the potato, minced onions, cracker meal, egg, and remaining salt and pepper. Stuff the pocket and skewer or sew the opening.

Heat the oil in a roasting pan and place the veal and sliced onions in it. Roast in a 325° oven 3 hours or until meat is tender; baste frequently and add a little of the water from time to time. Remove fastenings before serving.
Serves 6–8.

VARIATION:

A flour stuffing may be used in place of the potato mixture. Mix together 1½ cups sifted flour, ½ cup grated onion, 2 teaspoons salt, ½ teaspoon pepper, 2 teaspoons paprika, and ½ cup melted fat or butter. Proceed with the veal and roast as directed.

Mostek Nadziewany

POLISH ROLLED STUFFED BREAST OF VEAL

Breast of veal, boned and
pounded flat (reserve the
bones)
2 teaspoons salt
½ teaspoon freshly ground
black pepper
1 clove garlic, minced
½ pound sliced cooked
tongue
½ pound Swiss cheese, cut
into narrow strips

2 teaspoons chopped parsley
4 tablespoons butter
½ cup sliced onions
1 carrot, sliced
½ cup dry white wine
½ cup water
1 cup light cream (about)
½ pound mushrooms, sliced
2 tablespoons flour

Rub the veal with a mixture of the salt, pepper, and garlic.

Arrange a layer of tongue on the meat with a layer of cheese over it. Sprinkle with the parsley. Roll up the meat lengthwise and tie with string in a few places. Place in a greased shallow baking pan and dot with 2 tablespoons of the butter. Add the veal bones, the onions, carrot, wine, and water. Bake in a 375° oven 1¾ hours, or until tender, basting occasionally with the pan juices. Transfer the veal to a hot platter; remove the strings and keep warm. Discard the bones. Strain the pan juices and add enough cream to make 2 cups.

Melt the remaining butter; sauté the mushrooms 3 minutes. Blend in the flour. Add the pan juices and bring to the boiling point, stirring steadily. Cook 3 minutes longer. Taste for seasoning. *Serves 6–8.*

Zrazy ze Śmietaną

POLISH ROLLED BREAST OF VEAL WITH SOUR CREAM GRAVY

Breast of veal, boned and
  lightly pounded
2 cloves garlic, minced
6 anchovies, mashed
¼ teaspoon thyme
6 tablespoons butter
2 cups dry white wine

2 teaspoons salt
½ teaspoon freshly ground
  black pepper
2 tablespoons flour
¼ cup dry sherry
1 cup sour cream
2 tablespoons capers

Lay the meat flat with the boned surface up. Cream together the garlic, anchovies, thyme, and 2 tablespoons of the butter. Spread over the meat, roll up, and tie in several places. Place the veal in a glass or pottery bowl, pour the wine over it, and marinate at least 3 hours, or overnight, turning and basting occasionally.

Drain and dry the meat, reserving the marinade. Rub the meat with the salt and pepper. Heat the remaining butter in a Dutch oven or heavy skillet and brown the meat on all sides. Add the marinade, cover, and cook over low heat 2 hours or until the meat is tender. Transfer the meat to a hot serving platter and remove the strings.

Blend the flour with the sherry and stir into the gravy until thickened, then cook 2 minutes longer.

Blend in the sour cream and capers, taste for seasoning, and heat but do not let boil. Slice the meat, pour some of the gravy over it, and serve the rest separately.

Serves 6–8.

Kalbsschnitzel in Rahmsoss

AUSTRIAN VEAL CUTLETS IN SOUR CREAM SAUCE

6 tablespoons butter
2 pounds veal cutlet, cut
  in 12 pieces and pounded
  very thin

1¼ teaspoons salt
¾ cup sour cream
Lemon slices

Melt the butter in a skillet over low heat and lightly brown the veal on both sides. Sprinkle with the salt and add the sour cream; cook 5 minutes, basting frequently. Garnish with the lemon slices. *Serves 4–6.*

Welsh Rolled Stuffed Breast of Veal

**Breast of veal, boned and
pounded flat
2 teaspoons salt
½ teaspoon freshly ground
black pepper
1 pound pork sausage meat
½ pound ground veal
1 cup fresh bread crumbs
1 cup chopped onions
¼ teaspoon sage
¼ pound butter**

**3 onions, sliced
3 carrots, sliced
1 turnip, sliced
1 stalk celery, sliced
2 bay leaves, finely crushed
3 tablespoons minced
parsley
⅛ teaspoon thyme
8 peppercorns
2 cups water**

Season the veal with the salt and pepper. Mix together the pork sausage meat, veal, bread crumbs, onions, and sage. Spread on the meat. Roll tight and tie in several places. Melt the butter in a skillet and brown the meat on all sides.

Spread the sliced onions, carrots, turnip, celery, bay leaves, parsley, thyme, and peppercorns on the bottom of a Dutch oven or heavy casserole. Place meat over the vegetables, and pour all the drippings on top. Rinse the skillet with the water and pour over the meat. Cover and cook over low heat 2½ hours or until tender. Transfer meat to a hot platter, and remove the strings. Strain the gravy and pour some over the meat and serve the rest in a sauceboat.

Serves 6–8.

Holsteiner Schnitzel

BREADED VEAL CUTLETS WITH FRIED EGGS AND ANCHOVIES

1½ pounds veal cutlet, cut in 6 pieces and pounded very thin	1½ teaspoons salt
	¼ pound (1 stick) butter
Milk	6 fried eggs
¼ cup flour	12 anchovy fillets
½ cup dry bread crumbs	6 lemon wedges
	Minced parsley

Dip the veal in milk, then in a mixture of the flour, bread crumbs, and salt, coating the pieces thoroughly.

Melt half the butter in a large skillet; in it arrange as many veal slices as the pan will hold in a single layer. Cook over low heat until browned on both sides. Transfer to a hot serving dish and keep in a 225° oven while preparing the remaining veal in the remaining butter. Arrange the veal cutlets on the serving dish in a single layer. Put a fried egg on each cutlet, and arrange two anchovies over each egg. Garnish with a lemon wedge, sprinkled with parsley. *Serves 6.*

Escalopes de Veau à la Crème

FRENCH PROVINCIAL VEAL CUTLETS IN CREAM

1½ pounds veal cutlet, cut in 6 pieces and pounded thin	⅛ teaspoon white pepper
	4 tablespoons butter
¼ cup flour	¾ cup heavy cream
1¼ teaspoons salt	2 tablespoons lemon juice

Dip the veal in a mixture of the flour, salt, and pepper. Melt the butter in a skillet over low heat and sauté the veal on both sides until tender but not brown, about 10 minutes. Transfer to a hot platter.

Stir the cream and lemon juice into the skillet; cook over high heat 3 minutes, scraping the browned glaze from the skillet. Pour over the veal. *Serves 6.*

Scaloppine al Carciofi

ITALIAN VEAL CUTLETS WITH ARTICHOKE HEARTS

3 tablespoons butter
1 package frozen artichoke
   hearts, thawed and
   drained
2½ teaspoons salt
2 pounds veal cutlet, cut in
   12 pieces and pounded
   thin

1 egg, beaten
¼ cup flour
¼ teaspoon freshly ground
   black pepper
3 tablespoons olive oil
¼ cup beef broth
⅓ cup grated Parmesan
   cheese

Melt the butter in a skillet with an ovenproof handle; sauté the artichokes 5 minutes. Sprinkle with 1 teaspoon of the salt and remove. Dip the veal in the egg, then in a mixture of the flour, pepper, and remaining salt.

Heat the oil in the skillet over low heat and brown the veal on both sides. Arrange the artichokes over the veal, add the broth, and sprinkle with the cheese. Bake in a 375° oven 10 minutes or until top is browned. *Serves 6.*

Costolette di Vitello Veronese

ITALIAN VEAL CUTLETS WITH CHEESE SAUCE

1 pound veal cutlet, cut in
   8 pieces and pounded
   thin
1 teaspoon salt
3 tablespoons grated
   Parmesan cheese
¼ pound mozzarella cheese,
   cubed

½ cup heavy cream
½ cup julienne-cut ham
1 egg
¼ teaspoon freshly ground
   black pepper
4 tablespoons butter

Sprinkle the veal with the salt.

In the top of a double boiler combine the cheeses, cream, and ham. Place over hot water until cheese melts. Beat the egg and pepper in a bowl; add the cheese mixture, stirring steadily to prevent curdling. Return to double boiler and keep hot.

Melt the butter in a skillet over low heat and brown the cutlets on both sides. Spoon the cheese mixture over them, then place under a hot broiler until top is browned.

Serves 4.

Sformato di Vitello

ITALIAN VEAL AND ZUCCHINI LAYERS

1½ pounds small zucchini	¼ teaspoon nutmeg
2½ teaspoons salt	¾ cup grated Parmesan
6 tablespoons butter	cheese
½ teaspoon freshly ground	3 tablespoons olive oil
black pepper	
1½ pounds veal cutlet, cut	
in 16 pieces and	
pounded thin	

Scrub the unpeeled zucchini and slice very thin. Sprinkle with 1½ teaspoons of the salt and let stand 1 hour. Drain well. Melt half the butter in a skillet and lightly brown the zucchini in it. Sprinkle with half the pepper.

Melt the remaining butter in a skillet over low heat and lightly brown the veal on both sides. Season with the remaining salt and the pepper.

In a buttered shallow casserole or deep pie plate, spread ⅓ of the zucchini; sprinkle with a little nutmeg. Arrange half the veal over it; sprinkle with ¼ cup cheese and 1 tablespoon oil. Cover with ⅓ the zucchini, sprinkle with nutmeg; arrange remaining veal over it, sprinkle with ¼ cup of the cheese and 1 tablespoon of the oil. Cover with remaining zucchini, sprinkle with the remaining cheese and remaining oil.

Bake in a 350° oven 45 minutes.

Serves 6–8.

Saltimbocca

ITALIAN VEAL AND HAM MEDALLIONS

1½ pounds veal cutlet, cut
   in 12 scallops and
   pounded thin
1¼ teaspoons salt
¼ teaspoon freshly ground
   black pepper

12 fresh sage leaves or ½
   teaspoon dried sage
12 slices prosciutto (ham)
4 tablespoons butter
¾ cup dry white wine

Season the veal with the salt and pepper. Put a sage leaf on
each, or sprinkle with the dried sage. Fit a slice of ham over
each piece of the veal, so that the ham covers the veal. Fasten
with toothpicks.

Melt the butter in a skillet over medium heat; cook the ham
side for 1 minute, then turn over and cook until veal side browns.
Add the wine; cover and cook over low heat 5 minutes or until
the veal is tender. Remove toothpicks.

Serves 6.

Vitello alla Parmigiana

VEAL CUTLETS WITH CHEESE AND TOMATO SAUCE,
NORTH ITALIAN STYLE

2 eggs
½ teaspoon salt
¼ teaspoon freshly ground
   black pepper
1 cup dry bread crumbs
1 cup grated Parmesan
   cheese

1½ pounds veal cutlet, cut
   in 6 pieces and pounded
   thin
2 tablespoons butter
1 cup tomato sauce
6 slices mozzarella cheese

Beat together the eggs, salt, and pepper. Combine the bread
crumbs and Parmesan cheese on a piece of wax paper. Dip the
veal first in the eggs and then in the bread crumb-cheese mixture,
coating them well.

Melt the butter in a skillet. Fry the cutlets in it over medium heat until browned on both sides. Arrange the cutlets in a baking dish. Pour the tomato sauce over them. Place a slice of cheese on each cutlet. Bake on the upper level of a 375° oven 10 minutes.

Serves 6.

Veau à la Lucullus

VEAL CUTLETS WITH PÂTÉ

2 pounds veal cutlet, cut in 12 pieces and pounded thin
2½ teaspoons salt
¼ teaspoon white pepper
⅜ pound (1¼ sticks) butter
2 cups thinly sliced onions

2 tablespoons flour
1 cup chicken broth
¾ cup light cream
2 egg yolks
¾ pound mushrooms, sliced
1 3-ounce can pâté de foie gras

Season the veal with 1½ teaspoons of the salt and ⅛ teaspoon of the pepper. Melt 3 tablespoons of the butter in a saucepan over low heat and sauté the onions 15 minutes, but don't let them brown. Mix in the flour, then slowly stir in the broth until smooth. Add the cream and remaining salt and pepper and bring to the boiling point, stirring constantly. Cover and cook over low heat 30 minutes. Purée the mixture in an electric blender or force through a sieve. Beat the egg yolks in a bowl and gradually add a little of the hot sauce, stirring steadily to prevent curdling. Combine with balance of the sauce in the saucepan and cook over low heat, stirring until thickened; do not allow to boil. Melt half the remaining butter in a skillet; sauté the mushrooms 5 minutes. Melt the remaining butter in a skillet and sauté the veal cutlets 5 minutes on each side. Spread 6 slices of veal with the *pâté* and cover with the remaining slices. Arrange in a baking dish in a single layer and surround with the mushrooms. Cover with the sauce and place on the upper level of a 475° oven 10 minutes or until delicately browned.

Serves 6.

Carne de Vitel

RUMANIAN VEAL CUTLETS WITH CHICKEN LIVERS

2 pounds veal cutlet, cut in
12 pieces and pounded
thin
¼ cup flour
2½ teaspoons salt
¾ teaspoon freshly ground
black pepper

¼ pound (1 stick) butter
½ pound chicken livers,
diced
½ cup peeled, chopped
tomatoes
¼ teaspoon marjoram

Dip the veal in a mixture of the flour and half the salt and pepper.

Melt the butter in a skillet until it sizzles; brown the veal on both sides over high heat. Remove. Add the livers to the skillet; cook over high heat 3 minutes. Return the veal and add the tomatoes, marjoram, and the remaining salt and pepper; cook over medium heat 5 minutes longer. Serve with noodles or rice. *Serves 4–6.*

Carne de Vitel Stil Taranesc

RUMANIAN COUNTRY-STYLE VEAL CUTLETS

1½ pounds veal cutlet, cut
in 12 scallops and
pounded thin
¼ cup flour
1½ teaspoons salt
¼ teaspoon freshly ground
black pepper

5 tablespoons butter
3 tablespoons minced
green onions (scallions)
1 tablespoon tomato paste
1 cup sour cream

Dip the scallops in a mixture of the flour, salt, and pepper. Melt the butter in a skillet over medium heat and sauté the veal until browned on both sides and tender. Transfer to a heated platter and keep warm.

In the butter remaining in the skillet, sauté the green onions

3 minutes. Stir in the tomato paste; cook 1 minute. Blend in the sour cream. Heat, stirring steadily, but do not let boil. Taste for seasoning and pour over the scallops.
Serves 4.

Veau à la Stroganoff
VEAL STROGANOFF

1½ pounds veal cutlet, pounded thin
¼ cup flour
1½ teaspoons salt
¼ teaspoon freshly ground black pepper
4 tablespoons butter

½ cup sliced onions
½ cup dry white wine
½ pound mushrooms, sliced and sautéed
1 cup sour cream
1 tablespoon minced parsley

Cut the veal in narrow finger-length strips and toss in a mixture of the flour, salt, and pepper. Heat the butter in a skillet over medium heat and sauté the veal and onions, shaking the pan frequently to brown all sides. Add the wine; cook over low heat 10 minutes or until tender. Mix in the mushrooms, sour cream, and parsley. Taste for seasoning; heat, but do not let boil. Serve with rice or noodles. *Serves 4–6.*

Escalope et Riz de Veau
VEAL CUTLETS AND SWEETBREADS IN PORT WINE SAUCE

1 pound veal cutlet, cut in 8 scallops and pounded thin
1¼ teaspoons salt
¼ teaspoon freshly ground black pepper
6 tablespoons butter

1 pair Parboiled Calf's Sweetbreads*
½ cup port wine
1 tablespoon flour
1 cup heavy cream
½ pound mushrooms, sliced and sautéed

Season the veal with the salt and pepper. Heat 4 tablespoons of the butter in a skillet over medium heat and brown the veal on both sides. Transfer to a hot serving dish.

Remove the membranes and tubes of the sweetbreads, and dice the sweetbreads. Add the remaining butter to the skillet, and lightly brown the sweetbreads in it. Transfer to the serving dish.

Stir the port wine into the pan juices and cook over high heat 2 minutes. Mix the flour with a little cream until smooth, then add the rest of the cream; add to the skillet and bring to a boil, stirring constantly. Add the mushrooms, taste for seasoning, and cook over low heat 2 minutes. Pour sauce over the veal and sweetbreads and serve.

Serves 4.

Ternera con Berenjenas

SPANISH BAKED VEAL CUTLETS WITH EGGPLANT

6 tablespoons olive oil
1½ pounds veal cutlet, cut in 18 small scallops and pounded thin
1 eggplant, peeled and sliced thin
1 cup thinly sliced onions
2 cups cubed tomatoes
1 cup diced green peppers
1½ teaspoons salt
½ teaspoon freshly ground black pepper
½ teaspoon orégano

Heat 3 tablespoons of the oil in a skillet over medium heat and brown the meat on both sides. Rub a baking dish with 1 tablespoon of the oil; arrange successive layers of the eggplant, veal, onions, tomatoes, and green peppers, seasoning each layer with a mixture of the salt, pepper, and orégano. Sprinkle with the remaining oil. Cover and bake in a 350° oven 1¼ hours, removing the cover for the last 15 minutes.

Serves 6.

Kalbsschnitzel nach Schweizer Art

EMMENTAL VEAL CUTLETS

1½ pounds veal cutlet, cut
in 6 pieces and pounded
thin
¼ cup flour
1¼ teaspoons salt
⅛ teaspoon freshly ground
black pepper

2 eggs, beaten
¾ cup dry bread crumbs
6 tablespoons butter
6 slices Swiss cheese, cut ⅛
inch thick
6 fried eggs

Dip the veal in a mixture of the flour, salt, and pepper, then in the beaten eggs, and finally in the bread crumbs, coating all sides well.

Melt the butter in a skillet; sauté the veal over low heat until browned on both sides. Put a slice of cheese on each cutlet, and place under a hot broiler until melted. Serve with a fried egg on each cutlet. *Serves 6.*

Wiener Schnitzel

VIENNESE VEAL CUTLETS

1½ pounds veal cutlet, cut
in 6 pieces and pounded
thin
½ cup flour
1½ teaspoons salt
¼ teaspoon freshly ground
black pepper

2 eggs, beaten
¾ cup fine dry bread
crumbs
¼ pound (1 stick)
3 tablespoons lemon juice
3 tablespoons chopped
parsley

Dip each piece of veal in a mixture of the flour, salt, and pepper, then in the beaten eggs, and finally in the bread crumbs. Melt half the butter in a large skillet and sauté the veal in a single layer over medium heat until tender and well browned on both sides, about 5 minutes. Transfer to a hot serving platter. Add remaining butter to the skillet and allow to brown. Mix in the lemon juice and parsley. Pour over the veal and serve. *Serves 6.*

Piccata al Marsala
VEAL SCALOPPINE WITH MARSALA

1½ pounds veal cutlet, cut in 16 pieces and pounded thin
½ cup flour
2 teaspoons salt

½ teaspoon freshly ground black pepper
2 tablespoons butter
2 tablespoons olive oil
⅓ cup Marsala

Dip each piece of veal in a mixture of the flour, salt, and pepper.

Heat the butter and oil in a heavy skillet and brown the veal on both sides over high heat. Add the wine and bring to a boil and cook over medium heat 2 minutes. *Serves 4–6.*

Oiseaux de Veau sans Tête
FRENCH PROVINCIAL VEAL BIRDS

2 pounds veal cutlet, cut in 6 pieces and pounded thin
2 teaspoons salt
½ teaspoon freshly ground black pepper
¼ teaspoon nutmeg
¼ teaspoon thyme
¼ pound sausage meat
½ teaspoon marjoram

3 tablespoons grated onion
2 cloves garlic, minced
2 tablespoons minced parsley
4 tablespoons butter
1 cup dry white wine
12 small white onions
½ pound mushrooms, sliced and sautéed
1 bay leaf

Rub each cutlet with a mixture of 1½ teaspoons of the salt, ¼ teaspoon of the pepper, the nutmeg, and thyme.

Mix the sausage meat with the marjoram, grated onion, garlic, parsley, and remaining salt and pepper. Spread the mixture on the veal cutlets and roll up. Tie with string or fasten with skewers or toothpicks.

Melt the butter in a deep skillet over medium heat and brown the rolls on all sides. Add the wine, white onions, mushrooms, and bay leaf. Cover and bake in a 375° oven 45 minutes or until tender. Shake the pan once or twice but don't lift the cover. Transfer the rolls to a hot platter and remove the fastenings. Discard the bay leaf and taste the gravy for seasoning.
Serves 6.

Braciolette Ripiene

VEAL BIRDS, HUNTER'S STYLE

2 pounds veal cutlet, cut in 12 pieces and pounded thin	1 tablespoon parsley
	¼ teaspoon sage
	2 teaspoons flour
1¾ teaspoons salt	1 cup Marsala or sweet sherry
½ teaspoon freshly ground black pepper	12 slices Italian or French bread, toasted
½ pound chicken livers	2 tablespoons water
4 tablespoons butter	
2 slices prosciutto (ham)	

Season the veal with 1¼ teaspoons of the salt and ¼ teaspoon of the pepper. Sauté the chicken livers in 2 tablespoons of the butter 5 minutes; chop fine with the prosciutto, parsley, sage, and remaining salt and pepper. On each veal cutlet, spread some of the liver mixture. Roll up each slice, fasten with toothpicks or tie with string. Melt the remaining butter in a skillet over medium heat and brown the rolls on all sides. Sprinkle the flour over the birds, add the wine, and cook 20 minutes, turning the rolls frequently.

Arrange the toast on a serving platter. Remove the birds from the pan and place them on the slices of toast. Remove the fastenings. Mix the water into the pan juices, bring to a boil, and pour over veal birds. *Serves 6.*

Involto di Vitello alla Milanese
MILANESE VEAL BIRDS

½ pound ground veal
1 clove garlic, minced
¼ cup finely chopped
  parsley
2 tablespoons dry white
  wine
⅛ teaspoon nutmeg
2 teaspoons salt

½ teaspoon freshly ground
  black pepper
1½ pounds veal cutlet, cut
  in 6 pieces and pounded
  thin
⅓ cup flour
6 tablespoons butter
¼ teaspoon sage

Mix together the ground veal, garlic, parsley, wine, nutmeg, ¾ teaspoon of the salt, and ¼ teaspoon of the pepper. Spread some of the mixture on each of the cutlets, roll up, and tie with thread.

Mix the flour with the remaining salt and pepper; dip the rolls in the mixture. Melt the butter in a skillet; add the sage and rolls. Sauté over medium heat 20 minutes or until brown on all sides and tender. Remove the threads. *Serves 6.*

Perdices de Capellán
SPANISH VEAL BIRDS

¼ pound sausage meat
1½ pounds veal cutlet, cut
in 6 pieces and pounded
  thin
6 slices ham
½ cup flour
2 teaspoons salt

½ teaspoon freshly ground
  black pepper
2 tablespoons olive oil
2 tablespoons butter
1 clove garlic, minced
½ teaspoon thyme
1 tablespoon minced parsley
1 cup dry white wine

Form the sausage meat into 6 sausage shapes and brown lightly in a skillet. Drain well.

On each piece of veal, place a slice of ham and then a sausage.

Roll up and tie with thread or fasten with toothpicks. Dip the rolls in a mixture of the flour, salt, and pepper.

Heat the oil and butter in a skillet and brown the birds over medium heat on all sides. Add the garlic, thyme, parsley, and half the wine. Cover, bring to a boil, and cook over low heat 15 minutes. Add the remaining wine and cook 15 minutes longer, or until tender. Remove the fastenings.

Serves 6.

Rolinhos de Vitela com Anchovas
PORTUGUESE VEAL ROLLS WITH ANCHOVIES

1 pound veal cutlet, cut in 8 pieces and pounded thin

½ cup grated Parmesan cheese

8 anchovy fillets

1 teaspoon salt

¼ teaspoon freshly ground black pepper

4 tablespoons butter

½ cup beef broth

3 tablespoons chopped parsley

Sprinkle each slice of veal with some cheese, and then put an anchovy over it. Roll up and fasten with toothpicks or tie with thread. Season the veal with the salt and pepper. Melt half the butter in a skillet over medium heat and brown the rolls on all sides. Add 3 tablespoons of the broth; cook over low heat 15 minutes. Transfer rolls to a heated serving dish, and remove fastenings.

Mix the remaining broth into the skillet, scraping the bottom. Cook 3 minutes, remove from heat and mix in the remaining butter. Add the parsley and pour over rolls.

Serves 4.

Aleta de Ternera

SPANISH VEAL ROLL

Breast of veal, boned and
 pounded as thin as
 possible
1 clove garlic, minced
2½ teaspoons salt
½ teaspoon freshly ground
 black pepper
6 tablespoons olive oil
¼ pound ham, cut julienne
3 hard-cooked eggs, sliced
3 dill pickles, cut julienne

1 cup chopped onions
½ cup grated carrots
1 cup peeled, chopped
 tomatoes
3 tablespoons minced
 parsley
1 bay leaf
¼ teaspoon thyme
½ cup dry white wine
1 cup sliced pimiento-stuffed
 olives

Rub the veal with the garlic, salt, and pepper. Heat 2 table-spoons of the oil in a skillet; sauté the ham for 5 minutes. Arrange the sliced eggs on the meat, sprinkle with the ham, arrange the pickles over it. Roll up the meat and tie with thread.

Heat the remaining oil in a casserole or Dutch oven over medium heat and brown the meat on all sides. Remove the meat and sauté the onions and carrots until browned. Mix in the tomatoes; cook for 5 minutes. Return the meat and add the parsley, bay leaf, thyme, and wine. Cover and bake in a 350° oven for 2 hours, basting occasionally and adding a little water if necessary. Add the olives and bake 10 minutes longer. Remove the thread from the meat. Slice and serve. *Serves 6–8.*

Veal Chops, Anglo-Indian Style

6 veal chops, cut 1½ inches
 thick
½ cup cider vinegar
¼ cup vegetable oil
¼ cup ketchup
½ teaspoon turmeric
½ teaspoon ground
 cuminseeds

½ teaspoon crushed
 coriander seeds
1 teaspoon chili powder
¼ teaspoon dried ground
 chili peppers
1½ teaspoons salt
½ cup minced onion
1 clove garlic, sliced

Trim the fat from the chops. Combine the remaining ingredients in a bowl. Marinate the chops in the mixture 3 hours at room temperature.

Drain the chops and arrange on a broiling pan. Broil 5 inches from source of heat 20 minutes on each side, or until browned and tender, basting frequently with the marinade.

Serves 6.

Braciole di Vitello con Vino
BREADED VEAL CHOPS IN WINE SAUCE

6 loin veal chops, cut 1
  inch thick
1½ teaspoons salt
½ teaspoon freshly ground
  black pepper
6 tablespoons butter
1 cup dry bread crumbs
2 cloves
12 small white onions

½ pound mushrooms, sliced
1 clove garlic, minced
¾ cup dry white wine
1½ cups beef broth
1 bay leaf
¼ teaspoon thyme
2 tablespoons minced
  parsley

Trim the fat from the chops. Rub the chops with the salt and pepper. Melt the butter in a casserole or Dutch oven over medium heat and brown the chops on both sides. Remove the chops and stir the bread crumbs into the butter remaining in the pan until browned. Stick the cloves in 1 onion, and add the onions to the pan with the chops, the mushrooms, garlic, wine, broth, bay leaf, and thyme. Cover and bake in a 375° oven for 1 hour, removing the cover for the last 15 minutes. Sprinkle with the parsley.

Serves 6.

Côtes de Veau à la Bonne Femme

VEAL CHOPS, FRENCH HOME STYLE

6 veal chops, cut ¾ inch
   thick and pounded lightly
½ cup flour
1½ teaspoons salt
¼ teaspoon white pepper
6 tablespoons butter

12 small white onions
6 slices cooked bacon,
   crumbled
½ cup dry white wine
½ cup chicken broth

Trim the fat from the chops, then dip in a mixture of the flour, salt, and pepper. Melt half the butter in a skillet over medium heat and lightly brown the whole onions. Remove the onions. Add the remaining butter to the skillet and brown the chops on both sides. Return the onions, and add the bacon, wine, and broth. Cover and cook over low heat 25 minutes or until chops are tender. *Serves 6.*

Côtes de Veau aux Herbes

FRENCH PROVINCIAL VEAL CHOPS WITH HERBS

6 veal chops, cut 1 inch
   thick
2 tablespoons olive oil
6 tablespoons butter
1½ teaspoons salt
½ teaspoon freshly ground
   black pepper

¼ cup chopped onions
1 clove garlic, minced
½ teaspoon thyme
½ teaspoon basil
¼ cup minced parsley
½ cup dry white wine
¼ cup heavy cream

Trim the fat from the chops. Heat the oil and 2 tablespoons of the butter in a large skillet over medium heat and brown the chops on both sides. Transfer to a baking pan and sprinkle with the salt and pepper. Pour off the fat from the skillet. Melt 2 tablespoons of the remaining butter in the skillet; sauté the onions 5 minutes. Add the garlic, thyme, basil, parsley, and wine and bring to a boil, scraping the bottom of any browned particles.

Pour over the chops. Cover and bake in a 325°oven 30 minutes, or until chops are tender. Baste and turn a few times. Transfer the chops to a hot platter. Place the baking pan over direct heat. Stir the cream into the pan juices. Bring to a boil and cook over high heat 2 minutes. Taste for seasoning, then stir in small pieces of the remaining butter until just melted. Pour over the chops. *Serves 6.*

Côtes de Veau, Sauce Moutarde

FRENCH PROVINCIAL VEAL CHOPS WITH MUSTARD SAUCE

6 loin or rib veal chops, cut ¾ inch thick	2 tablespoons olive oil
1½ teaspoons salt	2 teaspoons prepared French mustard
¼ teaspoon white pepper	⅓ cup heavy cream
4 tablespoons butter	1 tablespoon minced parsley
2 tablespoons white wine vinegar	

Trim the fat from the chops. Season the chops with the salt and pepper. Melt the butter in a skillet and sauté the chops over very low heat for 15 minutes on each side or until tender. Transfer to a heated serving dish. To the juices in the pan, blend in the vinegar, oil, mustard, and cream. Heat, scraping the bottom of browned glaze, but do not let boil. Pour the sauce over the chops. Sprinkle with parsley and serve. *Serves 6.*

Borjúpörkölt

HUNGARIAN VEAL CHOPS

8 veal chops, cut ½ inch thick and pounded lightly	½ teaspoon freshly ground black pepper
4 tablespoons butter	2 cloves garlic, minced
2 cups thinly sliced onions	2 teaspoons paprika
1¼ teaspoons salt	¾ cup boiling water
	½ cup sour cream

Trim the fat from the chops. Melt the butter in a skillet over medium heat and sauté the onions 10 minutes. Add the chops and brown on both sides. Season with the salt, pepper, garlic, and paprika. Cover and cook over low heat 30 minutes, adding small quantities of the water from time to time as the pan becomes dry. Stir in the sour cream just before serving. Serve with parsley potatoes.

Serves 4.

Costolette di Vitello al Cartoccio
ITALIAN VEAL CHOPS PREPARED IN PAPER

6 veal chops, cut ¾ inch
thick
4 tablespoons butter
½ pound sausage meat
1 cup sliced mushrooms
1 clove garlic, minced

¼ teaspoon thyme
1½ teaspoons salt
½ teaspoon freshly ground
black pepper
2 tablespoons vegetable oil

Trim the fat from the chops. Melt 1 tablespoon of the butter in a skillet; add the sausage meat, mushrooms, garlic, and thyme. Cook over medium heat 5 minutes, stirring frequently. Taste for seasoning and drain off the fat.

Season the chops with the salt and pepper. Melt the remaining butter in a skillet and sauté the chops over low heat until browned on both sides.

Cut 6 pieces of parchment paper or aluminum foil large enough to wrap the chops completely. Brush each piece with oil. Using half the sausage mixture, spread some on each paper. Put the chops over it and cover with the remaining sausage mixture. Fold over the paper and seal the edges. Bake in a 425° oven 20 minutes. Serve in the papers.

Serves 6.

Costolette di Vitello

ITALIAN BREADED VEAL CHOPS

4 loin veal chops, cut 1
  inch thick and pounded
  lightly
1 cup dry bread crumbs
½ cup grated Parmesan
  cheese
1 tablespoon chopped
  parsley

1¼ teaspoons salt
¼ teaspoon freshly ground
  black pepper
1 egg
2 tablespoons water
4 tablespoons butter or
  vegetable oil

Trim the fat from the chops. Mix together the bread crumbs, cheese, and parsley on a piece of waxed paper. Rub the chops with the salt and pepper, dip them into the egg beaten with the water, then coat heavily with the bread crumb mixture.

Melt the butter or oil in a skillet, add the chops, and cook over medium low heat 15 minutes on each side or until tender. *Serves 4.*

Costolette de Vitello Valdostana

ITALIAN STUFFED VEAL CHOPS

6 veal chops, cut 1¼
  inches thick
¾ teaspoon salt
½ teaspoon freshly ground
  black pepper
6 slices prosciutto (ham)
6 slices fontina or
  mozzarella cheese

¼ cup flour
6 tablespoons butter
½ cup dry vermouth
¼ teaspoon thyme
½ teaspoon crushed bay leaf

Trim the fat from the chops and split each chop open by cutting through the middle horizontally, so that each opens like a book. Pound each side flat lightly. Season the outside of the chops with the salt and pepper. Place a slice of prosciutto and cheese on the cut sides of the chops and close the chops, pressing the edges together. Dip the chops in the flour.

Heat the butter in a skillet and sauté the veal over medium heat until browned on both sides. Add the vermouth, thyme, and bay leaf; cover and cook over low heat 25 minutes or until chops are tender.

Serves 6.

Costolette di Vitello nel Pomodori

ITALIAN VEAL CHOPS IN TOMATO SAUCE

6 veal chops, cut 1 inch thick
3 tablespoons butter
½ pound mushrooms, thinly sliced
1½ cups peeled, diced tomatoes
½ cup julienne-cut ham

¼ cup dry white wine
½ teaspoon thyme
2½ teaspoons salt
½ teaspoon freshly ground black pepper
3 tablespoons olive oil
2 tablespoons minced parsley

Trim the fat from the chops. Melt the butter in a saucepan; sauté the mushrooms over low heat 5 minutes. Add the tomatoes, ham, wine, thyme, 1 teaspoon of the salt, and ¼ teaspoon of the pepper. Bring to a boil and cook over low heat 15 minutes.

Season the chops with the remaining salt and pepper. Heat the oil in a skillet over medium heat and brown the chops on both sides. Spread half the sauce in a baking dish. Arrange the chops over it and cover with the remaining sauce. Sprinkle with the parsley; cover the pan. Bake in a 375° oven 15 minutes or until chops are tender.

Serves 6.

Piquant Braised Veal Chops

6 veal chops, cut 1 inch thick
2 teaspoons salt
½ teaspoon freshly ground black pepper
3 tablespoons flour
2 tablespoons vegetable oil
3 cups thinly sliced onions

2 tablespoons wine vinegar
2 tablespoons minced parsley
1 clove garlic, minced
¼ teaspoon thyme
1 bay leaf, crushed
¾ cup boiling water

Trim the fat from the chops. Rub the chops with the salt and pepper, then dip in the flour. Heat the oil in a skillet; spread the onions in the skillet and arrange the chops over them. Cover and cook over medium heat 10 minutes. Turn chops and cook 5 minutes. Add the vinegar, parsley, garlic, thyme, and bay leaf. Cover and cook 10 minutes, turning the chops several times. Add the water; cover and cook over low heat 45 minutes. *Serves 6.*

Côtelettes de Veau Lorraine

VEAL CHOPS, LORRAINE STYLE

4 loin veal chops, cut ½ inch thick
½ cup diced lean bacon
1 tablespoon butter
¾ teaspoon salt
¼ teaspoon freshly ground black pepper

2 shallots, finely chopped
1 teaspoon chopped parsley
½ cup dry white wine
½ cup chicken broth
2 egg yolks
1 teaspoon lemon juice

Trim the fat from the chops. Brown the bacon in a skillet; drain bacon and pour off all but 1 tablespoon fat. Add the butter to the skillet. Add the chops, sprinkle with salt and pepper, and cook over medium heat 20 minutes, turning to brown both sides. Remove chops and keep hot.

Add the shallots and parsley. Cook, stirring steadily, for 1 minute, but do not brown. Mix in the wine and broth, stirring the glaze from the pan. Simmer until liquid is reduced a little. Beat the egg yolks in a bowl. Gradually mix in a little of the hot liquid, stirring constantly to prevent curdling, then return mixture to pan, stirring steadily to prevent curdling. Reheat, stirring, but do not boil. Return chops and bacon to sauce and heat through. Taste for seasoning. Add lemon juice, stir, and serve.

Serves 4.

Costolette di Vitello con Salsa Piccante

NEAPOLITAN VEAL CHOPS WITH SPICY SAUCE

6 rib veal chops, cut 1 inch thick
2 teaspoons salt
¾ teaspoon freshly ground black pepper
6 tablespoons olive oil
4 green peppers, thinly sliced
¾ cup sliced onions

1 cup peeled, chopped tomatoes
¼ cup sliced green olives
1 tablespoon capers
1 clove garlic, minced
2 anchovies, minced
¼ cup flour
2 tablespoons wine vinegar

Have the bones of the chops cut down short and trim the fat. Rub the chops with 1½ teaspoons of the salt and ½ teaspoon of the pepper.

Heat 3 tablespoons of the oil in a skillet; sauté the peppers and onions 10 minutes. Mix in the tomatoes, olives, capers, and remaining salt and pepper. Cook over low heat 20 minutes. Stir in the garlic and anchovies. Prepare the chops meanwhile.

Dip the chops in the flour. Heat the remaining oil in a skillet over medium heat and sauté the chops until tender, turning to brown on both sides, about 25 minutes. Transfer to a heated serving dish. Stir the vinegar into the skillet, scraping the bottom well. Bring to a boil and pour over the chops. Spoon the pepper mixture over all.

Serves 6.

Kalbnuss, Elsasser Art
VEAL CHOPS WITH SAUERKRAUT

8 rib veal chops, cut 1 inch thick	1 cup dry white wine
1½ teaspoons salt	½ teaspoon caraway seeds
½ teaspoon freshly ground black pepper	4 tablespoons butter
2 pounds sauerkraut	1 cup chopped onions
	½ cup water

Trim the fat from the chops. Rub the chops with the salt and pepper.

Combine the sauerkraut, wine, and caraway seeds in a casserole. Cover and cook over low heat 1¼ hours, stirring frequently. While the sauerkraut is cooking, prepare the veal.

Melt the butter in a skillet over moderate heat and brown the veal on both sides. Add the onions, and cook 5 minutes. Add the water; cover and cook over low heat 30 minutes, or until the veal is tender, turning the chops several times. When the sauerkraut is cooked, arrange the veal over it, and pour pan juices on top. Cook 5 minutes longer.

Serves 8.

Smothered Veal Chops

6 veal chops, cut ¾ inch thick and pounded lightly	½ teaspoon freshly ground black pepper
½ cup cracker meal	2 eggs
¼ cup dry bread crumbs	6 tablespoons butter
2 teaspoons salt	1½ cups sliced onions
	¼ cup boiling water

Trim the fat from the chops. Mix together the cracker meal, bread crumbs, 1½ teaspoons of the salt, and the pepper. Beat the eggs and remaining salt. Dip the chops in the dry mixture, in the eggs, and then the dry mixture again. Let stand 15 minutes.

Melt half the butter in a skillet over medium heat and sauté the onions 10 minutes. Remove. Melt the remaining butter in the skillet; brown the chops on both sides. Spread the onions over the chops and add the water. Cover the skillet and cook over low heat 20 minutes, or until chops are tender, turning them once. *Serves 6.*

Southern Style Veal Chops

6 veal chops, cut ¾ inch
   thick and pounded lightly
1½ teaspoons salt
¼ teaspoon white pepper
1 cup crushed cornflakes

2 eggs
2 tablespoons light cream
2 tablespoons vegetable oil
3 tablespoons butter

Trim the fat from the veal. Season the chops with the salt and pepper. Dip in the cornflakes, then in the eggs beaten with the cream, and again in the cornflakes. Heat the oil and butter in a skillet (with an ovenproof handle). Brown the chops over medium heat on both sides. Cover and bake in a 325° oven 30 minutes or until tender; turn the chops after 15 minutes' baking time. *Serves 6.*

Chuletas de Ternera

VEAL CHOPS IN SPANISH SAUCE

6 veal chops, cut ¾ inch
   thick and pounded
   lightly
1½ teaspoons salt
½ teaspoon freshly ground
   black pepper
3 tablespoons olive oil
½ cup chopped mushrooms

¾ cup minced onions
¾ cup dry white wine
½ cup canned tomato sauce
2 teaspoons unsweetened
   cocoa
¼ teaspoon saffron
¼ cup ground almonds

Trim the fat from the chops and rub them with the salt and pepper. Heat the oil in a skillet over medium heat and brown the chops on both sides. Transfer to a baking dish in a single layer and cover with the mushrooms. To the oil remaining in the skillet add the onions. Sauté 10 minutes. Add the wine and tomato sauce; cook over low heat 10 minutes. Stir in the cocoa, saffron, and almonds. Taste for seasoning. Pour over the chops. Cover and bake in a 325° oven 40 minutes, removing the cover for the last 5 minutes.

Serves 6.

Kalbskoteletten nach Schweizer Art

SWISS BREADED STUFFED VEAL CHOPS

6 veal chops, cut 1 inch thick
6 slices boiled ham
6 thin slices Swiss cheese
2 eggs, beaten
¼ cup flour
2 teaspoons salt

½ teaspoon freshly ground black pepper
¾ cup dry bread crumbs
¼ pound (1 stick) butter
½ cup heavy cream
2 tablespoons minced parsley

Trim the fat from the chops and split them through the center from the outer edge to the bone, leaving the bone side connected. Open the chops like a book and pound each side as thin as possible. Place a slice of ham and cheese on each. Trim the cheese if it comes too close to the edge. Close the chops, moisten the edges with a little egg, and press together. Dip lightly in the flour mixed with the salt and pepper, then in the eggs, and finally in the bread crumbs.

Melt the butter in a skillet; sauté the chops over low heat 15 minutes on each side or until tender and browned. Transfer the chops to a heated serving dish. Stir the cream into the skillet, scraping the bottom of browned particles. Heat and pour over the chops. Sprinkle with the parsley.

Serves 6.

Panerade Kalukotletter Med Champinjoner

SWEDISH VEAL CHOPS WITH MUSHROOMS

4 loin veal chops, cut 1½
    inches thick
1½ teaspoons salt
½ teaspoon white pepper
2 tablespoons lemon juice
2 eggs beaten
¼ cup finely chopped
    mushrooms

2 tablespoons parsley
⅓ cup dry bread crumbs
2 tablespoons vegetable oil
6 tablespoons butter
½ cup sliced mushrooms
2 tablespoons flour
1 cup cream

Trim the fat from the chops. Rub the chops with the salt, pepper, and lemon juice. Dip the chops in the beaten eggs, then in a mixture of the chopped mushrooms, parsley, and bread crumbs. Heat the oil and butter in a skillet and sauté the chops over medium heat until brown on both sides and tender. Remove chops and keep warm. Add the sliced mushrooms; cook 3 minutes. Blend in the flour, then add the cream and bring to the boiling point, stirring steadily. Cook 3 minutes longer. Taste for seasoning. Serve sauce in a sauceboat.

Serves 4.

Geschmorte Kalbshaxe

BAVARIAN BRAISED VEAL KNUCKLES

3 tablespoons vegetable oil
4 pounds meaty veal
    knuckles, sawed into 6
    rounds
1 cup chopped onions
1 cup sliced carrots
1 cup sliced celery

½ cup chopped tomatoes
2 teaspoons salt
½ teaspoon freshly ground
    black pepper
½ teaspoon thyme
1 bay leaf
2 cups boiling water

Heat the oil in a Dutch oven or heavy saucepan over medium heat and brown the knuckles on all sides. Add the onions, carrots, celery, tomatoes, salt, pepper, and thyme and cook until vegetables brown lightly. Add the bay leaf and water; cover and cook over low heat 2½ hours, or until the meat is tender. Turn pieces occasionally, and add a little more boiling water if necessary. The gravy should be thick when finished. Arrange the knuckles on a hot serving dish, and pour gravy over them, discarding the bay leaf.

Serves 6.

Ossi Bucchi

ITALIAN BRAISED VEAL KNUCKLES

4 pounds meaty veal
knuckles, sawed into
3-inch pieces
¼ cup flour
2 tablespoons olive oil
2 tablespoons butter
2 teaspoons salt
½ teaspoon freshly ground
black pepper
¼ teaspoon rosemary
¾ cup chopped onions

¼ cup grated carrots
1 stalk celery, chopped
1 cup dry white wine
1 tablespoon tomato paste
½ cup water
2 tablespoons grated lemon
rind
1 clove garlic, minced
2 tablespoons minced
parsley

Roll the knuckles lightly in the flour. Heat the oil and butter in a Dutch oven or heavy saucepan over medium heat and brown the knuckles on all sides. Sprinkle with the salt, pepper, and rosemary. Add the onions, carrots, and celery. Cook 5 minutes. Add the wine, tomato paste, and water. Cover and cook over low heat 2 hours, or until tender. Add small amounts of boiling water from time to time if necessary. Mix together the lemon rind, garlic, and parsley; stir into the gravy. Cook 5 minutes longer.

Serves 4–6.

Kalbsgulyás

AUSTRIAN FRICASSEE OF VEAL

3 cups water
1 carrot
1 onion
1 bay leaf ⎫
Sprig parsley ⎪ tied
1 stalk ⎬ together
celery ⎭
¾ teaspoon salt
¼ teaspoon freshly ground
black pepper
2 pounds boneless lean
veal, cut into 1½-inch
cubes

3 tablespoons butter
¾ cup chopped onions
1 tablespoon flour
½ cup dry white wine
12 small white onions
½ pound mushrooms, sliced
2 egg yolks
½ cup heavy cream
Finely chopped parsley
and chives

Combine the water, carrot, onion, herb bundle, salt, and pepper; bring to a boil and cook over medium heat for 20 minutes. Add the veal and cook 5 minutes. Remove meat, strain and reserve stock. Melt the butter in a saucepan; add the chopped onions and cook 5 minutes, but do not brown. Add the veal and stir in the flour, wine, and the reserved stock. Cover and simmer ½ hour. Add the small white onions and mushrooms; cook 30 minutes longer. In a bowl, beat the egg yolks and cream; add a little hot sauce to egg-cream mixture, stirring steadily to prevent curdling. Return to balance of sauce. Reheat but do not boil. Adjust seasoning, sprinkle with chopped parsley and chives, and serve.

Serves 4.

Blanquette de Veau
FRICASSEE OF VEAL, CREAM STYLE

3 pounds boneless veal, cut
  ½ inch thick
1 carrot, quartered
2 onions
1 bay leaf
2 teaspoons salt
¼ teaspoon white pepper

½ teaspoon thyme
2 tablespoons butter
2 tablespoons flour
2 egg yolks
¼ cup light cream
1 cup sliced, sautéed
  mushrooms

Cut the veal into oblongs about 2 inches by 5 inches. Combine in a saucepan with cold water to cover and bring to a boil. Skim the surface of any foam and add the carrot, onions, bay leaf, salt, pepper, and thyme. Cover and cook over medium heat 1 hour or until veal is tender. Drain the meat. Strain the stock, reserving 2½ cups.

Melt the butter in a saucepan; blend in the flour. Gradually add the reserved stock, stirring steadily to the boiling point, then cook over low heat 10 minutes. Beat the egg yolks and cream in a bowl; gradually add a little hot sauce, stirring constantly to prevent curdling. Return to balance of sauce and cook until thickened, stirring steadily. Mix in the veal and mushrooms and taste for seasoning. Cook over very low heat 10 minutes, but do not allow to boil.

Serves 6–8.

Veau aux Noix d'Acajou
VEAL WITH CASHEW NUTS

3 tablespoons vegetable oil
3 pounds boneless shoulder
  of veal, cut in 1-inch
  cubes
2½ teaspoons salt
½ teaspoon freshly ground
  black pepper

16 small white onions
1 clove garlic, minced
1 8-ounce can tomato sauce
1 tablespoon Worcestershire
  sauce
½ cup boiling water
1 cup cashew nuts

Heat the oil in a Dutch oven or heavy casserole over medium heat and brown the veal on all sides. Add the salt, pepper, onions, and garlic; cook 5 minutes. Stir in the tomato sauce, Worcestershire, and boiling water. Bring to a boil, cover, and cook over low heat 45 minutes. Add the nuts. Re-cover and cook 25 minutes longer or until veal is tender.

Serves 6–8

Creole Veal Steak

4 tablespoons butter
3 pounds veal steak, cut
  in serving-sized pieces
3 teaspoons salt
¾ teaspoon freshly ground
  black pepper
½ pound ham, diced
3 sweet potatoes, peeled
  and sliced
2 tablespoons olive oil
1½ cups chopped onions

1 clove garlic, minced
1 16-ounce can tomatoes,
  drained and chopped
¼ teaspoon cayenne pepper
3 tablespoons minced
  parsley
¼ teaspoon thyme
1 bay leaf, crushed
¾ pound okra or 1 package
  frozen

Melt the butter in a deep skillet over medium heat and brown the veal on both sides. Season with 2 teaspoons salt and the pepper. Add the ham and sweet potatoes; cover and cook over low heat 20 minutes. Prepare the sauce meanwhile.

Heat the oil in a saucepan; brown the onions and garlic in it. Add the tomatoes, cayenne pepper, parsley, thyme, bay leaf, and remaining salt. Bring to a boil and cook over low heat 10 minutes. Add to the veal. Cover and cook 30 minutes.

Slice the okra and add to the veal. Cook 20 minutes longer. Taste for seasoning. *Serves 6–8.*

Prae tud Vasikaliha Hapukoore Soustiga
ESTONIAN VEAL STEW

2 tablespoons olive oil
2 tablespoons butter
¾ cup chopped onions
¼ cup chopped celery
Breast of veal, cut in
   serving-sized pieces, bone
   and all
2 cups peeled, cubed
   tomatoes

2 teaspoons salt
½ teaspoon freshly ground
   black pepper
½ teaspoon thyme
¾ cup hot beef broth
2 tablespoons minced
   parsley
1 cup sour cream

Heat the oil and butter in a Dutch oven or heavy casserole; sauté the onions and celery 5 minutes. Add the veal and cook over medium heat until well browned on all sides. Add the tomatoes, salt, pepper, and thyme. Cover and cook over low heat 1¼ hours, adding the broth from time to time. Skim the fat. Stir in the parsley and sour cream. *Serves 4–6.*

Étuvée de Veau
FRENCH PROVINCIAL VEAL IN RED WINE

24 small cubes lean bacon
2 tablespoons butter
24 small white onions
3 pounds boneless veal, cut
   in 1½-inch cubes
1½ teaspoons salt
½ teaspoon freshly ground
   black pepper
1 bay leaf
1 sprig   } tied
   parsley   } together
1 stalk celery

2 cloves garlic
2½ cups dry red wine
1 tablespoon potato flour
2 tablespoons water

Brown the bacon cubes in a Dutch oven or heavy skillet; drain and discard all but 2 tablespoons of fat. Add the butter and sauté the onions until lightly browned. Remove the onions, add the veal to the pan, and brown over medium heat on all sides. Season with the salt and pepper and add the bay leaf, parsley, celery, garlic, and wine. Replace onions and bacon, cover and cook over low heat 2 hours. Mix the potato starch with the water and stir into the gravy. Simmer 15 minutes. Remove bay leaf, parsley, celery, and garlic.

Serves 6–8.

Veau à la Marengo
VEAL IN WHITE WINE

3 tablespoons olive oil
2 pounds boneless veal, cut
  in 1½-inch squares
1 clove garlic, minced
¾ cup chopped onions
1½ cups peeled, diced
  tomatoes
1½ teaspoons salt
¼ teaspoon freshly ground
  black pepper

2 tablespoons flour
1 cup chicken broth
1 cup dry white wine
½ pound mushrooms, sliced
  and sautéed
4 slices French bread,
  sautéed

Heat the oil in a Dutch oven or heavy saucepan over medium heat and brown the veal on all sides. Add the garlic, onions, tomatoes, salt, and pepper. Brown lightly. Sprinkle with the flour and slowly mix in the broth and wine, stirring until smooth. Cover and cook over low heat 1 hour. Add the mushrooms, cover, and cook 15 minutes longer, or until veal is tender. Taste for seasoning. Serve garnished with the sautéed bread.

Serves 4.

Stufatino Firenze
FLORENTINE VEAL STEW

⅓ cup olive oil
Breast of veal, cut in
  serving-sized pieces, bone
  and all
1 tablespoon chopped
  parsley
2 cloves garlic, minced
1 bay leaf

½ teaspoon thyme
2 teaspoons salt
½ teaspoon freshly ground
  black pepper
1 cup dry white wine
1 8-ounce can tomato sauce
½ cup boiling water

Heat the oil in a Dutch oven or heavy saucepan; add the meat
and brown over medium heat on all sides. Mix in the parsley,
garlic, bay leaf, thyme, salt, pepper, and wine; cook over low
heat until wine is absorbed. Add the tomatoes and water; cover
and cook 1½ hours, or until meat is tender. Discard the bay leaf.
Serves 6–8.

Veau à la Guadeloupe
GUADELOUPE VEAL STEAK

3 pounds veal steak, cut
  1½ inches thick
3 teaspoons salt
¾ teaspoon freshly ground
  black pepper
4 tablespoons butter
½ pound ham, diced
2 sweet potatoes, peeled
  and quartered
1½ cups chopped onions

1 clove garlic, minced
3 tablespoons minced
  parsley
¼ teaspoon thyme
1 bay leaf, finely chopped
1 16-ounce can tomatoes,
  drained and chopped
¼ teaspoon cayenne pepper
¾ pound okra or 1 package
  frozen, sliced

Cut the veal steak into pieces about 2 inches wide and 3 inches
long. Season with 2 teaspoons of the salt and the pepper. Melt

2 tablespoons of the butter in a Dutch oven or heavy saucepan and brown the veal over medium heat. Add the ham and sweet potatoes; cover and cook over very low heat 20 minutes. Prepare the sauce meanwhile.

Melt the remaining butter in a skillet; brown the onions, garlic, parsley, thyme, and bay leaf. Add the tomatoes, cayenne pepper, and remaining salt. Bring to a boil and cook over low heat 10 minutes. Add to the veal. Cover and cook 1 hour. Add the okra. Cook 30 minutes longer. Taste for seasoning.
Serves 6–8.

Borjupaprikás

HUNGARIAN VEAL GOULASH

3 tablespoons butter	1 cup julienne-cut green
3 cups thinly sliced onions	peppers
3 pounds shoulder of veal,	1 cup peeled, diced
cut in 1½-inch cubes	tomatoes
1 tablespoon paprika	½ teaspoon caraway seeds
1½ teaspoons salt	½ cup sour cream
1 cup hot beef broth	

Melt the butter in a Dutch oven or heavy saucepan and brown the onions and meat over medium heat, stirring to brown all sides. Add the paprika, salt, and the broth; cover and cook over low heat 30 minutes. Add the green peppers, tomatoes, and caraway seeds. Re-cover and cook 30 minutes longer or until tender. Watch carefully and add a little boiling water if necessary. Blend in the sour cream, taste for seasoning. Serve with boiled egg noodles. *Serves 6–8.*

Vitello con Peperoni

NEAPOLITAN VEAL STEW WITH PEPPERS

3 tablespoons butter
3 tablespoons olive oil
2 cups thinly sliced onions
4 pounds boned shoulder
of veal, cut in 2-inch
cubes
2½ teaspoons salt
½ teaspoon freshly ground
black pepper

½ teaspoon orégano
2 cloves garlic, minced
¾ cup dry white wine
1½ cups peeled, diced
tomatoes
4 green peppers, seeded
and cut in eighths
lengthwise

Heat the butter and oil in a Dutch oven or heavy saucepan and sauté the onions 10 minutes. Add the veal and cook over medium heat until browned on all sides. Mix in the salt, pepper, orégano, garlic, and the wine. Cook over medium heat 5 minutes. Mix in the tomatoes and green peppers; cover and cook over low heat 2 hours. Taste for seasoning.
Serves 8–10.

Bryst av Kavestek

OSLO CRISP VEAL CUBES

4 cups water
3 teaspoons salt
Breast of veal, boned and
cut in 2-inch cubes
1 cup celery, chopped
2 egg whites
¼ teaspoon white pepper

½ cup dry bread crumbs
6 tablespoons butter
2 tablespoons flour
1 cup beef broth
1 teaspoon Worcestershire
sauce

Bring water to a boil, add half the salt, the veal, and celery. Cover and cook over low heat 45 minutes. Skim surface while meat is cooking. Remove meat, drain, and dry thoroughly. Lightly beat the egg whites, then mix in the pepper, remaining salt, and bread crumbs. Dip the meat cubes into this mixture. Melt the butter and sauté the veal over medium heat until crisp and brown on all sides. Transfer the meat to a heated serving dish. Stir the flour into the drippings, then mix in the broth, and bring to the boiling point, stirring constantly. Cook over low heat 5 minutes. Mix in the Worcestershire sauce. Pour over the meat.

Serves 6–8.

Lamb

Lamb, in the United States, is not as popular a meat as it is abroad. Most Americans are familiar with chops, leg of lamb and lamb stew. But foreign cooks offer a great variety of lamb recipes.

English lamb, or "joint" (too often mutton), served with mint sauce, is a favorite in the British Isles. The présalé lamb of France, which is very young spring lamb raised in the French salt marshes, is mouth-watering prepared in the French way: rare and pink.

But it is the Middle East that offers the widest scope in the preparation of lamb. The style of meat cookery in this area is based on it, to the exclusion of other meats. Meats are marinated and roasted on spits, on skewers, and in the oven; or with flavorful herbs and spices made into succulent stews; or they are ground and combined with native vegetables—eggplant, tomatoes, beans, onions, and peppers. And, of course, lamb curry is a menu staple.

Norwegian lamb too is of superior quality—the farther north one goes it seems the more delicate the lamb. The Norwegians prepare it in aspic, a delightful dish on a hot summer's night.

A lamb is a sheep of either sex which has not been allowed to come to maturity. Over twenty months old, it becomes mutton.

In purchasing lamb, look for the light pink lean meat of the young milk-fed animal. The color darkens with age. And the texture changes too; it should be fine and velvety, the fat firm, white, and of a waxy consistency. Genuine spring lamb, which comes from animals only about three to five months old, is available in spring and early summer. The next grade, usually called just plain "lamb," is marketed in fall and winter . . . the spring babies have been allowed to grow a bit older.

There is an old wives' tale that lamb has to be well done, so

Americans usually roast or broil it far longer than necessary. Try reducing the time and serve it as many Europeans do–a little bit pink. You'll be surprised how delicious it is.

LAMB CUTS[1]

Rib Rack (2) – There are two racks (12–16 ribs) in each animal, consisting of all the rib chops in one piece, similar to a rib roast. This is a tender cut and should be roasted. A rack may be cut into individual chops after roasting or cut in long horizontal pieces, in the French manner.

Crown Roast (2) – Two or more racks are shaped and tied into the shape of a crown. Usually the rib bones are scraped of meat. This is called "Frenched." The center of the crown is usually filled with a stuffing and then roasted.

Rib Chops (2) – The rack, cut into single or double chops. The rib bones can be merely cracked or Frenched. Broil or pan-broil rib chops, unless otherwise specified in recipes.

Loin Roast (3) – One side of the loin, containing all the loin chops. A loin may be boned and rolled. Roast a loin roast.

Saddle (3) – Both loins, with some bone removed and the flank ends trimmed and rolled. The saddle is then firmly tied, so that it holds its shape during roasting. To carve, slice in long horizontal strips, then turn it over and cut into the flank ends, thus reaching the tenderloin.

Loin Chops (3) – Similar in shape to porterhouse or T-bone steaks, and cut from the one side of the loin. Broil or pan-broil.

English Chops (3) – Chops cut from the saddle, which include two loins and tenderloins. One 1½-inch-thick English chop makes a serving. Broil or pan-broil.

Shoulder Chops (1) – Chops cut from the shoulder of the lamb, containing a large amount of bone. Shoulder chops are sometimes cut from a boned rolled shoulder. Boil, pan-broil, or braise.

Leg (6) – Usually sold whole, with the shank bone Frenched. Half a leg is also available, either the shank or loin half. Roast or braise.

Shank (4, 1) – Shank and elbow bones. Braise or stew.

[1] The numbers in parentheses refer to the Lamb Chart.

Steaks and Cutlets (6) – Cut from the leg. The center cuts look like small beef round steaks. Broil or pan-broil.

Sirloin roast (6) – A boneless roll, usually weighing no more than 3 pounds. Roast or braise.

Breast (5) – A fatty cut, that corresponds to breast of veal. The breast is sometimes cut into individual riblets, which correspond to spareribs. Roast, braise, or stew.

Gigot à la Bretonne

BRITTANY ROAST LEG OF LAMB WITH DRIED BEANS

6-pound leg of lamb	1 onion
5 teaspoons salt	1 bay leaf
1 teaspoon freshly ground	½ teaspoon thyme
black pepper	¼ teaspoon marjoram
5 cloves garlic	1 cup peeled, chopped
2 cups dried green	tomatoes
flageolets or white beans	2 tablespoons butter

Rub the lamb with 3 teaspoons of the salt, ¾ teaspoon of the pepper, and 3 cloves minced garlic. Let stand at room temperature until ready to roast, at least 2 hours.

Wash the beans, cover with cold water, and bring to a boil. Remove from heat and let soak 1 hour. Drain. Cover with fresh water, bring to a boil and add the onion, bay leaf, thyme, marjoram, and the remaining 2 cloves of garlic. Cook over low heat 1½ hours or until tender but firm. Discard onion, garlic, and bay leaf. Put beans in a casserole and mix with the tomatoes, butter, and the remaining salt and pepper. Bake in oven with lamb.

Place the lamb on a rack in a shallow roasting pan and roast in a 425° oven 30 minutes, turning to brown evenly. Reduce heat to 350° and roast 1¼ hours longer. The lamb should still be pink inside.

Add 4 tablespoons of the pan gravy to the beans and serve as an accompaniment to the carved roast lamb.

Serves 8–10.

Auckland Roast Leg of Lamb

5-pound leg of lamb
1 tablespoon salt
1 teaspoon freshly ground
    black pepper

2 cloves garlic, minced
1 teaspoon rosemary
½ cup melted butter

Rub the lamb with a mixture of the salt, pepper, garlic, and rosemary. Let stand 1 hour. Place on a rack in a roasting pan. Roast in a 375° oven 1 hour or until meat is tender but still pink, basting frequently with the melted butter. Place on a hot serving dish and let stand 20 minutes before carving.
Serves 6–8.

California Roast Leg of Lamb

5-pound leg of lamb
½ cup chili sauce
1 cup dry red wine
2 tablespoons cider vinegar
½ cup beef broth
2 tablespoons vegetable oil
2 teaspoons salt

½ teaspoon freshly ground
    black pepper
1 tablespoon sugar
1 bay leaf, crushed
1 cup minced onions
1 clove garlic, minced

Make a few gashes in the lamb; place in a glass or pottery container. Mix together all the remaining ingredients and pour over the lamb. Marinate the lamb in the refrigerator overnight, turning a few times.

Drain the lamb, and place on a rack in a roasting pan. Add half the marinade. Roast in a 325° oven 3¼ hours or until tender. Baste frequently and add the remaining marinade as needed.
Serves 6–8.

Abbacchio Marinato

FLORENTINE ROAST LEG OF LAMB

5-pound leg of lamb	1 teaspoon rosemary
1 tablespoon salt	½ cup olive oil
¾ teaspoon freshly ground black pepper	⅓ cup wine vinegar
	1 cup dry red wine

Prick the lamb in several places, then rub it with the salt, pepper, and rosemary. Place the lamb in a bowl; mix the oil and vinegar together and pour the mixture over the lamb. Marinate in the refrigerator overnight, turning a few times.

Drain the lamb and place on a rack in a shallow roasting pan. Reserve the marinade. Roast in a 350° oven 30 minutes. Pour off the fat. Mix the wine with the marinade. Add to the pan. Continue roasting the lamb a total of 15 minutes a pound, basting frequently. *Serves 6–8.*

Agneau à la Béarnaise

FRENCH PROVINCIAL ROAST LEG OF LAMB WITH BREAD CRUMB COATING

5-pound leg of lamb	½ teaspoon thyme
4 tablespoons softened butter	2 teaspoons salt
½ cup minced green onions (scallions)	½ teaspoon freshly ground black pepper
1 teaspoon powdered bay leaf	2 cups bread crumbs
3 tablespoons minced parsley	3 tablespoons lemon juice
	Lemon wedges
	Parsley

Rub the lamb with the softened butter. Mix together the green onions, bay leaf, parsley, thyme, salt, pepper, and 1½ cups of the bread crumbs. Press all over the lamb. Place the lamb on a rack in a shallow roasting pan and cover with a piece of buttered parchment or brown paper. Roast in a 350° oven 1¼ hours. Remove the paper, sprinkle with the remaining bread crumbs, and roast 15 minutes longer, or to desired degree of rareness. Transfer to a hot serving dish and sprinkle with the lemon juice. Garnish with lemon wedges and parsley. *Serves 8–10.*

Gigot à l'Ail

FRENCH PROVINCIAL ROAST LEG OF LAMB WITH GARLIC SAUCE

5-pound leg of lamb	**1 large head garlic**
2 teaspoons salt	**2 tablespoons raw rice**
½ teaspoon freshly ground black pepper	**1 cup milk**
	¼ teaspoon rosemary
2 tablespoons vegetable oil	**1½ cups beef broth**
2 tablespoons melted butter	

Trim the fat from the lamb, leaving a thin layer. Rub the meat with the salt and pepper, then brush with a mixture of the oil and butter. Place the lamb on a rack in a shallow roasting pan. Roast in a 425° oven 20 minutes, turning the leg to brown all sides. Reduce the heat to 350°, and roast 1 hour longer for medium rare or 1½ hours for well done. Transfer to a hot platter and let stand 20 minutes before carving.

While the lamb is roasting, prepare the sauce. Remove the outer covering of the head of garlic and separate the cloves. Cover the cloves with water, bring to a boil, and let stand 1 minute. Drain and peel the garlic. Cover the garlic with fresh water, bring to a boil and drain again.

Combine the rice, milk, and rosemary in a saucepan. Bring to a boil, add the garlic, and cook over low heat 45 minutes, stirring frequently.

Pour off the fat from the roasting pan after the roast is removed. Add the broth to the pan and bring to a boil over direct heat, scraping the bottom of any browned particles. Add to the garlic mixture; cook 2 minutes. Taste for seasoning. Purée the gravy in an electric blender or force through a sieve. Serve hot in a gravy boat.

Serves 6–8.

Karachi Roast Leg of Lamb

5-pound leg of lamb	½ teaspoon ginger
2 teaspoons salt	3 cloves garlic, minced
½ teaspoon dried ground chili peppers	½ cup ground almonds
	1½ cups yogurt
½ teaspoon powdered saffron	4 tablespoons butter

Trim the fat from the lamb, then prick the surface all over with a fork. Mix together the salt, red peppers, saffron, ginger, garlic, and almonds. Rub it into the meat very well. Place the meat in a bowl, and pour the yogurt over it. Cover and marinate in the refrigerator 2 hours before roasting time and baste frequently.

Drain the lamb, place on a rack in a shallow roasting pan and dot with the butter. Reserve the liquid. Roast in a 400° oven 30 minutes. Add the liquid, reduce heat to 325°, and roast 2 hours longer, basting frequently. Transfer the leg to a hot platter. Skim the fat from the pan juices and serve the sauce in a gravy boat.

Serves 6–8.

Stekt Lamm

SWEDISH ROAST LEG OF LAMB

5-pound leg of lamb	1 cup thinly sliced carrots
1 tablespoon salt	1 cup beef broth
¾ teaspoon freshly ground black pepper	1 cup strong brewed coffee
2 tablespoons butter	1 cup heavy cream
1½ cups thinly sliced onions	1 tablespoon sugar

Rub the lamb with the salt and pepper. Melt the butter in a shallow roasting pan and place the lamb and onions in it. Roast in a 425° oven 30 minutes, turning the lamb to brown all sides. Pour off the fat. Add the carrots and broth; roast in a 350° oven 45 minutes. Pour a mixture of the coffee, cream, and sugar over it and roast 45 minutes longer or to desired degree of rareness, basting frequently.

Transfer the lamb to a heated platter. Skim the fat from the gravy and purée gravy in an electric blender or force through a sieve. Taste for seasoning and serve in a gravy boat.

Serves 6–8.

Abbacchio al Vermouth

ROAST LEG OF LAMB WITH VERMOUTH

4-pound leg of lamb	¾ teaspoon freshly
3 cloves garlic, cut in	ground black pepper
slivers	4 tablespoons butter
¾ teaspoon rosemary	1½ cups dry vermouth
2½ teaspoons salt	

Make a few slits in the lamb, and in each insert some garlic slivers and rosemary. Rub the leg with the salt and pepper, and place it in a shallow roasting pan; dot with the butter. Roast in a 450° oven 25 minutes or until browned. Pour off the fat. Add the vermouth; reduce heat to 350° and roast 1 hour longer or to desired degree of rareness; baste frequently.

Serves 6–8.

Crown Roast of Lamb

Crown roast of lamb	¾ teaspoon freshly
½ cup minced onions	ground black pepper
2 cups fresh bread	½ cup melted butter
crumbs	2 cloves garlic, minced
½ teaspoons thyme	1½ cups dry sherry
3 teaspoons salt	Sautéed mushroom caps

Have the crown tied up, rib bones scraped, and the scraped meat ground. Mix the ground lamb with the onions, bread crumbs, thyme, ¾ teaspoon of the salt, ¼ teaspoon of the pepper, and ¼ cup of the melted butter.

Rub the crown with the garlic and remaining salt and pepper. Place the lamb in a roasting pan and fill the center with the stuffing. Cover the stuffing with a piece of aluminum foil. Place a potato cube or a piece of salt pork or aluminum foil on each bone to keep ends from burning. Roast in a 450° oven 20 minutes. Pour off the fat and add the remaining butter and sherry. Reduce heat to 350° and roast 2 hours longer, or to desired degree of rareness. Baste frequently and remove foil covering stuffing for the last 15 minutes of roasting time. Transfer to a heated platter, remove cubes of potato or salt pork or the aluminum foil, and replace with a sautéed mushroom cap or paper frill. Skim the fat from the gravy and serve with the roast.

Serves 6–8.

English Stuffed Crown Roast of Lamb

Crown roast of lamb	4 teaspoons rosemary
½ pound ground lamb	4 tablespoons butter
3 cloves garlic	½ cup minced onion
3½ teaspoons salt	½ cup chopped celery
1 teaspoon freshly ground black pepper	1 cup bread crumbs
	¼ cup chopped parsley

Have the bones of the lamb scraped and the meat ground. Buy enough extra ground lamb to make ½ pound. Cover the bone ends with aluminum foil to keep from burning.

Cut 2 cloves of the garlic into slivers. Make some incisions on the inside of the lamb and insert the garlic slivers. Rub the lamb with a mixture of 3 teaspoons of the salt, ¾ teaspoon of the pepper, and 2 teaspoons of the rosemary. Place the lamb on a rack in a roasting pan. Roast in a 375° oven 15 minutes a pound for pink meat or 22 minutes for well done. While the lamb is roasting, prepare the stuffing.

Mince the remaining garlic. Melt the butter in a skillet; sauté the garlic, onion, and celery 5 minutes. Add the ground lamb; cook until lightly browned, stirring frequently. Mix in the bread crumbs, parsley, and remaining salt, pepper, and rosemary.

About 45 minutes before end of roasting time, put the stuffing in the center of the crown and continue roasting.
Serves 6–8.

Selle d'Agneau au Four
ROAST SADDLE OF LAMB

Saddle of lamb (about 7 pounds)
2½ teaspoons salt
¾ teaspoon freshly ground black pepper

2 cloves garlic, minced
½ cup beef broth
½ cup dry red wine

Trim the fat from the lamb. Rub the lamb with a mixture of the salt, pepper, and garlic. Place in a shallow roasting pan. Roast in a 400° oven 20 minutes. Pour off the fat. Add the broth and wine; roast 1¼ hours longer or to desired degree of rareness, basting frequently. Carve parallel to the bones in long, thin bias-cut strips—don't cut into chops.
Serves 6–8.

Abbacchio alla Romana
ROMAN ROAST SADDLE OF LAMB

Saddle of baby lamb (about 7 pounds)
2 cloves garlic, minced
1 teaspoon freshly ground black pepper
12 anchovy fillets, finely minced
2 cloves

1 onion
1 bay leaf
3 sprigs parsley
½ cup beef broth
1 cup dry bread crumbs
½ teaspoon salt
½ teaspoon orégano
3 tablespoons cognac

Trim the fat from the lamb. Rub the lamb with a mixture of the garlic, pepper, and anchovy fillets. Place the lamb in a shallow roasting pan. Stick the cloves in the onion and add to the pan with the bay leaf, parsley, and beef broth. Roast in a 450° oven 15 minutes, then cover the lamb with a mixture of the bread crumbs, salt, and orégano. Reduce heat to 350° and continue roasting 10 minutes per pound for rare, 15 for medium, and 20 for well done. Baste several times with the pan juices. Just before serving, heat the cognac, set it aflame, and pour over the lamb. When flames die, transfer lamb to a heated platter. Strain the gravy into a sauceboat.
Serves 6–8.

Agneau à la Poitevine

FRENCH PROVINCIAL SPICED ROAST SHOULDER OF LAMB

1 tablespoon salt	1 clove garlic, minced
¾ teaspoon freshly ground black pepper	1 tablespoon lemon juice
⅛ teaspoon cayenne pepper	5-pound shoulder of lamb, boned, rolled, and tied
½ teaspoon ginger	2 tablespoons flour
1 teaspoon rosemary	2 cups beef broth

Mix together the salt, pepper, cayenne, ginger, rosemary, garlic, and lemon juice. Rub into the meat, forcing some into the rolled portion. Place the lamb on a rack in a shallow roasting pan. Roast in a 350° oven 3 hours. Transfer lamb to a heated serving dish. Pour off all but 2 tablespoons of fat. Place the pan over direct heat and stir the flour into it until browned. Add the broth and bring to a boil, stirring steadily. Cook over low heat 5 minutes. Taste for seasoning. Serve the gravy separately.
Serves 8–10.

Épaule d'Agneau à la Niçoise

RIVIERA BRAISED SHOULDER OF LAMB

4-pound shoulder of lamb, boned, rolled, and tied	2 cups drained canned tomatoes
2 cloves garlic, cut in slivers	1 cup beef broth
2 teaspoons salt	½ teaspoon orégano
½ teaspoon freshly ground black pepper	3 cups cubed eggplant
4 tablespoons olive oil	1 cup sliced black olives
1 cup thinly sliced onions	2 tablespoons minced parsley

Make a few slits in the lamb and insert the garlic; rub with the salt and pepper. Heat 2 tablespoons of the oil in a Dutch oven or heavy casserole and brown the lamb on all sides. Add the onions; cook 5 minutes. Pour off the fat. Mix in the tomatoes, broth, and orégano; cover and cook over low heat 2 hours. Baste and turn meat frequently.

Heat the remaining oil in a skillet; brown the eggplant in it. Add to the meat; cook 30 minutes, or until the meat is tender. Add the olives; cook 5 minutes longer. Remove the meat to a heated serving dish; skim the fat from the gravy, then mix in the parsley. Pour around the lamb. *Serves 6–8.*

Lammrücken

SCANDINAVIAN ROAST SHOULDER OF LAMB

5-pound shoulder of lamb, boned, rolled, and tied	3 slices bacon, diced
2½ teaspoons salt	¾ cup chopped onions
½ teaspoon freshly ground black pepper	½ cup water
	1 cup sour cream

Rub the meat with the salt and pepper. Lightly brown the bacon in a Dutch oven or heavy casserole. Pour off the fat, and add the meat and onions. Roast in a 400° oven 35 minutes, turning the meat to brown all sides. Add the water, reduce heat to 350°, and roast 30 minutes longer, or to desired degree of rareness. Transfer the meat to a heated serving dish. Skim the fat from the gravy, and blend in the sour cream. Serve in a sauceboat.

Serves 6–8.

Mostek Barani Duszony na Winie

POLISH BREAST OF LAMB IN WINE SAUCE

4 pounds breast of lamb	**2 stalks celery and**
2 tablespoons butter	**leaves**
1 cup sliced onions	**2 teaspoons salt**
1 cup diced carrots	**½ teaspoon freshly**
1 leek, sliced	**ground black pepper**
½ cup diced celery	**¾ cup beef broth**
root	**1½ cups dry white wine**
	2 egg yolks

Trim the fat from the lamb. Melt the butter in a Dutch oven or heavy casserole and brown the lamb on both sides. Add the onions, carrots, leek, celery root, celery, salt, and pepper. Cover and cook over low heat 10 minutes. Add ½ cup broth; re-cover and cook 30 minutes, turning the meat and adding some of the remaining broth from time to time. Add the wine, re-cover, and cook 1 hour. Cut the meat into serving-sized pieces and discard the celery.

Beat the egg yolks in a bowl; gradually add a little of the gravy, stirring steadily to prevent curdling. Stir this mixture into the pan. Taste for seasoning and heat but do not let boil.

Serves 6–8.

Abbacchio al Carciofi

ITALIAN BAKED SHOULDER OF LAMB WITH ARTICHOKES

2 tablespoons butter
3 pounds shoulder of lamb, cut in 1-inch cubes
2½ teaspoons salt
¼ teaspoon freshly ground black pepper
¼ cup dry vermouth

1 package frozen artichoke hearts, cooked and drained
4 eggs
½ cup grated Parmesan cheese
2 tablespoons minced parsley

Melt the butter in a deep skillet. Brown the lamb on all sides; sprinkle with 2 teaspoons of the salt and the pepper. Add the wine; cook over high heat 5 minutes. Cover and bake in a 350° oven 35 minutes; add the artichokes and a little boiling water if necessary. Re-cover and bake 10 minutes.

Beat together the eggs, cheese, parsley, and remaining salt. Pour over the lamb and artichokes. Bake, uncovered, 10 minutes longer. *Serves 6–8.*

Texas Breast of Lamb

4 pounds breast of lamb, cut in 6–8 pieces
½ cup chili sauce
¼ cup wine vinegar
½ cup water
½ cup thinly sliced onions
1 clove garlic, minced

2 teaspoons salt
1½ teaspoons chili powder
⅛ teaspoon Tabasco
1 tablespoon Worcestershire sauce
½ teaspoon garlic powder

Brown the lamb in a Dutch oven or heavy saucepan. Pour off the fat. Mix together all the remaining ingredients and add to the lamb. Cover and bake in a 350° oven 1½ hours, removing the cover for the last 15 minutes. Skim off the fat. *Serves 6–8.*

Melbourne Lamb Cutlets in Paper

6 lamb cutlets, cut ¼
inch thick
2 teaspoons salt
½ teaspoon freshly
ground black pepper
3 tablespoons olive oil
1 cup chopped onions

¾ cup chopped
mushrooms
¼ teaspoon nutmeg
2 tablespoons melted
butter
12 slices cooked ham

Trim the fat from the lamb. Season the cutlets with 1½ teaspoons of the salt and the pepper. Heat the oil in a skillet; sauté the onions 5 minutes; mix in the mushrooms, nutmeg, and remaining salt. Cook over very low heat 10 minutes. Cool 5 minutes.

Cut 6 pieces of parchment paper or aluminum foil large enough to cover each cutlet completely. Brush the foil with the butter, place a slice of ham on each piece, spread with the onion mixture, place a cutlet over it, and top with another slice of ham. Bring up the edges of the paper, seal, and place on a baking sheet. Bake in a 350° oven 45 minutes. Slit the paper and serve directly from it. *Serves 6.*

California Lamb Steaks

4 lamb steaks, cut ½
inch thick
2 tablespoons butter
1 teaspoon salt
¼ cup lemon juice

½ cup currant jelly
2 oranges, peeled,
sliced, and seeded
2 tablespoons grated
orange rind

Trim the fat from the lamb. Melt the butter in a skillet and brown the steaks on both sides. Sprinkle with the salt, and add the lemon juice and jelly. Cover and cook over low heat 25 minutes. Turn the steaks over and arrange the orange slices on them, recover, and cook 10 minutes longer. Stir the orange rind into the pan juices. *Serves 4.*

Agnello alla Parmigiana

ITALIAN BREADED LAMB STEAKS

6 lamb steaks, cut ½
   inch thick
1½ teaspoons salt
¼ teaspoon freshly
   ground black pepper
¼ teaspoon thyme

3 eggs
¼ cup cold water
¾ cup dry bread crumbs
¾ cup grated Parmesan
   cheese
⅓ cup vegetable oil

Trim the fat from the lamb. Season the steaks with the salt, pepper, and thyme. Beat the eggs with the water. Dip the steaks in the eggs, then in a mixture of the bread crumbs and cheese, and once more in the eggs.

Heat the oil in a heavy skillet; sauté the steaks 10 minutes on each side, or to desired degree of rareness. *Serves 6.*

Yoğurtlu Kebab

TURKISH LAMB STEAKS WITH YOGURT

1½ pounds lamb steak,
   cut in 4 pieces
½ cup grated onion
¼ cup olive oil
1½ teaspoons salt
6 peppercorns, crushed

4 slices whole-wheat bread,
   toasted
¾ cup hot beef broth
3 cups yogurt
Paprika

Trim the fat from the lamb. Mix together the onion, olive oil, salt, and peppercorns. Marinate the meat in the mixture for 2 hours at room temperature. Drain when ready to broil.

Put the toast in a heatproof serving dish. Pour the broth over it and keep in a warm oven until all the liquid is absorbed.

Broil the steaks to desired degree of rareness and arrange over the toast. While the lamb is broiling, beat the yogurt with a wooden spoon in a saucepan over low heat until warm. Pour over the meat and sprinkle with paprika. *Serves 4.*

Kouzou Kzartma

ARMENIAN MARINATED LAMB SHANKS

6 lamb shanks
1 cup dry red wine
1½ teaspoons salt
½ teaspoon freshly
　ground black pepper

1 clove garlic, minced
¼ teaspoon marjoram
1 bay leaf
1 tablespoon Worcestershire
　sauce

Wipe the shanks with a damp cloth. Combine the wine, salt, pepper, garlic, marjoram, and bay leaf. Pour over the shanks. Marinate at room temperature 1–2 hours or overnight in the refrigerator, turning a few times. Drain, reserving the marinade.

Place the shanks in a shallow roasting pan; brush with the Worcestershire sauce. Roast in a 400° oven 15 minutes. Add the marinade, reduce heat to 350°, and roast 45 minutes longer or until the shanks are tender. Baste frequently. Arrange on a platter and serve with rice or noodles.

Serves 6.

Australian Hot Pot

6 loin or shoulder lamb
　chops, cut 1 inch thick
4 tablespoons butter
3 teaspoons salt
1 teaspoon freshly ground
　black pepper
2 pounds potatoes, peeled
　and sliced

1½ pounds onions,
　sliced
1 cup sliced mushrooms
½ pound string beans,
　cut in half
1 cup beef broth
½ cup light cream

Trim the fat from the chops. Melt 2 tablespoons of the butter in a casserole; brown the chops on both sides. Sprinkle with 1 teaspoon of the salt and ½ teaspoon of the pepper. Arrange half the potatoes over the chops. Make successive layers of all of the onions, mushrooms, and string beans. Combine the broth, cream, and remaining salt and pepper and pour over the vegetables.

Arrange the remaining potatoes in an even overlapping design on top. Dot with the remaining butter. Cover and bake in a 350° oven 2½ hours. Remove cover and bake 20 minutes longer or until potatoes are brown on top. Serve from the casserole.
Serves 6.

Ghivetch

RUMANIAN LAMB AND VEGETABLE CASSEROLE

6 lamb chops, cut 1
   inch thick
1 cup olive oil
4 teaspoons salt
1 teaspoon freshly
   ground black pepper
2 cups diced potatoes
2 packages frozen mixed
   vegetables, thawed
1½ cups shredded
   cabbage

1 green pepper, cut
   julienne
2 cups diced eggplant
1 cup chopped onions
2 cloves garlic, minced
2 tomatoes, chopped
½ pound okra,
   sliced
⅛ teaspoon thyme
1 bay leaf

Trim the fat from the chops. Heat 2 tablespoons of the oil in a skillet and brown the chops on both sides. Sprinkle with half the salt and pepper.

Heat the remaining oil in a casserole until it bubbles. Add the potatoes, mixed vegetables, cabbage, green pepper, eggplant, onions, garlic, tomatoes, okra, thyme, bay leaf, and remaining salt and pepper. Mix lightly. Cover and bake in a 350° oven 30 minutes. Remove cover and arrange the chops over the vegetables. Bake 45 minutes longer, basting the chops occasionally. Discard the bay leaf.
Serves 6.

Côtelettes d'Agneau Panées

FRENCH PROVINCIAL BREADED LAMB CHOPS

6 rib or loin lamb chops,
cut 1 inch thick
1½ teaspoons salt
¼ teaspoon freshly
ground black pepper
¼ teaspoon thyme

2 eggs
2 tablespoons olive oil
¼ cup flour
¾ cup dry bread
crumbs
4 tablespoons butter

Trim the fat from the chops. Rub the chops with a mixture of the salt, pepper, and thyme. Beat the eggs with the olive oil. Dip the chops first in the flour, then in the beaten egg, and finally in the bread crumbs. Chill for ½ hour.

Melt the butter in a skillet and sauté the chops 7 minutes on each side or to desired degree of rareness.
Serves 6.

Báránypaprikás Tejfellel

HUNGARIAN BAKED LAMB CHOPS

6 loin lamb chops, cut
1½ inches thick
1½ teaspoons salt
½ teaspoon freshly
ground black pepper
1 teaspoon paprika

2 cups sliced green onions
(scallions)
½ cup sour cream
3 tablespoons grated
Parmesan cheese

Brown the chops on both sides in a skillet; pour off the fat. Season the chops with the salt, pepper, and paprika. Spread the green onions over the chops; add the sour cream. Bake in a 350° oven 30 minutes. Sprinkle with the cheese and bake 30 minutes longer.
Serves 6.

Cotelette di Agnello Positano
ITALIAN DEVILED LAMB CHOPS

8 loin lamb chops, cut 1
  inch thick
1 tablespoon olive oil
½ teaspoon salt
½ teaspoon pepper
½ teaspoon
  orégano
1 clove garlic, minced

4 anchovy fillets, chopped
½ teaspoon orégano
½ teaspoon salt
⅛ teaspoon freshly
  ground black pepper
2 teaspoons lemon juice
1 tablespoon prepared
  mustard

Remove the fat from the chops. Mix together the oil, salt, pepper, orégano, and garlic; rub the chops with the mixture and let stand at room temperature 2 hours. Mix together the anchovies, orégano, salt, pepper, lemon juice, and mustard. Arrange the chops on an oiled broiling pan and brush the top with the anchovy mixture; broil in a hot broiler 8 minutes. Turn over and brush the chops with the anchovy mixture again and broil 8 minutes, or to desired degree of rareness. Baste frequently. *Serves 4.*

Costolette d'Agnello al Vermouth
ITALIAN LAMB CHOPS WITH VERMOUTH

6 shoulder lamb chops,
  cut 1 inch thick
2 teaspoons salt
½ teaspoon freshly
  ground black pepper
¼ cup flour
3 tablespoons butter
1½ cups dry vermouth

½ teaspoon rosemary
1 clove garlic, minced
1 teaspoon grated lemon
  rind
1 bay leaf
2 tablespoons minced
  parsley

Trim the fat from the lamb and dip the chops in a mixture of the salt, pepper, and flour, coating them well. Melt the butter in a heavy skillet and brown the chops on both sides. Pour off the fat. Add the wine, rosemary, garlic, lemon rind, and bay leaf. Bring to a boil, cover, and cook over low heat 45 minutes or until tender. Sprinkle with the parsley before serving. *Serves 6.*

Chuletas de Cordero a la Navarra
SPANISH LAMB CHOPS

6 lamb chops, cut 1½
  inches thick
4 tablespoons olive oil
1 cup chopped onions
3 cups peeled, chopped
  tomatoes
2½ teaspoons salt

½ teaspoon freshly
  ground black pepper
½ cup diced ham
¼ pound chorizos
  (Spanish sausages),
  sliced

Trim the fat from the chops. Heat 3 tablespoons of the oil in a saucepan and sauté the onions 10 minutes. Add the tomatoes and 1 teaspoon of the salt. Cook over low heat 25 minutes.

Heat the remaining oil in a deep skillet and brown the chops on both sides. Pour off the fat. Season the chops with the pepper and remaining salt. Add the ham; cook 5 minutes. Poor the tomato mixture over the chops and arrange the sausage slices on top. Bake in a 350° oven 25 minutes. *Serves 6.*

Syltekjøti
NORWEGIAN LAMB CHOPS IN ASPIC

6 loin lamb chops, cut
  1 inch thick
3 cups water
2 tablespoons chopped
  parsley
½ cup sliced onions
¼ cup chopped celery

1 bay leaf
2 teaspoons salt
½ teaspoon white pepper
1 envelope (tablespoon)
  gelatin
2 tablespoons vinegar

Trim the fat from the chops. Combine in a saucepan with the water, parsley, onions, celery, bay leaf, salt, and pepper. Bring to a boil, cover, and cook over low heat 20 minutes. Remove the chops and arrange in a deep serving dish. Strain the lamb stock, reserving 2 cups. Sprinkle the gelatin into the vinegar. Let stand 5 minutes, then add to the reserved stock. Place over low heat, stirring until dissolved. Pour the gelatin mixture over the chops. Chill.

Serve with mint sauce or lingonberries.

Serves 6.

New Zealand Lamb Chops with Mustard

4 lamb chops, cut 1½
  inches thick
1¼ teaspoons salt
¼ teaspoon freshly ground
  black pepper

3 tablespoons prepared
  mustard
2 tablespoons honey

Trim the fat from the chops; season with the salt and pepper. Broil 8 minutes on 1 side, then turn over and broil 6 minutes. Mix together the mustard and honey; spread over the chops and broil 2 minutes longer. *Serves 4.*

Abbacchio alla Ciociara

ROMAN BRAISED LAMB IN COGNAC

3 pounds boneless lamb,
  cut in 1-inch cubes
3 tablespoons flour
2 teaspoons salt
½ teaspoon freshly
  ground black pepper
1 tablespoon vegetable
  oil

2 tablespoons butter
¼ pound prosciutto,
  (ham), cut julienne
½ cup cognac
¼ teaspoon thyme
1 clove garlic, minced

Trim the fat from the lamb. Toss the lamb in a mixture of the flour, salt, and pepper. Heat the oil and butter in a deep skillet and brown the lamb on all sides. Add the ham; cook 5 minutes. Mix in the cognac, thyme, and garlic; cover and cook over low heat 1 hour, or until lamb is tender. Watch carefully and add a little boiling water if necessary to keep from burning. There should be a very little gravy when meat is finished.
Serves 6–8.

Kokt Lamm med Dillsås

SWEDISH LAMB WITH DILL SAUCE

1 quart water	**4 tablespoons butter**
3 pounds boneless lamb	**4 tablespoons flour**
2½ teaspoons salt	**1½ tablespoons vinegar**
1 teaspoon white	**1 tablespoon sugar**
pepper	**1 egg yolk**
1 onion	**3 tablespoons chopped**
1 bay leaf	**dill**
10 dill sprigs	

Bring the water to a boil, add the lamb, bring to a boil again, and skim the foam from the top. Add the salt, pepper, onion, bay leaf, and dill sprigs. Cover and cook over low heat 1½ hours, or until lamb is tender. Remove meat and cut into cubes. Strain the stock. Keep meat warm while making sauce.

Melt the butter in a saucepan; blend in the flour. Add 2 cups of the lamb stock, stirring steadily to the boiling point. Add the vinegar and sugar. Cook over low heat 5 minutes. Beat the egg yolk in a bowl; gradually add a little of the hot sauce, stirring steadily. Return to balance of the sauce. Stir in the chopped dill. Pour over the lamb.
Serves 6–8.

Faarefrinkassee

NORWEGIAN FRICASSEE OF LAMB

3 pounds boneless lamb,
   cut in 1-inch cubes
2 teaspoons salt
½ teaspoon white pepper
2 cups chopped onions
4 cups beef broth

4 tablespoons butter
2 tablespoons flour
2 egg yolks
2 tablespoons chopped
   parsley
2 teaspoons chopped mint

Trim the fat from the lamb. In a saucepan, combine the lamb, salt, pepper, onions, and broth. Cover, bring to a boil, and cook over low heat 2 hours. Remove meat and keep warm. Strain the stock.

In a small saucepan melt the butter; blend in the flour and brown. Add 3 cups of the reserved stock. Bring to a boil, stirring constantly, then cook over low heat 5 minutes. Beat the egg yolks in a bowl; gradually add the hot sauce, stirring steadily to prevent curdling. Combine with the lamb and heat but do not let boil. Mix in the parsley and mint. *Serves 6.*

Ragoût d'Agneau

LAMB STEW

3 tablespoons olive oil
3 pounds boneless lamb,
   cut in 1½-inch cubes
¼ pound ham, diced
16 small white onions
2 teaspoons salt
½ teaspoon freshly
   ground black pepper

Dash ground allspice
1 bay leaf
1½ cups beef broth
2 cups peeled, diced
   potatoes
2 cups shelled green
   peas or 1 package
   frozen, thawed

Trim the fat from the lamb. Heat the oil in a Dutch oven or heavy skillet; add the lamb and ham and cook until browned. Add the onions and continue browning. Season with the salt, pepper, and allspice; add the bay leaf and broth. Cover and cook over low heat 45 minutes. Add the potatoes and peas, re-cover, and cook 25 minutes. Taste for seasoning. *Serves 6–8.*

Karitsa Muhennos

FINNISH LAMB STEW

3 pounds boneless lamb, cut in 1-inch cubes	1 tablespoon salt
2 pounds potatoes, peeled and diced	½ teaspoon freshly ground black pepper
1 cup diced carrots	3 cups boiling water
½ cup sliced leeks or onions	2 tablespoons minced dill or parsley

Trim the fat from the lamb. Arrange meat and vegetables in layers in a baking dish, sprinkling each layer with salt and pepper. Add the boiling water. Cover and bake in a 350° oven for 2½ hours. Sprinkle with the dill or parsley. *Serves 6–8.*

Gedünstete Lammkeule

AUSTRIAN LAMB STEW

3 pounds boneless lamb, cut in 1½-inch cubes	1 cup dry white wine
4 tablespoons butter	1 cup water
2 teaspoons salt	1 bay leaf
½ teaspoon freshly ground black pepper	2 cups peeled, diced tomatoes
½ teaspoon caraway seeds	16 small white onions
1½ cups sliced carrots	2 tablespoons minced dill or parsley

Trim the fat from the lamb. Melt the butter in a Dutch oven or deep skillet and brown the lamb on all sides. Add the salt, pepper, caraway seeds, carrots, wine, water, and bay leaf. Bring to a boil, cover, and cook over low heat 30 minutes. Add the tomatoes and onions; re-cover and cook 1 hour. Taste for seasoning and sprinkle with the dill or parsley. Serve with noodles.

Serves 6–8.

Lamm, Balkanishes Art

BALKAN LAMB STEW

3 pounds boneless lamb, cut in 2-inch cubes	3 tablespoons butter
¼ cup flour	1½ cups diced onions
2 teaspoons salt	¼ teaspoon cinnamon
½ teaspoon freshly ground black pepper	¼ teaspoon nutmeg
1 pound prunes	Dash ground allspice
	3½ cups chicken broth
	1 cup raw rice

Trim the fat from the lamb. Toss the lamb in a mixture of the flour, salt, and pepper.

Wash the prunes. Cover with boiling water and let soak while preparing the meat.

Melt the butter in a Dutch oven or heavy skillet and brown the lamb on all sides. Add the onions; cook 15 minutes. Add the cinnamon, nutmeg, allspice, and 1½ cups of the chicken broth. Bring to a boil, cover, and cook over low heat 1¼ hours. Add the drained prunes, rice, and remaining broth. Cook 25 minutes longer. Taste for seasoning.

Serves 6–8.

Haricot de Mouton

FRENCH LAMB STEW WITH WHITE BEANS

3 pounds boneless lamb, cut in 1-inch cubes	2½ teaspoons salt
2 tablespoons olive oil	½ teaspoon freshly ground black pepper
4 tablespoons butter	1 bay leaf
1 cup chopped onions	Boiling water
2 tablespoons flour	4 cups cooked white beans
1 tablespoon tomato paste	¼ cup chopped parsley
2 cloves garlic, minced	

Trim the fat from the lamb. Heat the oil and butter in a Dutch oven or heavy saucepan; brown the lamb on all sides. Add the onions; cook 5 minutes. Stir in the flour until browned. Add the tomato paste, garlic, salt, pepper, bay leaf, and boiling water to barely cover. Cover and cook over low heat 1½ hours. Add the beans and cook 30 minutes longer, or until the meat and beans are tender. Taste for seasoning, discard the bay leaf, and mix in the parsley. *Serves 6–8.*

Lammaskaali

FINNISH LAMB STEW WITH CABBAGE

2 pounds boneless lamb, cut in ½-inch cubes	1 teaspoon salt
2 tablespoons butter	¼ teaspoon ground allspice
½ cup grated carrots	1½ cups boiling water
2-pound head of cabbage, coarsely shredded	2 teaspoons parsley

Trim the fat from the lamb. Melt the butter in a heavy saucepan and brown the lamb on all sides. Spread the carrots and cabbage over the meat. Mix together the salt, allspice, and boiling water and pour into the pan. Cover, and cook over low heat 2 hours. Sprinkle with the parsley. *Serves 4–6.*

Creole Lamb Stew

3 pounds boneless lamb,
   cut in 1½-inch cubes
2 cups dry red wine
1 cup sliced onions
1 cup sliced green peppers
2 cloves garlic, minced
6 peppercorns
¾ teaspoon thyme

2 bay leaves
1½ teaspoons salt
½ teaspoon freshly
   ground black pepper
3 slices salt pork, diced
1 cup diced tomatoes
3 tablespoons minced
   parsley

Trim the fat from the lamb. Combine the wine, onions, green peppers, garlic, peppercorns, thyme, and bay leaves in a glass or pottery bowl. Add the meat and marinate overnight in the refrigerator.

Drain the lamb, reserving the marinade. Season the meat with the salt and pepper.

Brown the salt pork in a Dutch oven or casserole, then pour off the fat. Add the meat to the salt pork; cook over medium heat 10 minutes. Mix in the marinade and tomatoes. Cover tightly and bake in a 300° oven 3 hours. Skim the fat, taste for seasoning, and sprinkle with the parsley. *Serves 6–8.*

Agneau en Daube

FRENCH POTTED LAMB

3 pounds boneless lamb,
   cut in 1½-inch cubes
2 cups dry red wine
1 cup sliced onions
3 carrots, sliced
2 cloves garlic, minced
4 peppercorns
½ teaspoon thyme

2 bay leaves
3 slices salt pork, diced
1½ teaspoons salt
½ teaspoon freshly
   ground black pepper
3 tablespoons minced
   parsley
1 cup diced tomatoes

Trim the fat from the lamb. Mix together the wine, onions, carrots, garlic, peppercorns, thyme, and bay leaves. Add the lamb and let marinate in the refrigerator overnight.

Drain the meat, reserving the marinade. Brown the salt pork in an earthenware casserole or Dutch oven; pour off all but 2 tablespoons of the fat. Add the meat, salt, and pepper. Cook over medium heat 10 minutes. Add the marinade, parsley, and tomatoes. Cover tightly and bake in a 300° oven 3 hours. Skim the fat, taste for seasoning, and serve.

Serves 8–10.

Fassolia me Arni

GREEK LAMB STEW WITH WHITE BEANS

2 cups dried white beans
2 tablespoons olive oil
2 pounds boneless lamb, cut in 1½-inch cubes
1½ cups chopped onions
2 teaspoons salt
½ teaspoon freshly ground black pepper

½ teaspoon orégano
1 bay leaf
1½ cups peeled, chopped tomatoes
2 cloves garlic, minced
2 tablespoons minced parsley

Wash the beans, cover with water, and bring to a boil. Cook 5 minutes, remove from the heat, and let stand 1 hour. Drain; add fresh water to cover, bring to a boil, and cook over low heat 1½ hours. Drain, reserving 1½ cups liquid.

Trim the fat from the lamb. Heat the oil in a Dutch oven or heavy skillet and brown the lamb on all sides. Add the onions and continue browning. Add the beans, bean liquid, the salt, pepper, orégano, and bay leaf. Cover and cook over low heat 1 hour. Add the tomatoes and garlic; re-cover and cook 1 hour longer or until beans and lamb are tender. Sprinkle with the parsley.

Serves 6–8.

Navarin d'Agneau

FRENCH LAMB STEW IN RED WINE

3 pounds boneless lamb,
   cut in 1½-inch cubes
2 tablespoons lemon
   juice
¼ cup flour
2 teaspoons salt
¼ teaspoon freshly ground
   black pepper
½ teaspoon rosemary

2 tablespoons olive oil
2 tablespoons butter
3 tablespoons warmed
   cognac
2 cups dry red wine
2 cups diced onions
1 cup diced carrots
1 bay leaf

Trim the fat from the lamb. Sprinkle the lamb with the lemon juice and let stand 10 minutes. Drain and dry.

Roll the lamb in a mixture of the flour, salt, pepper, and rosemary. Heat the oil and butter in a Dutch oven or heavy skillet and brown the meat. Pour the warmed cognac over the meat and set it aflame. When the flames die, add the wine, onions, carrots, and bay leaf. Cover and bake in a 350° oven 2 hours. Skim the fat and discard the bay leaf.

Serves 6–8.

Báránygulyás

HUNGARIAN LAMB GOULASH

3 pounds boneless lamb,
   cut in 2-inch cubes
2 teaspoons salt
½ teaspoon freshly
   ground black pepper
2 cloves garlic, minced
2 tablespoons flour

2 tablespoons vegetable
   oil
3 cups chopped onions
2 green peppers, diced
2 tablespoons paprika
1 8-ounce can tomato
   sauce

Trim the fat from the lamb. Toss the lamb in a mixture of the salt, pepper, garlic, and flour. Heat the oil in a Dutch oven or heavy saucepan; spread the onions in it and put the lamb and green peppers over it. Sprinkle with paprika. Cover and cook over low heat 30 minutes. Add the tomato sauce. Re-cover and cook over low heat 2 hours. Watch carefully and add a very little boiling water if necessary.

Serves 6–8.

Abbacchio alla Cacciatore

LAMB, HUNTER'S STYLE

3 pounds boneless spring lamb, cut in 2-inch cubes
1½ teaspoons salt
½ teaspoon freshly ground black pepper
3 tablespoons olive oil
⅓ cup boiling water
3 anchovy fillets, minced
2 cloves garlic, minced
1 teaspoon rosemary
⅓ cup wine vinegar
2 tablespoons minced parsley

Trim the fat from the lamb. Season the lamb with the salt and pepper. Heat the oil in a Dutch oven or heavy deep skillet and brown the lamb on all sides. Add half the water; cover and cook over low heat 1 hour or until tender, adding some of the remaining water from time to time. If necessary, add very small amounts of boiling water to keep from burning.

Pound together the anchovies, garlic, and rosemary; mix in the vinegar. Stir into the lamb; cook over high heat 5 minutes. Sprinkle with the parsley.

Serves 6–8.

Gormeh Sabzee

IRANIAN LAMB AND PARSLEY STEW

3 pounds boneless lamb,
cut in 1-inch cubes
⅓ cup sesame or
vegetable oil
2 cups chopped green
onions (scallions)
8 cups chopped parsley
2½ teaspoons salt

¾ teaspoon freshly ground
black pepper
⅓ cup lemon juice
1 lemon, quartered
3 cups boiling water
2 16-ounce cans kidney
beans

Trim the fat from the lamb. Heat 2 tablespoons of the oil in
a Dutch oven or heavy skillet; brown the lamb on all sides and
remove from pan. Heat the remaining oil in the pan; add the green
onions and parsley; cook 5 minutes, stirring frequently. Return the
meat and add the salt, pepper, lemon juice, lemon quarters, and
boiling water. Cover and cook over low heat 1¼ hours. Skim the
fat; add the undrained beans. Taste for seasoning and cook 15
minutes longer. *Serves 6–8.*

Lamb

IRISH STEW

3 pounds shoulder of
lamb, cut in 1½-inch
cubes
2 pounds potatoes, peeled
and sliced ½ inch
thick
2 cups sliced onions
2½ teaspoons salt

½ teaspoon white
pepper
½ teaspoon thyme
1 bay leaf ⎫
3 sprigs ⎬ tied
parsley ⎬ together
1 stalk celery ⎭

Trim the fat from the lamb. In a Dutch oven or casserole, arrange
successive layers of the meat, potatoes, and onions; sprinkle each
layer with salt, pepper, and thyme. Add the bay leaf, parsley,

celery, and enough water to reach the top. Cover and bake in a 350° oven 2 hours or until the lamb is tender. *Serves 6–8.*

Damia

ISRAELI LAMB STEW WITH STRING BEANS

3 pounds boneless lamb, cut in 2-inch cubes	1 clove garlic, minced
3 tablespoons flour	1½ cups cubed tomatoes
2½ teaspoons salt	¼ teaspoon dried ground chili peppers
¼ teaspoon freshly ground black pepper	1 cup boiling water
2 tablespoons vegetable oil	1½ pounds string beans, cut in 2-inch lengths
1½ cups thinly sliced onions	

Trim the fat from the lamb. Toss the lamb with the flour, salt, and black pepper. Heat the oil in a Dutch oven or heavy saucepan and brown the lamb on all sides. Stir in the onions; cook until browned. Pour off the fat; add the garlic, tomatoes, red peppers, and water. Cover and cook over low heat 1 hour. Add the string beans; re-cover and cook 30 minutes or until the meat and string beans are tender. Serve with rice. *Serves 6–8.*

Sate Kambing

JAVANESE SPICED LAMB

3 pounds boneless lamb, cut in ½-inch cubes	2 teaspoons ground coriander
1 cup cider vinegar	1 teaspoon ground cumin
½ cup minced onions	½ teaspoon saffron
2 cloves garlic, minced	1 teaspoon powdered ginger
2 teaspoons salt	4 tablespoons oil
½ teaspoon dried ground chili peppers	½ cup water

Trim the fat from the lamb. Place the cubes in a bowl. Pour the vinegar over it and let stand 30 minutes. Drain. Pound or chop to a paste the onions, garlic, salt, chili peppers, coriander, cumin, saffron, and ginger; roll the lamb in the mixture. Let stand 30 minutes.

Heat the oil in a deep skillet and brown the lamb on all sides. Stir in the water; cover and cook over low heat 30 minutes or until tender.

Serves 6–8.

Fajoom

SYRIAN LAMB STEW WITH NAVY BEANS

2 pounds boneless lamb, cut in 1-inch cubes
1 pound dried navy beans
¼ pound (1 stick) butter
¾ cup chopped onions
1 clove garlic, minced
2 teaspoons salt
½ teaspoon freshly ground black pepper
½ teaspoon ground coriander
2 8-ounce cans tomato sauce
½ cup minced parsley

Trim the fat from the lamb. Wash the beans, cover with water, bring to a boil, remove from the heat, and let stand 1 hour. Drain, add fresh water to cover, bring to a boil, and cook over low heat 1 hour.

While the beans are cooking, melt the butter in a Dutch oven or heavy skillet; sauté the onions 5 minutes. Add the garlic, lamb, salt, pepper, and coriander; cook until meat browns, stirring frequently. Add the tomato sauce; cover and cook over low heat 30 minutes. Drain the beans and add to the meat. Cook 20 minutes longer or until the lamb and beans are tender. Taste for seasoning and stir in the parsley.

Serves 8–10.

Arnie me Bamies

MIDDLE EAST LAMB STEW WITH OKRA

2 pounds boneless lamb, cut
   in 1-inch cubes
¼ cup olive oil
1 cup chopped onions
1½ teaspoons salt
½ teaspoon freshly ground
   black pepper

3 tablespoons tomato paste
2 cups water
3 tablespoons lemon juice
1½ pounds fresh okra or 2
   packages frozen
¼ cup wine vinegar

Trim the fat from the lamb. Heat the oil in a Dutch oven or heavy casserole; brown the lamb and onions in it. Mix in the salt, pepper, tomato paste, water, and lemon juice. Bring to a boil, cover and cook over low heat 30 minutes.

While the lamb is cooking, prepare the okra. If fresh okra is used, wash it and cut off the stems. Pour the vinegar over the fresh or thawed frozen okra; marinate 30 minutes. Drain and rinse under cold water. Add the okra and cook 30 minutes longer, or until the lamb is tender. *Serves 6–8.*

Lam og Potater

NORWEGIAN LAMB STEW

2 pounds lamb, cut in 1-
   inch cubes
1½ pounds potatoes, peeled
   and sliced
1 cup grated carrots
4 cups shredded cabbage

2 teaspoons salt
½ teaspoon freshly ground
   black pepper
1 tablespoon flour
1 cup beef broth

Trim the fat from the lamb. Grease a baking dish and in it make layers of the meat, potatoes, carrots, and cabbage. Sprinkle each layer with a mixture of the salt, pepper, and flour. Add the broth. Cover, and bake in a 325° oven 3 hours. *Serves 6.*

Abbacchio con Piselli

PIEDMONT LAMB STEW WITH PEAS

3 pounds boneless lamb,
cut in 1½-inch cubes
3 tablespoons butter
2 teaspoons salt
½ teaspoon freshly ground
black pepper
1 tablespoon flour

16 small white onions
¾ cup boiling water
½ cup peeled, diced
tomatoes
2 pounds green peas,
shelled, or 2 packages
frozen

Trim the fat from the lamb. Melt the butter in a Dutch oven or heavy skillet and brown the lamb on all sides. Sprinkle with the salt, pepper, and flour. Add the onions; cook until onions turn yellow. Add the water and tomatoes; cover and cook over low heat 1 hour or until tender.

While the lamb is cooking, cook the peas in salted water until tender but firm. Drain and add the peas to the lamb; cook 5 minutes longer.

Serves 6–8.

Lammgryta

SWEDISH LAMB STEW

3 pounds boneless lamb,
cut in 1½-inch cubes
2 tablespoons flour
3 tablespoons butter
¾ cup chopped onions
1½ teaspoons salt
½ teaspoon freshly ground
black pepper

1 bay leaf
Dash ground allspice
1¼ cups beef broth
2 tablespoons tomato paste
2 cups diced potatoes
1½ cups sliced carrots
12 small white onions

Trim the fat from the lamb. Toss the lamb with the flour.

Melt the butter in a Dutch oven or heavy skillet and brown the lamb and chopped onions in it. Add the salt, pepper, bay leaf,

allspice, broth, and tomato paste. Bring to a boil and cook 20 minutes. Add the potatoes, carrots, and white onions. Cover and bake in a 400° oven 40 minutes. Taste for seasoning.
Serves 6–8.

Får i Kål

SWEDISH LAMB AND CABBAGE

3 pounds lamb shoulder,
  cut in 1½-inch cubes
2-pound head cabbage, cut
  in 8 wedges
1 cup sliced onions
2½ teaspoons salt

¾ teaspoon freshly ground
  black pepper
2 bay leaves
2 cups water
¼ cup chopped parsley

Trim the fat from the lamb. Place meat, cabbage, and onions in a saucepan. Add salt, pepper, bay leaves, and water. Bring to a boil, cover, and cook over low heat for 2 hours. Discard the bay leaves and sprinkle with parsley.
Serves 6–8.

Kuzu Güveci

TURKISH LAMB AND OKRA

3 pounds boneless lamb,
  cut in 1½-inch cubes
2 tablespoons vegetable oil
¾ cup finely chopped
  onions
1 29-ounce can tomatoes,
  drained and chopped
2 teaspoons salt

½ teaspoon freshly ground
  black pepper
½ teaspoon orégano
1 pound fresh okra, or 1
  package frozen, thawed
½ cup boiling water
2 tablespoons minced
  parsley

Trim the fat from the lamb. Heat the oil in a casserole and brown the lamb on all sides. Stir in the onions and cook until lightly browned. Add the tomatoes, salt, pepper, and orégano. Cover and cook over low heat 30 minutes. Add the okra, water, and parsley; re-cover and cook 45 minutes longer, or until the lamb is tender.

Serves 6–8.

Malai Korma

EAST INDIAN LAMB IN ALMOND CREAM

2 pounds boneless lamb, cut in small dice	1 cup ground, blanched almonds
½ teaspoon powdered ginger	½ cup heavy cream
3 teaspoons turmeric	1 bay leaf
2 cups chopped onions	1½ teaspoons salt
1 cup yogurt	¼ teaspoon dried ground chili peppers
4 tablespoons butter	
½ cup boiling water	

Trim the fat from the lamb. Toss the meat with the ginger and half the turmeric and onions. Add ¼ cup of the yogurt and let stand 30 minutes.

Melt the butter in a heavy skillet; sauté the remaining onions 10 minutes. Remove the onions and reserve. To the skillet, add the lamb mixture. Cook over medium heat, stirring frequently, for 5 minutes. Add the remaining yogurt, and cook until the liquid is absorbed. Add half the water, cover, and cook until the mixture is dry. Add the remaining water, re-cover, and cook 15 minutes.

Mix together the almonds, cream, bay leaf, salt, chili peppers, and the reserved turmeric and onions. Add to the meat; re-cover and cook over very low heat 15 minutes. Discard the bay leaf and taste for seasoning.

Serves 4–6.

Keema Korma Dal

BOMBAY LAMB CURRY WITH LENTILS

2 pounds boneless lamb, cut in 1-inch cubes	1 teaspoon turmeric
2 cups chopped onions	1 teaspoon ground cumin
2 cloves garlic, minced	1½ teaspoons salt
2 teaspoons ground coriander	½ cup yogurt
¼ teaspoon dried ground red peppers	2 cups lentils
	¼ pound butter
	4 cups boiling water

Trim the fat from the lamb. Pound together the onions, garlic, coriander, red peppers, turmeric, cumin, and salt; gradually blend in the yogurt. Add the lamb, tossing until well coated. Let stand 1 hour.

Wash the lentils thoroughly; cover with water, bring to a boil, and drain. Melt the butter in a casserole or Dutch oven; add the undrained meat. Cook over low heat 15 minutes, stirring frequently. Stir in the lentils and boiling water. Cover and cook over low heat 30 minutes, or until meat and lentils are tender and fairly dry. Taste for seasoning. *Serves 6–8.*

Ceylon Lamb Curry

3 pounds boneless lamb, cut in 1-inch cubes	¼ cup chopped preserved ginger
3 tablespoons butter	1½ cups beef broth
¾ cup finely chopped onions	2 tablespoons lime or lemon juice
2 teaspoons salt	½ cup packaged finely grated coconut
2 tablespoons curry powder	1 cup light cream

Trim the fat from the lamb. Melt the butter in a deep skillet or casserole; brown the onions and lamb in it. Stir in the salt and curry powder; cook 2 minutes. Add the ginger and broth, cover, and cook over low heat 1 hour. Stir the lime or lemon juice into the pan juices, then add the coconut and cream. Cook 10 minutes but do not let boil. Serve with rice. *Serves 6–8.*

Malai Korma

KASHMIR LAMB CURRY

2 pounds boneless lamb, cut in small cubes	2½ cups chopped onions
½ teaspoon powdered ginger	1 bay leaf
	1 cup yogurt
1 tablespoon turmeric	1½ teaspoons salt
¼ teaspoon ground cumin	¾ cup ground, blanched almonds
5 tablespoons butter	½ cup heavy cream

Trim the fat from the lamb. Toss together the ginger, turmeric, cumin, and lamb until lamb is coated with the spices. Let stand 20 minutes.

Melt 3 tablespoons of the butter in a Dutch oven or casserole; sauté the onions 10 minutes. Remove. Melt the remaining butter in the Dutch oven and lightly brown the meat on all sides. Return the onions and add the bay leaf, yogurt, and salt. Cover and cook over low heat 45 minutes or until lamb is tender. Mix together the almonds and cream; stir into the lamb; cook 10 minutes. Taste for seasoning. *Serves 4–6.*

Madras Lamb Curry

2 pounds boneless lamb, cut in 1-inch cubes	1 tablespoon curry powder
4 tablespoons butter	2 tablespoons flour
1½ cups chopped onions	1 cup beef broth
2 teaspoons salt	1 teaspoon drained capers
¼ teaspoon freshly ground black pepper	1 cup yogurt

Trim the fat from the lamb. Melt the butter in a saucepan; sauté the onions, lamb, salt, and pepper 15 minutes, stirring frequently. Blend in the curry powder and flour. Gradually add the broth, stirring constantly to the boiling point. Cook over low heat 45 minutes or until the lamb is tender. Add the capers and yogurt. Cook 5 minutes, stirring occasionally. Taste for seasoning. *Serves 4–6.*

Huzoor Pasand Pulao

PAKISTAN LAMB AND FRUIT CURRY

3 pounds boneless lamb, cut in 1-inch cubes
2 cups raw rice
¼ pound (1 stick) butter
1½ cups thinly sliced onions
2 cloves garlic, minced
4 cups yogurt
2 cloves
3 cardamom seeds, crushed
1 tablespoon salt
1 teaspoon crushed coriander seeds

1-inch piece fresh ginger, chopped, or 2 teaspoons powdered ginger
½ teaspoon freshly ground black pepper
1 teaspoon saffron
2 oranges, peeled, sectioned, and seeded
½ cup seedless grapes
½ cup sliced, blanched almonds
1 cup pistachio nuts

Trim the fat from the lamb. Wash the rice well in several waters. Soak in cold water 15 minutes. Drain well.

Melt the butter in a Dutch oven or heavy skillet and brown the lamb on all sides. Add the onions and continue browning. Add the garlic, yogurt, cloves, cardamom seeds, salt, coriander, ginger, and pepper. Stir well. Add rice and saffron, which has been dissolved in 2 tablespoons boiling water. Stir well. Arrange the oranges, grapes, and nuts on top, cover, and cook over medium heat 10 minutes. Reduce heat to low and cook 25 minutes longer, or until lamb and rice are tender. *Serves 8–10.*

Rogan Josh

PAKISTAN LAMB CURRY

2 pounds boneless lamb,
cut in 2-inch strips
6 tablespoons butter
2 pounds onions, minced
4 teaspoons crushed
coriander
2 teaspoons turmeric
2 teaspoons crushed
cuminseeds

½ teaspoon powdered
ginger
1½ teaspoons salt
½ teaspoon chili powder
½ cup yogurt
1 cup peeled, minced
tomatoes
½ cup boiling water

Trim the fat from the lamb. Melt the butter in a Dutch oven or casserole. Add the onions; cook over low heat, stirring frequently, until onions brown. Add the lamb, coriander, turmeric, cumin, and ginger. Cook, stirring frequently, for 10 minutes. Mix in the salt, chili powder, yogurt, and tomatoes; cook, stirring occasionally, until mixture is dry. Add the water; cover and cook 30 minutes, or until the meat is tender. Watch carefully and add a little more boiling water if necessary.
Serves 4–6.

Arni me Melitzanes

GREEK LAMB `AND EGGPLANT PUDDING

3 tablespoons olive oil
1 medium-sized eggplant,
peeled and cut in ½-inch
slices
1 cup sliced onions
3 cups chopped roast lamb
1 20-ounce can tomatoes,
drained

1 green pepper, cut julienne
2 tablespoons minced
parsley
2 teaspoons salt
¾ teaspoon freshly ground
black pepper
3 egg yolks
¾ cup light cream

Heat the oil in a skillet; sauté the eggplant 5 minutes. Remove. In the oil remaining sauté the onions 5 minutes. In a greased 2-quart casserole arrange successive layers of the eggplant, onions, lamb, tomatoes, and green peppers, sprinkled with the parsley, 1½ teaspoons of the salt, and ½ teaspoon of the pepper. Cover and bake in a 350° oven 1 hour. Beat together the egg yolks, cream, and the remaining salt and pepper; pour into the casserole. Re-cover and bake 15 minutes. Uncover and bake 5 minutes longer or until custard mixture is set.

Serves 6–8.

Pork and Ham

Charles Lamb's *A Dissertation upon Roast Pig* describes the succulent meat of the pig perfectly. Fresh pork is actually a misunderstood meat in the United States. It was formerly the least expensive meat, and thus relegated to everyday family meals. The basic form of preparation was, and still is, roast pork, with pan-fried pork chops a close second. In other countries, however, pork is often a holiday or party dish prepared in many different ways.

The Chinese, Italians, and French are particularly imaginative in the preparation of pork dishes. The Spanish specialize in serving suckling pig. The South Pacific islanders are notably fond of whole roast pigs for the many variations of the Hawaiian *luaus*.

Pork, the flesh of the swine (as older hogs are called), has been a staple in the diets of many people of the world since the Chinese caught the first wild one, said to be around 2900 B.C. Later, the pig so flourished in Ireland that the farmers there gave it the name of "the gentleman that pays the rent." The pig has also been called "man's best friend," for practically all parts of it are usable. The pig gives us ham, bacon, pork roasts, and chops, sausages, and lard—in addition to leather for shoes, gloves, and bags, and bristles for brushes. Next to beef, Americans eat more pork than any other meat.

The whole hog is called pork, but after it is butchered, the hind-leg cuts are called ham, either "fresh" or "smoked," the latter after the leg has gone through a curing process. Bacon is the smoked side meat, after the spareribs have been removed.

Fresh pork is available all year but is generally more plentiful from November to February. The hogs are usually slaughtered when they are between five and seven months old. The fat should be white and firm and the lean pinkish gray to delicate rose. Fresh pork should be well cooked but not dried out; 25–30 minutes a pound or 185° on a meat thermometer is the proper time. Just be sure no pink remains in the center. Thorough cooking not only brings out the full flavor but also kills any trichina organisms present.

Fresh ham and smoked ham are available in the same cuts, but there are two main kinds of smoked ham: Fully cooked hams which require nothing except serving, unless you wish to reheat them; and the cook-before-eating type which require some cooking. "Country style" and "Virginia" hams, which have been put through a long smoking and drying period, usually require soaking and simmering in water before baking. One may purchase a half of ham, either the shank or the butt end (the preference is yours), and either boned or bone-in. Slices for ham steaks may be removed from either half. There are also excellent canned smoked hams available, domestic or imported, neither of which requires cooking.

Smoked pork, or ham, is a favorite meat in the United States as well as in Scandinavia, the Central European countries, and Iceland. The type of curing and smoking varies from region to region, so always read the packer's directions for the preparation of a particular ham.

PORK AND HAM CUTS[1]

Ham (9) – The whole leg of the animal, available fresh or smoked. Half of the ham is also available, either the shank portion or the butt half, which is meatier.
Loin (7) – The whole loin, containing the tenderloin. In one piece, it is used for roasting. Choice chops are cut from the loin.
Rib (7) – Chops are cut from this piece, and only every other chop has a bone. Also made into crown roasts.
Tenderloin (10) – This is similar to the fillet of beef and is a long, tapering piece of meat, much used in Chinese cooking. A tenderloin weighs only ½ to 1 pound.
Sirloin Roast (7) – The end of the loin, containing the hipbone.
Shoulder (1, 2) – This portion contains the picnic (arm and shoulder), back and arm.
Boston Butt (1) – This cut is usually smoked.

[1] The numbers in parentheses refer to the Pork Chart.

Spareribs (5) – The breastbone and ribs, which have been removed from the bacon strip.

Canadian Style Bacon (7) – The cured, smoked boneless back strip.

Hocks and Knuckles (3) – Cut just above the foot.

Foot (4)

Salt Pork (8) – The fat of the back.

Barbecued Suckling Pig

A suckling pig is best when 4 to 6 weeks old. Gently rub the pig with olive oil, then stuff about two-thirds full (to allow room for swelling) with the following mixture:

1 cup chopped onions
1 cup chopped celery
2 tablespoons butter
6 cups crumbled corn
  bread
1 cup chopped crisp bacon
½ cup chopped pecans
6 pork sausages, sliced
2 teaspoons sage
½ teaspoon ground cloves
¼ teaspoon thyme
½ teaspoon nutmeg
1 teaspoon Worcestershire
  sauce
6 eggs, beaten
Hot water
Melted butter
Salt
Freshly ground black pepper

Sauté the onions and celery in the butter for 10 minutes. Mix with the corn bread, bacon, pecans, sausages, sage, cloves, thyme, nutmeg, Worcestershire sauce, and eggs.

Stuff the pig and close the opening securely with skewers. (If there is any stuffing left, bake it in a casserole.) Put the center barbecue spit through the mouth and out the other end. Place the smaller forked prongs in the body and bolt them securely. Put the revolving spit over the charcoal fire (burned down to coals). Roast 25 minutes a pound, or until tender and no pink remains. Baste very frequently with hot water and melted butter. Sprinkle liberally with salt and pepper before carving. The pig may also be roasted in a 350° oven or an electric rotisserie.

Crown Roast of Pork

Crown of pork	¾ cup chopped onions
5 teaspoons salt	4 cups soft bread crumbs
1 teaspoon freshly ground	¼ teaspoon thyme
black pepper	⅓ cup chopped parsley
¼ pound (1 stick) butter	1 egg, beaten

Have the butcher prepare the crown with the bones Frenched and backbone removed. Rub with 4 teaspoons of the salt and ¾ teaspoon of the pepper; place on a foil-covered rack in a shallow roasting pan.

Melt 2 tablespoons of the butter in a skillet; sauté the onions 5 minutes. Add the remaining butter. Mix in the bread crumbs, thyme, parsley, egg, and remaining salt and pepper. Fill the center of the crown and cover the stuffing with aluminum foil. Cover the bone ends with foil or potato cubes. Roast in a 350° oven 30 minutes a pound. Carefully transfer the crown to a platter. Discard the bone covering and replace with frills or sautéed mushrooms.

Serves 6–8.

Stuffed Crown Roast of Pork, Southern Style

Crown of pork	½ cup minced green
2 cloves garlic, minced	peppers
¾ teaspoon freshly ground	¾ cup diced celery
black pepper	3 tablespoons minced
4 teaspoons salt	parsley
4 tablespoons butter	3 cups cooked rice
1½ cups minced onions	½ cup seedless raisins

Rub the crown of pork with a mixture of the garlic, pepper, and 3 teaspoons salt. Place in a roasting pan.

Heat the butter in a skillet; sauté the onions, green peppers, and celery 10 minutes. Mix in the parsley, rice, raisins, and remaining salt.

Put the crown on a foil-covered rack in a roasting pan. Fill the center with the rice mixture and cover with a piece of aluminum foil. Cover the bone ends with foil or potato cubes. Roast in a 325° oven 3½ hours or until the pork is tender. Carefully transfer the crown to a hot serving dish, discard the covering of the stuffing and bones. Put paper frills on the bones.
Serves 8–10.

California Crown Roast of Pork

Crown of pork
2 teaspoons salt
½ teaspoon freshly ground
  black pepper
2 teaspoons Worcestershire
  sauce
1½ pounds prunes, pitted
2 cups water

3 cups peeled, sliced
  cooking apples
1 cup dry bread crumbs
¼ cup chopped green
  peppers
½ cup chopped celery
¼ cup melted butter

Rub the crown of pork with a mixture of the salt, pepper, and Worcestershire sauce. Place on a foil-covered rack in a roasting pan.

Wash the prunes, combine with the water and apples, and bring to a boil. Remove from the heat and let soak 5 minutes. Drain well, then mix with the bread crumbs, green peppers, celery, and butter. Cover the bone ends with foil or potato cubes. Fill the center of the crown. Cover the filling with aluminum foil. Roast in a 325° oven 3½ hours or until the pork is tender.
Serves 8–10.

Roast Fresh Ham

6-pound fresh ham
1 tablespoon salt
¾ teaspoon freshly ground
  black pepper

¼ teaspoon thyme
1 clove garlic, minced

Score the fat of the ham in an attractive design, then rub with a mixture of the salt, pepper, thyme, and garlic. Place on a rack in a roasting pan. Roast in a 325° oven 30 minutes a pound (185° on a meat thermometer), basting occasionally with the drippings. Let stand 15 minutes before carving.

Serves 10–12.

VARIATION:

Prepare ham as above. 1 hour before the roast is done, add 1 cup beef broth, small peeled potatoes, and small white onions; baste frequently during the remaining roasting time.

Schweineschlegel

FRESH ROAST HAM, BLACK FOREST STYLE

6-pound fresh ham	**1½ cups boiling water**
1 tablespoon salt	**2 tablespoons butter**
½ teaspoon freshly ground	**2 tablespoons flour**
black pepper	**¼ cup dry white wine**
1 cup sliced onions	

Score the ham in an attractive design and rub with the salt and pepper. Place in a roasting pan. Roast in a 400° oven 30 minutes. Pour off the fat and add the onions and water. Cover, reduce heat to 350°, and roast 3 hours longer, or until no pink remains. Remove cover for the last 30 minutes. Transfer the ham to a hot platter.

Place the pan over direct low heat and skim the fat from the pan juices. Stir in the butter, then the flour mixed with the wine. Bring to a boil, stirring steadily. If too thick, add a little boiling water. Cook 5 minutes longer. Carve the ham and serve the gravy in a sauceboat.

Serves 8–10.

Skinkestek med Tyttebaer

DANISH MARINATED FRESH HAM WITH LINGONBERRIES

6-pound fresh ham	3 bay leaves
1 tablespoon salt	3 cloves
¾ teaspoon freshly ground	6 peppercorns
black pepper	1 tablespoon cornstarch
2 cups dry white wine	2 tablespoons water
¼ cup vegetable oil	2 cups lingonberries

Have the butcher remove the skin of the ham. Rub with the salt and pepper. In a deep bowl, mix the wine, oil, bay leaves, cloves, and peppercorns. Marinate the ham in the mixture in the refrigerator 24 hours. Turn and baste frequently. Drain, reserving the marinade.

Place the ham in a roasting pan. Roast in a 350° oven 2 hours; pour off the fat. Heat the marinade and add to the ham. Roast 2 hours longer (185° on a meat thermometer), basting frequently. Transfer the ham to a heated serving dish. Let stand 15 minutes before carving. Skim the fat from the pan juices and pour into a saucepan. Add the cornstarch mixed with the water, stirring steadily to the boiling point. Add the lingonberries; cook 3 minutes longer.

Serves 8–10.

Schinken in Wein

GERMAN MARINATED FRESH HAM

6-pound fresh ham	¾ teaspoon freshly ground
1 quart dry red wine	black pepper
1 tablespoon vinegar	½ teaspoon thyme
1 cup chopped onions	2 bay leaves
2 cloves garlic, minced	1 slice salt pork
2 teaspoons salt	½ cup orange currant jelly

Trim the fat from the ham. In a saucepan, combine the wine, vinegar, onions, garlic, salt, pepper, thyme, and bay leaves. Bring to a boil and cook over low heat 10 minutes. Place the ham in a large glass or pottery bowl and pour the marinade over it. Marinate in the refrigerator 2 to 3 days, turning the meat and basting occasionally. Remove the meat, dry with paper towels, and reserve the marinade.

Dice the salt pork and render it in a Dutch oven or casserole; brown the ham in it on all sides. Pour off the fat. Heat the marinade and pour half of it over the meat. Cover and roast in a 350° oven 3½ hours or until tender, basting frequently and adding more marinade as needed. Remove cover for last half hour.

Transfer the meat to a platter. Strain the gravy into a saucepan and skim the fat. Stir the currant jelly into it and taste for seasoning. Thicken if necessary with a little cornstarch or flour mixed with water.

Serves 6–8.

Szynka Duszona na Czerwonym Winie
POLISH MARINATED FRESH HAM

6-pound fresh ham	2 tablespoons olive oil
3 cups dry red wine	1 cup beef broth
1 cup chopped onions	2 tablespoons minced
½ cup sliced carrots	parsley
2 cloves garlic, minced	3 hard-cooked egg yolks,
½ teaspoon marjoram	mashed
1 bay leaf	3 tablespoons capers
2 teaspoons salt	
½ teaspoon freshly ground	
black pepper	

Trim the fat from the ham and place in a glass or pottery bowl. Mix together the wine, onions, carrots, garlic, marjoram, bay leaf, salt, and pepper. Pour over the ham; marinate overnight, basting occasionally. Drain the meat, reserving the marinade.

Heat the oil in a Dutch oven or casserole and brown the ham

on all sides. Pour off the fat. Heat the marinade and pour over the meat. Cover and roast in a 350° oven 3 hours, or until tender. Add a little of the broth from time to time and baste frequently. Transfer the meat to a platter. Skim the fat from the gravy and stir in the parsley, egg yolks, and capers.
Serves 8–10.

Rôti de Porc Poêlé

BRAISED MARINATED LOIN OF PORK

4-pound boned loin of pork, rolled and tied	½ cup sliced carrots
1 tablespoon salt	8 peppercorns
½ cup wine vinegar	1 teaspoon thyme
1 cup dry white wine	2 bay leaves
¼ cup olive oil	3 tablespoons vegetable oil
2 cloves garlic, split	½ cup sliced green onions
½ cup sliced onions	(scallions)
	½ cup beef broth

Rub the meat with the salt. In a glass or pottery bowl, combine the vinegar, wine, olive oil, garlic, sliced onions, carrots, peppercorns, thyme, and bay leaves. Add the pork, and marinate in the refrigerator 2 days, basting and turning the meat frequently. Drain the meat and dry with paper towels.

Heat the vegetable oil in a casserole and brown the pork on all sides. Pour off all but 2 tablespoons of the fat. Add the green onions; cover and roast in a 325° oven 2¼ hours, basting and turning the meat a few times.

Transfer the meat to a hot serving platter. Remove the strings. Place the casserole over direct low heat. Add the broth to the casserole; bring to a boil and cook over high heat 3 minutes. Skim the fat and serve in a sauceboat. *Serves 8.*

Porc en Cidre

BRITTANY LOIN OF PORK IN CIDER SAUCE

6-pound boned loin of
  pork, rolled and tied
2½ teaspoons salt
¾ teaspoon freshly ground
  black pepper

8 baking apples, cored
8 large onions, peeled
1½ cups cider
2 tablespoons flour
¼ cup cognac

Rub the pork with the salt and pepper; place in a roasting pan. Roast in a 375° oven 1½ hours. Pour off the fat. Arrange the apples and onions around the pork and add 1 cup cider. Reduce heat to 325° and roast 1¼ hours longer, basting frequently.

Remove the strings from the pork. Arrange the pork, apples, and onions on a serving platter. Skim the fat from the gravy. Place pan over direct low heat and stir in the flour. Gradually add the cognac and remaining cider, stirring constantly and scraping the bottom of browned particles. Cook over low heat 5 minutes. Serve the gravy in a sauceboat. *Serves 8.*

Rôti de Porc en Cidre

NORMANDY LOIN OF PORK IN CIDER

10-rib loin of pork
1 tablespoon salt
¾ teaspoon freshly ground
  black pepper
8 baking apples, cored

8 small potatoes, peeled
8 large onions
1½ cups cider
2 tablespoons flour
¼ cup cognac

Rub the pork with the salt and pepper; place in a roasting pan. Roast in a 375° oven 1½ hours. Pour off the fat. Arrange the apples, potatoes, and onions around the pork and add 1 cup of the cider. Reduce heat to 325° and roast 1¼ hours longer, basting frequently.

Place the pork, apples, and onions on a serving platter. Skim the fat from the gravy. Place pan on direct low heat and stir in the flour. Gradually add the cognac and remaining cider, stirring constantly, scraping the bottom of any browned particles. Cook over low heat 5 minutes. *Serves 8.*

Chinese Braised Loin of Pork with Spinach

3-pound boned loin of pork	¼ cup soy sauce
1 clove garlic, minced	1 cup beef broth
1 teaspoon salt	2 tablespoons dry sherry
¼ teaspoon freshly ground	1½ pounds spinach, washed
black pepper	and drained
2 tablespoons honey	

Rub the pork with the garlic, salt, and pepper. In a deep skillet or heavy saucepan brown the pork on all sides. Pour off all but 2 tablespoons of the fat. Mix together the honey, soy sauce, broth, and sherry; bring to a boil and pour over the pork. Cover and cook over low heat 1½ hours, or until tender. Baste and turn the meat frequently. Remove the meat. Cook the spinach in the gravy 2 minutes. Heap the spinach in the center of a serving dish; slice the pork thin and arrange over the spinach. *Serves 4–6.*

Carré de Porc à la Paysanne

ROAST LOIN OF PORK, COUNTRY STYLE

6-pound loin of pork	6 potatoes, peeled and
2 teaspoons salt	quartered
½ teaspoon freshly ground	¾ cup dry white wine
black pepper	2 tablespoons minced
½ teaspoon paprika	parsley
12 small white onions	

Have the ribs of the pork cracked to facilitate carving. Rub the pork with a mixture of the salt, pepper, and paprika. Place in a roasting pan and roast in a 350° oven 1¼ hours. Pour off the fat;

arrange the onions and potatoes around the pork and add the wine. Roast 1¼ hours longer, basting frequently. Sprinkle with the parsley and serve.
Serves 6–8.

Pikante Schweinefleisch

GERMAN MARINATED PORK SLICES

8-rib loin of pork	**¼ teaspoon dried ground**
½ cup olive oil	**chili peppers**
3 tablespoons wine vinegar	**4 tablespoons grated onion**
1½ teaspoons salt	**3 cloves garlic**
	½ teaspoon orégano

Have the loin boned and cut in half lengthwise, making 2 long strips.

Mix together the oil, vinegar, salt, chili peppers, onion, garlic, and orégano. Marinate the pork strips in the mixture 4 hours, turning the meat frequently. Drain the pork, reserving the marinade.

Place the pork in a shallow roasting pan; roast in a 425° oven 10 minutes. Pour the reserved marinade over the meat, reduce heat to 350°, and roast 50 minutes longer, basting frequently. Serve the pork in thin slices. *Serves 6–8.*

Puerco Asado con Salsa di Naranja

MEXICAN ROAST LOIN OF PORK WITH ORANGE SAUCE

6-pound loin of pork	**2 cloves garlic, minced**
¾ teaspoon freshly ground	**1 tablespoon flour**
black pepper	**2 cups boiling water**
3 teaspoons salt	**¼ cup orange marmalade**
3 cups orange juice	**2 teaspoons prepared**
2 tablespoons grated	**mustard**
orange rind	

Rub the pork with the pepper and 2 teaspoons salt. Place in a shallow roasting pan; roast in a 375° oven 30 minutes. Pour off the fat. Mix together the orange juice, rind, garlic, and remaining salt; pour over the pork. Roast 2 hours longer, basting very frequently. Transfer the pork to a serving platter and skim the fat from the gravy.

Place the pan over direct heat and blend in the flour. Add the water, stirring and scraping the bottom of the pan. Cook over low heat 5 minutes. Mix in the marmalade and mustard. Carve the pork and serve the sauce in a sauceboat.

Serves 6–8.

Pieczén Wieprzowa Duszona na Czerwonem Winie

POLISH MARINATED LOIN OF PORK

6-pound boned loin of pork, rolled and tied	**3 cloves garlic, minced**
2½ teaspoons salt	**2 cups chopped onions**
1 teaspoon freshly ground black pepper	**2½ cups dry red wine**
½ teaspoon thyme	**3 tablespoons vegetable oil**
	2 tablespoons flour

Rub the pork with a mixture of the salt, pepper, thyme, and garlic. Place in a glass or pottery bowl; add the onions and 2 cups of the wine. Marinate the pork in the refrigerator overnight, basting occasionally.

Rub a roasting pan with the oil; put the undrained pork into it. Roast in a 350° oven 2½ hours, basting frequently. Transfer the pork to a heated platter and remove strings. Pour the gravy into a saucepan and skim the fat. Mix the flour with the remaining wine and stir into the gravy. Cook over low heat, stirring constantly, until thickened; then cook 5 minutes longer. Taste for seasoning. Serve in a sauceboat.

Serves 6–8.

Rôti de Porc Provençale

ROAST LOIN OF PORK, PROVENCE STYLE

6-pound loin of pork
2 cloves garlic, slivered
2 teaspoons salt
½ teaspoon freshly ground
black pepper

½ teaspoon thyme
2 cups dry white wine
¼ cup dry bread crumbs
½ cup chopped parsley

Have the bottom of the bones sawed at ¼-inch intervals; insert a garlic sliver in each cut. Rub the pork with the salt, pepper, and thyme. Place in a glass or pottery bowl and pour the wine over it. Marinate at room temperature 2 hours, basting and turning the meat several times. Drain, reserving the wine.

Place the pork in a roasting pan, fat side up, and pour 1 cup of the wine over it. Cover the pan with a piece of oiled aluminum foil and roast in a 350° oven 1½ hours.

Mix together the bread crumbs and parsley. Remove the foil from the pan and press the parsley mixture over the top of the pork. Pour the remaining wine into the pan (not over the pork). Reduce heat to 325° and roast 1 hour longer, basting frequently.
Serves 4–6.

Loin of Pork Stuffed with Prunes

6-pound loin of pork
2 teaspoons salt
½ teaspoon white pepper
¼ teaspoon powdered
ginger

16 pitted prunes
3 cups boiling water
2 tablespoons vegetable oil

Have the meat boned and a pocket cut in the center along the length of the roast. Rub the meat with the salt, pepper, and ginger.

Cover the prunes with the boiling water and soak 30 minutes. Drain, reserving the liquid. Stuff the pocket with the prunes. Tie the meat in several places with string.

Heat the oil in a Dutch oven or saucepan and brown the meat on all sides. Pour off the fat and add 1 cup of the prune liquid; cover and cook over low heat 2 hours; add more prune liquid as needed and baste frequently. Transfer the meat to a hot platter and remove the strings. Slice the meat and serve the gravy (skimmed of fat) in a sauceboat.

Serves 6–8.

Puerco Horneado

SPANISH SPICED ROAST LOIN OF PORK

3 cloves garlic, minced
2½ teaspoons salt
1 teaspoon freshly ground black pepper
½ teaspoon saffron
½ teaspoon ground cumin
½ teaspoon thyme
8-pound boned loin of pork, rolled and tied

½ cup boiling water
1 cup dry white wine
½ cup chopped onions, sautéed
2 tablespoons wine vinegar
3 tablespoons minced parsley
¼ teaspoon dried ground chili peppers

Pound together the garlic, salt, pepper, saffron, cumin, and thyme; rub into the pork. Wrap in waxed paper or foil and refrigerate overnight.

Place the pork in a shallow roasting pan. Roast in a 425° oven 25 minutes. Pour off the fat. Reduce heat to 350°, pour the water and ½ cup of the wine over the pork and roast 2 hours longer, basting frequently. Transfer the pork to a platter and remove the strings; skim the fat from the pan and place the pan over direct heat. Mix in the onions, vinegar, parsley, chili peppers, and remaining wine; bring to a boil, scraping the bottom of the pan of browned particles. Cook 2 minutes and serve in a sauceboat.

Serves 6–8.

Lomo a la Cádiz
SPANISH LOIN OF PORK IN SHERRY

6-pound loin of pork	2½ cups medium dry sherry
2½ teaspoons salt	1 tablespoon flour
½ teaspoon freshly ground	½ cup beef broth
black pepper	2 tablespoons minced
2 cloves garlic, minced	parsley
2 tablespoons olive oil	

Trim the fat from the pork. Rub the loin with a mixture of the salt, pepper, and garlic. Let stand at room temperature for 2 hours.

Heat the oil in a Dutch oven or casserole. Brown the pork in it on all sides. Pour off the fat. Add the sherry; cover and bake in a 350° oven, basting frequently, for 2½ hours or until the pork is tender. Transfer the pork to a hot platter and skim the fat from the pan juices. Put the pan over direct heat. Mix the flour with the broth, and stir into the pan juices until thickened and smooth. Mix in the parsley and taste for seasoning. Serve in a gravy boat.

Serves 6–8.

Australian Pork Chops with Apricots

6 pork chops, cut 1 inch	2 tablespoons vegetable oil
thick	½ cup dry white wine
1 cup dried apricots	2 tablespoons brown sugar
1 cup cider	2 tablespoons slivered,
¼ cup flour	blanched almonds
1½ teaspoons salt	
½ teaspoon freshly ground	
black pepper	

Trim the fat from the chops. Soak the apricots in the cider overnight. Purée the undrained apricots in an electric blender or force through a sieve.

Dip the chops in a mixture of the flour, salt, and pepper. Heat the oil in a deep skillet (with an ovenproof handle) and brown the chops on both sides. Spread with the apricot purée and pour the wine into the skillet. Cover and bake in a 350° oven 45 minutes. Sprinkle with the sugar and almonds. Bake uncovered 15 minutes longer.

Serves 6.

Schweinskoteletten mit Fruchtsauce

AUSTRIAN BAKED PORK CHOPS WITH FRUIT SAUCE

6 pork chops, cut 1½ inches thick	2 teaspoons chopped onions
1½ teaspoons salt	1 cup applesauce
½ teaspoon freshly ground black pepper	1 cup canned whole cranberries
⅛ teaspoon thyme	½ cup hot water
2 eggs, beaten	1 tablespoon Worcestershire sauce
1 cup dry bread crumbs	2 tablespoons sugar
3 tablespoons butter	

Trim the fat from the chops; rub with a mixture of the salt, pepper, and thyme. Dip the chops in the eggs, then in the crumbs, coating them well.

Melt the butter in a heavy skillet; sauté the onions 2 minutes. Add the chops and brown on both sides.

Mix together the applesauce, cranberries, water, Worcestershire sauce, and sugar; pour over the chops. Cover and bake in a 350° oven 50 minutes, or until chops are tender; remove the cover for the last 15 minutes.

Serves 6.

Schweinskoteletten in Rosinensauce
AUSTRIAN PORK CHOPS WITH RAISIN SAUCE

6 pork chops, cut 1 inch
thick
¼ cup flour
1½ teaspoons salt
1 tablespoon vegetable oil
1 tablespoon cornstarch
2 tablespoons brown sugar
½ teaspoon ginger

⅛ teaspoon nutmeg
1 cup orange juice
½ cup water
2 tablespoons lemon juice
2 oranges, peeled and
sectioned
¼ cup seedless raisins

Trim the fat from the chops; dip the chops in a mixture of
the flour and salt. Heat the oil in a skillet and brown the chops
on both sides. Pour off the fat. Mix together the cornstarch, sugar,
ginger, nutmeg, orange juice, water, and lemon juice. Add to the
skillet, stirring to the boiling point. Arrange the orange segments
on the chops and sprinkle with the raisins. Cover and cook over
low heat 45 minutes or until tender. *Serves 6.*

Schweinefleisch mit Sauerkraut
BAVARIAN BAKED PORK CHOPS WITH SAUERKRAUT

6 pork chops, cut 1 inch
thick
2 tablespoons vegetable oil
1½ teaspoons salt
½ teaspoon freshly ground
black pepper

1 cup sliced onions
1½ pounds sauerkraut
3 cups canned puréed
apricots
¼ teaspoon caraway seeds

Trim the fat from the chops; heat the oil in a skillet and brown
the chops on both sides. Season with the salt and pepper. Remove
the chops; in the fat remaining in the skillet, sauté the onions
5 minutes.
Rinse the sauerkraut under cold running water; drain well.

Mix the sauerkraut with the apricots, caraway seeds, and sautéed onions. Spread three-quarters of the sauerkraut mixture in a greased 2-quart baking dish, arrange the chops over it, and cover with the remaining sauerkraut. Cover and bake in a 350° oven 1¼ hours, removing the cover for the last 15 minutes. *Serves 6.*

Saures Schweinefleisch

BAVARIAN PIQUANT PORK CHOPS

8 loin pork chops, cut ½ inch thick	2 teaspoons salt
3 tablespoons lemon juice	½ teaspoon freshly ground black pepper
3 tablespoons olive oil	½ cup wine vinegar

Trim the fat from the chops. Sprinkle the chops with the lemon juice; let stand for 45 minutes. Heat the oil in a skillet; sauté the chops until very brown on both sides. Sprinkle with the salt, pepper, and vinegar. Cover and cook over low heat for 45 minutes, or until tender. *Serves 4.*

Schweinskoteletten mit Äpfeln

BAVARIAN PORK CHOPS WITH APPLES

4 pork chops, cut ¾ inch thick	¼ teaspoon freshly ground black pepper
3 tablespoons butter	3 apples, peeled and cut in ½-inch slices
1 teaspoon salt	

Trim the fat from the chops. Melt the butter in a skillet; cook the chops in it over low heat until browned on both sides and no pink remains. Season with the salt and pepper. Transfer the chops to a heated serving dish and keep hot. In the fat remaining in the skillet, lightly brown the apple slices. Arrange on the chops. *Serves 4.*

Svinekotelot med Aeble

DANISH PORK CHOPS WITH APPLES

8 loin pork chops, cut ½ inch thick	Flour
	4 slices bacon
2 pounds cooking apples, peeled, cored, and cut in 1-inch slices	1½ teaspoons salt
	½ teaspoon freshly ground black pepper
2 tablespoons lemon juice	½ cup sugar

Trim the fat from the chops. Sprinkle the apple slices with the lemon juice and dip lightly in flour.

Cook the bacon until crisp, then drain, crumble, and reserve. Pour off all but 2 tablespoons fat and reserve. Brown the pork chops on both sides in the fat remaining in the skillet. Cover and cook until done, about 15 minutes. Season with the salt and pepper. Remove pork chops and keep hot.

Add 2 tablespoons of the reserved fat to the skillet. Fry the apple slices in it until browned on both sides. Sprinkle both sides with the sugar, and cook until glazed. Arrange the pork chops on a heated platter with the apple slices around them. Sprinkle with the bacon. *Serves 4.*

Schweinskoteletten mit Äpfeln

VIENNESE PORK CHOPS WITH APPLES

6 pork chops, cut 1 inch thick	12 small white onions
	¼ cup seedless raisins
1½ teaspoons salt	½ cup sweet sherry
¼ teaspoon freshly ground black pepper	½ cup water
	3 tablespoons brown sugar
4 apples, peeled and quartered	⅛ teaspoon thyme
	¼ teaspoon nutmeg

In a skillet, brown the chops for 5 minutes on each side, then drain. Sprinkle with the salt and pepper. Arrange the chops in a baking dish. Cover with the apples, onions, and raisins. Add the sherry, water, brown sugar, thyme, and nutmeg. Cover and bake in a 375° oven 1¼ hours, removing the cover for the last 15 minutes. Taste for seasoning. *Serves 6.*

Baked Pork Chops, Catalina Style

6 loin pork chops, cut 1½ inches thick
5 cups toasted fresh bread crumbs
½ cup chopped green olives
1 8-ounce can whole-kernel corn, drained
3 tablespoons grated onion
1 teaspoon celery salt

1 cup beef broth
1½ teaspoons Worcestershire sauce
2 teaspoons salt
½ teaspoon freshly ground black pepper
¼ cup flour
12 pimiento-stuffed olives

Trim the fat from the chops. Slit the chops through the middle, from the outer edges to the bone. Mix together the bread crumbs, chopped olives, corn, onion, celery salt, broth, and Worcestershire sauce. Stuff the chops, closing the openings with toothpicks or skewers; reserve the remaining stuffing. Season the chops with the salt and pepper and dip lightly in the flour. Arrange the chops in a greased baking dish.

Bake in a 350° oven 35 minutes. Drain the fat, turn the chops, and spread remaining stuffing in the dish. Bake 40 minutes longer or until chops are tender. Garnish with the whole olives. *Serves 6.*

Pork Chops, Charleston Style

6 pork chops, cut 1½ inches thick
1 tablespoon vegetable oil
2 teaspoons salt
½ teaspoon freshly ground black pepper

3 tablespoons flour
2½ cups milk
2 cups sliced onions
¼ teaspoon thyme
2 bay leaves

Trim the fat from the chops. Heat the oil in a skillet; brown the chops on both sides. Season the chops with the salt and pepper, then remove from the skillet. To the fat in the skillet, add the flour, mixing until smooth. Gradually add the milk, stirring constantly to the boiling point. Return the chops and add the onions, thyme, and bay leaves.

Cover loosely and cook over low heat for 1 hour, turning the chops several times. Discard the bay leaves and taste for seasoning. *Serves 6.*

Côtelettes de Porc à la Courlandaise

PORK CHOPS WITH CHESTNUTS AND RED CABBAGE

6 loin pork chops, cut 1½ inches thick
1 egg, beaten
2 tablespoons butter
2 tablespoons flour
2 teaspoons salt
¼ teaspoon freshly ground black pepper

1 cup chicken broth
1 teaspoon lemon juice
2 teaspoons chopped parsley
1 pound chestnuts, cooked and peeled
1 3-pound head red cabbage, coarsely shredded
1 cup water

Trim the fat from the chops. Dip the chops in the egg. Heat the butter in a heavy skillet and brown the chops for 5 minutes on each side. Cover and cook over low heat 20 minutes. Remove chops and keep warm. Mix the flour, half the salt, and the pepper into the fat remaining in the pan. Add the broth, stirring steadily to the boiling point, then cook over low heat 10 minutes. Mix in the lemon juice and parsley.

While the chops are cooking, combine the chestnuts and cabbage in a saucepan, add the water and remaining salt, and cook over medium heat 15 minutes. Drain well. Arrange the chops in the center of a hot serving platter and surround with the cabbage and chestnuts. Serve the sauce separately. *Serves 6.*

Pork Chops Diane

6 loin pork chops, cut ¾
  inch thick and boned
3 tablespoons butter
¾ cup chopped onions
1 teaspoon cornstarch
1½ teaspoons salt
2 teaspoons prepared
  mustard

¼ teaspoon freshly ground
  black pepper
1 cup hot beef broth
1 teaspoon Worcestershire
  sauce

Trim the fat from the chops. Split the chops in half horizontally (to make thinner), but do not cut entirely through. Open
flat like a book.

Melt 2 tablespoons of the butter in a skillet; brown the chops
in it on both sides. Remove the chops. Heat the remaining butter
in the pan, add the onions, and sauté 3 minutes. Blend in the
cornstarch, salt, mustard, and pepper. Gradually add the broth,
stirring steadily to the boiling point. Add the Worcestershire
and return the chops. Baste the chops several times, cover and
cook over low heat 20 minutes or until the chops are tender.
Serves 6.

Côtes de Porc aux Pruneaux

FRENCH PROVINCIAL PORK CHOPS WITH PRUNES

6 pork chops, cut 1 inch
  thick
¼ cup flour
1½ teaspoons salt
¼ teaspoon freshly ground
  black pepper

1 pound prunes
1 cup port wine
2 tablespoons butter
2 tablespoons cognac
2 tablespoons heavy cream

Trim the fat from the chops. Dip the chops in a mixture of the
flour, salt, and pepper.

Soak the prunes in hot water 15 minutes. Drain. Add the port wine and cook over low heat 15 minutes, or until tender but firm.

Melt the butter in a skillet and sauté the chops 30 minutes, or until browned and no pink remains; turn frequently. Transfer the chops to a hot serving platter.

Drain the prunes, reserving ½ cup of the liquid, and arrange them around the chops. Heat the cognac and pour into the skillet in which the chops were cooked; set aflame. When flames die, add the ½ cup prune liquid and cream; cook over high heat 1 minute, scraping the browned particles from the pan. Pour over the chops.

Serves 6.

Schweinskoteletts mit Linsen

GERMAN BAKED PORK CHOPS WITH LENTILS

6 pork chops, cut 1 inch thick	¾ cup sliced onions
2½ teaspoons salt	1 bay leaf
½ teaspoon freshly ground black pepper	¼ teaspoon thyme
	2 tablespoons vegetable oil
2 cups lentils	1 cup chopped onions

Trim the fat from the chops and season with 1 teaspoon of the salt and ¼ teaspoon of the pepper.

Wash the lentils; combine in a saucepan with the sliced onions, bay leaf, and thyme; add water to cover. Bring to a boil and cook over low heat 1 hour. Mix in the remaining salt and pepper. Discard the bay leaf. Turn into a baking dish.

Heat the oil in a skillet and brown the chops on both sides. In the fat remaining in the skillet, sauté the chopped onions 10 minutes. Mix into the lentils and arrange the chops over the lentils. Cover and bake in a 350° oven 1 hour or until chops and lentils are tender, removing the cover for the last 15 minutes.

Serves 6.

Schweineschnitzel

GERMAN BRAISED PORK CHOPS WITH ONIONS

8 pork chops, cut ½ inch   1½ teaspoons salt
thick and pounded lightly   ½ teaspoon freshly ground
3 tablespoons butter   black pepper
¾ cup sliced onions

Trim the fat from the chops. Melt the butter in a skillet; add
the chops and onions; cook over medium heat until chops are
browned on both sides. Season with the salt and pepper. Cover and
cook over low heat 25 minutes. Add a tablespoon of boiling
water from time to time if necessary to keep the chops from
burning.
Serves 4.

Schweinskoteletts

GERMAN BREADED PORK CHOPS

4 pork chops, cut ¾ inch   1½ teaspoons salt
thick and pounded   ¼ teaspoon freshly ground
lightly   black pepper
1 egg, beaten   ½ cup dry bread crumbs
1 tablespoon grated onion   3 tablespoons butter
1 tablespoon minced parsley

Trim the fat from the chops. Mix the egg with the onion,
parsley, salt, and pepper. Dip the chops in the mixture, then in
the bread crumbs, coating them well.
Melt the butter in a skillet; sauté the chops over low heat until
browned on both sides and cooked through. To test, make a cut
near the bone and see that the meat is white.
Serves 4.

Costolette di Maiale alla Campania

ITALIAN PORK CHOPS WITH MUSHROOMS AND PEPPERS

6 loin pork chops, cut 1
inch thick
4 tablespoons olive oil
1½ teaspoons salt
½ teaspoon freshly ground
black pepper

2 green peppers, thinly
sliced
1 pound mushrooms, thinly
sliced
1 clove garlic, minced
¼ cup canned tomato sauce
2 tablespoons water

Trim the fat from the chops. Heat the oil in a skillet; brown the chops on both sides. Season with the salt and pepper. Remove and keep warm. To the oil remaining in the skillet add the peppers and sauté 10 minutes. Remove. Sauté the mushrooms and garlic 5 minutes. Mix in the tomato sauce and water; return the peppers and chops. Cover the skillet and cook over low heat 30 minutes or until chops are tender. Turn chops once or twice. *Serves 6.*

Costolette di Maiale Pizzaiola

ITALIAN PORK CHOPS PIZZAIOLA

8 loin or rib pork chops,
cut ½ inch thick
2 tablespoons olive oil
2 teaspoons salt
½ teaspoon freshly ground
black pepper
2 cloves garlic, minced
¼ cup canned tomato sauce

¼ cup dry red wine
¼ teaspoon orégano
2 green peppers, cut
julienne
½ pound mushrooms, sliced
3 Italian sausages, sliced
and browned

Trim the fat from the chops. Heat the oil in a skillet; brown the chops on both sides. Sprinkle with the salt, pepper, and garlic. Add the tomato sauce, wine, orégano, green peppers, and mushrooms. Cover and cook over low heat 15 minutes. Add the sausages and cook 10 minutes longer. Taste for seasoning. *Serves 4.*

Key West Pork Chops

6 pork chops, cut 1½ inches thick	2 limes or lemons
1½ cups raw rice	⅓ cup canned Spanish-style tomato sauce
3 tablespoons vegetable oil	2 cups tomato juice
2 teaspoons salt	1½ cups orange juice
6 small white onions	½ teaspoon Tabasco

Trim the fat from the chops. Wash the rice, cover with hot water, and let stand 10 minutes. Drain and dry the rice on paper towels.

Heat the oil in a Dutch oven or casserole; brown the chops in it on both sides. Remove the chops and drain off all but 4 table-spoons of the fat. Stir in the raw rice, stirring until well coated. Arrange the chops on top and sprinkle with the salt. Cut the onions in half lengthwise and cut each lime or lemon into thirds.

Place a slice of lime and a spoonful of tomato sauce on each chop. Add the onions, tomato juice, orange juice, and Tabasco; cover tightly and bake in a 325° oven 1 hour or until the chops are tender. *Serves 6.*

Costolette di Maiale Milanese

MILANESE PORK CHOPS WITH CHEESE COATING

4 rib pork chops, cut 1 inch thick	⅓ cup dry bread crumbs
1 egg, beaten	⅓ cup grated Parmesan cheese
1½ teaspoons salt	2 tablespoons olive oil
¼ teaspoon freshly ground black pepper	2 tablespoons butter

Have the bones of the chops cut down short and trim off the fat. Beat together the egg, salt, and pepper. Dip the chops in the mixture, then in the bread crumbs mixed with the cheese.

Heat the olive oil and butter in a skillet (with an ovenproof handle). Brown the chops over direct low heat on both sides. Cover and bake in a 350° oven 35 minutes or until chops are tender and no pink remains. Turn the chops twice, and remove cover for the last 10 minutes. *Serves 4.*

Kotlety Wieprzowe ze Śmietaną

POLISH STUFFED PORK CHOPS WITH SOUR CREAM

4 double rib pork chops	**1 cup fresh bread crumbs**
2 teaspoons salt	**¼ cup heavy cream**
½ teaspoon freshly ground	**2 tablespoons chopped**
black pepper	**parsley**
½ teaspoon thyme	**½ cup water**
¼ pound (1 stick) butter	**¾ cup sour cream**
¾ cup chopped onions	
¼ pound mushrooms,	
chopped	

Trim the fat from the chops. Split the chops through the middle to the bone, so that they open like a book. Rub with 1½ teaspoons of the salt, ¼ teaspoon of the pepper, and the thyme.

Melt half the butter in a skillet; sauté the onions 5 minutes. Add the mushrooms and sauté 3 minutes. Mix in the bread crumbs, cream, parsley, and remaining salt and pepper. Stuff the chops with the mixture and close the openings with skewers or toothpicks. Melt the remaining butter in a skillet; lightly brown the chops in it on both sides.

Arrange the chops in a baking pan, add the water, cover, and bake in a 350° oven 1 hour, removing the cover for the last 15 minutes. Transfer the chops to a heated serving dish. Skim the fat from the pan juices. Place pan over direct low heat. Stir in the sour cream. Heat, scraping the pan of any browned particles, but do not let boil. Pour over the chops. *Serves 4.*

New Mexican Pork Chops

6 pork chops, cut 1 inch
  thick
1½ teaspoons salt
½ teaspoon freshly ground
  black pepper
½ teaspoon ground ginger
¼ cup flour
2 tablespoons vegetable oil

½ cup chopped onions
1 clove garlic, minced
⅓ cup chili sauce
2 teaspoons Worcestershire
  sauce
3 tablespoons vinegar
1½ tablespoons brown sugar
¾ cup boiling water

Trim the fat from the chops and pound the chops lightly to flatten. Dip in a mixture of the salt, pepper, ginger, and flour. Heat the oil in a deep skillet (with an ovenproof handle) and brown the chops on both sides. Add the onions and garlic; cook 5 minutes. Pour off the fat. Mix together the chili sauce, Worcestershire sauce, vinegar, sugar, and water; add to the skillet. Cover and bake in a 375° oven 50 minutes, removing the cover for the last 10 minutes. *Serves 6.*

Schweinskoteletts mit Saurersahne

PORK CHOPS WITH SOUR CREAM

6 loin pork chops, cut 1
  inch thick
3 tablespoons butter
1½ teaspoons salt
½ teaspoon white pepper

1 cup sour cream
2 teaspoons capers
3 tablespoons diced dill
  pickle

Trim the fat from the chops. Melt the butter in a skillet; brown the chops on both sides. Season with the salt and pepper. Add the sour cream; cover and cook over low heat 40 minutes, turning the chops a few times. Mix in the capers and pickle.
Serves 6.

Southern Baked Pork Chops

6 pork chops, cut 1 inch
thick
2 teaspoons salt
1 teaspoon freshly ground
black pepper

1 clove garlic, minced
2 tablespoons lemon juice
2 cups grated Cheddar or
American cheese

Trim the fat from the chops. Mix the salt, pepper, and garlic to a paste. Rub into the pork chops; sprinkle with the lemon juice.

Arrange the chops in a greased baking dish. Bake in a 350° oven 20 minutes. Sprinkle with the cheese. Bake 20 minutes longer or until chops are tender. *Serves 6.*

Chuletas con Aceitunas

SPANISH PORK CHOPS WITH OLIVES

6 pork chops, cut 1 inch
thick
⅓ cup flour
2½ teaspoons salt
¾ teaspoon freshly ground
black pepper
2 tablespoons olive oil
1 cup sliced onions

2 cloves garlic, minced
2 cups peeled, chopped
tomatoes
¾ cup dry white wine
2 hard-cooked eggs,
chopped
½ cup sliced pimiento-
stuffed olives

Trim the fat from the chops; dip in a mixture of the flour, 1½ teaspoons of the salt, and ½ teaspoon of the pepper. Heat the oil in a skillet and brown the chops on both sides. Remove the chops. In the oil remaining in the skillet sauté the onions and garlic 10 minutes. Add the tomatoes and remaining salt and pepper. Cook over low heat 10 minutes. Stir in the wine and return the chops. Baste a few times. Cover and bake in a 375° oven 45 minutes or until the chops are tender; remove cover for last 10 minutes. Sprinkle with the eggs and olives. *Serves 6.*

Fläskkotlett

SWEDISH BAKED PORK CHOPS

6 loin pork chops, cut 1
   inch thick
2 tablespoons butter
1 teaspoon salt
¼ teaspoon freshly ground
   black pepper
½ pound mushrooms, sliced

4 slices bacon
¾ cup chopped onions
2 tablespoons flour
2 teaspoons paprika
¾ cup light cream
¾ cup beef broth
1 tablespoon tomato paste

Trim the fat from the chops. Melt the butter in a skillet; sauté the chops until browned on both sides. Season with salt and pepper. Transfer to a baking dish in a single layer. In the fat remaining, sauté the mushrooms 3 minutes. Spread over the chops. Fry the bacon until crisp. Drain and crumble. Pour off all but 2 tablespoons of fat; sauté the onions in it 5 minutes. Blend in the flour and paprika, then stir in the cream and broth. Cook, stirring steadily to the boiling point. Mix in the tomato paste and crumbled bacon; cook over low heat 5 minutes. Taste for seasoning and pour over the chops. Bake in a 375° oven for 30 minutes. *Serves 6.*

Fläskrulader

SWEDISH PORK BIRDS

8 rib pork chops, cut ¾
   inch thick, boned and
   pounded thin
2 teaspoons salt
½ teaspoon freshly ground
   black pepper

½ teaspoon ginger
1 17-ounce can prunes
3 tablespoons butter
2 tablespoons flour
½ cup light cream
1 teaspoon tomato paste

Trim the fat from the chops. Rub both sides of the chops with a mixture of the salt, pepper, and ginger. Drain and pit the prunes; reserve the juice. Place a prune on each chop, roll up, and tie with string or fasten with toothpicks.

Melt the butter in a skillet and brown the chops on both sides. Add the prune juice, cover, and cook over low heat 35 minutes. Transfer the chops to a hot serving dish and keep hot.

Mix the flour with the cream and tomato paste. Add to the pan juices, stirring steadily to the boiling point. Add any remaining prunes and cook over low heat 5 minutes. Pour over the chops. *Serves 4.*

Costolette di Maiale alla Toscana
TUSCAN BRAISED PORK CHOPS

8 pork chops, cut ½ inch thick	2 tablespoons olive oil
2 teaspoons salt	1 clove garlic, minced
½ teaspoon freshly ground black pepper	⅛ teaspoon fennel seeds
	½ cup dry white wine

Trim the fat from the chops; season with the salt and pepper. Heat the oil in a skillet and brown the chops on both sides over high heat. Pour off the fat and add the garlic, fennel, and the wine. Cover and cook over low heat 20 minutes, or until the chops are cooked through. *Serves 4.*

Puerco con Chili
VERA CRUZ PORK CHOPS WITH CHILI

8 pork chops, cut ½ inch thick	3 tablespoons butter
1 clove garlic	2 cups canned red beans
2 teaspoons chili powder	2 cups chopped tomatoes
3 teaspoons salt	½ teaspoon freshly ground black pepper

Trim the fat from the chops, then rub with the garlic, chili powder, and 2 teaspoons of the salt. Melt the butter in a deep skillet (with an ovenproof handle). Brown the chops in it on both sides. Cover with the beans and tomatoes and season with the pepper and remaining salt. Cover and bake in a 350° oven 45 minutes or until tender, removing the cover for the last 5 minutes. *Serves 4–6.*

Barbecued Spareribs

3 pounds spareribs, cut in
  serving-sized pieces
2 teaspoons salt
½ teaspoon freshly ground
  black pepper
1 clove garlic, minced
½ cup chopped onions
2 tablespoons paprika

½ cup brown sugar
1 tablespoon dry mustard
2 cups canned tomato sauce
2 cups chicken broth
½ cup cider vinegar
1 teaspoon pickling spice
  (in cheesecloth bag)

Rub the ribs with a mixture of the salt, pepper, and garlic. Place on a rack in a roasting pan; bake in a 375° oven 15 minutes, turning the ribs once. Pour off the fat and remove rack. Add the onions and paprika; bake 5 minutes. Add the sugar and mustard, then the tomato sauce, chicken broth, vinegar, and pickling spice; mix well. Bake 1 hour, basting frequently. Arrange the ribs on a platter and strain sauce over them or into a gravy boat. *Serves 4–6.*

Shew Pye Gult

CHINESE BARBECUED SPARERIBS

2 cloves garlic, minced
1 tablespoon sugar
½ teaspoon powdered ginger
6 tablespoons soy sauce
3 tablespoons cider vinegar

6 tablespoons honey
2 tablespoons dry sherry
1½ cups beef broth
2 racks spareribs, cut in
  individual ribs

Mix together the garlic, sugar, ginger, soy sauce, vinegar, honey, sherry, and broth. Put the ribs in a bowl. Pour the sauce over the ribs, then marinate at room temperature 3 hours, basting frequently. Or marinate overnight in the refrigerator.

Remove ribs from marinade and arrange in a shallow roasting pan. Bake in a 350° oven 20 minutes. Pour off the fat. Add the marinade and bake 40 minutes longer basting frequently. The ribs should be crisp but not dried out. *Serves 4–6.*

Chinese Spiced Spareribs

6 cloves garlic	1½ teaspoons salt
1 slice gingerroot or ½ teaspoon powdered ginger	1½ teaspoons sugar
	½ cup soy sauce
½ teaspoon cinnamon	2 tablespoons dry sherry
½ teaspoon anise	1 rack spareribs

Crush the garlic and gingerroot, or put through a press. Mix with the cinnamon, anise, salt, sugar, soy sauce, and sherry. Brush over both sides of the spareribs and let stand 1 hour, basting frequently.

Place a rack in a roasting pan. Add boiling water to reach the rack. Put the spareribs on the rack. Roast in a 400° oven 45 minutes, or until tender. Cut into ribs. *Serves 2–4.*

Spareribs with Beer and Honey

2 racks spareribs, cut in serving-sized pieces	¾ cup honey
	1 teaspoon dry mustard
2 cups beer	2 teaspoons salt
2 tablespoons lemon juice	

Marinate the ribs in a mixture of the remaining ingredients for 24 hours in the refrigerator, basting and turning a few times.

Drain; reserve the marinade. Arrange the ribs in a single layer in a shallow pan. Bake in a 350° oven 1½ hours, basting frequently with the marinade. *Serves 6–8.*

Costole di Maiale con Fagiolini

BRAISED SPARERIBS WITH GREEN BEANS

2 racks spareribs, cut in
  individual ribs
2 teaspoons salt
½ teaspoon freshly ground
  black pepper
2 cloves garlic, minced
1 tablespoon olive oil

¾ cup chopped onions
1 29-ounce can Italian-style
  tomatoes
1 bay leaf
1 pound green beans,
  cut, or 1 package frozen

Trim the fat from the ribs; season with the salt, pepper, and garlic. Heat the oil in a Dutch oven or heavy saucepan; brown the ribs in it on both sides. Add the onions and continue browning. Pour off the fat. Add the tomatoes and bay leaf; cover and cook over low heat 30 minutes. Skim the fat and add the beans; cook 30 minutes longer. Taste for seasoning. *Serves 4–5.*

Costillas de Cerdo

FRIED MARINATED SPARERIBS

1 cup cider vinegar
3 tablespoons grated onions
½ teaspoon marjoram
1 teaspoon Spanish paprika
½ teaspoon freshly ground
  black pepper
2½ teaspoons salt
2 racks spareribs, cut in
  individual ribs

5 eggs
¼ cup sifted flour
½ cup dry bread crumbs
4 tablespoons minced
  parsley
Vegetable oil for deep
  frying

Mix together the vinegar, onions, marjoram, paprika, pepper, and 1½ teaspoons salt. Marinate the ribs in the mixture for 3 hours at room temperature. Drain and place on a rack in a roasting pan. Roast in a 375° oven 20 minutes. Drain and cool.

Mix together the eggs, flour, bread crumbs, parsley, and remaining salt. Dip the ribs in the mixture, coating them well. Heat the fat to 370°. Fry the ribs in it until browned and crisp. Drain. *Serves 4–6.*

Hawaiian-Chinese Spareribs

½ cup soy sauce	1 clove garlic, minced
½ cup ketchup	½-inch piece gingerroot,
¼ cup dry sherry	crushed, or 1 teaspoon
¾ cup brown sugar	powdered ginger
1 teaspoon salt	1 rack of spareribs

Mix the soy sauce, ketchup, sherry, sugar, salt, garlic, and ginger. Rub into the spareribs very well, then let marinate for 3 hours. Remove ribs and place on a rack, with a shallow pan under it. Cover the bottom of the pan with ½ inch of water. Roast in a 350° oven 45 minutes, or until tender and browned. Baste with marinade and turn ribs frequently. Cut into individual ribs and serve with Chinese mustard and Chinese *duk* sauce for dunking.

Serves 6–8 as a starting course.

Pineapple Spareribs

2 racks spareribs, cut in	1 cup oil
individual ribs	1 20-ounce can pineapple
8 cups water	chunks
1½ cups cider vinegar	⅓ cup sugar
1 cup sifted cornstarch	2 green peppers, cut
¼ cup dark molasses	julienne
¼ cup soy sauce	

Trim the fat from the ribs. Bring 7 cups of the water to a boil. Add ½ cup of the vinegar and the ribs. Bring to a boil again and cook over medium heat 15 minutes. Drain.

Mix together the cornstarch, molasses, and soy sauce; dip the ribs in the mixture. Heat the oil in a skillet; brown the ribs in it. Drain. Drain the pineapple, reserving ¾ cup of juice.

In a deep skillet, mix the sugar, pineapple juice, remaining water and vinegar. Bring to a boil and add the ribs. Cover and cook over low heat 25 minutes, turning the ribs frequently. Add the green peppers and pineapple; cook 5 minutes longer.

Serves 6–8.

Kapusta z Wieprzowina

POLISH SPARERIBS AND SAUERKRAUT

2 racks spareribs, cut in individual ribs	1½ cups boiling water
2 tablespoons vegetable oil	1 apple, peeled, cored, and chopped
2 cloves garlic, minced	1½ pounds undrained sauerkraut
1 cup chopped onions	2 tablespoons fine barley
1 bay leaf	1 teaspoon caraway seeds
1 teaspoon salt	
½ teaspoon freshly ground black pepper	

Trim the fat from the ribs. Heat the oil in a Dutch oven or casserole. Cook the ribs over medium heat until browned on both sides. Add the garlic and onions and cook until browned. Add the bay leaf, salt, pepper, water, apple, sauerkraut, barley, and caraway seeds. Mix well and cook over low heat 1 hour longer, stirring frequently. Taste for seasoning. Remove bay leaf.

Serves 6.

Roast Stuffed Spareribs

2 racks spareribs	2 tablespoons butter
3 teaspoons salt	1½ cups chopped onions
1 teaspoon freshly ground	3 tablespoons minced
black pepper	parsley
½ teaspoon thyme	3 hard-cooked eggs, mashed
1 bay leaf, finely crushed	½ teaspoon sage
1½ cups diced bread	

Have the ribs cracked through the middle crosswise. Rub with a mixture of 2 teaspoons of the salt, ¾ teaspoon of the pepper, the thyme, and bay leaf.

Soak the bread in water, then drain well. Melt the butter in a skillet; sauté the onions 10 minutes. Mix in the bread, parsley, eggs, sage, and the remaining salt and pepper. Cook 5 minutes, stirring frequently. Spread between the racks of spareribs and skewer together. Place on a rack in a shallow roasting pan and bake in a 425° oven 30 minutes. Reduce the heat to 350° and roast 45 minutes longer, or until no pink remains in the pork. Serve with applesauce mixed with a little horseradish.

Serves 6–8.

Stegt Suinekam med Aebler og Svedsker

SWEDISH SPARERIBS WITH APPLES AND PRUNES

2 racks spareribs	4 apples, peeled, cored,
1½ teaspoons salt	and sliced ¼ inch thick
½ teaspoon freshly ground	2 tablespoons flour
black pepper	1 cup beef broth
1 cup water	¼ cup milk, scalded
1 pound prunes, pitted	

Have the spareribs cracked through the middle crosswise. Rub with the salt and pepper. Bring the water and prunes to a boil in a saucepan, remove from heat and soak 5 minutes. Add the apple slices. Let stand 5 minutes, then drain.

Put 1 rack of spareribs in a roasting pan. Spread the prunes and apples on it and cover with the other rack. Fasten the edges with skewers. Roast in a 350° oven, allowing 25 minutes per pound. Add a little hot water to the pan if it becomes too dry. About 15 minutes before the pork is done, remove 3 tablespoons of drippings from the pan and put in a small saucepan. Stir in the flour until smooth, gradually add the broth and milk, stirring to the boiling point. Serve in a gravy boat.
Serves 6.

Australian Pork Hocks with Vegetables

2 cloves	1 clove garlic, sliced
8 small white onions	1 bay leaf
4 pork hocks	4 sweet potatoes, peeled
2 teaspoons salt	and quartered
½ teaspoon freshly ground	4 carrots
black pepper	

Stick the cloves in 1 of the onions. Wash and scrub the pork hocks, then combine in a saucepan with the salt, pepper, garlic, bay leaf, and water to cover. Bring to a boil, cover, and cook over low heat 2 hours or until almost tender. Add the potatoes, carrots, and onions; cook 30 minutes longer. Drain the hocks and pull off the skin. Arrange on a serving dish with the vegetables around them. *Serves 4.*

Eisbein mit Sauerkraut

GERMAN PIG'S KNUCKLES AND SAUERKRAUT

6 fresh pig's knuckles	2 onions
2 pounds sauerkraut	3 cups dry white wine
1 tablespoon caraway seeds	6 thick frankfurters
4 cloves	

Wash the pig's knuckles; cover with boiling water and let stand 10 minutes. Scrub the knuckles with a brush and scrape with a knife to remove the tough, scaly skin. Wash under cold water and dry.

In a Dutch oven or heavy saucepan, spread half the sauerkraut, sprinkle with half the caraway seeds, and arrange the pig's knuckles over it. Cover with the remaining sauerkraut and caraway seeds. Stick the cloves in the onions and add with the wine. If the liquid doesn't cover the ingredients, add more wine or water. Cover, bring to a boil, and cook over low heat 3 hours, or until knuckles are almost tender. Add the frankfurters. Re-cover and cook 30 minutes longer. Serve with boiled potatoes, mustard, and pickles.

Serves 6.

Eisbein mit Sauerkraut

AUSTRIAN PIG'S KNUCKLES WITH SAUERKRAUT

3 pounds fresh pig's knuckles	1 parsnip
1 tablespoon salt	2 large onions
½ teaspoon freshly ground black pepper	2 pounds sauerkraut
	2 apples, peeled and diced
1 bay leaf	2 tablespoons flour
2 carrots	¼ cup dry white wine
1 stalk celery	2 tablespoons minced parsley

Wash the pig's knuckles, place in a large saucepan, and cover with cold water. Add the salt, pepper, bay leaf, carrots, celery, parsnip, and 1 of the onions. Bring to a boil, cover, and cook over low heat 3 hours.

Prepare the sauerkraut while the knuckles are cooking. Chop the remaining onion and combine with the undrained sauerkraut and apples. Cook over low heat 1½ hours, mixing frequently.

Drain the knuckles and arrange on a heated serving dish; keep warm. Strain and measure 2 cups of the stock into a saucepan. Mix the flour with the wine until smooth and add to the stock.

Cook, stirring steadily to the boiling point, then cook over low heat 5 minutes longer. Stir in the parsley.

Spread the sauerkraut around the knuckles, and put the gravy in a sauceboat. Serve with boiled potatoes, pickles, and mustard. *Serves 4–6.*

Pâté de Porc
FRENCH PROVINCIAL PORK PÂTÉ

12 thin slices salt pork	2 teaspoons salt
2 pounds loin of pork, boned	¾ teaspoon freshly ground black pepper
1 pound pork or beef liver	⅛ teaspoon ground allspice
2 cloves garlic	½ teaspoon sage
½ cup diced onions	½ cup dry white wine
1 bay leaf, crushed	3 tablespoons cognac
3 slices white bread, trimmed	¼ cup chopped truffles
¼ cup milk	2 eggs

Cover the salt pork with water, bring to a boil, and let stand 10 minutes. Drain and dry.

Grind the pork, liver, garlic, onions, and bay leaf through the medium blade of a food chopper.

Crumble the bread and soak it in the milk until soft, then mash smooth. Add to the pork mixture with the salt, pepper, allspice, sage, wine, cognac, truffles, and eggs. Mix very well with the hands.

Line a 12-inch loaf pan with 8 slices of the salt pork, then put the pork mixture into it. Arrange the remaining salt pork on the top. Cover the pan with a double piece of aluminum foil. Bake in a preheated 375° oven 3 hours. Cool, then chill before turning out. Serve in thin slices.

Serves 12–16.

Pieds de Cochon Diable

FRENCH PROVINCIAL DEVILED PIG'S FEET

4 small pig's feet, split
1 tablespoon salt
½ teaspoon freshly ground
  black pepper
2 onions
2 cloves garlic, sliced

2 tablespoons vinegar
4 cloves
¼ cup dry mustard
⅓ cup olive oil
1 cup dry bread crumbs

Be sure the feet are young and tender. Scrub the feet and pour boiling water over them; drain and scrape with a knife. In a saucepan combine the feet, salt, pepper, onions, garlic, vinegar, and cloves. Add water to cover. Bring to a boil; cover loosely and cook over low heat 2½ hours or until tender. Drain and cool.

Mix together the mustard and olive oil; brush the feet with the mixture and then roll in the bread crumbs, coating them completely. Place on a baking pan and broil until browned on all sides. Serve with pickles, mustard, and sauerkraut.

Serves 4.

Puerco con Frijoles

BRAISED PORK WITH BEANS

3 cups dried white or
  black beans
4 teaspoons salt
2 pounds boneless pork,
  cut in 2-inch cubes
¼ teaspoon freshly ground
  black pepper
2 cups boiling water

½ cup olive oil
2 cups chopped onions
2 cloves garlic, minced
¼ teaspoon dried ground
  chili peppers
¼ cup sliced onions
½ cup grated Cheddar
  cheese

Wash the beans. Cover with water and bring to a boil. Let soak 1 hour; drain, add fresh water to cover, and bring to a boil. Cook over low heat 2 hours or until tender, adding 2 teaspoons of the salt after 1 hour of cooking time. Drain if any liquid remains. Brown the pork lightly on all sides; season with the pepper and remaining salt, and add the 2 cups of boiling water. Cover and cook over low heat 20 minutes.

Heat the oil in a Dutch oven or casserole; sauté the chopped onions 10 minutes. Add the undrained pork, the garlic, beans, and the chili peppers. Cover and cook over low heat 30 minutes. Sprinkle with the sliced onions and grated cheese.

Serves 4–6.

Cazuela de Puerco

PORK CASSEROLE

2 pounds boneless pork, cut in ½-inch cubes
4 tablespoons olive oil
1 cup chopped onions
1 clove garlic, minced
1½ cups raw rice
¾ cup finely chopped green peppers

1 20-ounce can tomatoes
2½ cups beef broth
1½ teaspoons salt
½ cup chopped stuffed olives

Trim the fat from the pork. Heat the oil in a skillet; sauté the onions and garlic 5 minutes, stirring frequently. Remove from pan. To the oil remaining add the pork and cook over medium heat for 10 minutes, stirring frequently. Combine the pork with the sautéed onions, rice, green peppers, tomatoes, beef broth, and salt.

Turn into a greased 1½-quart casserole. Cover and bake in a 325° oven 50 minutes; add a little boiling water if casserole becomes dry. Add the olives and bake 5 minutes longer.

Serves 6–8.

Porkkana Riisilaatikko

FINNISH PORK CASSEROLE

3 cups diced cooked pork	1 tablespoon brown sugar
2 cups hot cooked rice	1 teaspoon salt
1½ cups grated carrots	3 tablespoons dry bread
¼ cup chopped almonds	crumbs
3 eggs, beaten	3 tablespoons butter

Mix together the meat, rice, carrots, almonds, eggs, sugar, and salt. Turn into a buttered 1½-quart baking dish. Sprinkle the top with the bread crumbs and dot with the butter. Bake in a 350° oven 25 minutes. *Serves 4.*

Puerco Mexicana

MEXICAN PORK-RICE CASSEROLE

1½ pounds boneless pork,	½ cup diced celery
cut ½ inch thick	1 20-ounce can tomatoes
2 tablespoons vegetable oil	⅛ teaspoon Tabasco
1½ teaspoons salt	3 cups drained half-cooked
½ teaspoon freshly ground	rice
black pepper	1 cup (¼ pound) grated
2 teaspoons chili powder	Cheddar cheese
1 cup chopped onions	

Trim the fat from the pork. Cut the pork in strips about 1 inch wide and 2 inches long. Heat the oil in a skillet; brown the pork on both sides. Add the salt, pepper, chili powder, onions, and celery; cook 5 minutes, stirring frequently. Mix in the to-matoes and Tabasco. Bring to a boil, cover and cook over low heat 30 minutes. Add the rice, mix lightly, and taste for seasoning. Turn into a greased 3-quart casserole. Sprinkle with the cheese. Bake in a preheated 350° oven 25 minutes.
Serves 6–8.

Bangkok Pork and Noodles

2 pounds boneless pork
1 pound fine egg noodles
1¼ cups vegetable oil
2 tablespoons soy sauce
2 tablespoons vinegar
2 teaspoons anchovy paste
4 teaspoons sugar

1½ teaspoons salt
4 eggs, beaten
1 cup bean sprouts, heated
4 tablespoons chopped
  green onions (scallions)
½ teaspoon ground
  coriander

Trim the fat from the pork. Cut the pork in matchlike pieces. Drop the noodles into boiling salted water; cook 1 minute and drain well. Spread on a flat surface and chill 2 hours. Heat 1 cup of the oil in a skillet; fry the noodles until crisp. Drain.

Heat the remaining oil in a skillet; sauté the pork 10 minutes, stirring frequently, then mix in the soy sauce, vinegar, anchovy paste, sugar, and salt; cook over low heat 5 minutes. Stir in the eggs until barely set. Mix in the fried noodles and bean sprouts; cook 2 minutes. Turn out onto a platter; sprinkle with the green onions and coriander.

Serves 6–8.

Cantonese Sweet and Sour Pork

2 pounds boneless pork,
  cut in 1-inch cubes
4 tablespoons dry sherry
½ cup soy sauce
6 tablespoons cornstarch
1 14-ounce can pineapple
  chunks
1½ cups vegetable oil
2 large onions, cut in sixths

4 green peppers, cut in
  strips
1 carrot, thinly sliced
½ cup diced water
  chestnuts
⅓ cup sugar
⅓ cup ketchup
3 tablespoons vinegar

Trim the fat from the pork and dip the cubes in a mixture of 2 tablespoons of the dry sherry and 4 tablespoons of the soy sauce. Let stand 10 minutes, then toss in 4 tablespoons of the cornstarch. Drain the pineapple, reserving the juice.

Heat the oil in a skillet; fry the pork until tender and browned on all sides. Drain the pork and keep hot. Pour off all but ¼ cup oil. In the oil remaining in the skillet; sauté the onions, green peppers, and carrot 3 minutes. Add the water chestnuts and pineapple chunks; cook 2 minutes.

Mix together the sugar, ketchup, vinegar, and the remaining sherry and soy sauce. Add to the skillet and bring to a boil. Stir in the pineapple juice mixed with the remaining cornstarch. Cook, stirring constantly, until thickened. Add the pork, mix well, heat, and serve. *Serves 6–8.*

Chinese Pork Chow Mein

1½ pounds boneless pork, cut in small dice
4 tablespoons vegetable oil
2 cups sliced onions
2 cups sliced celery
¼ cup soy sauce
1 19-ounce can bean sprouts, drained
3 tablespoons cornstarch
2 cups beef broth

Trim the fat from the pork. Heat 2 tablespoons of the oil in a large skillet. Add the pork and cook over low heat, stirring frequently, until no pink remains in the meat. Remove the pork.

Heat the remaining oil in the skillet; sauté the onions and celery 5 minutes. Mix in the pork, soy sauce, and sprouts; cook 2 minutes. Mix the cornstarch with the broth; add to the skillet, stirring steadily to the boiling point, then cook 3 minutes longer. Serve with rice and chow mein noodles. *Serves 6–8.*

Chinese Chop Suey

1 pound boneless pork
2 large onions
1 bunch celery
3 tablespoons vegetable oil
1½ teaspoons salt
½ teaspoon freshly ground black pepper
2 tablespoons soy sauce
1 tablespoon molasses
2 cups hot beef broth
1 10-ounce can bean sprouts
3 tablespoons cornstarch
¼ cup water

Trim the fat from the pork and cut the pork in matchlike pieces.

Cut each onion in 6 wedges and the celery in 1-inch pieces. Heat the oil, salt, and pepper in a skillet. Add the meat; cook over medium heat 5 minutes, stirring frequently. Add the onions, celery, and soy sauce. Cook over low heat 3 minutes, stirring almost constantly. Mix in the molasses and broth. Cover and cook over low heat 10 minutes. Add the sprouts; cook 3 minutes. Mix the cornstarch with the water and add to the skillet, stirring constantly until thickened. Cook 2 minutes and serve with rice. *Serves 4-6.*

Chinese Fried Pork with Green Onions

1 pound boneless pork, cut paper thin	¼ cup soy sauce
3 bunches green onions (scallions)	2 tablespoons dry sherry
	5 tablespoons vegetable oil
	1 teaspoon salt

Cut the pork in 1-inch squares. Cut the green onions crosswise into 2-inch pieces, green part and all. Toss the meat with the soy sauce and sherry. Let stand 20 minutes. Heat the oil in a skillet and sauté the pork until no pink remains, stirring frequently. Add the green onions and salt. Cook over high heat 30 seconds, stirring constantly. *Serves 4-6.*

Chinese Fried Pork and Vegetables

2 pounds boneless pork	½ teaspoon salt
½ cup vegetable oil	¼ cup soy sauce
½ pound mushrooms, sliced	2 tablespoons dry sherry
1 cup sliced green onions (scallions)	½ teaspoon monosodium glutamate
1 cup sliced water chestnuts	2 cups cooked rice, chilled

Trim the fat from the pork. Cut the pork in matchlike pieces.
Heat 3 tablespoons of the oil in the skillet; brown the pork in
it over low heat, stirring frequently. Remove about ½ cup of the
pork and keep hot. To the remaining pork, add the mushrooms,
green onions, and water chestnuts. Cook over medium heat 3
minutes, stirring frequently. Mix in the salt, soy sauce, sherry,
and monosodium glutamate. Cook over low heat 5 minutes;
preparing the rice during this time.

Heat the remaining oil in a skillet. Add the chilled rice; cook
over high heat, stirring almost constantly, until browned, about
5 minutes. Mix in the ½ cup pork. Heap in a bowl and cover with
the pork mixture.

Serves 4–6.

Chinese Pork and Fried Noodles

1 pound boneless pork	½ cup peanut or vegetable oil
1 tablespoon cornstarch	
2 tablespoons soy sauce	½ cup sliced bamboo shoots
1 tablespoon dry sherry	1 cup shredded cabbage
1 tablespoon grated gingerroot, or 1 teaspoon powdered ginger	(Chinese, if available)
	2 teaspoons salt
5 dried mushrooms	½ pound fine noodles, cooked, drained, and chilled
½ cup hot water	

Trim the fat from the pork. Cut the pork in matchlike pieces.
Mix together the cornstarch, soy sauce, sherry, and ginger. Pour
over the pork and let stand 10 minutes.

Soak the mushrooms in the hot water for 10 minutes. Drain
and slice.

Heat 3 tablespoons of the oil in a skillet and add the undrained
pork. Cook 6 minutes, stirring frequently. Remove.

Heat 2 tablespoons of the oil in the skillet. Add the bamboo
shoots and mushrooms; sauté 3 minutes. Add the cabbage and
1 teaspoon of the salt. Cook for 3 minutes, stirring very frequently.
Add the pork. Cook 2 minutes.

Heat the remaining oil in a skillet. Add the chilled noodles and remaining salt. Fry 5 minutes, turning the noodles frequently. Add the pork mixture and fry 2 minutes longer, stirring frequently.

Serves 4–6.

Chinese Spring Rolls with Pork Filling

FILLING:

½ pound boneless pork, cut very thin

⅓ cup vegetable oil

¾ teaspoon salt

1 teaspoon cornstarch

1 tablespoon dry sherry

¼ cup thinly sliced green onions (scallions)

½ cup julienne-cut water chestnuts

½ cup chopped mushrooms

½ cup bean sprouts

2 tablespoons soy sauce

Trim the fat from the pork. Cut the pork in ½-inch-long strips. Heat half the oil in a skillet; sauté the pork until browned, stirring frequently. Sprinkle with the salt, cornstarch, and sherry. Cook over low heat 5 minutes, stirring frequently. Turn mixture into a bowl.

Heat the remaining oil in the skillet; sauté the green onions, water chestnuts, mushrooms, and bean sprouts 5 minutes, stirring frequently. Mix in the soy sauce. Add to the pork mixture, mix thoroughly and cool.

PANCAKE:

1 cup sifted flour

2 eggs

1 cup water

Vegetable oil

Beat together the flour, eggs, and water until very smooth. Let stand 15 minutes.

Brush a hot 7-inch skillet with a little oil. Pour in 1 tablespoon batter, tilting the pan quickly to coat the bottom. Bake until the underside is lightly browned and the top dry. Turn out onto a napkin, browned side up. Stack while preparing the balance of the pancakes. Reserve a little batter for sealing the pancakes. Place 2 tablespoons of the filling along 1 side of the pancake. Brush all the edges with a little batter. Fold opposite sides in and roll up, pressing the edges together. Fry in deep 370° oil until browned and crisp. Cut each roll into 3 pieces. Serve with mustard and Chinese *duk* sauce.

Makes about 36 pieces.

Puerco con Maiz

CENTRAL AMERICAN PORK IN CORN MEAL CRUST

4 cups water	¾ cup chopped onions
3 teaspoons salt	½ teaspoon freshly ground
2 cups corn meal	black pepper
2 eggs, beaten	¾ cup tomato juice
1½ pounds boneless pork,	1 cup canned green peas
cut in ½-inch cubes	1 cup corn kernels
2 tablespoons vegetable oil	½ cup sliced olives

Bring the water and 2 teaspoons salt to a boil, stir in the corn meal until thickened, then cook over low heat 20 minutes. Cool 10 minutes, then beat in the eggs. Prepare the pork meanwhile.

Trim the fat from the pork. Heat the oil in a skillet; brown the pork and onions in it, stirring frequently. Add the pepper, tomato juice, and remaining salt. Cover and cook over low heat 45 minutes. Stir in the peas, corn, and olives. Taste for seasoning.

Spread half the corn meal mixture into a 1½-quart casserole, then spread the pork mixture over it. Cover with remaining corn meal mixture. Bake in a 375° oven 30 minutes, or until browned.

Serves 6–8.

Sianliha kanssa Juunikas Kastika

FINNISH PORK WITH BEET SAUCE

1 8¾-ounce can julienne
beets
2 tablespoons vinegar
2 pounds boneless pork
2 tablespoons butter
½ cup chopped onions

1 teaspoon salt
½ teaspoon freshly ground
black pepper
¼ cup water
3 tablespoons fresh bread
crumbs

Drain the beets and mix the juice with the vinegar.

Cut the pork into strips 2 inches long by ½-inch wide. Melt the butter in a skillet; brown the meat and onions in it. Season with the salt and pepper. Add the beet juice and water. Bring to a boil, and cook over low heat 15 minutes. Mix in the bread crumbs, then add the beets. Cook 5 minutes.

Serves 6–8.

Sianliha kanssa Makea Kaslike

FINNISH PORK WITH SWEET SAUCE

2 cups water
1 teaspoon salt
¼ teaspoon white pepper
1 onion
2 pounds boneless pork,
cut in 2-inch cubes
½ cup flour
1 egg, beaten
¼ cup bread crumbs
½ cup vegetable oil

2 cups beef broth
¼ cup currant jelly
2 tablespoons honey
1 teaspoon grated lemon
rind
½ teaspoon cinnamon
½ teaspoon ground cloves
1 tablespoon potato flour
or cornstarch
2 tablespoons dry sherry

Bring the water, salt, pepper, and onion to a boil; add the pork. Cook 15 minutes. Drain and dry the meat. Roll the meat in the flour, dip in the egg, and then in bread crumbs. Heat the oil in a skillet until it bubbles; fry the pork until browned on all sides.

Prepare the sauce meanwhile. Mix together the broth, jelly, honey, lemon rind, cinnamon, and cloves. Bring to a boil and cook over medium heat 15 minutes. Mix the starch with the sherry and stir into the sauce until thickened. Drain the meat, arrange on a heated platter, and pour sauce over the top. *Serves 4–6.*

Schweinsfilets mit Sauer Sahne

GERMAN PORK IN SOUR CREAM SAUCE

2 pounds boneless pork, cut in 1-inch cubes
2 tablespoons vegetable oil
½ cup chopped onions
1¼ teaspoons salt
¼ teaspoon freshly ground black pepper
1 8-ounce can tomato sauce
¼ cup chopped dill pickle
1 cup sour cream
3 tablespoons dry sherry

Trim the fat from the pork. Heat the oil in a skillet and brown the pork on all sides. Mix in the onions, salt, and pepper. Cover and cook over low heat 20 minutes, stirring frequently. Add the tomato sauce. Re-cover and cook 20 minutes longer or until the pork is tender. Mix in the pickle, sour cream, and sherry; heat but do not let boil. *Serves 4–6.*

Guisada de Puerco

GUATEMALAN PORK STRIPS

3 pounds boned fresh ham or shoulder of pork
2 cloves garlic, minced
2 cups chopped onions
1½ pounds tomatoes, peeled and chopped
2 teaspoons salt
½ teaspoon freshly ground black pepper
⅛ teaspoon powdered saffron
¼ cup olive oil
¾ cup water

Trim the fat from the meat. Cut pork into narrow strips about 2 inches long and ½ inch thick.

In a bowl, mix the garlic, onions, tomatoes, salt, pepper, and saffron. Add the pork, stir well, cover, and let stand 1 hour. Remove and drain the pork strips, reserving the vegetable mixture. Heat the oil in a deep skillet until it smokes. Cook the pork over high heat 10 minutes, stirring a few times. Add the vegetables and water. Cover and cook over low heat 1 hour. Taste for seasoning. Serve with boiled or fried rice.

Serves 6–8.

Sertésgerinc Sülve

HUNGARIAN PORK AND SAUERKRAUT

3 tablespoons vegetable oil	1 cup chopped onions
¾ cup thinly sliced onions	1 tablespoon paprika
1½ pounds sauerkraut, washed and drained	½ teaspoon thyme
	¾ cup beef broth
2 apples, peeled and sliced	1½ teaspoons salt
1 cup water	½ teaspoon freshly ground black pepper
½ teaspoon caraway seeds	
3 pounds shoulder of pork, cut in 1½-inch cubes	1 cup sour cream
	2 tablespoons minced dill
3 tablespoons flour	

Heat 2 tablespoons of the oil in a saucepan; sauté the sliced onions 10 minutes. Stir in the sauerkraut. Add the apples, water, and caraway seeds; cover and cook over low heat 2 hours. While the sauerkraut is cooking, prepare the pork.

Trim the fat from the pork. Toss the pork in the flour until coated. Heat the remaining oil in a skillet. Brown the pork and chopped onions in it. Stir in the paprika and thyme. Add the broth, salt, and pepper. Cover and cook over low heat 1½ hours. Add to the sauerkraut. Cook 10 minutes. Mix in the sour cream; taste for seasoning. Heat but do not let boil. Sprinkle with the dill and serve with boiled potatoes.

Serves 6–8.

Hong Kong Batter-Fried Sweet and Pungent Pork

1½ pounds boneless pork, cut in 1-inch cubes
2 eggs
½ teaspoon salt
½ cup flour
1¼ cups water
Vegetable oil for deep frying

½ cup vinegar
¼ cup brown sugar
1 tablespoon molasses
2 tablespoons cornstarch
1 8-ounce can pineapple wedges, drained
1 tomato, cut in 6 wedges

Trim the fat from the pork. Make a smooth batter of the eggs, salt, flour, and 3 tablespoons of the water. Dip the pork cubes in the mixture, coating the pieces on all sides. Heat the oil to 365°. Fry the pork until browned on all sides. Don't crowd the pan. Drain and keep hot.

In a saucepan, mix together the vinegar, brown sugar, molasses, and ¾ cup of the water. Bring to a boil. Mix the cornstarch with the remaining water; stir into the sauce until thickened. Add the pineapple and tomato; cook over low heat 3 minutes. Mix in the pork and serve. *Serves 4.*

Wienereintopf

AUSTRIAN PORK STEW

3 pounds boned shoulder of pork, cut in 1-inch cubes
⅓ tablespoon flour
3 teaspoons salt
¾ teaspoon freshly ground black pepper
¼ pound (1 stick) butter
2 cups thinly sliced onions

1½ pounds potatoes, peeled and thinly sliced
¾ teaspoon caraway seeds
3 carrots, cut julienne
2 cups finely shredded cabbage
3 cups beef broth (approximate)

Trim the fat from the pork. Toss the pork with the flour, 1½ teaspoons of the salt, and ¼ teaspoon of the pepper. Melt 2 tablespoons of the butter in a skillet and lightly brown the pork on all sides. Remove. In the same skillet, melt 2 tablespoons of the butter; sauté the onions until golden. Remove. Melt the remaining butter in the same skillet and reserve.

Arrange half the potato slices on the bottom of a buttered 3-quart casserole. Sprinkle with a little salt, pepper, and caraway seeds. Arrange alternate layers of the pork, onions, carrots, and cabbage, sprinkling each layer with salt, pepper, and caraway seeds. Cover with the remaining potatoes and sprinkle with salt, pepper, caraway seeds, and the reserved melted butter. Pour in enough of the broth to reach the top layer. Cover the casserole and bake in a 375° oven 1½ hours, removing the cover for the last 15 minutes.

Serves 6–8.

Pörkölt

HUNGARIAN PORK STEW

4 pounds boneless pork, cut in 1½-inch cubes
2 tablespoons butter
2 cups sliced onions
2 tablespoons paprika
2 teaspoons salt
½ teaspoon freshly ground black pepper
2 cloves garlic, minced
1 cup chopped green peppers
1 tablespoon lemon juice
2 tablespoons tomato paste
½ teaspoon basil
1 cup boiling water

Leave the fat on the meat. Melt the butter in a Dutch oven or heavy casserole; sauté the onions until golden. Remove from the heat and stir in the paprika, salt, and pepper. Add the meat, garlic, green peppers, lemon juice, tomato paste, basil, and the boiling water. Cover and cook over low heat 3 hours. Watch carefully, and add a little more boiling water if necessary.

Serves 8–10.

Adobong

PHILIPPINE PORK STEW

3 pounds boneless pork, cut
  in 1½-inch cubes
½ cup cider vinegar
2 teaspoons salt
½ teaspoon freshly ground
  black pepper
4 cloves garlic, minced

1 bay leaf
3 tablespoons oil
1 cup water
1¼ cups light cream
½ cup shredded coconut
3 drops yellow food coloring

Trim the fat from the pork. Marinate the pork in a mixture of the vinegar, salt, pepper, garlic, and bay leaf for 30 minutes. Drain, reserving the marinade.

Heat the oil in a casserole or heavy saucepan and brown the pork on all sides. Add the marinade and water. Cover and cook over medium heat 1 hour, or until tender and almost all the liquid has evaporated.

While the pork is cooking, combine the cream and coconut in a saucepan. Bring to a boil, remove from the heat, and let stand 30 minutes. Strain the cream. Discard the coconut. When the pork is tender, stir the cream into the pan with the food coloring. Cook 5 minutes longer. Taste for seasoning.

Serves 6–8.

Daging Ketjap

INDONESIAN BRAISED PORK

1½ pounds boneless pork,
  thinly cut
3 tablespoons vegetable oil
¾ cup minced onions
2 cloves garlic, minced

¼ teaspoon dried ground
  chili peppers
⅓ cup soy sauce
2 teaspoons brown sugar
1 teaspoon lemon juice

Trim the fat from the pork. Cut the pork in narrow strips. Heat the oil in a skillet; sauté the pork, onions, garlic, and chili peppers 10 minutes, stirring frequently. Add the soy sauce, sugar, and lemon juice. Cook over low heat 10 minutes, or until the pork is tender and no pink remains. *Serves 4–6.*

Porc a la Anisoara

RUMANIAN PORK AND ONION LAYERS

2 pounds boneless pork	1½ pounds onions, peeled
6 tablespoons butter	and chopped
1½ teaspoons salt	2 tablespoons flour
½ teaspoon freshly ground	¾ cup beef broth
black pepper	1 cup dry white wine

Trim the fat from the pork. Cut the pork in matchlike pieces; melt 2 tablespoons of the butter in a skillet. Lightly brown the pork in it. Season with ¾ teaspoon of the salt and ¼ teaspoon of the pepper. Remove.

Melt 3 tablespoons of the remaining butter in the skillet; mix in the onions and the remaining salt and pepper. Cook over low heat 20 minutes, stirring frequently. Spread half the onions on the bottom of a baking dish. Spread the pork over the onions and cover with the remaining onions.

Melt the remaining butter in the skillet; blend in the flour. Gradually add the broth, stirring steadily to the boiling point. Stir in the wine, then cook over low heat 5 minutes; pour over the onions. Bake in a 350° oven 1¼ hours. Serve with boiled potatoes. *Serves 4–6.*

TAIWAN PORK WITH ONIONS

2 pounds boneless pork	¾ cup beef broth
5 large onions	3 tablespoons oil
2 tablespoons soy sauce	1 clove garlic
1 teaspoon salt	1 teaspoon sherry
½ teaspoon sugar	2 teaspoons cornstarch

Trim the fat from the pork. Cut the pork into thin slices across the grain. Cut the onions in quarters and slice very thin. Mix together the soy sauce, salt, sugar, and broth.

Heat 2 tablespoons of the oil in a skillet. Sauté the onions and garlic 2 minutes, stirring steadily; remove. Heat the remaining oil in the skillet; sauté the pork 10 minutes. Add the sherry and half the broth mixture and return the onions. Cover and cook over low heat 5 minutes. Mix the cornstarch with the remaining broth mixture and stir into the skillet until thickened. Don't overcook. Serve with noodles or rice.

Serves 4–6.

Tourtière

CANADIAN PORK PIE

2 cups sifted flour	2 medium onions, peeled
2½ teaspoons salt	1 clove garlic
½ cup butter or lard	¾ cup boiling water
1 egg, beaten	3 tablespoons chopped
4 tablespoons milk	parsley
1½ pounds boneless lean	½ teaspoon freshly ground
pork	black pepper
2 slices bacon	Pinch of sage

Sift the flour with ¾ teaspoon of the salt and cut in the butter or lard with a pastry blender or 2 knives until the consistency of corn meal. Mix the egg and milk, add to the flour mixture, and toss lightly with a fork until dough forms a ball. Wrap in waxed paper and chill at least 1 hour.

Put the pork, bacon, onions, and garlic through a meat grinder. Cook in a heavy, ungreased saucepan over medium heat 5 minutes, stirring constantly. Mix in the water, parsley, pepper, sage, and remaining salt; cover and cook 20 minutes. Cool 15 minutes.

Divide the chilled dough into 2 pieces, one slightly larger than the other. Roll out the larger piece on a lightly floured surface. Line an 11-inch pie plate with it. Put the meat mixture in it, and cover with the smaller piece of rolled-out dough, sealing the edges.

Make a few slits on top. Bake in a preheated 450° oven 10 minutes, reduce heat to 350° and bake 25 minutes longer, or until well browned. *Serves 6–8.*

Baked Glazed Ham

1 uncooked tenderized ham	**1 cup packed brown sugar**
Whole cloves	**2 teaspoons dry mustard**

Scrub the rind with a stiff brush under cold running water. Dry well, and put in a roasting pan, fat side up.

Bake in a 300° oven 20 minutes a pound, or until tender (160° on a meat thermometer). Drain, reserving a little of the fat. With a sharp knife or kitchen shears, cut off the rind. Score the fat diagonally in a diamond pattern. Stud with cloves. Mix together the brown sugar, dry mustard, and reserved fat. Spread over the top of the ham. Raise the heat to 425° and bake the ham 30 minutes or until top is glazed. *Serves 14–16.*

Baked Ham with Beer Glaze

12-pound ham	**¼ cup bread crumbs**
2 cups beer	**1 teaspoon dry mustard**
1½ cups brown sugar	**Cloves**

Cook the ham according to the package directions or the type of ham it is. Drain and dry. Place the ham in a shallow roasting pan and add 1¼ cups beer. Bake in a 350° oven 1 hour, basting frequently. Remove ham from oven and score the fat in a diamond-shaped design.

Mix together the brown sugar, bread crumbs, mustard, and remaining beer. Press over the ham. Stud with cloves. Return to oven and bake 30 minutes longer, basting once or twice.

Serves 14–16.

California Style Ham with Apricots

10-pound ready-to-eat ham	1 cup brown sugar
1 No. 2½ can apricot halves	½ teaspoon ground cloves

Have the skin of the ham removed, and score the fat in a diamond pattern. Put the ham in a large roasting pan. Drain the apricots and pour the juice over the scored ham. Spread the brown sugar over the top of the fat, and sprinkle with the cloves. Bake the ham in a 425° oven for 45 minutes. Remove the ham from the oven for a few minutes.

Reduce the heat to 350°. Garnish the top of the ham with the apricots, fastening each one with a toothpick. Bake 25 minutes longer, basting every 10 minutes.
Serves 12–16.

Jambon au Champagne

HAM WITH CHAMPAGNE SAUCE

8- to 10-pound ham	2 bay leaves
3 onions	3 sprigs parsley
3 cloves garlic	1 bottle champagne or dry white wine
2 stalks celery	
6 cloves	1 cup sugar
1 teaspoon thyme	3 tablespoons flour

Soak the ham in water to cover for 24 hours, changing the water at least 3 times. Drain and scrub the rind with a stiff brush. Place the ham in a deep saucepan with cold water to cover; add the onions, garlic, celery, cloves, thyme, bay leaves, and parsley. Bring to a boil and cook 3 hours. Drain ham; strain and reserve 2 cups of the stock.

Remove the skin and as much fat as possible from the ham. Place in a roasting pan; pour the champagne or white wine and reserved stock over it. Cover and roast in a 350° oven 1 hour,

PORK

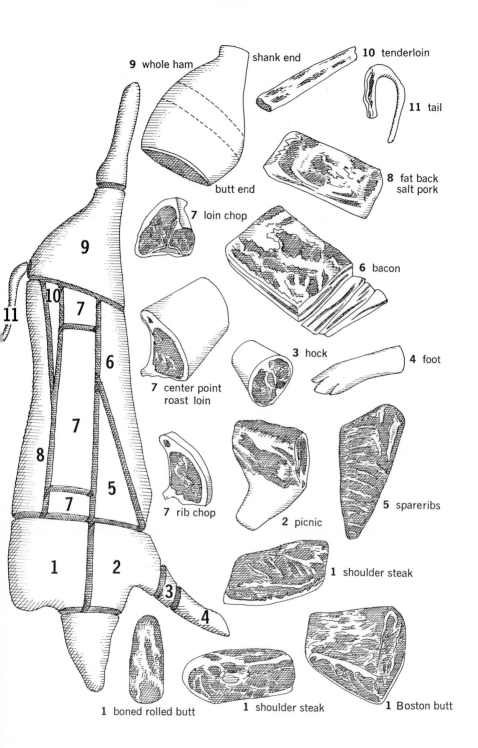

9 whole ham
shank end
10 tenderloin
11 tail
butt end
8 fat back salt pork
7 loin chop
6 bacon
7 center point roast loin
3 hock
4 foot
7 rib chop
2 picnic
5 spareribs
1 shoulder steak
1 boned rolled butt
1 shoulder steak
1 Boston butt

9
10
11
7
6
7
8
5
7
1
2
3
4

LAMB

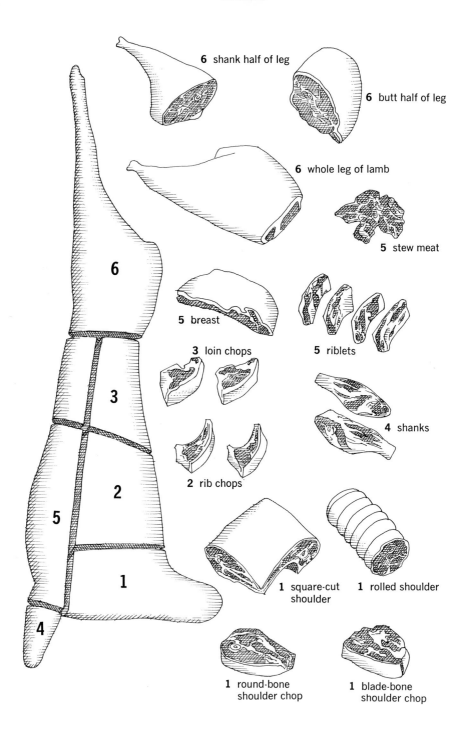

6 shank half of leg

6 butt half of leg

6 whole leg of lamb

5 stew meat

5 breast

3 loin chops

5 riblets

4 shanks

2 rib chops

1 square-cut shoulder

1 rolled shoulder

1 round-bone shoulder chop

1 blade-bone shoulder chop

VEAL

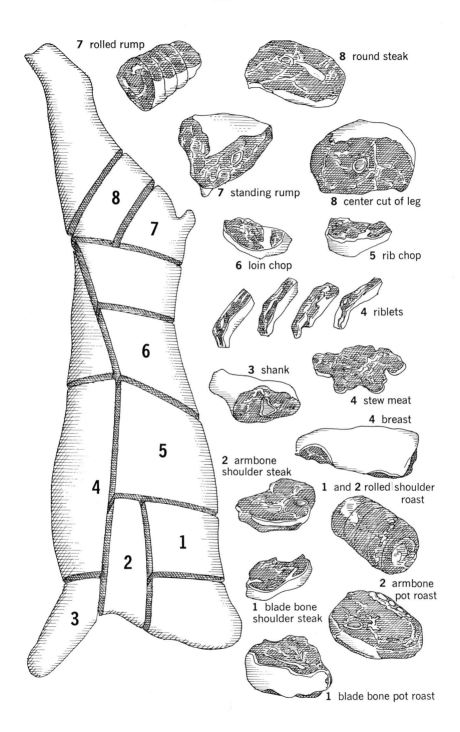

7 rolled rump

8 round steak

7 standing rump

8 center cut of leg

6 loin chop

5 rib chop

4 riblets

3 shank

4 stew meat

4 breast

2 armbone shoulder steak

1 and 2 rolled shoulder roast

1 blade bone shoulder steak

2 armbone pot roast

1 blade bone pot roast

BEEF

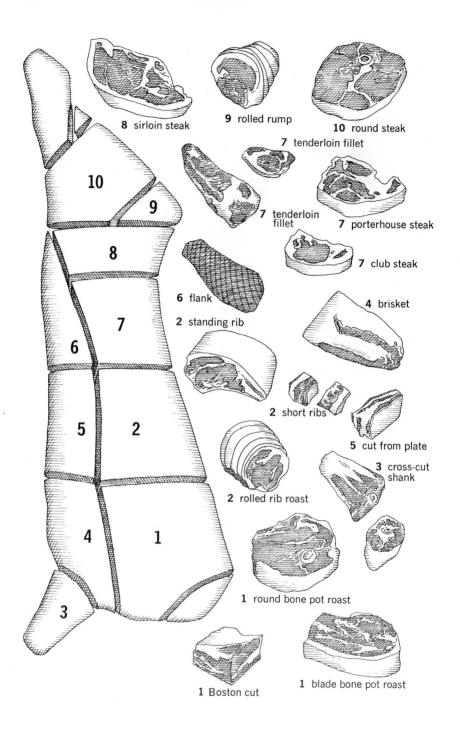

8 sirloin steak

9 rolled rump

10 round steak

7 tenderloin fillet

7 tenderloin fillet

7 porterhouse steak

7 club steak

6 flank

2 standing rib

4 brisket

2 short ribs

5 cut from plate

3 cross-cut shank

2 rolled rib roast

1 round bone pot roast

1 Boston cut

1 blade bone pot roast

4

basting frequently. Drain the ham again, reserving the liquid. Sprinkle the sugar on the ham; place in a 450° oven until browned and glazed.

Mix the flour with a little of the sauce until smooth, then add to all the sauce. Cook over low heat, stirring constantly to the boiling point, then cook over low heat 5 minutes.

Carve the ham and serve with the sauce.
Serves 12–14.

Jamón al Jerez

HAM IN SHERRY, IBERIAN STYLE

6 slices cooked ham, cut ½ inch thick
3 tablespoons butter
3 tablespoons chopped green onions (scallions)
3 tablespoons flour
¾ cup sweet sherry

¾ cup beef broth
2 teaspoons tomato paste
⅛ teaspoon freshly ground black pepper
1¼ cups heavy cream
3 tablespoons cognac

Trim the fat from the ham. Cut each slice in half crosswise. Melt the butter in a skillet; brown the ham on both sides. Remove the ham and keep warm. Pour off all but 2 tablespoons of the fat. Add the green onions; sauté 1 minute. Blend in the flour; cook 1 minute. Gradually add the wine and broth, stirring steadily to the boiling point. Blend in the tomato paste and pepper; cook over low heat 5 minutes. Stir in the cream, bring to a boil, and cook over low heat 5 minutes. Return the ham; cook 5 minutes, basting frequently. Heat the cognac; set aflame and pour over the ham.
Serves 6.

Jambon, Sauce Madère

HAM IN MADEIRA

10-pound tenderized ham	½ pound mushrooms,
1 cup chopped onions	chopped
1 cup chopped carrots	3 cups Madeira
1 bay leaf	

Cook the ham as the packer directs. Remove the skin and trim off some of the fat, leaving about a ½-inch layer. Arrange the onions, carrots, bay leaf, and mushrooms on the bottom of a roasting pan and put the ham on top. Pour the wine over the ham, cover, and roast in a 350° oven for 1 hour, basting several times. Remove ham to a hot serving platter, skim fat from pan juices, strain, thicken if necessary, and serve separately.
Serves 12–14.

Jambon au Ananas

HAM WITH PINEAPPLE

8-pound ham	1 can sliced pineapple
2 eggs, beaten	1½ cups dry white wine
1 cup brown sugar	2 tablespoons butter

Cook the ham according to the package directions or the type of ham it is and drain well. Score the fat in a diamond design, brush with the eggs, and spread with the brown sugar. Drain the pineapple and reserve ¾ cup juice. Put the ham in a roasting pan and pour the pineapple juice and wine around it. Bake in a 375° oven 1 hour, basting frequently to glaze. Transfer the ham to a hot serving platter. Skim the fat from the pan juices.

Melt the butter in a skillet and lightly brown the pineapple slices on both sides. Arrange around the ham. Serve the gravy separately.
Serves 10–12.

Schinken in Wein

HAM STEAK IN WINE, AUSTRIAN STYLE

2 pounds ready-to-eat ham
  steak in 1 piece
½ cup chopped onions
½ cup peeled, chopped
  tomatoes

1 cup dry red wine
½ cup beef broth
1 bay leaf
1 tablespoon butter
1 tablespoon flour

Put the ham steak in a skillet (with an ovenproof handle) or baking dish; add the onions, tomatoes, wine, broth, and bay leaf. Bake in a 375° oven 45 minutes, basting frequently. Knead the butter with the flour and add to the gravy in small pieces, stirring over direct heat until thickened.
Serves 4.

Jambon à la Montmorency

HAM STEAKS WITH CHERRY SAUCE

2 tablespoons butter
2 ready-to-eat ham steaks,
  cut 1 inch thick
1 No. 2½ can pitted black
  cherries
1 tablespoon cornstarch

2 tablespoons lemon juice
¼ cup water
1 tablespoon sugar
⅛ teaspoon nutmeg
⅛ teaspoon salt

Melt the butter in a skillet; lightly brown the ham steaks in it.
Drain the cherries and reserve ⅓ cup of the juice. Mix the juice with the cornstarch and lemon juice until smooth, then combine in a saucepan with the water, sugar, nutmeg, and salt. Cook over low heat, stirring constantly until thickened and clear. Add the cherries. Pour over the ham and bake in a 350° oven 30 minutes, basting frequently.
Serves 4–6.

Roulades de Jambon Argenteuil

HAM ROLLS WITH ASPARAGUS

3 tablespoons butter
½ cup chopped onions
1½ cups chopped
mushrooms
½ teaspoon salt
⅛ teaspoon freshly ground
black pepper
¼ teaspoon basil

¼ teaspoon dry mustard
¾ cup sour cream
2 hard-cooked egg yolks,
mashed
12 thin slices boiled ham
24 cooked or canned
asparagus spears

Melt the butter in a skillet; sauté the onions and mushrooms 5 minutes. Mix in the salt, pepper, basil, and mustard. Cook over low heat 3 minutes, or until dry. Remove from the heat and blend in the sour cream and egg yolks. Cool.

Spread the ham with the mushroom mixture and place 2 asparagus spears on each slice. Roll up the ham and serve cold. *Serves 6.*

Skinkrulader med Stuvad Spenat

SWEDISH HAM ROLLS

2 pounds spinach or 2
packages frozen spinach
2 tablespoons butter
2 tablespoons flour

1½ cups light cream
12 thin slices cooked ham
6 hard-cooked eggs, cut in
half

Cook the spinach, drain, and chop fine. Melt the butter; blend in the flour. Add the cream, stirring steadily to the boiling point. Add the spinach, and cook 5 minutes longer. Roll up the ham slices, fasten with toothpicks, and heat in a skillet.

Spread spinach on a hot platter. Arrange alternate rows of ham rolls and egg halves over it. *Serves 6.*

Hawaiian Style Ham Slices with Bananas

6 slices cooked ham, cut ¾ inch thick
3 bananas, sliced
¼ cup lemon juice

½ cup brown sugar
¾ cup flaked coconut
2 tablespoons butter

Cut the ham in half crosswise; arrange in a shallow, greased baking pan. Spread the banana slices over them; sprinkle with the lemon juice, brown sugar, and coconut. Dot with the butter. Bake in a 350° oven 25 minutes.
Serves 6.

Tranche de Jambon, Sauce Aurore

HAM SLICES WITH TOMATO-CREAM SAUCE

1½ cups dry white wine
½ cup chopped onions
3 cups beef broth
¾ cup peeled, chopped tomatoes
¼ teaspoon freshly ground black pepper

¼ teaspoon tarragon
2 tablespoons flour
1 cup heavy cream
2 tablespoons butter
8 slices cooked ham, cut ½ inch thick

Cook the wine and onions until the liquid is reduced to half. Add the broth, tomatoes, pepper, and tarragon. Bring to a boil and cook over low heat 1 hour. Purée in an electric blender or force through a sieve. Return to saucepan. Mix the flour and cream until smooth; add to the sauce, stirring constantly to the boiling point. Taste for seasoning and cook over low heat 10 minutes.

Melt the butter in a skillet; lightly brown the ham in it. Place on a heated platter and pour the sauce over it.
Serves 8.

Jambon à la Crème
HAM SLICES IN CREAM SAUCE

3 tablespoons butter	1 tablespoon flour
6 slices ready-to-eat ham, cut ½ inch thick	¾ cup dry white wine
	¾ cup heavy cream

Melt the butter in a skillet; cook the ham over low heat for 2 minutes on each side. Remove the ham. Blend the flour into the fat in the pan. Stir in the wine, and return the ham. Cook over medium heat until the liquid is reduced to about half. Transfer the ham to a hot platter. Stir the cream into the pan juices. Bring to a boil and immediately pour over the ham.
Serves 6.

Le Saupiquet Nivernaise
HAM SLICES IN WINE-CREAM SAUCE

5 tablespoons butter	¼ teaspoon white pepper
12 slices ready-to-eat ham, cut ¼ inch thick	2 tablespoons finely chopped onions
1 tablespoon flour	6 juniper berries
¾ cup beef broth	¼ cup heavy cream
¼ cup dry white wine	2 tablespoons chopped parsley
¼ cup wine vinegar	
¼ teaspoon salt	

Melt 3 tablespoons of the butter in a skillet and sauté the ham in it until lightly browned on both sides. Transfer to a hot serving platter.

Melt the remaining butter in a saucepan. Stir in the flour until browned. Gradually stir in the broth, then the wine, vinegar, salt, pepper, onions, and juniper berries, stirring steadily to the boiling point. Cook over low heat 10 minutes. Strain the sauce. Add the cream. Pour the sauce over the ham slices, sprinkle with the chopped parsley, and serve. *Serves 6.*

Southern Ham-Batter Pudding

¼ cup yellow corn meal
¼ cup flour
½ teaspoon salt
1 teaspoon baking powder
1 egg
½ cup milk
2 tablespoons melted butter

3 cups diced cooked ham
2 packages frozen succotash,
   cooked and drained
½ cup sour cream
2 teaspoons prepared
   mustard
¼ cup grated onion

Sift together the corn meal, flour, salt, and baking powder.
Beat the egg lightly, and mix in the milk and melted butter. Add
to the dry ingredients, stirring only until moistened.

In a greased 2-quart casserole mix the ham, succotash, sour
cream, mustard, and onion. Spread the corn meal batter over it.
Bake in a preheated 375° oven 30 minutes, or until the top is set
and golden in color.
Serves 4–6.

Southern Ham Croquettes

2 cups mashed potatoes
2 cups finely chopped
   cooked ham
2 tablespoons melted butter
2 tablespoons heavy cream

⅛ teaspoon cayenne pepper
3 egg yolks
½ cup dry bread crumbs
1 cup vegetable oil

Beat together the potatoes, ham, butter, cream, cayenne pepper,
and 2 egg yolks. Taste for seasoning. Form into 8 croquettes. Dip
in the remaining egg yolk, and then in the bread crumbs.

Heat the oil in a skillet; fry the croquettes until browned on
both sides. Drain and serve hot with heated ketchup.
Serves 4.

Skinka Royal

SWEDISH HAM CUSTARD

1 29-ounce can tomatoes	½ pound mushrooms, sliced
1 cup chopped onions	and sautéed
2 teaspoons salt	1½ cups grated Parmesan
¼ teaspoon freshly ground	cheese
black pepper	¼ pound butter
2 tablespoons bread crumbs	5 egg yolks
3 cups cooked rice	1½ cups light cream
1 pound cooked ham, cut	
julienne	

Cook the tomatoes, onions, 1½ teaspoons of the salt, and the pepper 15 minutes. Purée the mixture in an electric blender or force through a sieve. Butter a casserole and dust with the bread crumbs. Arrange successive layers (using half of each ingredient) of the rice, ham, mushrooms, tomato mixture, cheese, and dots of butter. Repeat the layers with remaining ingredients. Beat together the egg yolks and cream. Pour over the top. Bake in a 350° oven 35 minutes. *Serves 4–6.*

Torta di Prosciutto

ITALIAN HAM PIE

1½ pounds potatoes	¼ pound bel paese or
2 teaspoons salt	mozzarella cheese, cut
¼ teaspoon white pepper	julienne
⅛ teaspoon nutmeg	½ pound prosciutto (ham)
6 tablespoons butter	or cooked ham, cut
¼ cup dry bread crumbs	julienne
	4 hard-cooked eggs,
	quartered

Cook the unpeeled potatoes until tender. Drain, peel, and mash smooth with the salt, pepper, nutmeg, and 2 tablespoons butter. Spread 2 tablespoons butter in a 9-inch pie plate. Dust with half the bread crumbs, then cover with half the potatoes. Arrange the cheese, ham, and eggs over it, then cover with the remaining potatoes. Sprinkle with the remaining bread crumbs and dot with the remaining butter. Bake in a preheated 400° oven 25 minutes or until browned. Cut into wedges.

Serves 4.

New Zealand Style Potato-Ham Pie

1½ pounds potatoes
2 teaspoons salt
¼ teaspoon white pepper
⅛ teaspoon nutmeg
6 tablespoons butter
¼ cup dry bread crumbs

¼ pound Swiss cheese, cut julienne
1 pound cooked ham, cut julienne
4 hard-cooked eggs, quartered

Cook the unpeeled potatoes until tender. Drain, peel, and mash smooth. Beat in the salt, pepper, nutmeg, and 2 tablespoons of the butter.

Spread 2 tablespoons of the butter in a 9-inch pie plate. Dust with half the bread crumbs, then cover with half the potatoes. Arrange the cheese, ham, and eggs over it, then cover with the remaining potatoes. Sprinkle with the remaining bread crumbs and dot with the remaining butter. Bake in a preheated 400° oven 25 minutes or until browned. Cut into wedges.

Serves 4–6.

Ground Meats

The king in this category is the hamburger, a patty made of ground beef, broiled or pan-fried to individual taste, and placed between two toasted bun slices with a variety of complementary relishes, mustards, onions, tomatoes, or what-have-you. If you're a teen-ager, you probably have them all! They have an equally tantalizing flavor served on a plate. Hamburger is America's choice of individual meat dishes, whether it be in patties, in meat loaves, or as an ingredient in innumerable other recipes.

A group of food experts was once asked what one food they would want if they were cast away on an island, and the majority chose "hamburger." It's a good choice, because there are so many ways to prepare ground meat. Beef or a combination of meats, with herbs, spices, and sauces, can change the plain hamburger into an unusual dish. In Yugoslavia, for example, a national specialty is *čevapčiči,* a ground veal and beef mixture spiced and shaped into sausages, then broiled. The Chinese make meat balls of ground pork or beef, sometimes mixed with water chestnuts, roll them in cornstarch, dip them in beaten egg, and fry them. A variety of sauces change these basic meat balls into different dishes. Then, too, the Scandinavian countries favorite dish is the meat ball, sautéed and then cooked with cream.

Reputedly, the hamburger got its name from the German seaport of Hamburg, which it had reached by way of the Baltic Sea and the tribes of Tartary, those hearty riders (and meat eaters!) who pushed their way across Russia and Eastern Europe.

Today, hamburger is a symbol of all that's American, and it's understandable, too. For ground beef is good, fast and easy to prepare, inexpensive, and usually adored by children–which is not to say that it is not popular with adults as well.

Grinding meat is an easy way of tenderizing it, and hamburger can be made from any beef cut from fillet to heel. The price is determined by the amount of fat, which in turn governs the amount of shrinkage in the cooking process. About one-fourth fat is the desirable ratio. But if you are calorie conscious, choose your own cut (chuck is the best all-round buy) and grind it yourself. The meat should be a deep red color with flecks of fat. If you store it, make it into patties first, or at least keep it flat, for the center of a large round may spoil before it freezes.

Following the recipes for hamburgers, ground lamb is turned into lamburger. The lamb-eating countries of the Middle East find a variety of uses for it, in meat loaves, stuffings for vegetables, or in vegetable combinations as rolls, puddings, etc. Ground lamb is usually taken from the neck, breast, shank, flank, plate, or heel of the animal.

Ground veal may come from any part of the animal, but it is usually cut from the flank, breast, shank, and neck. Because of its subtle flavor, it is usually combined with other ground meats in the preparation of patties, loaves, or skillet dishes.

Ground pork, which is taken from stem to stern of the pig, lends itself to balls, rolls, stuffings, and in combination with other meats. It contains more fat than other ground meats, and is especially good as a meat loaf mixture. It can also readily be turned into sausage in the home kitchen. Any preparation with even a little pork in it must be thoroughly cooked.

Following you will find recipes for the basic ground meat preparations, as well as for some exotic dishes from around the world.

Basic Hamburger

1 pound ground beef	¼ teaspoon freshly ground
1 teaspoon salt	black pepper
	¼ cup ice water

With a fork, mix all the ingredients together lightly. Shape into 2, 4, or 6 patties. Broil 3 inches from source of heat to desired degree of rareness, turning once. The hamburgers may also be pan-broiled on a lightly greased heavy skillet.

VARIATIONS:

Cheeseburger: Place a slice of American or Cheddar cheese on the hamburger after the second side is browned. Broil until melted.

Bacon-Wrapped: Wrap a slice of bacon around the circumference of each hamburger before broiling; fasten with a toothpick. Proceed as for Basic Hamburger.

Stuffed Hamburger: Make twice the number of patties. Put 2 together with a filling of cheese, sautéed onions, relish, bread stuffing, mushroom stuffing, etc. Press edges together and proceed as for Basic Hamburger.

Nut Burgers: Add ½ cup ground nuts and 2 tablespoons minced onion. Proceed as for Basic Hamburger.

California Hamburgers

1 pound ground beef	½ cup dry red wine
1 4-ounce can deviled ham	3 tablespoons butter
¼ teaspoon salt	2 tablespoons minced
¼ teaspoon freshly ground	parsley
black pepper	

Mix together the beef, ham, salt, and pepper. Shape into 4 patties. Place in a bowl and add the wine; let marinate in the refrigerator 2 hours. Drain, reserving the wine.

Melt the butter in a skillet; brown the hamburgers on both sides, then add the wine. Cook to desired degree of rareness. Sprinkle with the parsley. Serve with the pan juices.

Serves 4.

Hamburger Cheese Patties

½ pound blue cheese	1½ teaspoons salt
¼ cup heavy cream	½ teaspoon freshly ground
2 pounds ground lean beef	black pepper

Mix the cheese and cream together until smooth. Mix the beef, salt, and pepper together. Form into 12 patties. Spread 6 patties with the cheese mixture, and cover with the remaining patties. Broil to desired degree of rareness, turning once.
Serves 6.

Carne Molida con Queso
MEXICAN CHEESE-HAMBURGERS

1 pound ground beef
¼ cup grated Parmesan
  cheese
1 cup finely chopped
  green onions (scallions)
1 cup finely chopped
  parsley

1 egg, beaten
2 tablespoons water
1 teaspoon salt
Dash cayenne pepper
1 cup dry bread crumbs
4 tablespoons butter

With the hand, mix together the beef, cheese, green onions, parsley, egg, water, salt, and cayenne pepper. Form into 1-inch balls (or walnut-sized for hors d'oeuvres) and flatten slightly. Dip in the bread crumbs, coating them thoroughly. Chill 1 hour. Melt the butter in a skillet and brown the balls on all sides.
Serves 4–5.

Boeuf Haché Bourguignon
BURGUNDY CHOPPED BEEF WITH RED WINE SAUCE

1½ pounds ground beef
½ cup heavy cream
2 tablespoons chopped
  onions
1½ teaspoons salt
½ teaspoon freshly ground
  black pepper
3 tablespoons butter
1 tablespoon cornstarch

½ cup beef broth
⅔ cup dry red wine
½ pound mushrooms, sliced
  and sautéed
6 slices French bread,
  sautéed
3 tablespoons chopped
  parsley

Mix together the beef, cream, onions, salt, and pepper; shape into 6 thick patties. Melt the butter in a skillet; cook the hamburgers to the desired degree of rareness, turning once. Remove and keep warm.

Mix the cornstarch with the broth and add to the skillet with the wine; cook, stirring steadily, to the boiling point. Taste for seasoning. Return the patties and add the mushrooms and cook over low heat for 3 minutes. Put a patty on each piece of sautéed bread, and pour the sauce over them. Sprinkle with the parsley. *Serves 6.*

Boeuf Haché à la Suisse

SWISS CHEESE GROUND BEEF

1½ pounds ground beef	2 tablespoons ice water
1½ teaspoons salt	6 slices Swiss cheese, cut
¼ teaspoon freshly ground	⅛ inch thick
black pepper	6 slices boiled ham

With the hand, lightly mix the beef, salt, pepper, and water. Shape into 12 patties. Place a slice of cheese and ham on 6 patties, then cover with the remaining patties. Press together gently. Broil on a greased pan 4 minutes on each side or to desired degree of rareness. Serve with a mushroom or tomato sauce if desired. *Serves 6.*

Hakkebøf

DANISH CHOPPED BEEFSTEAK

1½ pounds ground beef	½ cup light cream
1 teaspoon salt	½ cup flour
½ teaspoon freshly ground	4 tablespoons butter
black pepper	1 cup sliced onions

Mix the meat with the salt, pepper, and cream. Shape the meat into 4–6 flat, round patties, and dip in the flour. Melt the butter in a skillet; add the onions and sauté until transparent. Add the beef patties and sauté until crisp and brown on both sides. *Serves 4–6.*

Lihapullia

FINNISH BEEF PATTIES

1 pound ground beef	¼ teaspoon freshly ground
1½ cups grated raw potato	black pepper
¼ cup minced onions	2½ cups milk
1 egg, beaten	8 tablespoons butter
1¼ teaspoons salt	4 tablespoons flour

Mix together the beef, grated potato, onions, egg, salt, pepper, and ½ cup of the milk. Shape the mixture into 12 patties. Melt 4 tablespoons of the butter in a skillet; sauté the patties in it over low heat 10 minutes, turning them once. Remove and keep warm.

Add the remaining butter to the skillet. Blend in the flour. Gradually add the remaining milk, stirring steadily to the boiling point. Cook over low heat 5 minutes. Taste the gravy for seasoning. Pour over the hamburgers. *Serves 4–6.*

Crocchetti alla Parmigiana

MEAT CROQUETTES

2½ cups chicken broth	3 tablespoons minced
1 cup raw rice	parsley
1 cup minced cooked beef	2 eggs
or veal	½ cup flour
½ cup grated Parmesan	½ cup dry bread crumbs
cheese	Vegetable oil for deep
Dash cayenne pepper	frying

Bring the broth to a boil and add the rice. Cover and cook over low heat 20 minutes, or until tender and dry. Cool, then stir in the meat, cheese, cayenne pepper, parsley, and 1 beaten egg. Form into 12 croquettes. Dip the croquettes in the flour and chill 1 hour. Beat the remaining egg with a little water; dip the croquettes in it, then in the bread crumbs.

Heat the oil to 380°. Fry a few croquettes at a time until browned. Drain and serve with tomato sauce if desired.

Serves 6.

Biefballetjes

DUTCH BEEF CROQUETTES

1½ pounds ground beef	2 teaspoons paprika
1 cup cooked rice	1 teaspoon grated lemon
3 slices crisp bacon,	rind
crumbled	2 eggs, beaten
1 teaspoon salt	3 tablespoons butter
½ teaspoon freshly ground	½ cup sour cream
black pepper	

Mix together the beef, rice, bacon, salt, pepper, paprika, lemon rind, and eggs. Shape into 1-inch balls and flatten slightly.

Melt the butter in a skillet; brown the croquettes in it on both sides. Transfer the croquettes to a hot serving dish. Stir the sour cream into the skillet, scraping the bottom of browned particles. Heat but do not let boil; pour over the croquettes.

Serves 4–6.

Hampurinpihvi

FINNISH BREADED HAMBURGERS

1½ pounds ground beef
2½ teaspoons salt
½ teaspoon freshly ground
    black pepper
2 tablespoons minced
    parsley

2 eggs, beaten
¼ cup flour
½ cup dry bread crumbs
4 tablespoons butter

Mix together the meat, 1½ teaspoons of the salt, ¼ teaspoon of the pepper, and the parsley. Shape into 8 patties. Dip in the eggs, then in the flour mixed with the remaining salt and pepper, the eggs again, and finally the bread crumbs.

Melt the butter in a skillet; brown the patties on both sides. *Serves 4–6.*

Boeuf Haché

FRENCH GROUND BEEF

1 cup dry red wine
1 cup light cream
1¼ cups white bread cubes
2 pounds ground beef
½ cup finely chopped onions
2 teaspoons salt

½ teaspoon freshly ground
    black pepper
¾ cup dry bread crumbs
4 tablespoons butter

Mix together the wine and cream, then stir in the bread cubes. Let soak 5 minutes; mash smooth. Add to the meat with the onions, salt, and pepper. Shape into 12–16 flat cakes; dip in the bread crumbs. Chill 30 minutes.

Melt the butter in a skillet; brown the meat on both sides and cook to desired degree of rareness. *Serves 6–8.*

Deutsches Beefsteak

GERMAN HAMBURGERS

½ cup fresh bread crumbs	¼ teaspoon freshly ground
½ cup water	black pepper
1 pound ground beef	6 tablespoons butter
1 teaspoon salt	1½ cups thinly sliced onions

Soak the bread in the water, mash smooth, drain, and squeeze dry. Mix together the meat, bread, salt, and pepper. Shape into 8 flat, round patties.

Melt 3 tablespoons of the butter in a skillet; brown the onions in it. Remove and keep warm. Melt the remaining butter in the skillet; cook the hamburgers over high heat until browned on both sides, or to desired degree of rareness. Arrange on a heated serving dish, and cover with the onions.

Serves 4.

Italian Pizzaburger

2 tablespoons olive oil	¼ teaspoon orégano
½ cup chopped onions	1 egg, beaten
1½ pounds ground beef	6 English muffins, split
1 tablespoon minced	and lightly toasted
parsley	1 cup tomato sauce, heated
1 teaspoon salt	12 slices mozzarella or
¼ teaspoon freshly ground	American cheese
black pepper	

Heat the oil in a skillet; sauté the onions 5 minutes. Mix together the beef, parsley, salt, pepper, orégano, and egg. Add to the skillet and cook until browned, stirring to prevent lumps from forming. Spread mixture on the muffin halves. Spread some tomato sauce on each, then cover with a slice of cheese. Place under broiler until cheese melts.

Serves 6.

Boeuf Haché au Moelle
BEEF PATTIES WITH MARROW

3 tablespoons beef marrow
1½ pounds ground beef
3 tablespoons heavy cream

1½ teaspoons salt
½ teaspoon freshly ground
   black pepper

Ask the butcher to crack a marrowbone. Chop the marrow very fine, and mix with the beef, cream, salt, and pepper. Shape into 6 patties. Broil on a greased pan 3 minutes on each side or to desired degree of rareness. Serve with Béarnaise Sauce.*
Serves 6.

New Zealand Meat Patties

1 pound ground beef
1½ cups grated raw potato
3 tablespoons chopped
   onions
1 egg, beaten
½ cup light cream

1¼ teaspoons salt
¼ teaspoon freshly ground
   black pepper
¼ pound (1 stick) butter
4 tablespoons flour
2 cups milk

Mix together the beef, grated potato, onions, egg, cream, salt, and pepper. Shape into 12 thin patties. Melt 4 tablespoons of the butter in a skillet, and sauté the patties 15 minutes, turning them once. Remove and keep warm.

Melt the remaining butter in the skillet. Blend in the flour. Gradually add the milk, stirring steadily to the boiling point. Cook over low heat 5 minutes. Taste the gravy for seasoning. Pour over the patties.
Serves 4–6.

Oriental Hamburgers

1 pound ground beef	½ teaspoon ground
2 tablespoons soy sauce	coriander
¼ teaspoon freshly ground	½ cup chopped water
black pepper	chestnuts
½ teaspoon powdered ginger	2 tablespoons vegetable oil

Mix together lightly all the ingredients but the oil. Shape into 4 patties. Heat the oil in a skillet; cook the patties in it to desired degree of rareness, turning once.
Serves 4.

Bifteck au Poivre

PEPPERED HAMBURGERS

2 pounds ground beef	1 teaspoon Worcestershire
4 teaspoons coarsely	sauce
cracked black pepper	1 teaspoon lemon juice
4 tablespoons butter	2 tablespoons warm cognac
⅛ teaspoon Tabasco	Chopped parsley

Shape the beef lightly into 8 patties and dip each side into the pepper. Let stand 30 minutes.

Melt half the butter in a heavy skillet over high heat; add the hamburgers. Cook until well browned. Turn over and cook over high heat, then reduce heat to medium and cook to desired degree of rareness.

To the skillet, add the remaining butter, the Tabasco, Worcestershire, and lemon juice. Set the cognac aflame and pour into the skillet.

Transfer the patties to a warm platter. Scrape up the browned particles in the skillet and pour the pan juices over the patties. Sprinkle with the parsley.
Serves 4–6.

Bitok à la Russe

RUSSIAN HAMBURGERS

6 tablespoons butter
¼ cup finely chopped
  onions
1 pound twice-ground beef
1¼ teaspoons salt

¼ teaspoon freshly ground
  black pepper
1½ cups heavy cream
¼ cup flour

Melt 2 tablespoons of the butter in a skillet; sauté the onions 5 minutes. Cool, then mix the undrained onions with the beef, salt, and pepper. Very gradually mix in the cream with a wooden spoon. Chill 1 hour.

Shape the mixture into 8 cakes, then dip lightly in the flour. Melt the remaining butter in a skillet; sauté the cakes until browned on both sides. Serve with a mushroom sauce if desired. *Serves 4.*

Salisbury Steak

2 pounds ground beef
4 tablespoons grated onion
3 tablespoons finely chopped
  green peppers
1 clove garlic, minced
2 tablespoons minced
  parsley
2 teaspoons salt
½ teaspoon freshly ground
  black pepper
¼ teaspoon paprika

⅛ teaspoon marjoram
¼ cup flour
3 tablespoons olive oil
½ cup ketchup
3 tablespoons butter
⅛ teaspoon Tabasco
1 teaspoon Worcestershire
  sauce
½ teaspoon dry mustard
3 tablespoons dry sherry

Mix together the beef, onion, green peppers, garlic, parsley, salt, pepper, paprika, and marjoram. Form the mixture into 6–8 steak-shaped patties about ¾ inch thick. Dip lightly in the flour and brush with the oil. Arrange on a broiling pan. Broil 3 inches from source of heat 5 minutes on each side, or to desired degree of rareness. While the meat is broiling, prepare the sauce.

In a saucepan, combine the ketchup, butter, Tabasco, Worcestershire sauce, and mustard. Cook until butter melts, then stir in the sherry. Arrange the patties on a hot platter and pour the sauce over them. *Serves 6–8.*

Hamburg Squares

⅔ cup dry bread crumbs
⅔ cup milk
2 pounds ground beef
1½ teaspoons salt
¼ teaspoon freshly ground
   black pepper
¼ teaspoon sage
½ teaspoon thyme
½ cup chopped onions

⅓ cup chopped green
   peppers
1 4-ounce can chopped
   mushrooms
8 slices bacon
3 tablespoons melted butter
¼ cup ketchup
2 teaspoons Worcestershire
   sauce

Soak the bread crumbs in the milk for 5 minutes, add the ground beef, salt, pepper, sage, thyme, onions, green peppers, and mushrooms. Mix well. Put the mixture in a greased baking dish 13×9×2 inches. Arrange the bacon over the top and bake in a 350° oven for 30 minutes. Mix together the melted butter, ketchup, and Worcestershire sauce. Pour over the meat and bake 10 minutes longer. Cut into squares.
Serves 8.

Texas Hamburgers

1½ pounds ground beef
⅓ cup chili sauce
⅓ cup dry bread crumbs
1¼ teaspoons salt
½ teaspoon freshly ground
   black pepper

2 teaspoons chili powder
⅛ teaspoon Tabasco
¼ teaspoon dry mustard
2 tablespoons minced onions
1 clove garlic, minced
¼ cup ice water

Mix all ingredients together with the hand. Shape into 6 patties. Arrange on an oiled broiling pan. Broil 4 minutes on each side or to desired degree of rareness. *Serves 6.*

Biftecks à la Miremonde

MEAT PATTIES IN WINE SAUCE

¾ cup white bread cubes
6 tablespoons light cream
1 pound ground beef
¾ cup finely chopped
  sautéed onions
2 eggs, beaten
1 tablespoon uncooked
  farina

1 teaspoon salt
¼ teaspoon freshly ground
  black pepper
⅛ teaspoon grated nutmeg
4 tablespoons butter
½ cup dry white wine
1 tablespoon minced parsley

Soak the bread in the cream for 10 minutes, then mash smooth. Combine with the ground beef, sautéed onions, eggs, farina, salt, pepper, and nutmeg. Mix well and chill 1 hour. Form the mixture into 4 patties.

Melt the butter in a skillet; add the patties; cover and cook over low heat 10 minutes on each side. Transfer the patties to a heated platter. Stir the wine and parsley into the pan juices. Bring to a boil, scraping the bottom of browned particles. Cook over high heat 1 minute and pour over the patties. *Serves 4.*

Steak Tartare

1 pound fillet of beef or
  sirloin steak
½ cup finely chopped
  onions
1 clove garlic, minced
1¼ teaspoons salt

¾ teaspoon freshly ground
  black pepper
3 tablespoons capers
5 egg yolks
Capers, chopped onions,
  and minced parsley for
  garnish

Trim all the fat from the meat. Grind the meat just before serving. If you have the butcher do it, buy it as close as possible to serving time and be sure all the fat is trimmed. Mix in the onions, garlic, salt, pepper, capers, and 1 egg yolk. Shape lightly into 4 patties and make an indentation in each. Place a raw egg yolk in each, and surround with capers, chopped onions, and minced parsley. *Serves 4.*

VARIATION:

Steak Tartare Lucullus

Omit the onions, garlic, pepper, and capers and decrease the salt to ½ teaspoon. Spread the meat on hot buttered toast. Garnish each serving with a tablespoon of caviar and chopped green onions.

Note: Small balls of steak Tartare rolled in chopped parsley or small squares of steak Tartare Lucullus make excellent hors d'oeuvres.

Carne Cruda
ITALIAN STEAK TARTARE

1 pound trimmed sirloin steak	¼ teaspoon freshly ground black pepper
½ cup lemon juice	1 teaspoon prepared mustard
6 anchovy fillets	¼ cup capers
¼ cup olive oil	Pitted black olives
½ teaspoon salt	

It is better to grind the steak at home for this dish, but if you can't, buy it no more than 2 or 3 hours before using.

Mix the ground beef with ⅓ cup of the lemon juice and let stand in the refrigerator 1 hour. Mash the anchovies and beat with the oil until creamy, then add to the meat with the salt, pepper, mustard, and remaining lemon juice. Mix well and form into 4 mounds; garnish with the capers and olives. *Serves 4.*

CARVING A HAM

Step 1

Step 2

Step 3

CARVING A LOIN OF PORK

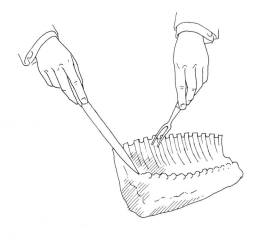

Step 1

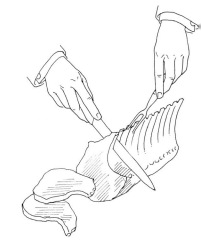

Step 2

CARVING A
FLANK STEAK

CARVING A
RACK OF LAMB

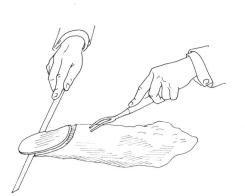

CARVING A LEG OF LAMB

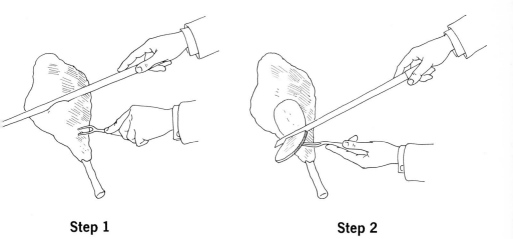

Step 1   Step 2

CARVING A SADDLE OF LAMB

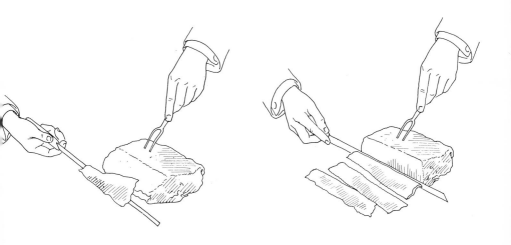

CARVING A
SIRLOIN OF BEEF

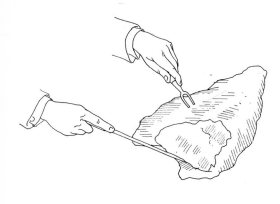

CARVING A
FILLET OF BEEF

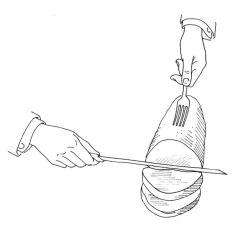

CARVING A STANDING RIB ROAST

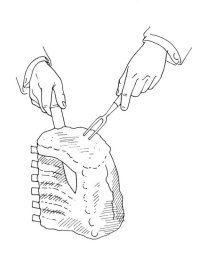

Step 1

Step 2

Frihed Smørrebrød

DANISH RAW BEEF SANDWICH

4 slices rye bread
1 pound ground lean
   sirloin steak

4 egg yolks
2 cups tiny Danish shrimp
   (canned)

Trim crusts from bread, and spread each slice with ¼ of the meat. Make a depression in the middle of each and carefully place a raw egg yolk in the center. Arrange shrimp in diagonals from each corner of the bread.
Serves 4.

Raaka Naudanliha

FINNISH RAW BEEF

1½ pounds fillet of beef
¾ cup diced cooked or
   canned beets
2 tablespoons vinegar
1 teaspoon salt

½ teaspoon freshly ground
   black pepper
1 cup chopped onions
6 egg yolks

Be sure the meat is free of fat. Grind the meat twice, at home if possible. Marinate the beets in vinegar for 30 minutes. Drain. Season the meat with the salt and pepper and shape into 6 patties. Arrange the patties on a serving plate or 6 individual plates. Drain the beets and place separate mounds of onions and beets around the beef. Place a raw egg yolk in the center of each mound. Everything is mixed together before eating.
Serves 6.

Couftah

EGYPTIAN BEEF BALLS

1½ pounds ground beef
¼ cup minced parsley
2½ teaspoons salt
½ teaspoon freshly ground
  black pepper
3 eggs
¼ cup vegetable oil

2 cups chopped onions
1 pound tomatoes, peeled
  and diced
1 cup water
½ teaspoon dry mustard
2 tablespoons vinegar

Mix together the beef, parsley, 1½ teaspoons of the salt, ¼ teaspoon of the pepper, and 1 beaten egg. Form into 1-inch balls.

Heat the oil in a skillet and brown the balls on all sides. Remove. To the fat remaining in the skillet add the onions, tomatoes, water, mustard, vinegar, and remaining salt and pepper. Bring to a boil and cook over low heat 15 minutes. Purée the mixture in an electric blender or force through a sieve.

Beat the remaining eggs in a bowl; add the hot sauce, stirring steadily to prevent curdling. Return to the skillet and add the meat balls. Heat but do not let boil.

Serves 6–8.

Lihapyörykät

FINNISH BEEF BALLS IN DILL SAUCE

1 pound ground beef
1½ cups grated raw
  potatoes
½ cup minced onions
½ cup chopped green
  peppers
1½ teaspoons salt
½ teaspoon freshly ground
  black pepper

1 tablespoon minced dill
  or ½ teaspoon dill seed
2 tablespoons vegetable oil
¾ cup canned tomato sauce
1 tablespoon Worcestershire
  sauce
½ cup water
¼ cup chopped dill pickles

Mix together the beef, potatoes, onions, green peppers, salt, pepper, and dill. Shape into 2-inch balls.

Heat the oil in a skillet and brown the balls on all sides. Add a mixture of the tomato sauce, Worcestershire sauce, water, and pickles. Bring to a boil, cover, and cook over low heat 35 minutes. Serve with noodles or rice.

Serves 4–6.

Fleischklösse mit Pilzen

GERMAN BEEF BALLS WITH MUSHROOMS

1 pound ground beef	3 cups beef broth
¼ cup finely chopped onions	1 pound mushrooms, sliced
2 tablespoons cracker meal	3 tablespoons butter
1 egg	2 tablespoons flour
¼ cup ice water	2 egg yolks
2 teaspoons salt	2 tablespoons lemon juice
½ teaspoon freshly ground black pepper	½ cup dry white wine
	2 tablespoons minced parsley

Mix together the meat, onions, cracker meal, egg, water, 1¼ teaspoons of the salt, and ¼ teaspoon of the pepper. Shape into walnut-sized balls. Bring 2½ cups of the broth to a boil and drop the meat balls into it. Cook over low heat 10 minutes. Drain.

While the meat balls are cooking, prepare the mushrooms. Melt the butter in a skillet; sauté the mushrooms 3 minutes. Blend in the flour, add the remaining salt and pepper, and stir until the flour browns. Add the remaining broth; cook over low heat 5 minutes. Beat the egg yolks; stir in the lemon juice and wine. Add to the mushrooms very gradually, stirring steadily to prevent curdling. Add the meat balls, mixing lightly. Heat but do not let boil. Sprinkle with the parsley.

Serves 4–6.

Keftedes

GREEK BEEF BALLS

1½ pounds ground beef
2 eggs, beaten
½ cup fresh bread crumbs
1 cup finely chopped onions
2 tablespoons chopped
parsley
1 tablespoon chopped fresh
mint

1½ teaspoons salt
½ teaspoon freshly ground
black pepper
¼ teaspoon cinnamon
¼ teaspoon ground allspice
½ cup vegetable oil

Mix together all the ingredients but the oil. Chill 3 hours. Shape the mixture into ½-inch balls.

Heat the oil in a skillet; fry the balls in it until browned, shaking the pan frequently to turn the balls. Serve hot or cold. *Serves 6–8.*

Kubiedeh

IRANIAN BEEF BALLS

2 tablespoons raw rice
3 tablespoons split peas
3 cups water
1 pound ground beef
1 cup chopped green
onions (scallions)
1 cup chopped parsley
1½ teaspoons salt

½ teaspoon freshly ground
black pepper
1 egg, beaten
3 tablespoons butter
½ cup chopped onions
1½ cups beef broth
2 tablespoons tomato paste
1 tablespoon lemon juice

Cook the rice and split peas in the water 30 minutes. Drain well. Mix together the beef, green onions, parsley, salt, pepper, egg, and cooked rice and peas. Shape into 2-inch balls.

Melt the butter in a skillet; sauté the onions 10 minutes. Stir in the broth, tomato paste, and lemon juice; bring to a boil and cook over low heat 10 minutes. Add the meat balls; cover and cook over low heat 30 minutes. Shake the pan and baste occasionally. *Serves 4–6.*

Polpette

ITALIAN BEEF BALLS

½ cup white bread cubes
½ cup milk
1½ pounds ground beef
2 teaspoons finely grated
  lemon rind
2 cloves garlic, minced
1 tablespoon minced parsley
2 eggs, beaten

1½ teaspoons salt
½ teaspoon freshly ground
  black pepper
⅛ teaspoon nutmeg
¼ cup grated Parmesan
  cheese
½ cup flour
⅓ cup olive oil

Soak the bread in the milk; drain and mash smooth. Mix together lightly the beef, lemon rind, garlic, parsley, eggs, salt, pepper, nutmeg, Parmesan cheese, and bread.

Shape round 1-inch cakes, ½ inch thick, roll them lightly in the flour. Make a dent on the top. Heat the oil in a skillet and fry the cakes 2 minutes on each side or to desired degree of rareness. Drain. *Serves 6–8.*

Arangi

ITALIAN BEEF-RICE BALLS

3 tablespoons vegetable oil
¼ cup chopped onions
¼ cup chopped green
  peppers
1 clove garlic, minced
1½ pounds ground beef
½ cup raw long-grain rice
1½ teaspoons salt

¼ teaspoon freshly ground
  black pepper
2 8-ounce cans tomato
  sauce
1 teaspoon sugar
1 bay leaf
⅛ teaspoon ground allspice

Heat 1 tablespoon of the oil in a skillet; sauté the onions, peppers, and garlic 5 minutes. Mix with the beef, raw rice, salt, and pepper. Shape into 2-inch balls.

Heat the remaining oil in the skillet and brown the balls on all sides. Add the tomato sauce, sugar, bay leaf, and allspice. Cover and cook over low heat 20 minutes. The rice will stick up around the meat balls. *Serves 4–6.*

Low-Calorie Beef Balls

1 pound lean top round	1 teaspoon salt
1 slice white bread, trimmed	¼ teaspoon freshly ground black pepper
¼ cup skim milk	1 egg white
2 teaspoons grated lemon rind	3 tablespoons flour
2 teaspoons minced parsley	2 tablespoons corn oil

Be sure all the fat is trimmed from the meat, then have it ground or do it yourself. Soak the bread in the milk, drain, and mash smooth. Mix together the meat, bread, lemon rind, parsley, salt, pepper, and egg white. Sprinkle the flour onto a board and form the meat into 1-inch round cakes ½ inch thick.

Heat the oil in a skillet and brown the cakes in it 2 minutes on each side, or to desired degree of rareness. *Serves 6.*

Albóndigas y Maíz

MEXICAN BEEF BALLS AND CORN

1½ pounds ground beef	¾ cup chopped onions
1½ teaspoons salt	1 cup bottled chili sauce
½ teaspoon freshly ground black pepper	½ cup water
2 tablespoons olive oil	1 tablespoon chili powder
¼ cup chopped green peppers	1 clove garlic, minced
	1½ cups canned or frozen corn kernels

Lightly mix together the beef, salt, and pepper. Shape the mixture into 1-inch balls. Heat the oil in a skillet and brown the meat balls on all sides. Remove the meat balls. To the oil remaining add the green peppers and onions; sauté 10 minutes. Return the meat balls to the skillet. Add the chili sauce, water, chili powder, and garlic. Cover and cook over low heat 10 minutes. Add the corn; cook over low heat 10 minutes.
Serves 6.

Beef Balls in Paprika Sauce

4 tablespoons butter
2½ cups thinly sliced onions
1 tablespoon paprika
1½ pounds ground beef
⅓ cup dry bread crumbs
1 egg, beaten
½ cup ice water
2 tablespoons ketchup
1½ teaspoons salt

¼ teaspoon freshly ground
　black pepper
1 clove garlic, minced
½ cup flour
1½ cups beef broth
¾ cup sour cream
2 tablespoons minced
　parsley

Melt 2 tablespoons of the butter in a skillet; add the onions, cover, and cook over low heat 15 minutes, stirring occasionally. Transfer the onions to a saucepan and stir in the paprika.

Mix together the beef, bread crumbs, egg, water, ketchup, salt, pepper, and garlic. Shape into 1-inch balls. Roll in the flour, reserving 1½ tablespoons of the flour. Melt the remaining butter in the skillet and brown the balls on all sides. Add to the onions in the saucepan. Blend the reserved flour into the fat remaining in the skillet. Add the broth, stirring steadily, to the boiling point. Add to the meat balls, cover, and cook over low heat 20 minutes, shaking the pan frequently. Stir in the sour cream and parsley.
Serves 6–8.

Polpette Parmigiana

PARMA BEEF-CHEESE BALLS

1½ pounds ground beef
¾ cup grated Cheddar
cheese
1 cup chopped, cooked,
drained spinach
1 clove garlic, minced
¾ cup chopped onions
3 tablespoons minced
parsley

1½ teaspoons salt
½ teaspoon freshly ground
black pepper
½ cup flour
¼ cup vegetable oil
2 8-ounce cans tomato
sauce
⅓ cup grated Parmesan
cheese

Mix together the meat, Cheddar cheese, spinach, garlic, onions, parsley, salt, and pepper. Chill 30 minutes. Shape into 2-inch balls. Roll in the flour. Heat the oil in a skillet and brown the balls on all sides. Pour off all the fat. Pour the tomato sauce over the meat balls. Cover and bake in a 375° oven 20 minutes. Sprinkle with the Parmesan cheese and bake uncovered 10 minutes longer. *Serves 6–8.*

Beef Balls in Pineapple Sauce

1½ pounds ground beef
¼ cup grated onions
1 egg
2 teaspoons salt
⅛ teaspoon freshly ground
black pepper
¼ cup cornstarch

1 8-ounce can pineapple
chunks
2 tablespoons vegetable oil
1 cup beef broth
2 tablespoons lemon juice
1 lemon, thinly sliced
4 tablespoons brown sugar
¼ cup gingersnap crumbs

Mix the meat, onions, egg, 1 teaspoon salt, and the pepper. Form the mixture into 1-inch balls; lightly roll them in the cornstarch.

Drain the pineapple and reserve ½ cup of the juice.

Heat the oil in a skillet and brown the meat balls on all sides. Add the broth, reserved pineapple juice, lemon juice, lemon, sugar, and remaining salt. Cover and cook over low heat 35 minutes. Stir in the gingersnaps, add the pineapple, and cook 10 minutes longer. *Serves 6.*

Bitki w Śmietanie

POLISH BEEF BALLS IN SOUR CREAM SAUCE

4 tablespoons butter	½ teaspoon freshly ground
½ cup chopped onions	black pepper
¾ cup white bread cubes	¼ teaspoon thyme
⅓ cup milk	½ cup flour
1½ pounds ground beef	1 cup beef broth
2 eggs	1½ cups sour cream
2 teaspoons salt	

Melt 1 tablespoon of the butter in a skillet; sauté the onions 5 minutes. Soak the bread cubes in the milk for 5 minutes, then mash smooth. Mix together the onions, soaked bread, beef, eggs, salt, pepper, and thyme. Chop until very smooth. Shape into 1-inch balls and roll in the flour.

Melt the remaining butter in a skillet; brown the meat balls on all sides. Mix in the broth and sour cream. Cover and cook over low heat 30 minutes. Serve with boiled potatoes or noodles. *Serves 4–6.*

Bitki z Kapusta

POLISH BEEF BALLS WITH SAUERKRAUT

2 pounds ground beef	1 pound potatoes, peeled
2 teaspoons salt	and sliced
½ teaspoon freshly ground	1 large apple, peeled,
black pepper	cored, and sliced
½ cup chopped onions	4 slices bacon, cut into
1 pound sauerkraut	thirds
	1 bay leaf

Combine the beef, salt, pepper, and onions and form into 12 large balls. Spread half the sauerkraut in a greased casserole. Arrange the potato and apple slices over the sauerkraut. Place the meat balls in the casserole and put a piece of bacon on each. Spread with the remaining sauerkraut and add the bay leaf. Cover and bake in a 375° oven 1¼ hours, removing the cover for the last 15 minutes. Watch carefully and add a little water if necessary, if sauerkraut begins to burn.

Serves 6–8.

Hackad Biff med Lök

SCANDINAVIAN BEEF BALLS

1½ pounds ground beef	2 tablespoons vegetable oil
2 tablespoons minced parsley	6 whole cloves
1½ teaspoons salt	3 tablespoons sugar
½ teaspoon freshly ground black pepper	1 tablespoon tomato paste
⅛ teaspoon marjoram	1 cup water
½ cup minced onions	2 tablespoons cider vinegar
1 egg	1 bay leaf
	½ cup crushed gingersnaps

Combine the beef, parsley, salt, pepper, marjoram, onions, and egg; mix together thoroughly. Form into 1-inch balls. Heat the oil in a skillet and fry the meat balls until browned on all sides.

Add a mixture of the cloves, sugar, tomato paste, water, cider vinegar, bay leaf, and gingersnaps. Cover and cook over low heat for 35 minutes. Mix occasionally. Remove bay leaf.

Serves 4–6.

Hachad Sjömansbiff

SWEDISH FLUFFY BEEF BALLS

6 eggs, separated
1 pound ground beef
1 teaspoon salt
¼ teaspoon freshly ground
black pepper
½ teaspoon baking powder

¼ cup grated onion
2 tablespoons minced
parsley
¼ teaspoon thyme
½ cup vegetable oil

Beat the egg yolks until thickened. Mix in the meat, salt, pepper, baking powder, onion, parsley, and thyme. Fold in the egg whites.

Heat the oil in a skillet; drop the mixture into it by the tablespoon. Fry until puffed and brown around the edges, then turn over to brown the other side.

Serves 4–6.

Små Köttbullas

SWEDISH BEEF BALLS IN SOUR CREAM

½ cup white bread cubes
1½ cups buttermilk
1½ pounds ground beef
1½ teaspoons salt
½ teaspoon freshly ground
black pepper

½ cup flour
2 tablespoons vegetable oil
2 tablespoons butter
¼ cup dry sherry
1 cup sour cream
Paprika

Soak the bread cubes in the buttermilk and mash smooth; mix with the beef, salt, and pepper until smooth. Shape into 2-inch balls; roll lightly in the flour. Heat the oil and butter in a skillet; brown the balls in it, shaking the pan to turn them. Mix the sherry and sour cream; add to the skillet. Cook over low heat 3 minutes, shaking the pan frequently. Sprinkle with the paprika. Serve with rice or noodles.

Serves 6–8.

Taipei Sweet and Sour Beef Balls

1 pound ground beef
1 egg
1 teaspoon salt
¼ teaspoon freshly ground
  black pepper
3 tablespoons diced green
  onions (scallions)
3 tablespoons cornstarch

1 8-ounce can pineapple
  wedges
3 tablespoons vegetable oil
1 tablespoon soy sauce
3 tablespoons vinegar
⅓ cup sugar
⅓ cup water
2 green peppers, cut
  julienne

Mix together the beef, egg, salt, pepper, green onions, and 1 tablespoon cornstarch. Shape into marble-sized balls. Drain the pineapple, reserving the juice.

Heat 2 tablespoons of the oil in a skillet and brown the meat balls on all sides. Remove. Add the remaining oil to the skillet. Mix together the remaining cornstarch, the soy sauce, vinegar, sugar, water, and pineapple juice. Add to the skillet, stirring steadily until thickened. Add the pineapple, green peppers, and meat balls. Bring to a boil and cook 3 minutes.
Serves 4–6.

New England Ground Beef in Blankets

1¼ pounds ground beef
1½ teaspoons salt
¼ teaspoon freshly ground
  black pepper
3 eggs
¾ cup milk
⅛ teaspoon white pepper

12 slices white bread
3 tablespoons butter
3 teaspoons prepared
  mustard
2 cups grated Cheddar
  cheese

Mix together the beef, 1 teaspoon of the salt, and the black pepper. Form into 12 rolls about 2-inches long.

Beat together the eggs, milk, white pepper, and remaining salt. Dip the bread in the mixture. Melt the butter in a skillet; brown the bread on both sides. Spread each slice with mustard,

and 1 tablespoon of cheese. Place a hamburger on it diagonally across the center. Fold over the bread and fasten with a toothpick. (The bread won't close completely.) Arrange on a buttered baking pan. Pour any remaining egg mixture over the tops and sprinkle with the remaining cheese. Bake in a 325° oven 15 minutes.
Serves 6–8.

Aruba Beef-Stuffed Red Cheese

1 whole 4-pound Edam cheese	1½ cups peeled, chopped tomatoes
2 tablespoons butter	½ cup dry bread crumbs
1 cup minced onions	2 eggs, beaten
1 pound ground beef	½ cup chopped stuffed olives
1 teaspoon salt	
Dash cayenne pepper	

Leave the wax coating on the cheese. Cut a 1-inch horizontal piece off the top. Scoop out the cheese, leaving a ½-inch thick shell. Cover shell with water and let soak 1 hour. Drain. Grate enough of the scooped-out cheese to measure 2 cups.

Melt the butter in a skillet; sauté the onions 5 minutes. Add the meat; cook over medium heat 5 minutes, stirring frequently. Add the salt, pepper, and tomatoes; cook 5 minutes. Remove from heat and mix in the bread crumbs, eggs, olives, and grated cheese. Stuff the cheese and replace the top. Wrap the cheese in cheesecloth or foil, to help retain the shape. Place in a greased baking pan. Bake in a 375° oven 1½ hours. Remove from pan and let stand 5 minutes. Remove the wrapping and peel off the outer wax skin. Cut the cheese into wedges, and serve.
Serves 6–8.

Californian Beef-Cheese Sausages in Bacon

1 pound ground beef
1 teaspoon salt
¼ teaspoon freshly ground
black pepper
1 egg
¼ cup grated American or
Cheddar cheese
½ cup chopped pimiento-
stuffed olives

¼ cup finely chopped green
peppers
¼ cup chopped onions
¾ cup dry bread crumbs
2 tablespoons lemon juice
½ cup water
8 slices bacon, cut in half

Mix together all the ingredients but the bacon. Shape into 16 sausage shapes. Wrap a piece of bacon around each sausage, fastening it with a toothpick.

Place on a rack in a baking pan. Bake in a 375° oven 35 minutes. *Serves 4–6.*

Kibbeh Chalab

ISRAELI BEEF-POTATO CROQUETTES

⅔ cup vegetable oil
1 cup minced onions
1 pound ground beef
2 cups mashed potatoes
2 teaspoons salt
½ teaspoon freshly ground
black pepper

2 tablespoons minced
parsley
1 egg
½ cup vegetable oil

Heat 2 tablespoons of the oil in a skillet; sauté the onions 5 minutes. Cool. Mix the meat with the onions, potatoes, salt, pepper, parsley, and egg until well blended. Shape into 12 croquettes.

Heat the remaining oil in a skillet; fry the croquettes until browned on both sides and to desired degree of rareness. *Serves 4–6.*

Sacramento Beef Cups

1 pound ground beef	½ teaspoon marjoram
2 eggs, separated	2 tablespoons flour
1 teaspoon salt	Dash cayenne pepper
¼ teaspoon freshly ground	½ cup dry red wine
black pepper	½ cup canned tomato sauce

Mix together the beef, egg yolks, salt, pepper, marjoram, flour, cayenne, wine, and tomato sauce. Beat the egg whites until stiff, then fold into the meat mixture gently but thoroughly.

Divide the meat mixture among 6 buttered custard cups. Bake in a preheated 400° oven 25 minutes. Turn out carefully.

Serves 6.

Chili Sandwiches

1 tablespoon vegetable oil	¼ teaspoon freshly ground
¾ pound ground beef	black pepper
½ cup minced onions	2 teaspoons chili powder
1 clove garlic, minced	Softened butter
½ cup minced green	12 slices sandwich bread
peppers	¾ cup grated American
⅓ cup tomato sauce	cheese
1 teaspoon salt	

Heat the oil in a skillet; add the beef, onions, garlic, and green peppers. Cook over medium heat, stirring frequently, until browned. Mix in the tomato sauce, salt, pepper, and chili powder. Cook over low heat 15 minutes, stirring frequently. Taste for seasoning.

Butter 1 side of each slice of bread. Put 6 slices on a piece of waxed paper, butter side down. Spread the slices with the chili mixture to within ½ inch of the edges. Sprinkle with the cheese, and cover with the remaining bread—butter side up.

Heat a heavy skillet and brown the sandwiches on both sides.

Makes 6 sandwiches.

Australian Ground Beef Rarebit

2 tablespoons butter
¾ cup chopped onions
½ cup chopped green
  peppers
1 pound ground beef

1 teaspoon salt
Dash cayenne pepper
1 cup beer
3 cups (¾ pound) grated
  Cheddar cheese

Melt the butter in a deep skillet; sauté the onions and green peppers 5 minutes. Add the meat; cook over medium heat until browned, stirring almost constantly. Mix in the salt, cayenne pepper, and beer. Add the cheese, stirring until melted. Serve on toasted English muffins or toast. *Serves 6–8.*

Ceylon Ground Beef

4 tablespoons butter
1 cup finely chopped
  onions
2 cloves garlic, minced
3 tablespoons minced
  parsley
1½ pounds ground beef
1½ teaspoons salt

1 tablespoon curry powder
1½ pounds tomatoes, peeled
  and thinly sliced
½ cup slivered, blanched
  almonds
2 cups cooked or canned
  green peas

Melt the butter in a skillet; sauté the onions, garlic, and parsley 5 minutes. Add the meat; cook over medium heat 5 minutes, stirring frequently. Mix in the salt, curry powder, and tomatoes. Cover and cook over low heat 25 minutes, stirring occasionally. Add the almonds and peas; re-cover and cook 5 minutes longer. Serve with rice.
Serves 4.

Chinese Ground Beef

2 tablespoons vegetable oil
1 pound ground beef
1½ cups chopped onions
2 cups thinly sliced celery
½ teaspoon salt

1¼ cups beef broth
1 16-ounce can bean
   sprouts, drained
2 tablespoons cornstarch
2 tablespoons soy sauce

Heat the oil in a skillet; brown the beef and onions in it. Add the celery, salt, and beef broth; cook over low heat 10 minutes. Add the bean sprouts, then a mixture of the cornstarch and soy sauce. Cook, stirring steadily until thickened. Serve with boiled rice.

Serves 4–6.

Ground Beef Curry

4 tablespoons butter
1 cup chopped onions
1½ pounds ground beef
½ cup boiling water
1½ teaspoons salt

½ teaspoon freshly ground
   black pepper
1 tablespoon curry powder
1 egg
1 cup yogurt

Melt the butter in a skillet; sauté the onions 10 minutes. Stir in the beef until browned. Add the water, salt, pepper, and curry powder. Cover and cook over low heat 15 minutes.

Beat the egg in a bowl and blend in the yogurt. Gradually add a little of the meat mixture, stirring steadily, then mix into the skillet; cook over low heat 5 minutes, stirring almost steadily, but do not let boil. Serve with rice.

Serves 6.

Picadillo

CUBAN MEAT HASH

¼ cup olive oil
1 cup chopped onions
1 cup chopped green
  peppers
1 clove garlic, minced
1½ pounds ground pork
1½ teaspoons salt

½ teaspoon freshly ground
  black pepper
½ cup canned tomato sauce
2 tablespoons water
½ cup seedless raisins
½ cup sliced stuffed olives
2 pimientos, cut julienne

Heat the oil in a skillet; sauté the onions and green peppers
5 minutes. Mix in the garlic and pork; cook over medium heat
until browned, stirring almost constantly. Blend in the salt, pepper,
tomato sauce, water, and raisins; cook over low heat 25 minutes,
stirring frequently. Mix in the olives. Serve with rice, garnished
with the pimiento strips.
Serves 6–8.

Barbecued Beef Loaves

1½ pounds ground beef
1 egg, beaten
½ cup ice water
⅓ cup dry bread crumbs
¼ cup minced onions
2 tablespoons minced
  parsley
2 tablespoons prepared
  horseradish

1½ teaspoons salt
¼ teaspoon freshly ground
  black pepper
1 cup chili sauce
½ teaspoon dry mustard
1½ teaspoons Worcestershire
  sauce

Mix together the beef, egg, water, bread crumbs, onions, parsley,
horseradish, salt, and pepper. Shape into 6 loaves. Place in an
oiled shallow pan. Cover the tops and sides with a mixture of
the chili sauce, mustard, and Worcestershire sauce. Bake in a
350° oven 45 minutes, basting occasionally with the pan drippings. *Serves 6.*

Canadian Beef-Cheese Loaf

1½ pounds ground beef
1½ cups chopped onions
¼ cup cracker meal
1½ teaspoons salt
¼ teaspoon freshly ground
   black pepper
¼ teaspoon mace

¾ cup currants or seedless
   raisins
2 eggs, beaten
¼ cup water
1 cup grated Cheddar
   cheese

Mix together thoroughly all the ingredients but the cheese. Spread half the mixture into an oblong shape about 8×10 inches. Sprinkle the cheese over it and cover with the remaining meat mixture, pressing down the edges. Transfer to a greased baking dish. Bake in a 350° oven 1 hour.
Serves 4–6.

Hienontaat Pihvi

FINNISH GROUND BEEF LOAF SLICES

2 pounds ground beef
1 cup cooked or canned
   beets
1 cup grated raw potatoes
3 eggs, beaten
2 tablespoons chopped
   onions
2 tablespoons capers
2 teaspoons salt

½ teaspoon freshly ground
   black pepper
6 tablespoons butter
1 cup sliced onions
1 tablespoon flour
1 tablespoon tomato juice
1 tablespoon prepared
   mustard
½ cup light cream

Grind the meat, beets, and potatoes in a food chopper twice. Add the eggs, chopped onions, capers, salt, and pepper; mix well. Shape into a loaf. Cut the uncooked meat loaf carefully into ½-inch slices. Melt half the butter in a skillet and sauté the meat slices 6 minutes on each side and add butter as needed. Transfer the slices to a warm serving platter and keep warm.

278 THE COMPLETE ROUND-THE-WORLD MEAT COOKBOOK

Add the sliced onions to the skillet and let brown. Put the browned onions on top of the meat slices. Blend the flour into the skillet, stirring well to pick up all the glaze in the pan. Mix in the tomato juice and mustard, then add the cream and stir continuously until sauce thickens. Pour the sauce over the meat. *Serves 8.*

Carne Molida

VENEZUELAN BEEF LOAF

½ cup olive oil
½ cup chopped onions
½ cup white bread cubes
¼ cup milk
1½ pounds ground beef
2 eggs
½ cup grated Cheddar
    cheese
2 teaspoons salt

¾ teaspoon freshly ground
    black pepper
¼ cup flour
1½ cups sliced onions
1 cup peeled, chopped
    tomatoes
¼ teaspoon thyme
3 tablespoons minced parsley

Heat half the oil in a skillet; sauté the chopped onions in it 10 minutes. Soak the bread in the milk and mash smooth. Mix the soaked bread with the sautéed onions, the meat, eggs, cheese, 1 teaspoon of the salt, and ¼ teaspoon of the pepper. Shape the meat mixture into a loaf and sprinkle with the flour.

Heat the remaining oil in a baking dish; sauté the sliced onions in it for 5 minutes. Add the tomatoes, thyme, parsley, and the remaining salt and pepper. Place the loaf in it. Cover and bake in a 375° oven 1 hour, basting frequently. Remove cover and bake 10 minutes longer.
Serves 6–8.

Albondigón Mexicana

MEXICAN BEEF LOAF

2 pounds ground beef	⅛ teaspoon Tabasco
½ cup minced onions	2 teaspoons chili powder
½ cup minced green	2 eggs
peppers	2 tablespoons butter
1 clove garlic, minced	2 tablespoons bread crumbs
1½ teaspoons salt	2 pimientos, cut julienne

Buy beef, pork, or veal or a combination of the three meats. Mix together the meat, onions, green peppers, garlic, salt, Tabasco, chili powder, and eggs. Shape into a loaf and place in a baking dish. Dot with the butter and sprinkle with the bread crumbs. Bake in a 400° oven 1 hour. Decorate with the pimientos 5 minutes before the end of baking time. Serve hot or cold. *Serves 8–10.*

Sformato di Carne e Riso

ITALIAN RICE-BEEF MOLD

1 pound ground beef	½ cup peeled, chopped
1½ teaspoons salt	tomatoes
¾ teaspoon freshly ground	4 cups cooked, drained
black pepper	rice
½ teaspoon orégano	3 tablespoons butter
2 egg yolks	¼ cup grated Parmesan
¼ cup minced onion	cheese

Mix together thoroughly the meat, salt, ½ teaspoon of the pepper, the orégano, egg yolks, onion, and tomatoes. Mix the rice with the remaining pepper and add additional salt if necessary.

Line the bottom and sides of a buttered 2-quart mold with 3 cups of the rice. Put the meat mixture in the center and spread the remaining rice on top. Dot with butter and sprinkle with the

cheese. Cover the mold and place in a shallow pan of water. Bake in a 350° oven 45 minutes, removing the cover for the last 5 minutes. Unmold onto a heated platter and serve with a spicy tomato sauce if desired.
Serves 4–6.

Ground Beef with Fried Noodles

1 pound ground beef
2 tablespoons dry sherry
⅓ cup soy sauce
2 cups chopped red or green peppers
½ cup chopped onions
1 teaspoon salt
2 tablespoons cornstarch

Vegetable oil for deep frying
2 cups raw fine noodles
¼ cup vegetable oil
¾ cup beef broth
½ teaspoon monosodium glutamate

Mix together the beef, sherry, soy sauce, peppers, onions, salt, and cornstarch. Heat the oil to 370°. Fry the noodles in it 3 minutes, or until golden brown. Drain the noodles and place in deep dish.

Heat the ¼ cup of oil in a skillet and sauté the meat mixture in it for 10 minutes, or until browned, stirring frequently. Add the broth and monosodium glutamate, mix thoroughly, and pour over the fried noodles.
Serves 4–6.

African Beef-Spinach Pie

3 tablespoons butter
¾ cup chopped onions
1 pound ground beef
1 cup chopped spinach
¼ cup minced parsley

1¼ teaspoons salt
¼ teaspoon freshly ground black pepper
1 tablespoon curry powder
4 eggs, beaten

Melt the butter in a skillet; sauté the onions 5 minutes. Stir in the meat until browned. Mix in the spinach, parsley, salt, pepper, and curry, then the eggs. Spread in a greased 9-inch pie plate. Bake in a preheated 350° oven 35 minutes or until set. Cut in wedges.

Serves 4.

Pastel de Carne
MEXICAN HAMBURGER PIE

PASTRY:

1½ cups sifted flour	⅔ cup shortening
¾ teaspoon salt	⅓ cup ice water

Sift the flour and salt into a bowl. Cut in the shortening with a pastry blender or 2 knives until mixture looks like coarse corn meal. Add just enough of the water, tossing with a fork, until a dough is formed. Roll out ⅔ of the dough and line a 9-inch pie plate with it. Chill the pie plate and remaining dough while preparing the filling.

FILLING:

2 tablespoons vegetable oil	¼ teaspoon freshly ground
½ cup chopped onions	black pepper
½ cup chopped green	1 tablespoon chili powder
peppers	1 8-ounce can Spanish-style
1 pound ground beef	tomato sauce
1 teaspoon salt	½ cup sliced stuffed olives

Heat the oil in a skillet; sauté the onions and green peppers 5 minutes. Mix in the beef until browned. Stir in the salt, pepper, chili powder, and tomato sauce. Cook over low heat 15 minutes. Cool. Mix in the olives.

Spread the meat mixture in the lined pie plate. Roll out the remaining pastry and cut into strips. Cover the meat in a lattice design. Bake the pie in a preheated 400° oven 35 minutes or until pastry is browned. Serve cut into wedges.
Serves 4–6.

Sformato di Carne alla Siciliana

SICILIAN BEEF PIE

1½ pounds ground beef	⅓ cup cold water
¾ cup chopped onions	1 egg, beaten
1 clove garlic, minced	¼ cup dry bread crumbs
½ cup chopped green peppers	1 16-ounce can Italian-style tomatoes, drained
2 teaspoons salt	½ teaspoon orégano
¼ teaspoon freshly ground black pepper	¼ cup grated Parmesan cheese

Mix together the beef, onions, garlic, green peppers, 1¼ teaspoons of the salt, the pepper, water, egg, and bread crumbs. Spread in a greased 11-inch pie plate. Bake in a 375° oven 20 minutes. Pour off the fat. Mix the tomatoes, orégano, and remaining salt; spread over the meat and sprinkle with the cheese. Bake 20 minutes longer. Cut into wedges. *Serves 6–8.*

Babottee

SOUTH AFRICAN GROUND BEEF PIE

3 tablespoons butter	1 teaspoon salt
2 cups chopped onions	2 eggs
¾ cup white bread cubes	3 tablespoons lemon juice
¾ cup milk	3 tablespoons honey
2 pounds ground beef	¼ cup ground almonds
2 tablespoons curry powder	3 bay leaves

Melt the butter in a skillet and sauté the onions 10 minutes. Soak the bread in the milk, drain, and squeeze dry. Reserve milk and mash bread. In a bowl combine the beef, bread, sautéed onions, curry powder, salt, 1 egg, lemon juice, honey, and almonds. Mix well. Put the bay leaves on the bottom of a buttered baking dish. Cover with the meat mixture. Beat the remaining egg with the reserved milk and pour over the meat. Bake in a 350° oven 1¼ hours. Serve hot. *Serves 6–8.*

Pastichio

GREEK BEEF-MACARONI PUDDING

3 tablespoons olive oil	¾ cup grated Parmesan
1 cup chopped onions	cheese
1 pound ground beef	1 pound elbow macaroni,
¾ cup peeled, chopped	cooked and drained
tomatoes	2 tablespoons butter
2 teaspoons salt	1 tablespoon flour
½ teaspoon freshly ground	⅛ teaspoon white pepper
black pepper	1 cup milk
¼ teaspoon orégano	1 egg yolk

Heat the oil in a skillet; cook the onions and meat in it over high heat, stirring steadily, for 5 minutes. Mix in the tomatoes, 1½ teaspoons of the salt, the black pepper, and orégano; cook over low heat 5 minutes. Mix in ½ cup of the cheese. Taste for seasoning.

In a buttered 2½-quart casserole spread half the macaroni. Spread the meat mixture over it and cover with the remaining macaroni.

Melt the butter in a saucepan; gradually blend in the flour, white pepper, and remaining salt. Add the milk gradually, stirring steadily to the boiling point. Cook over low heat 5 minutes. Beat the egg yolk and remaining cheese in a bowl; add the hot sauce slowly, stirring steadily to prevent curdling. Pour over the macaroni. Bake in a 375° oven 30 minutes or until top is set and golden brown. *Serves 4–6.*

Liha-Makaromilaatikko

FINNISH BEEF PUDDING

½ pound macaroni
4 tablespoons butter
½ cup chopped onions
1 pound ground beef
½ cup beef broth
2 teaspoons salt

½ teaspoon freshly ground
black pepper
4 eggs
1½ cups milk
2 tablespoons dry bread
crumbs

Break the macaroni up into small pieces; let soak in boiling salted water for 10 minutes. Drain and rinse under cold water.

Melt 2 tablespoons of the butter in a skillet; sauté the onions until transparent. Add the beef; cook until browned, stirring frequently. Mix in the broth, salt, and pepper. Grease a 1½-quart baking dish. Make layers of the macaroni and meat, starting and ending with the macaroni.

Beat the eggs well, then mix in the milk. Pour the mixture over the macaroni. Sprinkle the bread crumbs on top and dot with the remaining butter. Place the dish in a pan and add water to it. Bake in a preheated 375° oven 45 minutes or until the top is set and lightly browned.

Serves 4–6.

Csángó Gulyás

HUNGARIAN GROUND BEEF GOULASH

3 tablespoons butter
2 cups thinly sliced onions
2 teaspoons paprika
1¼ teaspoons salt
2 pounds ground beef
1 green pepper, cut julienne

½ cup tomato sauce
1 cup beef broth
2 cups cubed, cooked
potatoes
½ cup sour cream

Melt the butter in a saucepan; sauté the onions 10 minutes. Blend in the paprika and salt, then add the beef and green pepper.

Cook over medium heat 5 minutes, stirring almost constantly. Stir in the tomato sauce and broth. Cover and cook over low heat 20 minutes. Add the potato cubes; cook 5 minutes longer. Stir in the sour cream. Taste for seasoning. *Serves 6–8.*

Youverlakia

ISTANBUL GROUND BEEF IN EGG SAUCE

3 tablespoons butter	¼ teaspoon nutmeg
½ cup chopped onions	¼ cup beef broth
1½ pounds ground beef	2 egg yolks
1 pound mushrooms, sliced	2 tablespoons lemon juice
1¼ teaspoons salt	2 tablespoons dry sherry
½ teaspoon freshly ground	
black pepper	

Melt the butter in a skillet; sauté the onions 5 minutes. Add the beef and mushrooms; cook over high heat 5 minutes, stirring almost constantly. Mix in the salt, pepper, nutmeg, and broth; cook over low heat 10 minutes.

Beat the egg yolks, lemon juice, and sherry in a bowl. Add a little meat mixture, stirring steadily to prevent curdling. Return to the skillet; heat but do not let boil. Serve with rice or noodles. *Serves 4–6.*

Moussaka

BEEF-EGGPLANT CASSEROLE, NEAR EAST STYLE

1 medium-sized eggplant	½ teaspoon freshly ground
4 teaspoons salt	black pepper
¼ cup flour	3 tablespoons minced parsley
3 tablespoons vegetable oil	½ teaspoon orégano
2 pounds ground beef	2 cups drained canned
½ cup chopped onions	tomatoes

Peel the eggplant and cut lengthwise, then crosswise in half-inch slices. Sprinkle the eggplant with 2 teaspoons of the salt and let stand 30 minutes. Drain well. Dip the slices in the flour, then brown in the oil. Mix together the beef, onions, pepper, parsley, orégano, and remaining salt. In a greased 2-quart casserole, arrange successive layers of the eggplant, beef, and tomatoes, ending with the tomatoes. Bake in a 350° oven 1 hour.
Serves 6–8.

Scottish Minced Beef

4 tablespoons butter
2 pounds ground beef
3 tablespoons boiling water
1½ cups chopped onions

1½ teaspoons salt
½ teaspoon freshly ground
   black pepper

Melt the butter in a skillet; add the meat and cook over high heat, stirring constantly, until browned. Mix in the water, onions, salt, and pepper. Cover and cook 20 minutes over low heat, stirring frequently.
Serves 6–8.

Southern Beef-Batter Pudding

1½ pounds ground beef
2½ teaspoons salt
½ teaspoon freshly ground
   black pepper
¼ cup chili sauce
¾ cup minced onions

2 tablespoons minced parsley
5 eggs
1½ cups sifted flour
1½ teaspoons baking powder
1½ cups milk
3 tablespoons melted butter

With the hand mix together the beef, 1½ teaspoons of the salt, the pepper, chili sauce, onions, parsley, and 1 egg. Shape into 1-inch balls and arrange evenly in a greased baking pan 12× 18 inches.

Sift together the flour, baking powder, and the remaining salt. Beat the remaining eggs well, then beat in the milk and melted butter. Add the flour mixture, beating until smooth. Pour over the meat balls. Bake in a preheated 350° oven 50 minutes or until set and browned. Cut into squares. *Serves 4–6.*

Vietnamese Ground Beef

3 tablespoons vegetable oil	1 teaspoon salt
¾ cup flaked coconut	1 tablespoon curry powder
1 pound ground beef	2 tablespoons lemon juice
½ cup finely chopped onions	1 tablespoon plum jelly
	1 tablespoon soy sauce
1 clove garlic, minced	¼ cup water

Heat 1 tablespoon of the oil in a skillet; add the coconut and stir over low heat until lightly browned. Remove. Heat the remaining oil in the skillet; add the meat, onions, and garlic. Cook over medium heat, stirring frequently, until browned. Mix in the salt, curry powder, lemon juice, jelly, soy sauce, and water. Cook over low heat 10 minutes. Mix in the coconut. Serve on rice or noodles. *Serves 4.*

Note: Equal parts of plum jelly and lemon juice are used as a substitute for tamarind, not normally available.

Yorkshire Pudding with Ground Beef

1 cup sifted flour	3 tablespoons grated onion
2 teaspoons salt	½ teaspoon freshly ground black pepper
⅛ teaspoon nutmeg	
Dash cayenne pepper	1 clove garlic, minced
1 cup milk	1 tablespoon minced parsley
2 eggs	3 tablespoons vegetable oil
1½ pounds ground beef	

Sift together the flour, ½ teaspoon of the salt, the nutmeg, and cayenne pepper. Gradually beat in the milk, then 1 egg at a time. Chill 30 minutes, then beat with a rotary beater until frothy.

Combine the beef, onion, pepper, garlic, parsley, and remaining salt. Mix together thoroughly. Rub a shallow pan 8×12 inches with the oil. Place in a 425° oven until oil bubbles. Pour half the batter into it. Quickly spread the meat mixture over it, and pour remaining batter over the meat. Bake in a 425° oven 15 minutes. Reduce heat to 350° and bake 20 minutes longer, or until puffed and browned. Cut into squares and serve immediately with a mushroom or tomato sauce. *Serves 6–8.*

Aardappel-Purée met Bief

DUTCH BEEF-POTATO ROLL

¾ cup white bread cubes	¼ teaspoon freshly ground
½ cup milk	black pepper
3 tablespoons butter	¼ teaspoon marjoram
½ cup chopped onions	3 tablespoons dry bread
1 clove garlic, minced	crumbs
1 pound ground beef	2 cups hot seasoned mashed
1 teaspoon salt	potatoes
	2 tablespoons minced parsley

Soak the bread in the milk for 10 minutes. Drain well and mash smooth.

Heat 1 tablespoon of the butter in a skillet; sauté the onions and garlic 10 minutes. Mix together the beef, soaked bread, sautéed onions, salt, pepper, and marjoram. Sprinkle the bread crumbs on a piece of waxed paper. Spread the meat mixture onto it and form a rectangle about ½ inch thick. Mix the potatoes with the parsley and spread over the meat. Lift the paper at one end and roll up the meat like a jelly roll.

Melt the remaining butter in a shallow baking pan. Place the roll in it. Bake in a 375° oven 50 minutes, basting a few times with the pan juices. Serve cut into 1-inch slices, with a mushroom sauce if desired. *Serves 4–6.*

Beef Ring

2 pounds ground beef
½ cup grated onions
2 cups fresh bread crumbs
⅜ pound (1½ sticks) soft
  butter
2½ teaspoons salt

½ teaspoon freshly ground
  black pepper
½ teaspoon dry mustard
2 tablespoons minced parsley
½ cup chili sauce

With the hand mix together thoroughly all the ingredients but
the chili sauce. Pack into an oiled 9-inch ring mold. Spread the
chili sauce on top. Bake in a 400° oven 45 minutes or until meat
is browned and shrunk away from the sides of the pan. Run a knife
around the edges and turn out onto a hot serving dish. Fill the
center with creamed vegetables or mushrooms.
Serves 8–10.

Polpettone alla Siciliana

SICILIAN BEEF ROLL

1½ pounds ground beef
½ cup tomato juice
2 eggs, beaten
½ cup soft bread crumbs
1½ teaspoons salt
½ teaspoon freshly ground
  black pepper

¼ teaspoon orégano
2 cloves garlic, minced
3 tablespoons minced parsley
8 slices cooked ham
8 slices mozzarella cheese

Mix together all the ingredients but the ham and cheese. On a
large piece of wax paper, pat out the meat mixture into a
rectangle 10×16 inches. Arrange the ham and cheese on it, then
roll up like a jelly roll, lifting the paper as you roll. Place the roll
in a greased baking dish. Bake in a 350° oven 1 hour. Let the
roll stand at room temperature for 15 minutes before slicing.
Serves 6–8.

Pita s Mesom

YUGOSLAVIAN BEEF AND PASTRY ROLL

1 tablespoon vegetable oil	2 tablespoons minced parsley
1 pound ground beef	1 10½-ounce can beef
½ cup finely chopped	gravy
onions	1¾ cups sifted flour
½ cup chopped mushrooms	2½ teaspoons baking
2 teaspoons salt	powder
¼ teaspoon freshly ground	3 tablespoons minced parsley
black pepper	5 tablespoons shortening
¼ teaspoon dry mustard	⅔ cup milk
¼ cup chopped black	
olives	

Heat the oil in a skillet; add the beef, onions, and mushrooms. Cook, stirring frequently, for 10 minutes. Mix in 1 teaspoon of the salt, the pepper, mustard, olives, 2 tablespoons of parsley, and ¼ cup of the gravy; cook over low heat 5 minutes. Cool.

Sift the flour, remaining salt, and baking powder into a bowl. Mix in 3 tablespoons of parsley, then cut in the shortening until the consistency of coarse corn meal. Stir in the milk until a ball of dough is formed. Turn out onto a lightly floured surface and knead lightly for a few seconds.

Roll out the dough into a rectangle 10×14 inches. Spread the meat mixture on the dough to within ½ inch of the edges. Roll up like a jelly roll. Brush the edge with water and press together. Place on a greased baking pan. Bake in a preheated 400° oven 30 minutes or until browned. Heat the remaining gravy and serve with the sliced roll.

Serves 4–5.

Ground Beef Stroganoff

4 tablespoons butter
¾ cup chopped onions
1½ pounds ground beef
1 pound mushrooms, sliced
2 teaspoons salt

½ teaspoon freshly ground
   black pepper
½ cup beef broth
1 cup sour cream
2 tablespoons minced chives
   or parsley

Melt the butter in a skillet; sauté the onions over low heat 10 minutes. Add the beef and mushrooms; cook over medium heat, stirring frequently until browned. Add the salt, pepper, and broth; cook over low heat 10 minutes. Mix in the sour cream; heat but do not let boil. Serve on noodles, rice, or toast, sprinkled with the chives or parsley.
Serves 6–8.

Kaulo

GREEK LAMB ROLLS

1½ pounds ground lean
   lamb
¾ cup soft bread crumbs
¾ cup tomato sauce
3 tablespoons minced parsley
¾ teaspoon ground cumin
2 cloves garlic, minced

2½ teaspoons salt
¾ teaspoon freshly ground
   black pepper
3 tablespoons vegetable oil
2 8-ounce cans tomato sauce
¼ cup dry white wine
2 tablespoons honey

Mix together the lamb, bread crumbs, tomato sauce, parsley, cumin, garlic, 1½ teaspoons of the salt, and ½ teaspoon of the pepper. Shape into 12 rolls about 4 inches long by 1 inch in diameter. Heat the oil in a deep skillet and brown the rolls on all sides. Add the tomato sauce, wine, honey, and remaining salt and pepper. Bring to a boil, cover, and cook over low heat 20 minutes. Serve with rice.
Serves 6–8.

Moussaka à la Grecque

GREEK LAMB AND EGGPLANT LAYERS

2 medium-sized eggplants
⅜ pound (1½ sticks) butter
3½ teaspoons salt
1½ cups chopped onions
1½ pounds ground lean lamb
1 tablespoon tomato paste
⅓ cup dry red wine
½ teaspoon freshly ground black pepper

¼ teaspoon cinnamon
¼ cup chopped parsley
3 tablespoons flour
2 cups hot milk
1 cup cottage cheese, drained
2 eggs, beaten
⅛ teaspoon nutmeg
¾ cup dry bread crumbs
¾ cup grated Parmesan cheese

Peel the eggplants and cut into slices ½ inch thick. Melt 4 tablespoons of the butter in a skillet; brown the eggplant slices on both sides. Remove and sprinkle with 1 teaspoon of the salt.

In the same skillet, melt 4 tablespoons of the remaining butter; sauté the onions 10 minutes. Add the meat; cook 10 minutes, stirring frequently. Stir in the tomato paste, wine, pepper, cinnamon, parsley, and 1½ teaspoons of the remaining salt. Cook over low heat, stirring frequently, until mixture is fairly dry. Taste for seasoning. Cool.

Melt the remaining butter in a saucepan, blend in the flour and remaining salt. Add the milk, stirring steadily to the boiling point, then cook 5 minutes longer. Remove from the heat, cool 5 minutes, then mix in the cottage cheese, eggs, and nutmeg.

Grease a baking pan 8×12 inches, and dust lightly with some bread crumbs. Arrange layers of the eggplant and meat, sprinkling each layer with bread crumbs and Parmesan cheese. Start and end with eggplant. Pour the sauce over the top. Bake in a preheated 375° oven 1 hour, or until the custard top is set and golden brown. Let stand 30 minutes at room temperature before cutting into squares.

Serves 6–8.

Soutzoulakia

GREEK GROUND LAMB AND GREEN BEANS

½ cup olive oil
2 cups chopped onions
1 pound ground lean
 lamb
1½ cups canned tomatoes
1 cup water
1½ teaspoons salt

½ teaspoon freshly ground
 black pepper
1 bay leaf
2 tablespoons minced parsley
1½ pounds green beans or
 2 packages frozen,
 thawed

Heat the oil in a saucepan; sauté the onions 5 minutes. Mix
in the lamb until browned. Add the tomatoes, water, salt, pepper,
bay leaf, and parsley. Bring to a boil and add the beans; cover
and cook over low heat 30 minutes. *Serves 4–6.*

Daoud Basha

ARABIAN LAMB BALLS

2 pounds lean lamb,
 ground twice
2½ teaspoons salt
1 teaspoon freshly ground
 black pepper
½ cup ice water
4 tablespoons butter

2 cups finely chopped
 onions
½ cup tomato sauce
¼ cup pine nuts or sliced
 almonds
¼ cup minced parsley

Combine the lamb, 1½ teaspoons of the salt, and ½ teaspoon of
the pepper in a chopping bowl. Gradually add the water, chopping
all the time. Form the mixture into 1-inch balls.

Melt the butter in a large skillet. Fry the meat balls until well
browned on all sides. Add the onions, tomato sauce, and remaining salt and pepper. Cover, and cook over low heat for 25
minutes, stirring occasionally. Add the nuts and cook 5 minutes
longer. Watch carefully and add a little boiling water if necessary to prevent burning. Mix in the parsley. *Serves 6–8.*

Kibbi ib Sa-Nee-Yee

IRAQI LAMB LOAF

½ cup white bread cubes
½ cup water
1½ pounds ground lean
  lamb
¼ cup finely chopped
  celery leaves
¼ cup minced parsley
¾ cup finely chopped green
  onions (scallions)

¼ cup pine nuts or slivered
  almonds
1½ teaspoons salt
½ teaspoon freshly ground
  black pepper
¼ teaspoon cinnamon
2 eggs, beaten
2 tablespoons tomato paste
2 tablespoons vegetable oil

Crumble the bread and soak in the water 5 minutes. Mash smooth, then drain. Mix together the bread, meat, celery leaves, parsley, green onions, almonds, salt, pepper, cinnamon, eggs, and tomato paste. Shape into a loaf; place in an oiled baking pan. Bake in a 350° oven 1 hour. Serve hot or cold.

Serves 6–8.

Kibbe

LEBANESE BAKED GROUND LAMB

½ pound cracked wheat
  (bourghol)
1 clove garlic, minced
3 onions
1½ pounds boneless lean
  lamb, ground three times

1 teaspoon salt
6 tablespoons olive oil
¼ teaspoon cinnamon
¾ cup coarsely chopped
  walnuts

Soak the cracked wheat (available in specialty food shops) in warm water 10 minutes. Drain, then knead for 1 minute. Grind in a food chopper with the garlic and 2 of the onions. Combine in a chopping bowl with half the ground lamb and ½ teaspoon of the salt; chop until very fine. Reserve. Chop the remaining onion.

Heat 2 tablespoons of the oil in a skillet and sauté the chopped onion, the remaining ground lamb, remaining salt, and the cinnamon 20 minutes, stirring frequently. Heat 2 tablespoons of the oil in another pan and sauté the walnuts 5 minutes, stirring frequently. Drain and add to the sautéed lamb, mixing well. Rub an 8-inch-square baking dish with 1 tablespoon of the oil. Pat half the reserved wheat-lamb mixture on the bottom of the dish. Cover with the lamb-walnut mixture. Cover with the remaining wheat-lamb mixture, pressing down firmly. Sprinkle with the remaining oil. With a sharp knife, cut in slices, cutting down to the bottom of the dish before baking. Bake in a 350° oven 45 minutes. *Serves 6–8.*

Kufta

EGYPTIAN LAMB CROQUETTES

2 pounds ground lean lamb
¾ cup minced onions
1½ teaspoons salt
⅛ teaspoon cayenne pepper
¼ teaspoon orégano
3 tablespoons chopped parsley

2 eggs, beaten
½ cup milk
1½ cups dry bread crumbs
¼ pound (1 stick) butter

Combine the lamb, onions, salt, pepper, orégano, parsley, eggs, milk, and 1 cup of the bread crumbs. Mix thoroughly and shape into 16 croquettes. Dip the croquettes in the remaining bread crumbs. Melt half the butter in a skillet and fry the croquettes slowly over low heat until browned on all sides, about 20 minutes, adding more butter as needed. *Serves 8.*

Kebabs

MIDDLE EAST LAMB CROQUETTES

1 cup cracked wheat	½ teaspoon freshly ground
1 pound ground very lean	black pepper
lamb	¼ teaspoon cinnamon
½ cup grated onion	2 tablespoons vegetable oil
1 teaspoon salt	

Cover the wheat (available in specialty food shops) with water and let stand 2 hours. Pick up the wheat several times and rub between the hands. Drain well.

Mix the wheat with the meat, onion, salt, pepper, and cinnamon. Put through a food chopper. (If the mixture is stiff, knead in a tablespoon or two of ice water.) Shape into 12 patties.

Heat the oil in a skillet; sauté the patties over very low heat 10 minutes on each side.

Serves 4–6.

VARIATION:

Kebabs in Tomato Sauce

Shape the meat mixture into ½-inch balls. Arrange in an oiled casserole. Cover with a mixture of:

1 cup thinly sliced onions	1¼ teaspoons salt
1 green pepper, cut julienne	½ teaspoon freshly ground
1 29-ounce can tomatoes,	black pepper
drained	

Bake in a 350° oven 50 minutes. Serve with rice.
Serves 4–6.

Keema Huzoor Pasandh

DELHI GROUND LAMB CURRY

1½ pounds ground lean
  lamb
½ cup minced onions
2 cloves garlic, minced
2 teaspoons salt
6 tablespoons butter

¾ cup thinly sliced onions
1½ tablespoons curry
  powder
1 tablespoon tomato paste
2 cups yogurt

Mix together the lamb, minced onions, garlic, and 1¼ teaspoons of the salt. Shape into 1-inch balls.

Melt the butter in a heavy saucepan; brown the sliced onions in it. Add the meat balls; sauté until browned on all sides. Mix together the curry powder, tomato paste, yogurt, and remaining salt; add to the meat balls. Cook over low heat 30 minutes, stirring frequently. Serve with rice.

Serves 6–8.

Ma Ho

CHINESE PORK-STUFFED ORANGES

8 large oranges
2 tablespoons vegetable oil
1 tablespoon minced garlic
1½ pounds ground lean
  pork
¼ cup chopped peanuts
¼ teaspoon ground
  coriander

½ teaspoon dried ground
  chili peppers
2 teaspoons soy sauce
2 tablespoons dry sherry
¾ teaspoon salt

Wash the unpeeled oranges and make four cuts in each running from the top to within ½-inch of the bottom. Spread the oranges open. Remove the pits.

Heat the oil in a skillet; sauté the garlic 2 minutes. Add the pork, peanuts, coriander, chili peppers, soy sauce, sherry, and salt.

Cook over low heat 15 minutes, stirring frequently. Stuff the oranges with the mixture.

Arrange the oranges in a baking pan. Add the water and bake in a 350° oven 15 minutes.

Serves 4–8.

Chinese Batter-Fried Pork Balls

1 pound finely ground pork	¼ teaspoon white pepper
½ cup finely chopped green onions (scallions)	2 eggs
	¼ cup flour
½ cup chopped water chestnuts	Vegetable oil for deep frying
2¼ teaspoons salt	

Chop together the pork, green onions, water chestnuts, 1¼ teaspoons of the salt, and the pepper until very fine. Shape into marble-sized balls. Chill 30 minutes.

Beat together the eggs and remaining salt. Stir in the flour until smooth. Dip the balls in the mixture. Heat the oil to 365°. Fry the balls in it 10 minutes, turning to brown all sides. Drain well.

Serves 4, or pierce with cocktail picks and serve as a hot hors d'oeuvre.

Chinese Sweet and Sour Pork Balls

1 pound ground lean pork	4 tablespoons cornstarch
¼ cup chopped green onions (scallions)	2¼ cups vegetable oil
	¾ cup sliced, cooked carrots
½ teaspoon ground ginger	1 package frozen snow pea pods
½ teaspoon monosodium glutamate	
	5 tablespoons sugar
1 egg	4 tablespoons vinegar
2 tablespoons dry sherry	½ cup beef broth
5 tablespoons soy sauce	1 cup water
1 teaspoon salt	

Mix together the pork, green onions, ginger, monosodium glutamate, egg, 1 tablespoon of the sherry, 2 tablespoons of the soy sauce, ½ teaspoon of the salt, and 2 tablespoons of the cornstarch. Shape the mixture into walnut-sized balls. Heat 2 cups of the oil until it bubbles. Fry the balls until browned. Drain.

Heat the remaining oil in a skillet; sauté the carrots and snow pea pods 3 minutes. In a saucepan combine the sugar, vinegar, beef broth, and the remaining sherry, soy sauce, and salt. Pour over the vegetables and bring to a boil, then stir in the remaining cornstarch, mixed with the water, until thickened. Add the meat balls and cook 5 minutes.

Serves 4–6.

Pork Balls, Thai Style

1½ cups white bread cubes	½ cup cornstarch
1 cup milk	½ cup sesame seeds
2 pounds ground pork	6 tablespoons butter
3 eggs, separated	½ cup minced onions
½ cup minced, sautéed onions	1 cup sliced onions
	2 cups beef broth
2 teaspoons salt	1 bay leaf
½ teaspoon freshly ground black pepper	1 teaspoon ground coriander
	1 clove garlic, minced
½ teaspoon ground cumin	3 tablespoons minced parsley

Soak the bread in the milk; drain and mash smooth. Mix together the soaked bread, pork, egg yolks, sautéed onions, salt, pepper, and cumin. Beat the egg whites until stiff and fold into the meat mixture. Shape into 1-inch balls.

Mix together the cornstarch and sesame seeds, and roll the balls in the mixture. Melt the butter in a skillet; brown the balls. Add the minced and sliced onions and continue browning. Add the broth, bay leaf, coriander, and garlic. Cover and cook over low heat 25 minutes. Taste for seasoning, discard bay leaf, and sprinkle with the parsley.

Serves 6–8.

Svenska Köttbullar

SWEDISH PORK BALLS

¾ pound potatoes	½ teaspoon freshly ground
1 pound ground lean pork	black pepper
3 eggs, beaten	½ cup heavy cream
1 cup finely chopped onions	¼ pound (1 stick) butter
2 teaspoons salt	

Peel and grate the potatoes. Mix together the grated potatoes, ground pork, eggs, onions, salt, pepper, and cream. Mix well. Shape into 1-inch balls. Melt the butter in a skillet. Fry the balls in it over low heat 25 minutes, or until no pink remains in the pork. Shake the pan frequently.
Serves 4–6.

Puerco con Huevos

MEXICAN SPICY PORK WITH SCRAMBLED EGGS

2 tablespoons olive oil	½ teaspoon orégano
1 pound ground lean pork	1½ teaspoons salt
2 cloves garlic	3 tablespoons tomato juice
¼ teaspoon dried ground	4 eggs, beaten
chili peppers	

Heat the oil in a skillet; add the pork and cook over high heat, stirring almost constantly, until browned. Mix in the garlic, chili peppers, orégano, salt, and tomato juice. Cook over low heat 15 minutes, stirring occasionally. Pour the eggs over the mixture and cook, stirring steadily, until the eggs set.
Serves 4–6.

Sopa Seca

PERUVIAN PORK STEW

½ cup olive oil
2½ cups chopped onions
1½ pounds ground lean
  pork
2 cloves garlic, minced
1½ cups chopped fresh
  tomatoes
2 cans chick-peas, drained
3½ teaspoons salt
¼ teaspoon dried ground
  chili peppers

2 cups raw rice
½ cup chopped green
  peppers
1 16-ounce can tomatoes
2 cups boiling water
½ teaspoon freshly ground
  black pepper
½ teaspoon orégano
½ cup seedless raisins
½ cup sliced almonds

Heat half the oil in a saucepan; brown half the onions in it. Mix in the pork and half the garlic until browned. Add the fresh tomatoes, chick-peas, 1½ teaspoons of the salt, and the chili peppers. Cover and cook over low heat 45 minutes. Prepare the rice meanwhile.

Heat the remaining oil in a saucepan; sauté the rice, green peppers, and remaining onions until browned. Mix in the canned tomatoes, boiling water, pepper, orégano, and the remaining garlic and salt. Cover and cook over low heat for 25 minutes. Mix in the raisins and almonds. Combine with the meat mixture.

Serves 6–8.

Musaca cu Tatei

RUMANIAN PORK AND POTATO PUDDING

1 slice white bread, trimmed
¼ cup milk
1 pound boneless lean pork,
  ground twice
½ cup chopped parsley
1 cup grated onion
3 teaspoons salt
½ teaspoon freshly ground
  black pepper

4 tablespoons butter
1 pound potatoes, peeled
  and thinly sliced
2 eggs, beaten
½ cup heavy cream
⅓ cup grated Parmesan
cheese

Soak the bread in the milk for 5 minutes; mash smooth. Mix together the bread, pork, 2 tablespoons of the parsley, 2 tablespoons of the onion, 1½ teaspoons of the salt, and ¼ teaspoon of the pepper.

In a buttered casserole, arrange successive layers of the potatoes and pork mixture; sprinkle the potato layer with some of the remaining parsley and onions and dot with butter. Make as many layers as possible, starting and ending with the potatoes. Cover and bake in a 350° oven for 35 minutes.

Beat the eggs with the cream, cheese, and remaining salt and pepper. Pour over the potatoes and bake uncovered 20 minutes longer, or until the egg mixture is set and lightly browned on top. *Serves 4–6.*

Kroppkakor

SWEDISH PORK DUMPLINGS

1½ pounds potatoes	**¼ cup chopped onions**
1 egg yolk, beaten	**¼ teaspoon freshly ground**
5 teaspoons salt	**black pepper**
½ cup flour	**3 quarts water**
1 tablespoon vegetable oil	**Melted butter**
½ pound ground lean pork	

Cook the unpeeled potatoes in boiling salted water 20 minutes or until tender. Drain, peel, mash, and cool. Beat in the egg yolk and 1½ teaspoons of the salt. Turn out onto a floured board. Knead in the flour.

Shape the potato dough into a long roll and cut into 10 even pieces. Flatten each piece slightly and make a depression in the middle.

Heat the oil in a skillet; sauté the pork and onions until no pink remains in the pork. Mix in ½ teaspoon of the salt and the pepper. Put 1 tablespoon of this mixture into the depression of each dumpling. Fold over the dough and shape into balls. Bring the water to a boil, add the remaining salt. Drop the dumplings into water and cook 10 minutes. Don't crowd the pan. Drain and serve with melted butter. *Makes 10 dumplings.*

Mousse au Jambon

HAM MOUSSE

2 envelopes (2 tablespoons)
 gelatin
⅔ cup cold water
4 egg yolks
¾ teaspoon salt
Dash Tabasco
2 teaspoons dry mustard

1¼ cups beef broth
2 cups ground cooked ham
¼ cup minced onions
½ cup mayonnaise
½ cup heavy cream,
 whipped

Sprinkle the gelatin into the cold water to soften. Combine
the egg yolks, salt, Tabasco, and mustard in the top of a double
boiler. Beat until thick and lemon-colored. Add the broth. Place
over boiling water and cook, stirring constantly until mixture
thickens and coats a spoon. Stir in the softened gelatin until
dissolved. Cool. Fold in the ham, onions, mayonnaise, and cream.
Pour into an oiled 2-quart mold. Chill until firm. Unmold onto
shredded lettuce. *Serves 8.*

Soufflé au Jambon

HAM SOUFFLÉ

1 cup light cream
½ cup chicken broth
6 tablespoons quick-cooking
 tapioca
½ teaspoon salt
¼ teaspoon freshly ground
 black pepper
½ teaspoon nutmeg

1 tablespoon grated onion
½ teaspoon dry mustard
1 cup ground cooked ham
2 tablespoons minced
 parsley
3 eggs, separated
Grated Parmesan cheese
(optional)

In a saucepan, combine the cream, broth, tapioca, salt, pepper,
nutmeg, and onion. Cook over medium heat, stirring constantly,
until the mixture boils. Remove from the heat and stir in the
mustard, ham, and parsley. Cool 10 minutes.

Beat the egg yolks in a bowl; add the ham mixture, stirring steadily. Fold in the egg whites. Turn into a greased 1½-quart soufflé dish. Sprinkle the top with grated Parmesan cheese if desired. Bake in a preheated 350° oven 45 minutes or until browned and firm. Serve at once.

Serves 4–6.

Schönbrunner Lunch

AUSTRIAN HAM PIE

¼ pound (1 stick) butter	1 pound ground cooked
6 eggs, separated	ham
½ cup sour cream	1 cup cooked or canned
¾ teaspoon salt	green peas
4 tablespoons flour	1 cup sliced sautéed
¾ cup grated Parmesan	mushrooms
cheese	

Cream the butter, then beat in the egg yolks, sour cream, salt, flour, and 2 tablespoons of the cheese. Beat the egg whites until stiff, then fold into the yolk mixture. Spread half the mixture in a 2-quart buttered baking dish. Make successive layers of the ham, peas, and mushrooms, sprinkling each layer with some of the remaining cheese. Cover with the remaining egg mixture.

Place in a cold oven, turn on, and set at 350°. Bake 50 minutes, or until set and browned. Serve immediately, directly from the dish.

Serves 4–6.

Hachis

DANISH HAM HASH

2 tablespoons butter	1 teaspoon salt
¾ cup chopped onions	¼ teaspoon paprika
1 teaspoon flour	1 tablespoon cognac
1 tablespoon chopped sweet pickle	1 teaspoon meat extract
	3 cups ground cooked ham
2 teaspoons sugar	6 fried eggs

Melt the butter in a skillet; sauté the onions 5 minutes. Blend in the flour until browned. Add a mixture of the pickle, sugar, salt, paprika, cognac, and meat extract. Mix well, add the ham, and mix again. Cook over medium heat 10 minutes, stirring occasionally. Heap in 6 mounds and place a fried egg on top of each mound.
Serves 6.

Australian Veal Loaf

1½ pounds ground lean veal	½ cup chopped green peppers
1½ teaspoons salt	½ cup chopped onions
½ teaspoon freshly ground black pepper	½ cup chopped celery
	1½ cups grated carrots
¼ cup dry bread crumbs	¼ teaspoon dry mustard
1 egg, beaten	⅔ cup chili sauce

Combine the veal, salt, pepper, bread crumbs, egg, green peppers, onions, celery, carrots, mustard, and ½ cup of the chili sauce. Grease an 11-inch loaf pan and pack the mixture into it. Spread the remaining chili sauce on top. Bake in a 350° oven 1¼ hours. Slice and serve hot or cold.
Serves 6–8.

Pain de Veau

BELGIAN VEAL LOAF

2 pounds ground lean veal
¼ cup finely chopped
onions
1 egg, beaten
1 cup sour cream
1 cup soft bread crumbs

3 tablespoons minced
parsley
2 teaspoons salt
½ teaspoon white pepper
⅛ teaspoon nutmeg
4 tablespoons melted butter

Using the hand, mix all the ingredients together (reserve 2 tablespoons of the butter). Pack into a greased 9-inch loaf pan and brush with the remaining butter. Bake in a 350° oven 1½ hours. Let stand 5 minutes before turning out onto a heated serving dish. Slice and serve with creamed spinach and potato balls. *Serves 6–8.*

Mousse de Veau

FRENCH VEAL MOUSSE

2 pounds ground lean veal
1½ teaspoons salt
½ teaspoon white pepper

3 egg whites
1½ cups light cream

Put the meat in a mixing bowl, and with an electric mixer or a wooden spoon beat in the salt, pepper, and unbeaten egg whites; gradually beat in the cream. Turn the mixture into a well-greased 9-inch ring mold. Cover the mold with a piece of greased waxed paper or foil, and place in a pan containing 1 inch of boiling water. Bake in a 350° oven 45 minutes or until set. Remove from oven and let stand 5 minutes. Run a knife around the edges and turn out onto a heated serving dish. Serve with hollandaise, mushroom, or tomato sauce. *Serves 8–10.*

Mitzri

EGYPTIAN VEAL BURGERS

1½ pounds ground veal	2 tablespoons minced parsley
2 teaspoons salt	2 eggs, beaten
½ teaspoon freshly ground black pepper	½ cup dry bread crumbs
	½ cup vegetable oil

Mix together the meat, salt, pepper, and the parsley. Shape into 12 flat patties. Dip in the eggs, and then in the bread crumbs, coating them thoroughly.

Heat the oil in a skillet; sauté the patties until cooked through and browned on both sides, about 10 minutes on each side. *Serves 4–6.*

VARIATION:

Serve with a fried egg and 2 anchovy fillets on top of each patty.

Fricadelles de Veau à la Crème

FRENCH VEAL CROQUETTES WITH CREAM SAUCE

1 cup white bread cubes	¼ cup minced parsley
½ cup light cream	½ cup flour
1 pound ground lean veal	3 tablespoons vegetable oil
1¼ teaspoons salt	4 tablespoons butter
½ teaspoon white pepper	½ cup dry white wine
⅛ teaspoon nutmeg	½ teaspoon marjoram
1 egg, beaten	½ cup heavy cream

Soak the bread in the light cream until very soft, then mash smooth. Mix with the veal, salt, pepper, nutmeg, egg, and 3 tablespoons of the parsley. Shape into 8 croquettes. Dip in the flour.

Heat the oil and 2 tablespoons of the butter in a large skillet. Brown the croquettes in it on all sides. Pour off most of the fat, cover the skillet, and cook over low heat 15 minutes, turning the patties once.

Transfer the croquettes to a hot serving platter. Pour off the fat. Add the wine and marjoram. Bring to a boil, scraping the bottom of any browned particles. Add the heavy cream; cook over high heat 3 minutes. Stir in small pieces of the remaining butter until melted. Pour over the patties and sprinkle with the remaining parsley.

Serves 4.

Kalbfleischhaschee

GERMAN-STYLE GROUND VEAL

2 tablespoons vegetable oil	¼ teaspoon fennel seeds
1 cup chopped onions	1 tablespoon flour
1½ pounds ground lean veal	½ cup canned tomato sauce
1½ teaspoons salt	1 cup sour cream
½ teaspoon freshly ground black pepper	2 tablespoons minced parsley

Heat the oil in a skillet; sauté the onions 5 minutes. Add the veal; cook over medium heat, stirring almost steadily, until browned. Mix in the salt, pepper, fennel, and flour, then the tomato sauce. Cover and cook over low heat 20 minutes. Mix in the sour cream; heat but do not let boil. Taste for seasoning and sprinkle with the parsley.

Serves 6–8.

Gnocchi di Vitello

VEAL DUMPLINGS, NORTH ITALIAN STYLE

1 pound ground lean veal
¼ pound prosciutto (ham)
or cooked ham, finely
chopped
4 tablespoons grated
Parmesan cheese
2 eggs, beaten

2 teaspoons salt
1 cup dry bread crumbs
6 tablespoons butter
4 tablespoons dry vermouth
1 pound tomatoes, chopped
¼ teaspoon freshly ground
black pepper

Mix together the veal, prosciutto or ham, cheese, eggs, and 1 teaspoon of the salt. Shape tablespoons of the mixture into little balls. Roll in the bread crumbs.

Melt the butter in a saucepan and brown the balls on all sides. Add the wine; cook until absorbed, add the tomatoes, pepper, and remaining salt; cook over low heat 30 minutes. Taste for seasoning. Serve with steamed rice or noodles and a bowl of grated cheese. *Serves 4–6.*

Kotlety Cielęce Siekane

POLISH VEAL PATTIES

5 tablespoons butter
¾ cup chopped onions
1½ cups diced bread
1 cup milk
1½ pounds ground lean
veal

1½ teaspoons salt
¼ teaspoon white pepper
2 tablespoons minced parsley
3 eggs
¾ cup dry bread crumbs

Melt 2 tablespoons of the butter in a skillet; brown the onions in it. Soak the bread in the milk and mash until smooth. Mix together the browned onions, mashed bread, veal, salt, pepper, parsley, and 1 egg. Shape into 12 patties. Dip the patties in the remaining eggs, beaten, and then in the bread crumbs.

Heat the remaining butter in a skillet. Sauté the patties over low heat 15 minutes on each side. *Serves 6.*

Teftely

RUSSIAN GROUND VEAL WITH GREEN BEANS

2 tablespoons olive oil	¼ teaspoon fennel seeds
1 cup chopped onions	1 tablespoon flour
1½ pounds ground lean veal	½ cup canned tomato sauce
1½ teaspoons salt	1½ pounds green beans, cooked and drained
½ teaspoon freshly ground black pepper	1 cup sour cream
	2 tablespoons minced parsley

Heat the oil in a skillet; sauté the onions 5 minutes. Add the veal; cook over medium heat, stirring almost steadily, until browned. Mix in the salt, pepper, fennel, and flour, then the tomato sauce. Cover and cook over low heat 20 minutes. Add the beans; cook 5 minutes longer. Mix in the sour cream; heat but do not let boil. Taste for seasoning; sprinkle with the parsley. *Serves 6–8.*

Telece Cuvte

SERBIAN VEAL BALLS

1½ pounds ground lean veal	½ cup grated drained potatoes
1½ teaspoons salt	¼ pound (1 stick) butter
½ teaspoon white pepper	¼ cup minced onions
1 clove garlic, minced	1 cup sliced mushrooms
2 tablespoons minced parsley	2 tablespoons flour
1 egg, beaten	1 cup beef broth
½ cup light cream	1 cup sour cream
	½ teaspoon paprika

Mix together the veal, salt, pepper, garlic, parsley, egg, cream, and potatoes. Shape into 1-inch balls.

Melt the butter in a skillet and brown the balls on all sides; remove from pan. To the fat remaining, add the onions and mushrooms; sauté 5 minutes. Blend in the flour, then add the broth, stirring steadily to the boiling point. Return the meat balls. Cover and cook over low heat 20 minutes. Stir in the sour cream and paprika; heat but do not let boil. Serve with noodles or dumplings.
Serves 4–6.

Polpette di Vitello

VEAL BALLS IN TOMATO SAUCE

1½ pounds ground lean
   veal
2 eggs, beaten
1 tablespoon Marsala or
   sweet sherry
½ cup grated Parmesan
   cheese
2½ teaspoons salt
½ teaspoon freshly ground
   black pepper

¼ cup flour
4 tablespoons butter
½ cup chopped onions
1 clove garlic, minced
1 29-ounce can Italian-style
   tomatoes
2 tablespoons minced
   parsley

Mix together the veal, eggs, wine, cheese, and half the salt and pepper. Shape into 1-inch balls and roll lightly in the flour.

Melt the butter in a saucepan; sauté the onions 10 minutes. Add the garlic, tomatoes, and remaining salt and pepper. Bring to a boil and cook over low heat 20 minutes. Add the meat balls to the sauce; cover and cook over low heat 1 hour. Taste for seasoning and sprinkle with the parsley. Serve with rice or noodles.
Serves 6–8.

Pljeskavice

YUGOSLAVIAN VEAL AND SAUSAGE BALLS

5 tablespoons butter	1 egg, beaten
½ cup chopped green onions (scallions)	1 teaspoon salt
1 slice white bread	¼ teaspoon freshly ground black pepper
¼ cup milk	¼ teaspoon orégano
1 pound ground lean veal	1 tablespoon minced parsley
½ pound sausage meat	

Melt 2 tablespoons butter in a skillet; brown the onions in it. Soak the bread in the milk; drain, squeeze dry, and mash.

Mix together the veal, sausage, egg, salt, pepper, orégano, sautéed onions, and bread. Shape into 1-inch balls. Melt the remaining butter in a skillet; brown the balls in it over low heat, shaking the pan frequently. Sprinkle with the parsley. Serve with tomato or mushroom sauce.

Serves 4–6.

African Meat Loaf

1 pound ground beef	1½ teaspoons salt
1 pound ground lean pork	½ teaspoon freshly ground black pepper
¾ cup cracker meal	
3 eggs, beaten	2 cups chopped peanuts
½ cup chopped onions	⅔ cup brown sugar

Mix together the beef, pork, cracker meal, eggs, onions, salt, pepper, and 1¼ cups of the peanuts. Combine the remaining peanuts and brown sugar.

Grease a 9-inch loaf pan heavily. Line the bottom and sides with the brown sugar mixture. Fill with the meat mixture. Bake in a 375° oven for 1¼ hours. Turn out carefully onto a platter, with the glazed side up.

Serves 8–10.

Lammauflauf

AUSTRIAN LAMB-VEAL LOAF

1 cup soft bread crumbs
½ cup water
1½ pounds ground lean
 lamb
½ pound ground veal
½ cup minced onions
1 clove garlic, minced

¼ cup minced green
 peppers
3 tablespoons minced parsley
1 egg, beaten
2 teaspoons salt
½ teaspoon freshly ground
 black pepper

Soak the bread crumbs in the water, then mix lightly with the remaining ingredients. Press into a lightly greased 9-inch loaf pan. Bake in a 350° oven 1½ hours. Cool 10 minutes before turning out. Slice and serve with a mushroom or tomato sauce if desired. *Serves 6–8.*

Hackbraten

GERMAN MEAT LOAF

4 tablespoons butter
1½ cups chopped onions
2 slices white bread,
 trimmed and diced
2 tablespoons chopped
 parsley
¾ pound ground beef

¾ pound ground pork
1 egg, beaten
2 teaspoons salt
½ teaspoon freshly ground
 black pepper
½ cup dry bread crumbs
¾ cup hot beef broth

Melt 2 tablespoons of the butter in a skillet; sauté half the onions 5 minutes. Mix in the diced bread and parsley; sauté 2 minutes. Combine this mixture with the beef, pork, egg, salt, and pepper. Mix well and shape into a loaf; sprinkle with the bread crumbs.

Melt the remaining butter in a baking pan. Place the loaf in it and add the broth and remaining onions. Bake in a 375° oven 1¼ hours, basting frequently.

Serves 4–6.

Hawaiian Meat Loaf

1 pound ground beef
1 pound ground pork
2 teaspoons salt
½ teaspoon freshly ground
   black pepper
½ cup cracker meal
1 cup peeled, chopped
   tomatoes

2 eggs, beaten
⅓ cup brown sugar
½ cup canned crushed
   pineapple
¼ teaspoon powdered
   ginger
2 tablespoons melted butter

With the hand mix together the beef, pork, salt, pepper, cracker meal, tomatoes, and eggs. Pack into a 7-inch greased loaf pan. Bake in a 350° oven 1 hour.

Mix together the brown sugar, pineapple, ginger, and butter. Spread over the meat loaf. Bake 15 minutes longer, or until top is glazed and browned.

Serves 6–8.

Polpettone alla Fiorentina

ITALIAN PROVINCIAL BEEF-VEAL LOAF

1 pound ground round steak
1 pound ground veal
¼ cup grated onion
1 clove garlic, minced
2 teaspoons salt
¼ teaspoon freshly ground
   black pepper

¼ cup dry bread crumbs
¼ cup ketchup
¼ cup ice water
3 tablespoons vegetable oil
2 eggs, beaten

Mix all the ingredients together lightly. Shape into a loaf and place in an oiled baking pan. Bake in a 375° oven 50 minutes.

Serves 6–8.

Kufteh Gusht

IRANIAN LAMB-BEEF LOAF

¾ cup white bread cubes
½ cup water
1 pound ground lean lamb
½ pound ground lean beef
¼ cup finely chopped
celery leaves
¼ cup minced parsley
¾ cup finely chopped green
onions (scallions)

1½ teaspoons salt
½ teaspoon freshly ground
black pepper
¼ teaspoon cinnamon
2 eggs, beaten
2 tablespoons tomato paste
2 tablespoons vegetable oil

Soak the bread in the water for 5 minutes; mash smooth, then drain. Mix together the soaked bread, meats, celery leaves, parsley, green onions, salt, pepper, cinnamon, eggs, and tomato paste. Shape into a loaf; place in an oiled baking pan. Bake in a preheated 350° oven 1 hour. Serve hot or cold.
Serves 6–8.

Albondigón de Carne

MEXICAN MEAT LOAF

2 pounds ground pork or
beef, or a mixture of both
½ cup minced onions
½ cup minced green
peppers
1 clove garlic, minced
1½ teaspoons salt
⅛ teaspoon dried ground
chili peppers

1 tablespoon chili powder
2 eggs, beaten
2 tablespoons olive oil
2 tablespoons dry bread
crumbs
2 pimientos, cut julienne

Mix together the meat, onions, green peppers, garlic, salt, red peppers, chili powder, and eggs. Shape into a loaf and place in a greased baking dish. Sprinkle with the oil and bread crumbs.

Bake in a 400° oven 55 minutes. Arrange the pimientos on top and bake 5 minutes longer. Serve hot or cold.
Serves 6–8.

Carne Tocata Latava

RUMANIAN MEAT LOAF

1 cup white bread cubes	⅛ teaspoon ground fennel
½ cup water	2 tablespoons minced parsley
1 cup chopped, sautéed	1 clove garlic, minced
onions	½ cup beef broth
1½ pounds ground beef	2 eggs, beaten
½ pound ground pork	3 hard-cooked eggs, chopped
2 teaspoons salt	6 slices bacon
½ teaspoon freshly ground	
black pepper	

Soak the bread cubes in the water for 5 minutes, then mash smooth. Mix together the bread, sautéed onions, beef, pork, salt, pepper, fennel, parsley, and garlic. Mix in the broth and beaten eggs, then the hard-cooked eggs. Form into a loaf.

Arrange 3 slices of bacon on the bottom of a baking dish. Put the loaf over the bacon and arrange the remaining bacon on top. Bake in a 350° oven 1½ hours, basting occasionally with the pan drippings. Serve hot or cold.
Serves 8–10.

Čevapčiči

BALKAN VEAL AND BEEF SAUSAGES

1 pound ground fat beef	¾ teaspoon freshly ground
1 pound ground veal	black pepper
1½ teaspoons salt	1½ teaspoons paprika
	1 cup minced onions

Chop all the ingredients together until very fluffy and fine. Shape into sausages between floured hands. Broil as close to the heat as possible (or over a charcoal fire) turning the sausages frequently to brown all sides. Serve with chopped onions and spicy peppers.
Serves 6–8.

Frikadeller

DANISH MEAT BALLS

½ pound ground lean pork
½ pound ground beef
1 cup minced onions
5 tablespoons flour
1 teaspoon salt

½ teaspoon freshly ground
  black pepper
1 cup light cream
Vegetable oil for deep frying

Mix together the pork, beef, onions, flour, salt, and pepper. With a wooden spoon gradually beat in the cream. Shape the mixture into walnut-sized balls.

Heat the oil to 365°. Fry the balls in it 10 minutes, or until the pork is cooked through. Drain and serve hot.
Serves 4.

Lihapyörykät

FINNISH MEAT BALLS

½ cup fresh bread crumbs
1 cup milk
½ pound ground pork
½ pound ground veal
½ pound ground beef
½ cup chopped onions
1 egg, beaten

2 teaspoons salt
½ teaspoon freshly ground
  black pepper
4 tablespoons butter
1 tablespoon flour
¾ cup heavy cream

Soak the bread crumbs in the milk for 5 minutes. Mash smooth and add the meats, onions, egg, salt, and pepper. Mix well. Shape into walnut-sized balls. Melt the butter in a skillet. Add the meat balls and cook over low heat 20 minutes, shaking the pan frequently. Transfer the meat balls to a hot platter and keep warm. Mix together the flour and cream. Stir into the pan juices, scraping up all the bits and pieces. Cook, stirring steadily. Pour the sauce over the meat balls.

Serves 6–8.

Königsberger Klopse

GERMAN MEAT BALLS

½ cup white bread cubes	1 tablespoon anchovy paste
½ cup milk	3 cups boiling water
1 pound ground beef	2 tablespoons lemon juice
½ pound ground pork	2 bay leaves
¾ cup chopped, sautéed onions	2 cloves
2 eggs, beaten	2 tablespoons cold water
1½ teaspoons salt	2 tablespoons flour
¼ teaspoon freshly ground black pepper	¼ cup capers

Soak the bread in the milk and mash very smooth. Mix with the beef, pork, onions, eggs, ½ teaspoon salt, the pepper, and anchovy paste. Shape into 2-inch balls.

In a saucepan, combine the boiling water, lemon juice, bay leaves, cloves, and remaining salt. Bring to a boil and place the meat balls in it. Cook over low heat 30 minutes.

Mix the cold water with the flour and carefully stir it into the gravy until thickened, then cook 5 minutes longer. Add the capers.

Serves 4–6.

Boulettes de Boeuf

MEAT BALLS, FRENCH PROVINCIAL STYLE

½ cup white bread cubes
¼ cup milk
1 pound ground lean beef
¼ pound sausage meat
1 cup minced onions
1 tablespoon minced parsley
1 teaspoon salt

¼ teaspoon freshly ground
  black pepper
2 eggs
½ cup flour
¾ cup dry bread crumbs
Vegetable oil for deep frying
Parsley sprigs

Soak the bread cubes in the milk, then mash smooth. In a bowl combine the beef, sausage meat, onions, and parsley. Mix in the bread, salt, pepper, and 1 egg thoroughly. Chill. With wet hands shape the mixture into small balls or ovals; roll in the flour, then in the remaining egg, beaten, and finally in the bread crumbs.

Heat the oil to 375° and fry the meat balls until browned, turning frequently to brown all sides. Drain and arrange on a hot serving dish. Drop the parsley into the hot oil and remove almost immediately with a skimmer. Garnish the meat balls with the fried parsley. *Serves 6.*

Köttbuller

SWEDISH MEAT BALLS

1 cup white bread cubes
1 cup light cream
1 pound ground beef
½ pound ground lean pork
½ pound ground veal
1 cup minced, sautéed
  onions
2 teaspoons salt

½ teaspoon white pepper
¼ teaspoon nutmeg
2 eggs, beaten
2 tablespoons minced
  parsley
½ cup flour
5 tablespoons butter
2 cups heavy cream

Soak the bread cubes in the light cream for 10 minutes; mash smooth.

Mix together the beef, pork, veal, sautéed onions, salt, pepper, nutmeg, eggs, parsley, and soaked bread. Shape into 1-inch balls and roll in the flour, reserving 2 tablespoons. Melt the butter in a skillet; add the balls and cook over medium heat 10 minutes, shaking the pan frequently to turn balls and brown all sides. Transfer the meat to a casserole. Blend the reserved flour into the butter remaining in the skillet. Gradually add the heavy cream, stirring steadily to the boiling point; cook over low heat 5 minutes. Pour the sauce over the meat balls and cook over low heat 15 minutes.

Serves 6–8.

Couftah

ARABIAN MEAT CROQUETTES

1 cup white bread cubes	¼ teaspoon crushed
½ cup milk	cuminseed
1 pound ground lean beef	3 tablespoons chopped
1 pound ground lean	parsley
lamb	2 eggs, beaten
¾ cup finely chopped	½ cup dry bread crumbs
onions	¼ pound (1 stick) butter
1½ teaspoons salt	
¼ teaspoon cayenne	
pepper	

Soak the bread in the milk for 5 minutes; mash smooth.

Mix together thoroughly the beef, lamb, onions, salt, pepper, cumin, parsley, eggs, and soaked bread. Shape into 12 croquettes. Dip in the dry bread crumbs. Melt half the butter in a skillet and sauté the croquettes over low heat until browned on both sides, adding more butter as needed.

Serves 6.

Keema Korma Curry
BENGAL GROUND MEAT CURRY

2 pounds ground beef
2 cups yogurt
4 teaspoons curry powder
1½ teaspoons salt

2½ cups minced onions
2 cloves garlic, minced
4 tablespoons butter

Combine the meat, yogurt, curry powder, salt, onions, and garlic. Mix thoroughly. Let stand in the refrigerator 3 hours.

Melt the butter in a heavy saucepan. Add the meat mixture; cover and cook over very low heat 1 hour, stirring frequently. Serve with rice.

Serves 8.

Chinese Omelets with Meat Stuffing

3 eggs
1 teaspoon salt
½ pound ground cooked
  beef or pork
2 teaspoons soy sauce
2 teaspoons dry sherry
½ teaspoon ground ginger

2 teaspoons cornstarch
3 tablespoons chopped
  onions
3 tablespoons flour
3 tablespoons water
1 cup vegetable oil

Beat together the eggs and ½ teaspoon of the salt. Pour about 2 tablespoons of the egg mixture into a hot greased 6-inch skillet. Fry until lightly browned and set. Repeat with remaining eggs. You should have 6 omelets.

Combine the ground meat, soy sauce, sherry, ginger, cornstarch, onions, and remaining salt; mix thoroughly. Spread on the egg pancakes. Turn opposite sides in and roll up. Seal the edges with the flour mixed with the water. In a skillet heat the oil to 370° and fry the rolls in it until browned on both sides. Drain the rolls. Serve hot with mixed salt and pepper for dipping.

Serves 6–12.

Aeggah
MIDDLE EAST MEAT PUFFS

6 eggs
1 teaspoon salt
¼ teaspoon freshly ground
black pepper

½ pound ground raw beef
½ cup chopped parsley
1 cup vegetable oil

Beat together the eggs, salt, and pepper. Stir in the beef and parsley.

Heat the oil in a skillet until it boils; drop the mixture into it by the tablespoon. Fry until browned on both sides. Drain and serve hot or cold.

Serves 4–6.

Mixed Meats

Every good cook knows how to combine leftover meats into a tempting dish, but relatively few cooks start out fresh to make mixed-meat dishes. For instance, steak and kidney pie is a staple on English menus, but it was left to the Australians to come up with a pudding made of these two ingredients—plus oysters! The Brazilians have an equally unusual dish which is made up of dried beef, raw corned beef, and pork. The well-known cassoulet of the French provinces combines lamb and pork with garlic sausages, and from this same region we also have the lesser known *tourte Lorraine,* which is a veal-pork pie.

With these ideas as a launching pad, try your own ingenuity at innovations, and avoid family grumblings such as, "What, lamb stew again!"

Australian Steak, Kidney, and Oyster Pudding

PASTRY:

3 cups sifted flour
1 teaspoon salt
4 tablespoons butter

¼ pound suet, chopped,
or ½ cup shortening
1 egg, beaten
3 tablespoons water

Sift the flour and salt into a bowl; cut in the butter with a pastry blender or 2 knives, then cut in the suet or shortening With a fork, stir in the egg and water, until a soft ball of dough is formed. Divide dough in 2 pieces, one larger than the other. Roll out the larger piece, and line a 2-quart casserole with it.

FILLING:

3 veal kidneys

2 pounds rump steak, cut
in 1-inch cubes

½ pound mushrooms,
sliced

¾ cup chopped onions

1½ teaspoons salt

½ teaspoon freshly ground
black pepper

16 shucked oysters

¾ cup dry red wine

½ cup beef broth

Wash the kidneys and soak in cold water. Cut in half and remove the white core; slice the kidneys. Toss together the kidneys, steak, mushrooms, onions, salt, and pepper. Turn into the lined casserole. Arrange the oysters over the mixture, then pour in a mixture of the wine and broth. Roll out the remaining dough and cover the casserole, sealing the edges well. Cut a slit in the top. Cut a large piece of aluminum foil double the size of the casserole, butter it, and pleat it. Tie it over the casserole. Place the casserole in a large kettle, and add water to reach halfway up the casserole. Cover the kettle, bring to a boil, and cook over low heat 6 hours. Add hot water to the kettle when necessary to keep level halfway up. Serve directly from the casserole.

Serves 6–8.

Cripulja

BALKAN BEEF AND LIVER RAGOUT

2 pounds fillet of beef

1 pound calf's liver

¼ cup flour

2 teaspoons salt

½ teaspoon freshly ground
black pepper

6 tablespoons butter

1½ cups thinly sliced
onions

½ cup beef broth

½ cup dry red wine

Cut the beef into ½-inch-thick slices, then into strips 1 inch wide and 2 inches long. Cut the liver in the same manner. Toss the beef and liver in a mixture of the flour, salt, and pepper.

Melt half the butter in a large skillet; sauté the onions until golden. Remove. Melt the remaining butter in the skillet; brown the meat and liver in it. Return the onions and add the broth and wine. Bring to a boil and cook over low heat 10 minutes. Taste for seasoning. *Serves 6–8.*

Feijoada

BRAZILIAN ASSORTED MEATS WITH BLACK BEANS

1 pound dried beef
3 cups dried black beans
1 pound raw corned beef
¼ pound salt pork
4 pounds loin of pork
1½ teaspoons salt
½ teaspoon freshly ground
  black pepper

1 cup orange juice
3 tablespoons olive oil
1 cup chopped onions
2 cloves garlic, minced
½ pound Spanish sausages,
  sliced
¼ teaspoon dried ground
  chili peppers

Soak the dried beef in cold water for 2 hours. Drain, cover with fresh water, and bring to a boil. Cook 5 minutes. Drain and cut in small pieces.

Wash the beans, cover with water, and bring to a boil; let soak 1 hour. Drain, add fresh water to cover, and bring to a boil; add the dried beef; cook over low heat 2½ hours. While the beans are cooking, prepare the other meats. Combine the corned beef and salt pork in a saucepan. Add water to cover. Bring to a boil; cover and cook over low heat 2½ hours.

Season the pork with the salt and pepper; roast in a 375° oven 1¾ hours. When the beans are tender, drain the corned beef and salt pork and add to the beans. Remove 1 cup of the beans and purée in an electric blender or mash to a paste. Return to the remaining beans with the orange juice. Cook over low heat 1 hour.

Heat the oil in a skillet; sauté the onions and garlic 5 minutes. Add the sausages and let brown. Add to the beans with the chili peppers. Cook 30 minutes. Taste for seasoning.

Slice the meats and arrange on a platter. Put the beans in a deep bowl. Serve with rice, sliced oranges, and pickled onions. *Serves 12.*

Karjalanpaisti

FINNISH MEAT STEW

1 pound boneless pork	1 teaspoon ground allspice
1 pound boneless lamb	1 bay leaf
1 pound boneless beef	½ teaspoon powdered ginger
1 cup chopped onions	2 teaspoons salt
1½ cups boiling beef broth	

Cut the meats in 1-inch cubes.

In a 2-quart baking dish, combine the meats, onions, broth, allspice, bay leaf, ginger, and salt. Bake in a 475° oven 20 minutes; cover dish tightly, reduce heat to 325°, and bake 2½ hours longer. *Serves 6–8.*

Tourte Lorraine

FRENCH PROVINCIAL VEAL-PORK PIE

PASTRY:

2 cups sifted flour	½ pound (2 sticks) butter
1 teaspoon salt	⅓ cup light cream

Sift the flour and salt into a bowl; cut in the butter with a pastry blender or 2 knives until mixture looks like coarse corn meal. Add the cream and toss with a fork until a ball of dough is formed. Chill several hours or overnight.

FILLING:

1 pound boneless veal	1¾ teaspoons salt
1 pound boneless lean pork	¼ teaspoon freshly ground
1 cup dry white wine	black pepper
1 clove garlic, minced	3 eggs, beaten
¼ cup chopped onions	2 cups cream
1 tablespoon chopped parsley	

Cut the veal and pork into ½-inch cubes.

In a glass or pottery bowl, mix together the wine, garlic, onions, parsley, 1½ teaspoons of the salt, and the pepper; marinate the pork and veal in the mixture 24 hours in the refrigerator.

Divide the pastry in two, making one piece larger than the other. Roll out the larger piece and fit it into a deep 11-inch pie plate. Drain the meats and dry well, and spread in the lined pie plate. Cover with the remaining rolled out pastry and seal the edges. Cut a small hole in the center of the top crust. Bake the pie in a preheated 425° oven 25 minutes.

Beat together the eggs, cream, and remaining salt. Insert a small funnel in the hole in the pie crust and slowly pour in the egg-cream mixture. Reduce heat to 325° and bake 20 minutes longer. Serve hot.

Serves 6–8.

Cassoulet

FRENCH PROVINCIAL MIXED MEATS AND BEANS

4 cups pea beans
2 quarts water
2 cloves garlic, minced
2 onions
2 cloves
½ teaspoon thyme
1 bay leaf
⅛ pound salt pork, diced
2 tablespoons vegetable oil
2 pounds boneless lamb,
　cut in 1-inch cubes

2 pounds boneless pork,
　cut in 1-inch cubes
1½ cups chopped onions
1 8-ounce can tomato
　sauce
1 cup dry white wine
1 tablespoon salt
2 garlic sausages, sliced

Wash the beans, add the 2 quarts of water, and bring to a boil. Cook 2 minutes, remove from heat, and let soak 1 hour. Add the garlic, onions stuck with the cloves, thyme, bay leaf, and salt pork. Bring to a boil and cook over medium heat 1 hour.

Heat the oil in a skillet; brown the lamb and pork in it. Add to the beans. In oil remaining in the skillet brown the onions. Add to

the bean mixture with the tomato sauce, wine, and salt. Cover and cook over low heat 1 hour. Transfer the mixture to a large casserole and add the sausages. Mix lightly. Taste for seasoning. Bake in a 325° oven 50 minutes.
Serves 8–10.

Fegato e Prosciutto con Risotto

LIVER AND HAM WITH RICE, ITALIAN STYLE

½ pound prosciutto (ham)
½ pound calf's liver
6 tablespoons butter
¾ cup finely chopped
onions
2 cups raw rice
⅓ cup Marsala or sweet
sherry
5 cups hot chicken broth
1½ teaspoons salt

¾ cup thinly sliced onions
½ pound mushrooms,
sliced
1 cup beef broth
1 teaspoon salt
¼ teaspoon freshly ground
black pepper
1 bay leaf
¼ teaspoon thyme

Cut the ham in narrow slivers. Wash, dry, and dice the liver.
Melt half the butter in a saucepan; sauté the chopped onions until yellow and transparent. Stir in the rice until lightly browned. Add ¼ cup wine; cook until absorbed. Add 2 cups of the broth and the salt; cover and cook over low heat 25 minutes, adding the remaining chicken broth as it becomes absorbed by the rice. Prepare the sauce while the rice is cooking.
Melt the remaining butter in a small saucepan; sauté the sliced onions and ham 5 minutes. Add the liver and mushrooms; sauté 5 minutes, stirring frequently. Mix in the beef broth, salt, pepper, bay leaf, thyme, and remaining wine. Cook over low heat 10 minutes. Taste for seasoning. Discard the bay leaf, then mix half the sauce with the rice. Heap the rice in a bowl and pour the remaining sauce over the top.
Serves 4–6.

Picadillo

SOUTH AMERICAN MIXED MEAT HASH

¼ cup olive oil
1 cup chopped green
    peppers
1 cup chopped onions
1 clove garlic, minced
1 pound ground beef
½ pound ground pork
1½ teaspoons salt

½ teaspoon freshly ground
    black pepper
½ cup canned tomato sauce
¼ cup dry white wine
½ cup seedless raisins
¼ cup capers
½ cup sliced almonds

Heat the oil in a large skillet; sauté the green peppers, onions,
and garlic 5 minutes. Add the beef and pork; cook over medium
heat, stirring constantly until browned. Season with the salt and
pepper. Mix in the tomato sauce, wine, and raisins. Cook over low
heat 25 minutes, mixing frequently. Add the capers and almonds;
cook 5 minutes longer.
Serves 4–6.

Gevetsch

YUGOSLAVIAN MEAT AND VEGETABLE STEW

3 tablespoons vegetable oil
1 pound
    boneless beef
½ pound   } cut in
    boneless veal   1-inch
1 pound   cubes
    boneless pork
2 cups sliced onions
1 cup beef broth

2 cups peeled, sliced
    potatoes
2 carrots, sliced
2 tomatoes, cut into eighths
1 green pepper, cut julienne
2 teaspoons salt
½ teaspoon freshly ground
    black pepper
1 tablespoon paprika

Heat the oil in a Dutch oven or casserole and brown the meats
on all sides. Remove. To the fat remaining add the onions; cook
until golden, stirring frequently. Add the broth and bring to a

boil. Return the meat with the potatoes, carrots, tomatoes, green pepper, salt, pepper, and paprika. Bake in a 350° oven 2 hours.
Serves 6–8.

Carne Estufada

PORTUGUESE MIXED MEAT STEW

1 pound boneless beef	½ teaspoon freshly ground
1 pound boneless veal	black pepper
1 pound boneless pork	2 teaspoons paprika
4 tablespoons butter	2 tablespoons tomato paste
3 cups thinly sliced onions	1 cup dry white wine
2 teaspoons salt	1 cup sour cream

Cut the beef, veal, and pork into 1-inch cubes.

Melt the butter in a casserole; sauté the onions 10 minutes. Add the cubed meat; cook over medium heat until browned. Stir in the salt, pepper, paprika, tomato paste, and ¼ cup of the wine. Cover and cook over low heat 30 minutes. Add the remaining wine and cook 1½ hours longer. Stir the sour cream into the pan juices. Heat but do not let boil.
Serves 6–8.

Moskovskaya Solyanka

BEEF WITH SAUERKRAUT, RUSSIAN STYLE

2 tablespoons vegetable oil	1½ pounds sauerkraut,
3 pounds cross rib or chuck	drained
of beef, cut in 2-inch	1 bay leaf
cubes	1½ cups chopped canned
1½ cups sliced onions	tomatoes
1½ teaspoons salt	6 frankfurters, cut in thirds
½ teaspoon freshly ground	1 cup sour cream
black pepper	

Heat the oil in a casserole; brown the meat and onions in it. Sprinkle with the salt and pepper. Cover and cook over low heat 30 minutes. Watch carefully and add a very little water if necessary to keep from burning. Mix in the sauerkraut. Cook 10 minutes, stirring frequently. Add the bay leaf and tomatoes. Cover and cook 1 hour. Add the frankfurters and cook 30 minutes longer or until the meat is tender. Discard the bay leaf and mix in the sour cream.

Serves 8–10.

Variety Meats

The French name given to the innards of animals, *abats de boucherie,* makes them sound almost as delicious as they are. (Don't translate it literally!) *Abats* include brains, kidneys, heart, liver, sweetbreads, tripe, tails (oxtails), and feet. Less than fifty years ago, butchers gave away many of these parts because they couldn't sell them. Today brains, liver, kidneys, and sweetbreads are considered as delicacies and command high prices.

Dieticians discovered the nutritional value of *abats* and suddenly they became valuable and expensive. Besides contributing to our health, they broaden the scope of menu planning. Europeans are very aware of this, and their cuisines utilize these delicate foods with great imagination. Of course, all animals have these parts, but the calf produces the best brains, kidneys, liver, and sweetbreads. Lamb and beef kidneys and liver are good, but most people prefer those from the calf.

Besides innards, variety meats include feet, tails, and other excrescences. Calf's feet are more tender than steer feet, and pig's feet are greatly favored by the Germans.

Variety meats are very perishable, so always keep them refrigerated until cooking time, and be sure to use them within twenty-four hours after purchase.

The tenderness of variety meats, as with muscle meats, determines the cooking method to be used. All brains and sweetbreads are tender, but if you plan to serve liver or kidneys you will find they are best when they come from young animals. Beef liver and kidneys, and the tongue and heart of all animals, are less tender and require long, slow cooking by moist heat. Pork liver should be braised. Brains, sweetbreads, and tripe are usually first simmered in water, then prepared for serving according to the particular recipe.

Except for calf's liver, which is sometimes served medium, variety meats should all be cooked until well done.

Brochettes de Foie de Veau
CALF'S LIVER ON SKEWERS

1¼ pounds calf's liver, cut
 in 1-inch cubes
½ teaspoon salt
⅛ teaspoon freshly ground
 black pepper

12 slices bacon (about)
18 mushroom caps
¼ cup melted butter

Rinse the liver and dry on paper towels. Season with the salt
and pepper. Cut the bacon in half crosswise and wrap a piece
around each piece of liver. Cut the mushrooms in half; sprinkle
with a little salt and pepper. On 6 skewers thread the liver and
mushrooms on them alternately. Brush with the butter. Broil
until browned, turning the skewers frequently.
Serves 6.

Chinese Style Fried Calf's Liver

1 pound calf's or beef liver
2 tablespoons dry sherry
1 teaspoon salt
½ teaspoon powdered
 ginger
3 tablespoons soy sauce
⅓ cup cornstarch

1 cup vegetable oil
1 cup sliced onions
½ cup sliced celery
½ cup julienne-cut green
 peppers
½ teaspoon sugar

Rinse the liver, cut in bite-sized pieces, and dry on paper
towels. Marinate the pieces in a mixture of the sherry, salt, ginger,
and 1 tablespoon of the soy sauce for 15 minutes. Drain the liver
and roll in the cornstarch.
Heat the oil in a skillet until it bubbles; fry the liver until
browned. Remove the liver. Pour off all but 3 tablespoons of
the oil. In the oil remaining sauté the onions, celery, and green
peppers 5 minutes. Add the sugar, remaining soy sauce, and the
liver. Cook 1 minute, stirring constantly.
Serves 4.

Chinese Calf's Liver with Pineapple

1 pound calf's liver
¼ cup soy sauce
1 12-ounce can pineapple juice
¼ cup cider vinegar
¼ teaspoon salt

¼ cup sugar
2 tablespoons cornstarch
1 8-ounce can pineapple chunks, drained
½ cup blanched almonds
¼ cup vegetable oil

Rinse the liver, cut into narrow strips, and dry on paper towels.

Combine the soy sauce, pineapple juice, vinegar, salt, sugar, and cornstarch in a saucepan; cook over low heat, stirring steadily, until thickened and smooth. Add the pineapple chunks and almonds; keep hot while preparing the liver.

Heat the oil in a skillet; add the liver, and cook over high heat until browned. Heap the liver on a hot serving dish and pour the sauce over it. Serve with rice. *Serves 4.*

Äpfel mit Leberfulle

LIVER-STUFFED APPLES

½ pound calf's or beef liver
6 large baking apples
¾ teaspoon salt

⅛ teaspoon thyme
2 tablespoons butter
¾ cup dry white wine

Rinse the liver and dry on paper towels.

Wash the apples, remove the core, then carefully scoop out some of the pulp and reserve. Chop the liver, then add the apple pulp and chop until fine. Mix in the salt and thyme. Stuff the apples.

Rub a baking dish with the butter; arrange the apples in it and add the wine. Cover and bake in a 325° oven 35 minutes, or until the apples are tender and the liver cooked; remove the cover for the last 5 minutes. Serve as an accompaniment with meat or poultry dishes. *Serves 6.*

Kananmaksaa Omenien Kanssa

FINNISH CALF'S LIVER WITH APPLES

1½ pounds calf's liver
¼ pound (1 stick) butter
6 apples, peeled, cored, and
cut into sixths
4 tablespoons sugar
1½ teaspoons salt
½ teaspoon freshly ground
black pepper

¼ cup chicken broth
1 cup apple juice
1½ tablespoons cornstarch
1 tablespoon lemon juice
2 tablespoons currant jelly

Rinse the liver, cut in narrow strips, and dry on paper towels.

Melt half the butter in a skillet, add the apples, sprinkle them with the sugar, and cook over low heat 8 minutes, or until soft, turning frequently. Do not break the slices.

Melt the remaining butter in another skillet and sauté the liver 3 minutes. Add the salt, pepper, and broth. Cook over medium heat 3 minutes. In a saucepan mix 2 tablespoons of the apple juice with the cornstarch until smooth; combine with the remaining apple juice, lemon juice, and jelly. Cook over low heat until thick, stirring constantly. Arrange the apples on a hot serving dish and spoon the liver mixture over them. Serve the sauce in a sauceboat.

Serves 6.

Leber mit Äpfeln und Zwiebeln

GERMAN CALF'S LIVER AND APPLES

1 pound calf's liver
¼ cup dry bread crumbs
1 teaspoon salt
¼ teaspoon white pepper
¼ pound butter

2 cups thinly sliced onions
3 apples, peeled and sliced
½-inch thick
3 tablespoons sugar

Rinse the liver. Cut into pencil-thin 2-inch pieces and dry on paper towels. Toss the pieces with a mixture of the bread crumbs, salt, and pepper. Melt 3 tablespoons butter in a skillet; sauté the liver 3 minutes or until browned. Remove and keep warm. In the same skillet, melt half the remaining butter; sauté the onions until browned.

In a separate skillet, melt the remaining butter; sauté the apples until golden on one side, sprinkle with sugar, turn, and sauté the other side until golden. Arrange the onions and apples over the liver.

Serves 4–5.

Liver and Macaroni au Gratin

1 pound calf's or beef
  liver
6 tablespoons butter
1½ cups chopped onions
1 29-ounce can tomatoes
2 tablespoons tomato paste
2 teaspoons salt
⅛ teaspoon dried ground
  chili peppers

½ pound mushrooms, sliced
1 pound elbow macaroni,
  cooked and drained
¼ cup dry bread crumbs
½ cup grated Gruyère or
  Swiss cheese

Rinse and dice the liver and dry on paper towels.

Melt half the butter in a saucepan; sauté the onions 5 minutes, stirring frequently. Mix in the tomatoes, tomato paste, salt, and dried peppers. Cook over low heat 45 minutes, stirring occasionally.

Melt the remaining butter in a skillet; sauté the liver and mushrooms 5 minutes, stirring frequently. Add to the sauce. Cook 5 minutes. Taste for seasoning.

Spread the macaroni in a buttered casserole. Arrange the liver and mushrooms on top. Pour the sauce over it. Sprinkle a mixture of the bread crumbs and cheese on top. Bake in a 350° oven for 25 minutes.

Serves 4–6.

Martinique Baked Calf's Liver

2 pounds calf's liver in 1
   piece
½ cup flour
3 teaspoons salt
1 teaspoon freshly ground
   black pepper
3 tablespoons butter
1 cup thinly sliced onions
1 cup thinly sliced green
   peppers

1 cup sliced mushrooms
¼ cup chopped ham
1 20-ounce can tomatoes
1 clove garlic, minced
3 tablespoons minced parsley
½ teaspoon marjoram
1 bay leaf
⅔ cup dry white wine

Rinse the liver and dry on paper towels. Dip the liver in a mixture of the flour, 2 teaspoons of the salt, and ½ teaspoon of the pepper.

Melt the butter in a deep skillet or casserole; brown the liver in it on all sides. Add the onions, green peppers, mushrooms, ham, tomatoes, garlic, parsley, marjoram, bay leaf, wine, and the remaining salt and pepper. Cover and bake in a 375° oven 1 hour. Taste for seasoning. Slice the liver and serve with the sauce. *Serves 6–8.*

Pilaff de Foie de Veau

MOROCCAN CALF'S LIVER AND RICE

1 pound calf's liver
¼ cup olive oil
6 slices eggplant
1 small zucchini, sliced
1 tomato, peeled and sliced
1 cup raw rice
1½ cups chicken broth

3 tablespoons butter
½ pound mushrooms,
   sliced
¼ cup port
1½ teaspoons salt
½ teaspoon freshly ground
   black pepper

Rinse the liver, cut in ½-inch cubes, and dry on paper towels. Heat the oil in a deep skillet; add the eggplant, zucchini, and tomato; cook over medium heat 5 minutes. Stir in the rice until translucent. Add the broth; cover and cook over low heat 12 minutes.

While the rice is cooking, melt the butter in another skillet; brown the liver in it. Remove. In the butter remaining in the skillet, sauté the mushrooms 3 minutes. Remove. Pour the port into the skillet. Cook over high heat 2 minutes, scraping the bottom of browned particles; add to the rice with the salt, pepper, liver, and mushrooms; mix lightly with 2 forks and cook over low heat 5 minutes, or until the rice is tender.

Serves 4.

Watróbka Duszona ze Śmietana

POLISH CALF'S LIVER IN SOUR CREAM

2 pounds calf's liver in 1 piece	¼ cup beef broth
	1½ teaspoons salt
2 cups milk	½ teaspoon freshly ground
4 tablespoons butter	black pepper
1 cup chopped onions	1 cup sour cream

Rinse the liver and place it in a bowl. Pour the milk over it and let stand in the refrigerator for 3 hours. Drain and dry on paper towels.

Melt the butter in a skillet; brown the liver in it. Add the onions and cook 5 minutes. Add the broth, salt, and pepper. Cover and cook over low heat 20 minutes, basting and turning the liver several times. Blend the sour cream into the pan juices. Heat but do not let boil. Slice and serve with the gravy. The liver may be sliced before cooking, if you prefer. Cook only 10 minutes after browning.

Serves 6–8.

Fígado

PORTUGUESE CALF'S LIVER IN NUT SAUCE

1 pound calf's liver	¼ teaspoon freshly ground
3 tablespoons vegetable oil	black pepper
¾ cup chopped onions	1 teaspoon grated lemon
1 clove garlic, minced	rind
½ cup ground walnuts	½ cup chicken broth
¾ teaspoon salt	

Rinse the liver, cut in narrow strips, and dry on paper towels. Heat the oil in a skillet, sauté the onions and garlic 10 minutes. Add the liver; sauté until no pink remains. Mix in the nuts, salt, pepper, lemon rind, and broth; cook over low heat 5 minutes, stirring frequently. *Serves 4.*

Fegatini di Vitello al Vino

ITALIAN CALF'S LIVER IN WINE SAUCE

1 pound calf's liver	⅛ teaspoon sage
4 slices bacon, diced	½ cup Marsala or sweet
4 tablespoons butter	sherry
1¼ teaspoons salt	
¼ teaspoon freshly ground	
black pepper	

Rinse the liver, cut in pencil-thin 2-inch strips, and dry on paper towels.

In a skillet, lightly brown the bacon; pour off the fat. Add the butter to the skillet, and, when foaming, the liver. Sauté 2 minutes; season with the salt, pepper, and sage. Sauté 2 minutes longer. Remove and keep hot.

Stir the wine into the skillet, scraping the bottom of browned particles. Cook over medium heat 1 minute. Pour over the liver. Serve on sautéed bread if you like.

Serves 4.

Leberragout

VIENNESE LIVER RAGOUT

1 pound calf's liver	1 teaspoon salt
4 tablespoons butter	2 teaspoons paprika
1 cup thinly sliced onions	½ cup sour cream

Rinse the liver, cut in narrow strips, and dry on paper towels. Melt 2 tablespoons of the butter in a skillet; sauté the onions until golden. Remove. Melt the remaining butter in the skillet; sauté the liver 5 minutes. Return the onions; season with the salt and paprika. Mix in the sour cream, heat but do not let boil. Serve on rice or toast if desired.
Serves 4.

Lefver Kroketter

SWEDISH LIVER BALLS

1 pound calf's liver	1 teaspoon paprika
3 tablespoons butter	1 teaspoon salt
¾ cup chopped sweet pickle	½ teaspoon pepper
	½ cup mayonnaise

Rinse the liver, cut in small pieces, and dry on paper towels. Melt the butter in a skillet. Add the liver, cover, and cook over low heat 10 minutes. Purée the undrained liver in an electric blender, or chop to a paste, or put through a food chopper. Mix the purée with the sweet pickle, paprika, salt, pepper, and mayonnaise. Taste for seasoning. Shape mixture into 1-inch balls.
Serves 8 as an appetizer.

Kalvlever Pudding
SWEDISH LIVER CUSTARD

1 pound calf's liver	Dash cayenne pepper
6 egg yolks	2 tablespoons minced parsley
⅓ cup heavy cream	¼ cup finely chopped,
1½ teaspoons salt	sautéed mushrooms
¼ teaspoon freshly ground	2 tablespoons melted butter
black pepper	

Rinse and drain the liver. Purée the raw liver in an electric blender or force through a food mill.

Beat the egg yolks, then mix in the liver, cream, salt, pepper, cayenne pepper, parsley, mushrooms, and butter. Beat well. Divide among 6 buttered ramekins or custard cups. Place the ramekins in a shallow pan of hot water. Bake in a preheated 350° oven 20 minutes, or until a knife inserted in the center comes out clean. Serve hot.

Serves 6.

Foies de Veau en Aspic
CALF'S LIVER IN ASPIC

1 pound calf's liver	¼ teaspoon salt
1½ envelopes (4½	Dash freshly ground black
teaspoons) gelatin	pepper
2½ cups chicken broth	¼ cup medium-dry sherry
2 tablespoons butter	
3 tablespoons minced green	
onions (scallions)	

Rinse and dice the liver, dry on paper towels.

Soften the gelatin in ½ cup of the broth, then place over hot water, stirring until dissolved. Add to the remaining broth. Rinse 6 ½-cup molds or teacups with cold water, shake out, then pour the gelatin mixture into them to a depth of ⅛ inch. Chill until firm. Let the remaining gelatin mixture stand until syrupy.

Melt the butter in a skillet; sauté the liver 3 minutes. Add the green onions; sauté 1 minute. Pour off the fat and add the salt, pepper, and sherry. Cover and cook over low heat 5 minutes. Mix in ½ cup of the gelatin mixture. Chill until the mixture barely begins to set. Divide the liver mixture among the molds and pour the remaining gelatin mixture over it. Chill until firm. Carefully unmold onto shredded lettuce.

Serves 6.

Parboiled Calf's Brains

3 calf's brains	1 onion
2 tablespoons vinegar	1 bay leaf
1 teaspoon salt	2 sprigs parsley

Wash the brains under cold running water; remove the membranes. Cover with cold water and let soak 2 hours, changing the water twice. Drain and cover with fresh water; add the vinegar, salt, onion, bay leaf, and parsley. Bring to a boil, cover, and cook over low heat 20 minutes. Remove from heat and let stand in the stock until cool enough to handle. If you want to parboil the brains several hours before using, leave them in the stock, cover, and refrigerate until needed. Drain and use as directed in recipes.

Cervelles au Buerre Noir

BRAINS IN BLACK BUTTER

3 Parboiled Calf's Brains*	½ pound butter
¼ cup flour	3 teaspoons capers
1 teaspoon salt	2 tablespoons wine vinegar

Dry the brains and cut each in half lengthwise. Dip in a mixture of the flour and salt. Melt 3 tablespoons of the butter in a skillet; brown the brains in it. Transfer the brains to a heated serving platter, sprinkle with the capers, and keep warm. Put the remain-

ing butter in the same skillet and heat until it browns; remove
from the heat and stir in the vinegar. Return the skillet to heat
and bring to a boil. Pour over the brains.
Serves 3–4.

Cervello all' Aceto
BRAINS IN BROWN BUTTER, ITALIAN STYLE

1 pound calf's brains	3 cups water
1 carrot, quartered	3 tablespoons butter
1 stalk celery, sliced	2 tablespoons wine vinegar
¼ teaspoon thyme	2 tablespoons minced parsley
¼ teaspoon orégano	1 tablespoon capers
1½ teaspoons salt	

Wash the brains, remove the membranes, and soak in cold
water 30 minutes. Drain. Combine the brains in a saucepan with
the carrot, celery, thyme, orégano, salt, and water. Bring to a boil
and cook over low heat 25 minutes. Drain well and place on a hot
serving dish.

Put the butter in a skillet and heat until browned. Mix in the
vinegar and parsley. Pour the butter sauce over the brains and
sprinkle with the capers.
Serves 4.

Cervello alla Milanese
BREADED BRAINS

3 calf's brains	¼ cup grated Parmesan
¼ cup flour	cheese
1 egg	4 tablespoons butter
1 teaspoon salt	Lemon wedges
¼ cup dry bread crumbs	

Wash the brains, remove the veins and connective tissues, and soak in ice water 30 minutes. Drain and dry, then cut in ½-inch cubes. Dip the pieces in the flour, then in the egg beaten with the salt, and finally roll in the bread crumbs mixed with the cheese.

Melt the butter in a skillet; brown the brains in it on all sides. Garnish with lemon wedges. *Serves 3–4.*

Cervello Fritto

ITALIAN FRIED BRAINS

3 Parboiled Calf's Brains*	1 teaspoon salt
½ cup olive oil	¼ teaspoon white pepper
3 tablespoons lemon juice	2 eggs, beaten
2 tablespoons minced parsley	½ cup vegetable oil
¾ cup flour	

Cut the parboiled brains in half horizontally. Mix together the oil, lemon juice, and parsley. Marinate the brains in the mixture for 15 minutes. Drain. Mix together the flour, salt, and pepper; dip the brains in the mixture, then in the eggs.

Heat the oil in a skillet; brown the brains in it on both sides. Serve with lemon wedges.

Serves 6 as a first course.

New Zealand Braised Brains

1 cup julienne-cut ham	3 Parboiled Calf's Brains*
1 cup chicken broth	4 tablespoons butter
2 teaspoons lemon juice	

In a saucepan, combine the ham, broth, and lemon juice. Bring to a boil and cook over low heat 10 minutes. Add the brains; cook 10 minutes. Drain and slice the brains and place on a heated serving dish.

Put the butter in a skillet and heat until it browns; pour over the brains. *Serves 4.*

Inkha Mishwee

SYRIAN BAKED BRAINS

4 Parboiled Calf's Brains*   1 cup peeled, chopped
3 tablespoons butter   tomatoes
¼ cup chopped onions   ½ teaspoon salt
2 tablespoons chopped   ⅛ teaspoon white pepper
  green peppers   1 bay leaf
2 tablespoons flour   ⅛ teaspoon thyme
¾ cup beef broth

Cube the parboiled brains.

Melt the butter in a saucepan; sauté the onions and green peppers 5 minutes. Blend in the flour, then add the broth and tomatoes, stirring steadily to the boiling point. Add the salt, pepper, bay leaf, and thyme; cook over low heat 20 minutes. Discard the bay leaf, and gently stir the brains into the sauce. Taste for seasoning, and turn into a baking dish. Bake in a 350° oven 15 minutes. *Serves 4–6.*

Crocchette di Cervella

BRAIN CROQUETTES

1 pound Parboiled Calf's   1 egg, beaten
  Brains*   ¼ cup flour
1¼ teaspoons salt   4 tablespoons butter
¼ teaspoon white pepper   Lemon wedges
½ cup chopped, sautéed
  onions

Mash the parboiled brains to a paste. Mix in the salt, pepper, and onions. Chill the mixture for 2 hours. Form into 8 croquettes; dip in the egg, then in the flour.

Melt the butter in a skillet; brown the croquettes on both sides. Serve with lemon wedges.

Serves 4.

Creeri de Vitel

RUMANIAN CHOPPED BRAINS

3 Parboiled Calf's Brains*
1 cup chopped onions
¼ cup vegetable oil

¼ teaspoon freshly ground
black pepper
¼ cup lemon juice

Chop together the parboiled brains, onions, oil, pepper, and lemon juice. Taste for seasoning. Chill.
Serves 6 as a first course.

Peceni Mozak C Lukom

SERBIAN CALF'S BRAINS SAUTÉED

3 Parboiled Calf's Brains*
4 tablespoons butter
½ cup minced onions
2 tablespoons chopped
   celery leaves

1 teaspoon salt
¼ teaspoon white pepper
1 teaspoon Worcestershire
   sauce

Dice the parboiled brains.
Melt the butter in a skillet; sauté the onions and celery leaves 5 minutes. Add the brains; sauté 5 minutes, stirring almost constantly. Sprinkle with the salt, pepper, and Worcestershire sauce.
Serves 3–4.

Parboiled Calf's Sweetbreads

Calf's sweetbreads are very delicate and spoil quickly, so always keep them refrigerated and use within 24 hours. Try to get slaughterhouse sweetbreads—these are not frozen.

Wash the sweetbreads and soak them in ice water for 1 hour. Drain, then cover with water, and add 2 teaspoons of vinegar or lemon juice and about 1 teaspoon of salt (for 2 or 3 pairs). Bring to a boil and cook over low heat 15 minutes. Drain, cover with cold water and let cool. Drain and remove the membranes, tubes, and connective tissues. Use as directed in recipes, but keep them in the refrigerator until ready to use.

Ris de Veau Clamart

BRAISED SWEETBREADS WITH GREEN PEAS

4 pairs Parboiled Calf's Sweetbreads*	1½ cups chicken broth
6 tablespoons butter	2 cups cooked or canned green peas
1½ cups chopped onions	2 teaspoons potato flour or cornstarch
2 carrots, grated	2 tablespoons water
¾ teaspoon salt	
¼ teaspoon white pepper	

Slice the parboiled sweetbreads diagonally. Melt 4 tablespoons of the butter in a baking dish; sauté the onions and carrots 10 minutes. Arrange the sweetbreads over the vegetables, season with salt and pepper, and add the chicken broth. Bake in a 425° oven 30 minutes, basting frequently.

Transfer the sweetbreads to a hot serving dish. Toss the peas in the remaining butter until coated and pour over the sweetbreads.

Mix the potato flour or cornstarch and water to a paste and stir into the baking dish. Cook over direct heat, stirring, until thickened. Taste for seasoning and pour over the sweetbreads.

Serves 4–6.

Animelle alla Ciociara

ITALIAN BRAISED SWEETBREADS

3 pairs Parboiled Calf's
    Sweetbreads*
¼ cup flour
4 tablespoons olive oil
4 tablespoons butter
¼ teaspoon white pepper
1 cup sliced, sautéed
    mushrooms

½ cup julienne-cut
    prosciutto (ham) or
    cooked ham
¾ cup peeled, diced
    tomatoes
½ cup dry white wine
1 teaspoon salt

Dry the parboiled sweetbreads thoroughly and leave whole. Dip lightly in the flour. Heat the oil in a skillet; brown the sweetbreads in it on both sides. Pour off the oil. Add the butter, pepper, mushrooms, ham, tomatoes, wine, and salt. Bring to a boil and cook over low heat 10 minutes.
Serves 6.

Mollejas a la Española

SPANISH BRAISED SWEETBREADS

3 pairs Calf's sweetbreads
1 tablespoon vinegar
1½ teaspoons salt
4 tablespoons butter
1 cup diced onions

1 cup thinly sliced carrots
10 slices crisp bacon,
    crumbled
¾ cup chicken broth
¼ teaspoon white pepper

Wash the sweetbreads and soak in ice water 1 hour. Drain, add fresh water to cover, the vinegar, and ¾ teaspoon of the salt. Bring to a boil and cook over low heat 15 minutes. Drain, add cold water to cover, and let soak 15 minutes. Remove the membranes and tubes of the sweetbreads and slice.

Melt the butter in a skillet; sauté the onions and carrots 5 minutes. Add the sweetbreads and bacon; cook until sweetbreads brown lightly. Add the broth, remaining salt, and pepper. Cover and cook over low heat 15 minutes, stirring occasionally. Serve on sautéed bread if desired.

Serves 4–6.

Ris de Veau Grillé

BROILED SWEETBREADS

3 pairs Parboiled Calf's Sweetbreads*	**1½ teaspoons salt**
⅓ cup flour	**¼ teaspoon white pepper**
	½ cup melted butter

Cut the parboiled sweetbreads in half horizontally, to make them thinner. Dip the pieces in a mixture of the flour, salt, and pepper, then in the melted butter. Broil until delicately browned on both sides, basting frequently with the remaining butter. *Serves 3–6.*

Virginia Broiled Sweetbreads

3 pairs Parboiled Calf's Sweetbreads*	**1 cup bread crumbs**
1¼ teaspoons salt	**6 slices cooked ham, cut ⅛ inch thick**
¼ teaspoon freshly ground black pepper	**6 mushroom caps**
¾ cup melted butter	**6 slices buttered toast**

Split the parboiled sweetbreads in half. Season with the salt and pepper, then dip in the melted butter, then roll in the crumbs. Sprinkle with ¼ cup of the butter and broil about 5 inches from the source of heat until well browned on both sides. Broil the ham at the same time. Sauté the mushrooms in 2 tablespoons of the remaining butter.

Place a slice of ham on each slice of toast, arrange the sweetbreads over the ham, and top with a mushroom. Lightly brown the remaining butter and pour over the top. *Serves 6.*

Ris de Veau aux Beurre Noir

SAUTÉED SWEETBREADS IN BLACK BUTTER

2 pairs Parboiled Calf's
　Sweetbreads*
¼ cup flour
1 teaspoon salt
¼ teaspoon freshly ground
　black pepper

6 tablespoons butter
1 clove garlic, minced
1 teaspoon lemon juice
½ cup dry white wine
2 tablespoons minced
　capers

Split the parboiled sweetbreads in half. Dip the sweetbreads in a mixture of the flour, salt, and pepper. Melt 3 tablespoons of the butter in a skillet; brown the sweetbreads in it. Remove and keep warm. Add the remaining butter to the skillet. Cook over very low heat until browned. Add the garlic, then the lemon juice, wine, and capers. Bring to a boil and pour over the sweetbreads. *Serves 4.*

Stuvad Kalvbräss

CREAMED SWEETBREADS

3 pairs Parboiled Calf's
　Sweetbreads*
2 tablespoons butter
2 tablespoons flour
1 cup chicken broth

½ cup heavy cream
1 teaspoon salt
½ teaspoon white pepper
1 tablespoon lemon juice

Cube the parboiled sweetbreads. Melt the butter in a saucepan; blend in the flour and mix well. Add the chicken broth, stirring steadily to the boiling point. Add the cream, and cook over low heat 5 minutes. Add the salt, pepper, lemon juice, and sweetbreads; cook 5 minutes. Serve on toast. *Serves 4–6.*

Ris de Veau Sauté à la Crème
SWEETBREADS SAUTÉED IN CREAM

3 pairs Parboiled Calf's
  Sweetbreads*
¼ cup flour
3 tablespoons butter
2 tablespoons warm cognac
½ pound mushrooms,
  sliced

2 truffles, sliced
1 teaspoon salt
⅛ teaspoon white pepper
⅛ teaspoon nutmeg
½ cup sweet sherry
1 cup heavy cream

Slice the parboiled sweetbreads diagonally; dip them in the flour. Melt the butter in a skillet; lightly brown the sweetbreads in it. Pour the cognac over them and set aflame. When the flames die, add the mushrooms, truffles, salt, pepper, and nutmeg. Cook over low heat 5 minutes. Stir in the sherry; cook 5 minutes. Blend in the cream; heat but do not let boil. Taste for seasoning. *Serves 4–6.*

Ris de Veau au Gratin
SWEETBREADS AU GRATIN

3 pairs Parboiled Calf's
  Sweetbreads*
3 tablespoons butter
¼ pound mushrooms,
  sliced
1 clove garlic, minced
2 teaspoons flour

¾ cup chicken broth
1 teaspoon salt
½ teaspoon freshly ground
  black pepper
½ cup sour cream
½ cup grated Parmesan
  cheese

Cut the parboiled sweetbreads in thin slices. Melt 2 tablespoons of the butter in a skillet; brown the sweetbreads in it. Remove and keep warm. Add the remaining butter to the skillet; sauté the mushrooms 3 minutes. Blend in the garlic and flour; add the broth, stirring steadily to the boiling point. Mix in the salt, pepper, and sour cream; return the sweetbreads. Cover and cook over low

heat 5 minutes. Turn into an ovenproof serving dish and sprinkle with the cheese. Place under the broiler until browned. Serve directly from the dish.
Serves 4–6.

Animelle al Prosciutto

ITALIAN SWEETBREADS AND HAM

3 pairs Parboiled Calf's
Sweetbreads*
2 tablespoons butter
2 tablespoons olive oil
½ teaspoon salt
⅛ teaspoon white pepper

4 slices Parma or prosciutto
ham, cut julienne
3 tablespoons Marsala or
sweet sherry
2 tablespoons minced
parsley

Cube the parboiled sweetbreads. Heat the butter and oil in a skillet; sauté the sweetbreads until browned. Add the salt, pepper, and ham; sauté 3 minutes. Stir in the wine and parsley. Cook over high heat 2 minutes.
Serves 4–6.

Kalbräss med Schinken

SWEDISH SWEETBREADS AND HAM

3 pairs sweetbreads
1½ cups water
1½ cups dry white wine
1 small bay leaf
¼ teaspoon thyme
1 teaspoon salt
4 tablespoons butter

¼ cup flour
1 cup milk
½ pound boiled ham,
cubed
½ cup sliced stuffed olives
⅛ teaspoon white pepper

Soak the sweetbreads in ice water to cover for 1 hour. Drain. In a saucepan, combine and bring to a boil the 1½ cups water, the wine, bay leaf, thyme, and salt. Add the sweetbreads and cook over low heat 15 minutes. Drain the sweetbreads and place in ice water. Strain and measure 2 cups of the stock.

Drain the sweetbreads, remove the membranes and tubes, then cut into large cubes.

Melt the butter in a saucepan; blend in the flour. Add the reserved stock and milk, stirring steadily to the boiling point. Add the sweetbreads, ham, olives, and pepper; cook over low heat 10 minutes. Taste for seasoning. Serve in hot patty shells or on toast. *Serves 6–8.*

Ris de Veau à la Bourbonnaise

SWEETBREADS IN HERB SAUCE

4 pairs Parboiled Calf's Sweetbreads*
6 tablespoons butter
1 teaspoon salt
⅛ teaspoon white pepper
1 clove garlic, minced
½ teaspoon tarragon
1 tablespoon minced parsley
3 tablespoons chopped chives or green onions (scallions)
1¼ cups chicken broth
1 egg yolk
1 teaspoon lemon juice

Cut the parboiled sweetbreads in half lengthwise and then into quarters crosswise. Melt the butter in a skillet; lightly brown the sweetbreads in it on both sides. Add the salt, pepper, garlic, tarragon, parsley, chives, and broth. Bring to a boil and cook over low heat 5 minutes.

Beat the egg yolk and lemon juice in a bowl; gradually add a little of the hot sauce, beating steadily to prevent curdling. Return to skillet; heat but do not let boil. Taste for seasoning. Serve in patty shells or *croustades.*
Serves 4–6.

Geschmorte Kalbsmilch

BAVARIAN BAKED SWEETBREADS AND CHICKEN LIVERS

3 pairs Parboiled Calf's
Sweetbreads*
1 pound chicken livers
6 tablespoons butter
1 teaspoon salt

¼ teaspoon freshly ground
black pepper
½ cup dry white wine
½ pound mushrooms,
sliced and sautéed

Cut the parboiled sweetbreads in half crosswise. Wash the livers, removing any discolored areas.

Spread the butter in a 1½-quart baking dish. Arrange the sweetbreads in it and cover with the livers. Season with the salt and pepper and add the wine. Bake in a 425° oven 10 minutes. Mix in the mushrooms; reduce heat to 325° and bake 10 minutes longer. *Serves 6.*

Ris de Veau Lucullus

SWEETBREADS AND MUSHROOMS LUCULLUS

3 pairs Parboiled Calf's
Sweetbreads*
6 tablespoons butter
1 cup port
1 pound mushrooms,
sliced

2 teaspoons beef extract
1 teaspoon salt
¼ teaspoon white pepper
2 cups heavy cream

Cut the parboiled sweetbreads in half horizontally to make thinner, then cut them in half crosswise. Heat 4 tablespoons of the butter in a casserole; lightly brown the sweetbreads in it. Add the port; cook over low heat until the wine is reduced to half. Melt the remaining butter in a skillet; sauté the mushrooms 5 minutes. Mix into the casserole with the beef extract, salt, pepper, and cream. Cover and bake in a 350° oven 20 minutes. Thicken sauce, if necessary, with 1 tablespoon flour kneaded with 1 tablespoon butter. *Serves 4–6.*

Stekt Kalbräss med Svamp och Bacon

FRIED SWEETBREADS WITH MUSHROOMS AND BACON,
SWEDISH STYLE

4 pairs Parboiled Calf's Sweetbreads*	¾ pound mushrooms
½ cup dry bread crumbs	¼ pound (1 stick) butter
2 teaspoons salt	8 slices crisp bacon
¼ teaspoon freshly ground black pepper	

Cut the parboiled sweetbreads into ½-inch slices. Mix together the bread crumbs, salt, and pepper. Dip the sweetbreads into the mixture.

Cut the mushrooms in half. Melt 2 tablespoons of the butter in a skillet; add the mushrooms, cover, and cook over low heat 5 minutes. Remove and keep warm. Melt the remaining butter in the skillet; add the sweetbreads and brown on both sides. Arrange the sweetbreads on a hot platter and surround with the bacon and mushrooms.

Serves 6–8.

Ris de Veau aux Champignons

SAUTÉED SWEETBREADS WITH MUSHROOMS

2 pairs Parboiled Calf's Sweetbreads*	¼ cup chicken broth
⅓ cup flour	½ teaspoon tomato paste
3 tablespoons butter	1 clove garlic, minced
1 teaspoon salt	Sautéed bread or toast
¼ teaspoon white pepper	8 mushroom caps, sautéed
2 tablespoons warm cognac	2 tablespoons minced parsley
¾ cup dry white wine	

Cut the parboiled sweetbreads horizontally in half to make them thinner. Dip in the flour, reserving 1 tablespoon. Melt the

butter in a skillet; brown the sweetbreads on both sides. Season
with the salt and pepper. Pour the cognac over them and set
aflame. When the flames die, remove the sweetbreads from the
pan and keep warm. Blend the reserved flour into the pan. Add
the wine, broth, tomato paste, and garlic, stirring steadily to the
boiling point; cook over low heat 5 minutes. Place the sweetbreads
on sautéed bread or toast with a mushroom on top. Pour the
sauce over all and sprinkle with the parsley.

Serves 2–4.

Geschmorte Kalbsmilch

GERMAN SWEETBREADS AND MUSHROOMS

3 pairs Parboiled Calf's Sweetbreads*	**2 cups chicken broth**
3 tablespoons butter	**1 teaspoon salt**
1 cup diced onions	**¼ teaspoon white pepper**
2 tablespoons vegetable oil	**1 16-ounce can green peas, drained**
1 pound mushrooms, sliced	**3 tablespoons minced parsley**
3 tablespoons flour	

Dice the parboiled sweetbreads. Melt 2 tablespoons of the butter
in a skillet and brown the onions in it. Remove the onions and
reserve. Heat the oil and remaining butter in the skillet. Cook the
mushrooms in it for 5 minutes. Mix the flour and broth until
smooth and stir into the mushrooms. Cook over low heat 5 minutes, stirring constantly. Add the browned onions, the sweetbreads,
salt, pepper, peas, and parsley. Heat and serve on toast or in patty
shells.

Serves 4–6.

Animelle alla Campania
NEAPOLITAN SWEETBREADS

4 pairs Parboiled Calf's Sweetbreads*	⅛ teaspoon white pepper
	1 teaspoon capers
3 tablespoons olive oil	½ cup sliced black olives
1 teaspoon salt	2 tablespoons bread crumbs

Cut the parboiled sweetbreads into large cubes. Heat 1½ table-spoons of the olive oil in a shallow casserole; add the sweetbreads, salt, pepper, capers, and olives. Sprinkle with the bread crumbs and pour the remaining olive oil over the crumbs. Bake in a 400° oven 15 minutes. Serve from the casserole.
Serves 4–6.

Ris de Veau Lyonnaise
SWEETBREADS WITH ONION PURÉE

3 pairs Parboiled Calf's Sweetbreads*	2 carrots, grated
	1 bay leaf
¼ cup raw rice	¼ teaspoon thyme
1 quart boiling water	¾ cup dry white wine
6 tablespoons butter	½ cup chicken broth
4 cups chopped onions	½ pound mushrooms,
1 teaspoon salt	sliced and sautéed
⅛ teaspoon white pepper	½ cup diced ham
2 cloves garlic, minced	½ cup grated Swiss cheese

Dry the parboiled sweetbreads on paper towels. Put between 2 plates with a weight on top and cool.

Cook the rice in the boiling water for 5 minutes. Drain well. Melt half the butter in a heavy saucepan. Add 3 cups of the onions and stir over low heat for 1 minute. Stir in the rice, salt, and pepper. Cover and bake in a 300° oven 50 minutes, stirring occasionally. Purée the mixture in an electric blender or force through a sieve.

Melt the remaining butter in a saucepan; add the remaining onions, garlic, carrots, bay leaf, thyme, and sweetbreads. Sauté until the sweetbreads are browned on both sides. Stir in the wine and broth, cover, and simmer gently 5 minutes. Remove the sweetbreads, slice, and keep warm. Strain the pan juices into another pan and mix in the onion purée. Arrange the sweetbreads on a serving dish and over them place the sliced mushrooms and diced ham. Cover with the sauce and sprinkle with the cheese; place on the upper level of a 425° oven until delicately browned. *Serves 4–6.*

Zwezerikballetjes

DUTCH SWEETBREAD CROQUETTES

3 pairs Parboiled Calf's Sweetbreads*	2 tablespoons minced shallots or green onions (scallions)
4 tablespoons butter	2 tablespoons minced parsley
2 tablespoons grated onion	2 eggs
½ cup flour	2 tablespoons milk
1 cup chicken broth	¾ cup dry bread crumbs
1 cup light cream	Vegetable oil for deep frying
2 teaspoons salt	Parsley sprigs
⅛ teaspoon cayenne pepper	

Dice the parboiled sweetbreads. Melt the butter in a saucepan; stir in the onion and half the flour, then add the broth and cream, stirring steadily to the boiling point. Cook over low heat 10 minutes, stirring occasionally. Stir in 1½ teaspoons of the salt and the cayenne pepper. Cool 10 minutes, then fold in the sweetbreads, shallots or green onions, and parsley. Chill the mixture, and form into 12 croquettes.

Beat together the eggs, milk, and remaining salt. Dip the croquettes in the remaining flour, the beaten eggs, and finally in the bread crumbs, coating them thoroughly.

Heat the oil to 390° and fry a few croquettes at a time until browned. Drain and place on a hot platter. Garnish with parsley sprigs. *Serves 6.*

Moletas de Vitela com Porto
SWEETBREADS IN PORT WINE

3 pairs Parboiled Calf's
    Sweetbreads*
3 tablespoons flour
6 tablespoons butter
1 cup chopped onions

1 teaspoon salt
⅛ teaspoon white pepper
1 cup port
6 shallots, sliced

Cube the parboiled sweetbreads and toss them with the flour. Melt the butter in a skillet; lightly brown the sweetbreads. Add the onions, salt, and pepper; sauté 5 minutes. Mix in the port; cook over low heat 5 minutes. Stir in the shallots; cook 5 minutes. Taste for seasoning. Serve with green peas and sautéed bread.
Serves 3–6.

Ris de Veau au Vin Blanc
SWEETBREADS IN WHITE WINE

4 pairs Parboiled Calf's
    Sweetbreads*
3 tablespoons butter
1½ cups sliced onions
1 cup grated carrots
3 tablespoons minced
    parsley
1 bay leaf

1½ teaspoons salt
¼ teaspoon white pepper
1 tablespoon sweet sherry
½ cup dry white wine
¼ cup chicken broth
2 cups fresh or frozen
    green peas
¾ cup chopped mushrooms

Cut the parboiled sweetbreads in quarters. Melt the butter in a casserole; sauté the onions and carrots 10 minutes, stirring frequently. Arrange the sweetbreads over them and add the parsley, bay leaf, salt, pepper, sherry, white wine, broth, peas, and mushrooms. Bake in a 375° oven 30 minutes, turning the sweetbreads once or twice. Discard bay leaf.
Serves 6–8.

Kalvbrässpastej

SWEDISH SWEETBREAD LOAF

2 pairs Parboiled Calf's Sweetbreads*	4 eggs, beaten
4 tablespoons butter	1 teaspoon salt
4 tablespoons flour	Dash cayenne pepper
1 cup light cream	12 cooked or canned
¾ cup grated Gruyère cheese	asparagus tips

Chop the parboiled sweetbreads. Melt the butter in a saucepan. Blend in the flour. Gradually add the cream, stirring constantly to the boiling point. Add the cheese. Cook over low heat 5 minutes, stirring occasionally. Cool 15 minutes, then beat in the eggs.

Add the sweetbreads, salt, and pepper. Taste for seasoning. Arrange the asparagus on the bottom of a buttered 9-inch loaf pan and slowly pour the sweetbread mixture over them. Bake in a 300° oven 40 minutes, or until a knife inserted in the center comes out clean. Carefully run a knife around the pan and turn out onto a heated platter.

Serves 4–6.

Queue de Boeuf Bourguignonne

BRAISED OXTAILS IN RED WINE

2 oxtails, cut in 1-inch lengths	1 teaspoon salt
½ cup flour	½ teaspoon freshly ground black pepper
3 slices salt pork, diced	4 cups dry red wine
1 cup diced onions	1 cup water
1 carrot, grated	2 teaspoons tomato paste

Cover the oxtails with boiling water, drain, and dry; roll in the flour. Brown the salt pork in a Dutch oven or casserole; drain off all but 2 tablespoons fat. Add the oxtails, onions, and carrot and cook until browned. Mix in the salt, pepper, and 2 cups of the wine. Cook over high heat until the wine evaporates. Add the water, tomato paste, and remaining wine; cover and cook over low heat 3 hours. Taste for seasoning.

Serves 4–6.

Potrawa z Ogona

POLISH OXTAIL RAGOUT

2 oxtails, cut in 2-inch lengths	1½ pounds tomatoes, peeled and chopped
1 carrot	½ teaspoon freshly ground black pepper
3 sprigs parsley	⅛ teaspoon nutmeg
3 teaspoons salt	¼ cup sliced, blanched almonds
2 tablespoons butter	3 tablespoons seedless raisins
¾ cup chopped onions	
¾ cup diced celery	
¼ pound ham, cut julienne	
¾ cup dry white wine	

Cover the oxtails with boiling water and drain. Place in a saucepan, add the carrot, parsley, half the salt, and water barely to cover. Bring to a boil and cook over medium heat 1½ hours. Drain well.

Melt the butter in a saucepan; sauté the onions, celery, and ham 5 minutes. Add the oxtails; cook 10 minutes. Mix in the wine; cook until evaporated. Add the tomatoes, pepper, nutmeg, and remaining salt. Cover and cook over low heat 50 minutes. Mix in the nuts and raisins; cook 5 minutes longer.

Serves 6–8.

Ragoût de Queue de Boeuf

OXTAIL STEW

2 2-pound oxtails, cut in 2-inch lengths	4 cups dry red wine
¾ cup flour	3 sprigs parsley
2 teaspoons salt	2 stalks celery	tied together
½ teaspoon freshly ground black pepper	1 leek
½ teaspoon thyme	1 bay leaf
4 tablespoons olive oil	1 clove garlic, minced
2 cloves	½ pound mushrooms, sliced
12 small white onions	
1 cup boiling water	

Cover the oxtail pieces with boiling water, drain, and dry. Roll in a mixture of the flour, salt, pepper, and thyme. Heat the oil in a Dutch oven; brown the oxtail pieces in it on all sides. Pour off the fat. Stick the cloves in an onion and add with all the onions, the water, wine, parsley, celery, leek, bay leaf, and garlic. Cover tightly and bake in a 300° oven 3 hours. Add the mushrooms. Re-cover and bake 30 minutes longer. Discard the herb bundle. Skim the fat and taste for seasoning. *Serves 4–6.*

Geschmorte Nieren

GERMAN BRAISED KIDNEYS

6 veal kidneys	¼ teaspoon freshly ground black pepper
2 cups water	
2 tablespoons vinegar	½ cup sour cream
4 tablespoons butter	2 tablespoons minced parsley
1 cup chopped onions	
1½ teaspoons salt	

Wash the kidneys, cut in half, and discard the cores. Soak in the water mixed with the vinegar 1 hour. Drain and slice very thin.

Melt the butter in a skillet; sauté the onions 5 minutes. Add the kidneys and cook until browned. Mix in the salt, pepper, and sour cream; cook over low heat 5 minutes. Sprinkle with the parsley. *Serves 6.*

Rignoni al Marsala
ITALIAN BRAISED KIDNEYS

4 veal kidneys	1 teaspoon grated lemon
3 cups boiling water	rind
2 tablespoons lemon juice	½ cup Marsala or sweet
4 tablespoons butter	sherry
1¼ teaspoons salt	3 tablespoons minced
¼ teaspoon freshly ground	parsley
black pepper	

Wash the kidneys, cut in half, and remove the cores. Soak in the boiling water mixed with the lemon juice for 3 minutes. Drain, dry, and slice thin.

Melt the butter in a skillet; sauté the kidneys 5 minutes. Mix in the salt, pepper, lemon rind, and wine. Cook over medium heat 5 minutes. Sprinkle with the parsley. *Serves 4.*

Rognons de Veau au Cognac
VEAL KIDNEYS IN COGNAC SAUCE

4 veal kidneys	1½ teaspoons salt
1½ cups water	¼ teaspoon freshly ground
2 teaspoons vinegar	black pepper
5 tablespoons butter	⅛ teaspoon dry mustard
1 cup sliced mushrooms	¼ cup heavy cream
½ cup warm cognac	

Wash the kidneys, trim the fat, and remove the cores. Soak in a mixture of the water and vinegar for 1 hour. Drain and rinse in cold water. Dry the kidneys and cut in ½-inch-thick slices.

Melt 2 tablespoons of the butter in a skillet; sauté the mushrooms 5 minutes. Remove. Melt the remaining butter in the skillet; sauté the kidney slices 2 minutes on each side. Pour the cognac over them and set aflame. When the flames die, return the mushrooms and sprinkle with the salt, pepper, and mustard. Cook 1 minute. Stir in the cream; heat but do not let boil.

Serves 4.

Riñones con Jamón

KIDNEYS WITH HAM, SPANISH STYLE

6 veal kidneys	⅓ cup dry sherry
¼ cup flour	2 tablespoons minced parsley
4 tablespoons butter	6 slices ham
½ cup chopped onions	6 slices sautéed bread
1½ teaspoons salt	
¼ teaspoon freshly ground black pepper	

Wash the kidneys and soak in cold water to cover for 1 hour. Drain; slice the kidneys and discard the white cores. Dip the kidney slices in the flour.

Melt the butter in a skillet; sauté the onions 5 minutes. Add the kidneys; cook over high heat 1 minute on each side. Add the salt, pepper, sherry, and parsley. Cover and cook over low heat 6 minutes. While the kidneys are cooking, heat the ham in a skillet without browning.

Place a slice of ham on each piece of bread and spoon the kidneys and pan juices over it.

Serves 6.

Rognons Clamart

KIDNEYS WITH PEAS

6 veal kidneys
2 cups water
2 tablespoons vinegar
⅓ cup flour
1½ teaspoons salt
½ teaspoon freshly ground
black pepper
2 tablespoons vegetable oil

2 tablespoons butter
½ cup finely chopped
onions
2 tablespoons minced parsley
½ cup dry red wine
⅛ teaspoon thyme
2 cups cooked green peas

Wash the kidneys, trim the fat, and remove the cores. Mix together the water and vinegar; soak the kidneys in the mixture 1 hour. Drain, dry, and slice. Toss the pieces in a mixture of the flour, salt, and pepper. Heat the oil and butter in a skillet; brown kidneys on both sides over high heat. Mix in the onions; cook 2 minutes. Add the parsley, wine, thyme, and peas. Cook over medium heat 5 minutes. *Serves 6.*

Rim, Molho de Madeira

KIDNEYS IN MADEIRA WINE

6 veal kidneys
6 tablespoons butter
1½ teaspoons salt
¼ teaspoon freshly ground
black pepper

⅓ cup meat glaze
2 tablespoons lemon juice
⅓ cup Madeira
2 tablespoons minced
parsley

Wash the kidneys well and soak in cold water 1 hour. Drain. Remove the cores and cut each kidney in 6 slices. Melt 2 tablespoons of the butter in a skillet and sauté the kidneys over high heat, 2 minutes on each side. Season with the salt and pepper. Transfer to a hot serving dish.

Stir the meat glaze, lemon juice, Madeira wine, parsley, and remaining butter into the pan and cook over high heat, stirring until the meat glaze melts. Pour over the kidneys.

Serves 6.

Rognons à la Créole

KIDNEYS, NEW ORLEANS STYLE

4 veal kidneys
½ cup flour
2 teaspoons salt
½ teaspoon freshly ground
black pepper
4 slices bacon, cut in small
pieces
2 tablespoons vegetable oil
1 cup thinly sliced onions
1 cup thinly sliced green
peppers

1 19-ounce can tomatoes
1 clove garlic, minced
1 bay leaf, finely chopped
¼ teaspoon thyme
2 tablespoons minced parsley
½ cup sliced green olives
⅛ teaspoon cayenne pepper
2 tablespoons butter

Wash the kidneys and soak in cold water 1 hour. Drain, remove the cores, and cut the kidneys in ¾-inch slices. Dip in a mixture of the flour, 1 teaspoon of the salt, and ¼ teaspoon of the pepper.

Prepare the sauce while the kidneys are soaking. Brown the bacon in a saucepan, pour off most of the fat. Add the oil, onions, and green peppers; cook 5 minutes. Mix in the tomatoes, garlic, bay leaf, thyme, parsley, olives, cayenne pepper, and the remaining salt and pepper. Bring to a boil and cook over low heat 30 minutes.

Melt the butter in a skillet; brown the kidneys in it. Add to the sauce; cook 10 minutes longer. Taste for seasoning. Serve with rice.

Serves 4.

Kidneys St. Louis

4 veal kidneys
5 tablespoons butter
¾ teaspoon salt
¼ teaspoon freshly
ground black pepper

2 teaspoons prepared
French-style mustard
½ teaspoon lemon juice
1 teaspoon Worcestershire
sauce

Wash the kidneys, cut in half, and remove the fat and cores. Soak in cold water 1 hour. Drain and cut the kidneys into small pieces.

Melt the butter in a skillet; sauté the kidneys 2 minutes. Add the salt, pepper, mustard, and lemon juice. Cook over medium heat 2 minutes, stirring almost constantly. Mix in the Worcestershire. *Serves 4.*

Nieren Lelia

KIDNEYS IN MUSTARD SAUCE, SALZBURG STYLE

4 veal kidneys
4 tablespoons butter
¼ pound mushrooms, sliced
1 clove garlic, minced
2 tablespoons flour
1¼ teaspoons salt

¼ teaspoon freshly ground black pepper
1 teaspoon dry mustard
1½ cups beef broth
2 tablespoons minced parsley

Wash the kidneys, cut in half, and remove the cores. Soak in cold water 50 minutes. Drain and cut into thick slices. Melt 2 tablespoons of the butter in a skillet, sauté the kidneys 1 minute on a side. Remove the kidneys. Melt the remaining butter in the skillet; sauté the mushrooms and garlic 3 minutes. Blend in the flour, salt, pepper, and mustard. Add the broth, stirring steadily to the boiling point; cook over low heat 5 minutes. Return the kidneys; cook 3 minutes. Sprinkle with the parsley and serve with rice. *Serves 4.*

Guiso de Riñones

SPANISH SAUTÉED KIDNEYS

6 veal kidneys
3 tablespoons olive oil
1 cup chopped onions
2 teaspoons Spanish paprika

1½ teaspoons salt
¼ cup dry bread crumbs
2 hard-cooked eggs, chopped

Wash the kidneys and soak in cold water 1 hour. Drain and remove the skin, fat, and cores of the kidneys, then cut into cubes. Heat the oil in a skillet; sauté the onions 5 minutes. Add the kidneys and paprika; sauté 5 minutes. Sprinkle with the salt and bread crumbs; cook 1 minute. Garnish with the chopped eggs. *Serves 6.*

Njur Sauté

SWEDISH SAUTÉED KIDNEYS

2 beef kidneys	½ cup chopped onions
½ cup flour	½ cup chopped green
1½ teaspoons salt	peppers
½ teaspoon freshly ground	½ teaspoon celery salt
black pepper	½ teaspoon paprika
3 tablespoons butter	1 teaspoon Worcestershire
1 cup tomato juice	sauce
½ cup beef broth	

Wash the kidneys and cut off any fat. Pour boiling water over them. Drain and remove skin and cores. Slice the kidneys. Combine the flour, salt, and pepper. Dip the kidney slices in the mixture. Melt the butter in a skillet. Brown the kidneys in it, cover, and cook over low heat for 15 minutes. Mix together the tomato juice, broth, onions, green peppers, celery salt, paprika, and Worcestershire sauce. Cook in a saucepan for 15 minutes. Add to the kidneys and cook for 3 minutes. *Serves 6.*

Riñones al Jerez

KIDNEYS IN SHERRY

4 veal kidneys	2 tablespoons minced
3 tablespoons butter	parsley
¾ cup chopped onions	¼ teaspoon freshly ground
1 tablespoon flour	black pepper
1 cup beef broth	2 tablespoons olive oil
	3 tablespoons dry sherry

Wash the kidneys and soak in cold water 1 hour. Drain and discard the cores. Slice the kidneys thin.

Melt the butter in a saucepan; sauté the onions until browned. Sprinkle with the flour, stirring until browned. Add the broth, mixing steadily to the boiling point; cook over low heat for 15 minutes. Mix in the parsley and pepper.

Heat the oil in a skillet; sauté the kidneys over high heat for 1 minute. Add to the sauce with the sherry. Cook over low heat 5 minutes. *Serves 6.*

Riñones en Salsa de Tomate

KIDNEYS IN TOMATO SAUCE, SPANISH STYLE

6 veal kidneys
3 tablespoons olive oil
1 cup chopped onions
1 cup canned tomato sauce
1 cup sliced mushrooms
2½ teaspoons salt
3 tablespoons butter
2 cups canned tiny green
  peas

½ teaspoon freshly ground
  black pepper
1 tablespoon minced
  parsley
¼ cup dry white wine
3 hard-cooked eggs, sliced

Wash the kidneys and soak in cold water 1 hour. Drain, discard the cores, and slice thin.

Heat the oil in a saucepan; sauté the onions for 10 minutes. Add the tomato sauce, mushrooms, and 1½ teaspoons salt; cook over low heat for 15 minutes.

Melt the butter in a skillet; cook the kidneys over high heat for 2 minutes. Add the peas, pepper, parsley, wine, and remaining salt; cook for 1 minute. Combine with the sauce and cook for 2 minutes, or until kidneys are tender. Garnish with the sliced eggs and serve with rice. *Serves 6.*

Rognoni al Vino Bianco

KIDNEYS IN WHITE WINE, ITALIAN STYLE

4 veal kidneys	2 cups thinly sliced onions
½ cup warm dry white wine	1½ teaspoons salt
	¼ teaspoon freshly ground black pepper
4 tablespoons butter	

Wash the kidneys, cut in half, and remove the cores. Soak in boiling water 5 minutes. Drain, dry, and slice, then marinate in the wine 1 hour. Drain and dry, reserving the wine.

Melt the butter in a skillet; sauté the onions over very low heat until soft and yellow. Sprinkle with the salt and pepper. Add the kidneys and ¼ cup of the reserved wine; cover and cook over low heat 10 minutes, adding the remaining wine after 5 minutes. Serve with sautéed Italian or French bread.

Serves 4.

Saure Nieren

KIDNEYS IN SOUR WINE SAUCE, GERMAN STYLE

6 veal kidneys	½ cup beef broth
4 tablespoons butter	¾ teaspoon salt
1 tablespoon flour	¼ teaspoon freshly ground black pepper
1 tablespoon wine vinegar	
½ cup dry white wine	1 tablespoon minced parsley

Wash the kidneys and soak in cold water for 1 hour. Drain, split, and remove the cores. Slice the kidneys crosswise.

Melt the butter in a skillet; sauté the kidneys over high heat for 2 minutes on each side. Remove and keep warm. Blend the flour into the skillet; then add the vinegar, wine, and broth. Cook over medium heat 5 minutes. Return the kidneys and add the salt, pepper, and parsley; heat but don't let mixture boil. Taste for seasoning.

Serves 6.

Borjuvese Frikandó

HUNGARIAN KIDNEY STEW

6 veal kidneys
2 tablespoons vinegar
¼ cup olive oil
2 cups chopped onions
2 cloves garlic, minced
1½ teaspoons salt
½ teaspoon freshly ground
  black pepper

1 cup boiling water
1 bay leaf
¼ cup minced parsley
1 teaspoon caraway seeds
1 cup sour cream

Wash the kidneys, cover with cold water, add the vinegar, and let soak 30 minutes. Slice thin, and remove the cores. Dry well.

Heat the oil in a skillet; brown the kidneys in it. Add the onions and garlic; cook 5 minutes. Pour off the fat. Add the salt, pepper, water, bay leaf, parsley, and caraway seeds. Cover and cook over low heat 45 minutes. Blend in the sour cream. Heat but do not let boil.

Serves 6.

Callos a la Chilena

CHILEAN TRIPE

2 pounds tripe
2 tablespoons lemon juice
¼ cup olive oil
1 cup sliced onions
1 teaspoon salt
1 cup tomato juice

1 cup corn kernels
¼ pound cream cheese,
  mashed
¼ pound Cheddar cheese,
  grated
⅛ teaspoon cayenne pepper

Wash the tripe in several changes of water and place it in a saucepan. Add the lemon juice and water to cover. Bring to a boil and cook over high heat 5 minutes. Drain well. Add fresh water to cover. Bring to a boil and cook over medium heat for 2 hours, or until tender. Drain and slice in matchlike strips.

Heat the olive oil in a skillet. Sauté the onions 10 minutes. Add the salt, tomato juice, corn, and tripe. Cook over low heat 20 minutes. Blend in the cream cheese, Cheddar cheese, and cayenne pepper. Cook 10 minutes, stirring occasionally. Taste for seasoning.

Serves 6–8.

Tripe à la Mode de Caen

TRIPE, CAEN STYLE

3 pounds tripe	**½ teaspoon freshly ground**
3 slices salt pork	**black pepper**
2 cups sliced onions	**¼ teaspoon thyme**
2 carrots, sliced	**¼ teaspoon marjoram**
½ cup thinly sliced celery	**2 sprigs parsley**
1 green pepper, chopped	**4 cups beef broth**
2 calf's feet, cut up	**4 cups cider**
2 bay leaves	**½ cup tomato paste**
2 teaspoons salt	**¼ cup Calvados or apple**
	brandy

Start the preparation of the tripe the day before it is to be served.

Wash the tripe under running water, then soak in water to cover 1 hour, changing the water 3 times. Drain. Cut tripe in strips 3 inches long by ½ inch wide.

Spread the salt pork on the bottom of a Dutch oven or heavy earthenware pot with a tight-fitting cover. Arrange the onions, carrots, celery, and green pepper over the salt pork, then add the tripe, calf's feet, bay leaves, salt, pepper, thyme, marjoram, parsley, broth, and cider. Cover tightly, and press aluminum foil around the edge of the cover to keep the steam from escaping. Bake in a 225° oven 12 hours (overnight is a good time). Place pan on direct low heat and stir the tomato paste and apple brandy into the pan juices. Cook 30 minutes longer. Taste for seasoning. Discard the calf's feet and serve in deep bowls.

Serves 8–10.

Tripe, Creole Style

2 pounds tripe
1 tablespoon vinegar
1 tablespoon salt
2 tablespoons butter
1½ cups sliced onions
2 tablespoons flour
2 cloves garlic, minced
¼ cup chopped ham

1 bay leaf, chopped
½ teaspoon thyme
¼ teaspoon cayenne
  pepper
1 20-ounce can tomatoes,
  drained
¾ cup julienne-cut green
  peppers

Wash the tripe in several changes of water. Combine in a saucepan with the vinegar, salt, and water to cover. Bring to a boil and cook over medium heat 4 hours or until tender. Drain and cut into strips 2 inches long by ½ inch wide.

Melt the butter in a saucepan; sauté the onions 10 minutes. Mix in the flour, garlic, and ham; sauté 3 minutes. Add the bay leaf, thyme, cayenne pepper, tomatoes, and green peppers. Bring to a boil, cover, and cook over low heat 45 minutes. Taste for seasoning. Serve with rice. *Serves 4–6.*

Trippa alla Fiorentina

TRIPE IN MEAT SAUCE

2 pounds tripe
2 tablespoons butter
½ pound stewing beef in
  1 piece
¾ cup chopped onions
½ cup grated carrots
¾ cup dry red wine

¾ cup peeled, chopped
  tomatoes
2 teaspoons salt
½ teaspoon freshly ground
  black pepper
½ teaspoon thyme
½ cup grated Parmesan
  cheese

Wash the tripe, cover with water, and bring to a boil; cook over low heat 1 hour. Drain, cool, and cut into 2-inch-long, ½-inch-wide strips. Prepare the sauce while the tripe is cooking.

Melt the butter in a saucepan; add the beef, onions, and carrots. Cook over medium heat until browned. Add the wine, tomatoes, salt, and pepper; bring to a boil, cover, and cook over low heat 1 hour. Add the thyme and tripe; re-cover and cook 1 hour longer. Cut the beef into very small pieces and return to the tripe. Serve in deep plates, sprinkled with the cheese.
Serves 6–8.

Boiled Beef Tongue

5-pound smoked or pickled beef tongue	**1 bay leaf**
1 onion	**2 stalks celery**
1 clove garlic	**½ teaspoon pickling spice**

Wash the tongue and cover with cold water. Bring to a boil and cook over low heat 30 minutes. Taste the water. If salty, drain and add fresh boiling water to cover. Add the onion, garlic, bay leaf, celery, and pickling spice. Cover loosely and cook over low heat 2¾ hours or until tender. Remove the tongue, peel off the skin, and trim the root ends. Slice diagonally and serve with mustard, or use as directed in recipes. *Serves 8–10.*

Note: Some smoked tongues require overnight soaking—ask the butcher or read instructions on the wrappings. Fresh tongue may be cooked in the same manner, but add salt to taste.

Lengua a la Madrileña

MADRID BAKED TONGUE

5-pound fresh beef tongue	**½ teaspoon basil**
1½ cups sliced onions	**2 cloves garlic, minced**
2 teaspoons salt	**1 bay leaf**
½ teaspoon freshly ground black pepper	**1 16-ounce can tomatoes**
	2 cups boiling water

Cover the tongue with boiling water and cook 10 minutes. Drain, and when cool enough to handle remove the skin and root.

Place the tongue in a roasting pan with the onions around it. Sprinkle with the salt, pepper, basil, and garlic. Add the bay leaf, tomatoes, and water. Cover the pan and bake in a 325° oven 3 hours or until the tongue is tender. Baste frequently and remove the cover for the last 30 minutes. Discard the bay leaf.
Serves 6–8.

Langue de Boeuf Bourguignonne

BURGUNDY BRAISED TONGUE

5-pound fresh beef tongue	**1 bay leaf**
2 tablespoons butter	**2 stalks celery**
2 cups sliced onions	**1 cup peeled, diced**
1 cup sliced carrots	**tomatoes**
1½ cups dry red wine	**1½ teaspoons salt**
2 tablespoons flour	**½ teaspoon freshly ground**
3 cups beef broth	**black pepper**
3 sprigs parsley	**½ teaspoon thyme**

Cover the tongue with water and bring to a boil. Cook 5 minutes. Drain, peel off the skin, and trim the root end.

Melt the butter in a Dutch oven or casserole; brown the tongue, onions, and carrots in it. Pour off the fat. Add the wine and cook over low heat 15 minutes. Mix the flour with the broth and gradually add to the pan, stirring until thickened. Tie together the parsley, bay leaf, and celery. Put in the pan with the tomatoes, salt, pepper, and thyme. Cover and cook over low heat 2½ hours or until the tongue is tender. Taste for seasoning. Remove the tongue and slice. Strain the gravy and serve separately.
Serves 8–10.

Naudanliha Kieli

FINNISH TONGUE

5-pound fresh beef tongue	1 onion
1 tablespoon salt	3 tablespoons butter
½ teaspoon freshly ground black pepper	¾ cup chopped onions
	2 cups chopped mushrooms
4 bay leaves	2 tablespoons flour
2 cloves	2 tablespoons dry sherry
2 stalks celery	1 tablespoon minced parsley

Wash the tongue, cover with water, and bring to a boil. Add the salt, pepper, bay leaves, cloves, celery, and whole onion. Cover and cook over low heat 2½ hours, or until tongue is tender. Drain, reserving 3 cups of stock. Remove the skin, bones, and roots of the tongue.

Melt the butter in a saucepan; sauté the chopped onions 5 minutes. Add the mushrooms; sauté 5 minutes. Blend in the flour until browned. Gradually add the reserved stock, stirring steadily to the boiling point. Cook over low heat 10 minutes. Stir in the sherry and parsley. Taste for seasoning. Slice the tongue and serve with the sauce. *Serves 8–10.*

Israeli Glazed Tongue

5-pound fresh beef tongue	2 cups dry white wine
2 cloves	¼ cup honey
1 onion	1 teaspoon cinnamon
1 bay leaf	4 thin slices lemon
6 peppercorns	

Wash the tongue and place in a saucepan with water to cover. Add the cloves, onion, bay leaf, and peppercorns. Bring to a boil, cover, and cook over low heat 3 hours. Drain and cool 30 minutes. Remove the skin, bones, and roots of the tongue. Cut the tongue in ¼-inch slices.

Arrange the sliced tongue in a casserole or baking dish; add a mixture of the wine, honey, cinnamon, and lemon slices. Cover and bake in a 375° oven 30 minutes, or until liquid is almost absorbed.

Serves 8–10.

Lengua a la Española

FRESH TONGUE IN SPANISH SAUCE

5-pound fresh beef tongue
¼ cup olive oil
1 cup sliced onions
2 carrots, sliced
2 cloves garlic, minced
2 green peppers, cut in strips
3 cups diced tomatoes
1½ teaspoons salt
½ teaspoon freshly ground black pepper
2 sprigs parsley
1 bay leaf
¼ teaspoon thyme
1 tablespoon unsweetened cocoa
1 cup boiling water

Wash the tongue and place in a deep kettle of boiling water. Cook over high heat 15 minutes. Drain, cool, and remove the root ends, bones, and skin.

Heat the oil in a Dutch oven or heavy saucepan. Lightly brown the tongue in it. Add the onions, carrots, garlic, green peppers, tomatoes, salt, pepper, parsley, bay leaf, and thyme. Cover and cook over low heat 30 minutes. Mix the cocoa with the boiling water and add to the tongue; re-cover and cook 2 hours longer or until the tongue is tender. Place the tongue on a hot platter. Force the gravy through a sieve. Slice the tongue and pour the gravy over it.

Serves 8–10.

Langue de Boeuf Provençale

BEEF TONGUE, PROVENCE STYLE

4 tablespoons butter
4 tablespoons flour
2 cups tongue stock or beef
broth
½ cup sugar
½ cup wine vinegar
½ cup seedless raisins

3 tablespoons grated orange
rind
1 cup chopped walnuts
5-pound smoked or
pickled beef tongue,
cooked

Melt the butter in a saucepan; blend in the flour. Cook over low heat until browned, stirring steadily to the boiling point, then gradually add the stock or broth, stirring steadily. Cook 5 minutes longer. Combine the sugar and vinegar in a saucepan and cook until the mixture caramelizes. Add to the sauce with the raisins, orange rind, and chopped walnuts. Slice the tongue, arrange on a serving platter, and pour the sauce over it.
Serves 8–10.

Limba cu Masline

RUMANIAN TONGUE WITH OLIVES

5-pound fresh or pickled
beef tongue
3 tablespoons butter
1 clove garlic, minced
1½ cups chopped onions
2 tablespoons flour
½ cup dry white wine

½ cup canned tomato sauce
3 tablespoons lemon juice
1 bay leaf
½ teaspoon powdered ginger
½ teaspoon freshly ground
black pepper
1 cup ripe olives

Wash the tongue, cover with water, bring to a boil, and cook 3 hours, or until tender. (If fresh tongue is used, add 2 teaspoons of salt.) Drain, reserving 1½ cups of the stock. Remove the skin, bones, and roots and cut into ¼-inch slices.

Melt the butter in a saucepan; sauté the garlic and onions 5 minutes. Blend in the flour until smooth. Combine the reserved stock, wine, tomato sauce, and lemon juice. Gradually add to the onions, stirring to the boiling point. Add the bay leaf, ginger, pepper, olives, and sliced tongue. Cook over low heat 15 minutes. Taste for seasoning and add more salt if necessary. Serve hot with tiny boiled potatoes. *Serves 6–8.*

Haifa Tongue with Sweet-and-Sour Sauce

2 tablespoons fat	½ teaspoon salt
1 cup chopped onions	¼ cup seedless raisins
2 tablespoons flour	¼ cup sliced, blanched
2 cups tongue stock or	almonds
beef broth	1 lemon, thinly sliced
⅓ cup cider vinegar	5-pound pickled beef
¼ cup brown sugar	tongue, cooked

Melt the fat in a saucepan and lightly brown the onions. Blend in the flour; gradually add the stock or broth, stirring constantly until thickened. Stir in the vinegar, brown sugar, salt, and raisins. Cook over low heat 5 minutes. Add the almonds and sliced lemon. Cook 5 minutes.

Slice the cleaned tongue and serve with the sauce.
Serves 8–10.

Lengua con Salsa de Almendras

TONGUE IN ALMOND SAUCE

5-pound pickled beef	¼ teaspoon marjoram
tongue	1 cup ground almonds
2 tablespoons butter	½ cup dry bread crumbs
¾ cup chopped onions	½ cup chopped olives
2 cloves garlic, minced	¼ cup capers
¾ cup chopped tomatoes	

Wash the tongue, cover with water, bring to a boil, and cook over low heat for 3 hours, or until tender. Drain, reserving 2½ cups of stock. Remove the skin, bones, and roots of the tongue.

Melt the butter in a saucepan; sauté the onions and garlic 5 minutes. Add the tomatoes; cook over low heat 5 minutes. Stir in the marjoram, almonds, and reserved stock. Cook over low heat 5 minutes. Add the bread crumbs and olives; cook for 5 minutes.

Slice the tongue, add to the sauce, and cook 5 minutes. Arrange the slices on a platter and sprinkle with the capers.

Serves 8–10.

Lengua en Salsa de Huevos

SLICED TONGUE IN EGG SAUCE

5-pound pickled beef tongue	**2 egg yolks, beaten**
2 tablespoons butter	**¾ cup coarsely chopped almonds**
¼ cup minced onions	**¼ cup chopped green olives**
1 clove garlic, minced	**1 tablespoon capers**
¾ cup diced tomatoes	**1 tablespoon minced parsley**
1 bay leaf	

Wash the tongue, cover with water, and bring to a boil. Cover loosely and cook over medium heat 3 hours or until tender. Drain, reserving 3 cups of stock. Remove the skin, bones, and root ends of the tongue.

Melt the butter in a saucepan; sauté the onions 5 minutes. Add the garlic, tomatoes, bay leaf, and reserved stock. Cook over low heat 20 minutes. Beat the egg yolks in a bowl; gradually add the hot sauce, stirring steadily to prevent curdling. Return to the saucepan and add the almonds, olives, capers, and parsley. Heat but do not let boil. Slice the tongue and pour the sauce over it.

Serves 8–10.

Zunge mit Meerrettich Sauce

BAVARIAN-STYLE TONGUE WITH HORSERADISH SAUCE

5-pound smoked or pickled
  beef tongue
½ cup prepared horseradish
⅓ cup soft bread crumbs
1 cup sour cream

2 tablespoons butter
1 egg yolk
1 teaspoon prepared
  mustard

Wash the tongue, cover with water, and bring to a boil. Cover loosely and cook over low heat 3 hours, or until tongue is tender. As the water boils out, add boiling water so the tongue is covered at all times. Drain the tongue, reserving 1 cup of liquid. Remove the root ends, bones, and skin of the tongue.

In a saucepan, combine the tongue liquid, horseradish, and bread crumbs. Bring to a boil; blend in the sour cream and butter until the butter melts.

Beat the egg yolk and mustard in a bowl; gradually add the hot sauce, stirring steadily to prevent curdling. Return to the saucepan; heat but do not let boil. Slice the tongue and serve with the sauce.

Serves 8–10.

Lengua con Salsa de Hongos

TONGUE IN MUSHROOM SAUCE

5-pound smoked beef
  tongue
2 cloves garlic, minced
3 tablespoons butter
¾ cup chopped onions

2 cups chopped mushrooms
2 tablespoons flour
1½ cups dry red wine
1 tablespoon minced
  parsley

Wash the tongue, cover with water, and bring to a boil. Drain, add the garlic and fresh boiling water to cover. Cover and cook over low heat 3 hours or until tender. Drain, reserving 1½ cups of liquid. Remove the skin, bones, and roots.

Melt the butter in a saucepan; sauté the onions 5 minutes. Add the mushrooms; sauté 5 minutes. Stir in the flour until browned. Gradually add the wine and reserved liquid, stirring steadily to the boiling point. Cook over low heat 10 minutes. Stir in the parsley. Slice the tongue and serve with the sauce. *Serves 8–10.*

Lingua Portuguesa

PORTUGUESE TONGUE IN WINE SAUCE

5-pound fresh beef tongue	½ teaspoon freshly ground
2 tablespoons butter	black pepper
1½ cups sliced onions	½ teaspoon thyme
1 cup sliced carrots	3 sprigs parsley
2 cups dry white wine	2 stalks celery
2 tablespoons flour	1 bay leaf
3 cups beef broth	2 tomatoes, diced
1½ teaspoons salt	

Wash the tongue and trim the root end. Cover with water and bring to a boil; let cook 5 minutes. Drain, peel the skin, and remove the root ends.

Melt the butter in a Dutch oven or heavy saucepan. Brown the tongue, onions, and carrots in it. Pour off the fat and add the wine. Cook over low heat 15 minutes. Mix the flour with a little of the broth until smooth and add with all the broth, stirring steadily until thickened. Add the salt, pepper, thyme, parsley, celery, bay leaf, and tomatoes. Cover and cook over low heat 2¾ hours or until the tongue is tender. Taste for seasoning. Transfer the tongue to a serving platter and strain the gravy. *Serves 8–10.*

Zungen-Ragout

GERMAN TONGUE RAGOUT

5-pound fresh beef tongue
1 onion
1 bay leaf
6 peppercorns
3 teaspoons salt
2 Parboiled Calf's Brains*
2 pairs Parboiled Calf's
Sweetbreads*
6 tablespoons butter

½ pound ground pork
1 egg
3 tablespoons dry bread
crumbs
⅛ teaspoon freshly ground
black pepper
4 tablespoons flour
1 cup sliced mushrooms
¼ cup sweet sherry

Wash the tongue, cover with water, and bring to a boil. Add the onion, bay leaf, peppercorns, and 2 teaspoons of the salt. Cover, bring to a boil, and cook over low heat 2½ hours, or until tender. Drain, reserving the stock. Trim the tongue of the root ends, bones, and skin.

Cube the parboiled brains and sweetbreads. Melt 3 tablespoons of the butter in a skillet and lightly brown the cubes in it.

Mix together the pork, egg, bread crumbs, pepper, and ½ teaspoon of the remaining salt. Shape into walnut-sized balls and cook in the reserved stock 20 minutes. Drain. Strain and reserve 3 cups stock.

Melt the remaining butter in a saucepan; blend in the flour. Gradually add the stock, stirring steadily to the boiling point. Add the mushrooms and remaining salt; cook over low heat 10 minutes. Mix in the sherry. Slice the tongue and add to the sauce with the pork balls and half the brains and sweetbreads. Heat. Arrange on a hot serving dish and garnish with the remaining brains and sweetbreads.

Serves 10–12.

Rinderzunge mit Kartoffel

AUSTRIAN TONGUE AND POTATO HASH

3 tablespoons vegetable oil
3 cups diced potatoes
1 cup chopped onions
¾ teaspoon salt
3 cups diced cooked beef
  tongue

1½ cups drained canned
  tomatoes
½ cup chicken broth
½ teaspoon freshly ground
  black pepper
¼ teaspoon marjoram

Heat the oil in a skillet; sauté the potatoes and onions 10 minutes. Season with the salt. Lightly mix in the tongue, tomatoes, broth, pepper, and marjoram. Bake in a 350° oven 45 minutes.
Serves 4–6.

Australian Tongue in Aspic

5-pound Boiled Beef
  Tongue*
1 egg white and shell
2 envelopes (2 tablespoons)
  gelatin

½ cup dry white wine
1 teaspoon Worcestershire
  sauce
⅛ teaspoon Tabasco
Salt if needed

Cook the tongue as directed in the Boiled Beef Tongue recipe, and cool in the broth. Remove the root, bones, and skin and chill. Strain the broth, chill, and remove the fat.

Beat the egg white in a saucepan with a fork till frothy and crush the eggshell. Add 3½ cups of the broth, bring to a boil, and cook over low heat 10 minutes. Cool and then strain through several thicknesses of cheesecloth.

Soften the gelatin in the wine. Heat the cleared broth and stir in the gelatin until dissolved. Add the Worcestershire, Tabasco, and salt if necessary. Pour a thin layer into a 9-inch loaf pan and chill until firm. Chill the remaining aspic in another pan until it begins to set. Cut the tongue into thin slices and arrange in layers in the lined loaf pan with the aspic between each layer.

Chill until firm. Turn out and serve surrounded with cucumbers, quartered hard-cooked eggs, sliced stuffed olives, tomatoes, and crisp greens.
Serves 8–10.

Stegte Hjerter
DANISH STUFFED HEARTS

2 calf's hearts	2 tablespoons butter
¼ pound (1 stick) butter	½ teaspoon salt
½ cup finely chopped parsley	1 tablespoon flour
	¼ cup cranberry sauce

Cut out the veins and arteries of the hearts. Wash very well in cold water. Cream all but 3 tablespoons of the butter and blend in the parsley. Using half the mixture for each, stuff the hearts and sew up or skewer the openings. Melt 2 tablespoons of the butter in a deep skillet and sauté the hearts until brown. Add the salt and enough water to cover the hearts. Bring to a boil, cover, and cook over low heat 3 hours. Turn the hearts over once. Place the hearts on a platter, remove the fastening, and keep warm. Blend the remaining butter with the flour and add to the liquid in the skillet. Cook, stirring until thickened, then add the cranberry sauce. Pour the sauce over the hearts.
Serves 4.

Anticuchos
PERUVIAN BARBECUED HEART

1 beef heart	¼ teaspoon saffron
1½ teaspoons salt	3 cloves garlic, minced
½ teaspoon dried ground chili peppers	1 cup tarragon vinegar
6 peppercorns	½ cup water
	¼ cup olive oil

Wash the heart, remove the skin, veins, and arteries, and cut in 1-inch cubes. In a bowl, mix together the salt, peppers, peppercorns, saffron, garlic, vinegar, and water. Marinate the heart in the mixture overnight in the refrigerator.

Drain the heart, and reserve the marinade. Thread the pieces on 4–6 skewers. Brush with the olive oil. Broil 5 inches from the heat 45 minutes, or until the heart is tender. Turn the skewers frequently and baste frequently with the marinade.

Serves 4–6.

Mocoto

SOUTH AMERICAN CALF'S FEET STEW

4 calf's feet	1 tablespoon salt
3 quarts water	½ teaspoon freshly ground
1 cup sliced onions	black pepper
3 sprigs parsley ⎫	1 cup peeled, chopped
2 stalks ⎪ tied	tomatoes
celery, cut in ⎬ together	½ cup dry red wine
pieces ⎪	2 egg yolks
1 bay leaf ⎭	

Have the feet chopped up into small pieces. Pour boiling water over them and scrape. Combine the feet with the water, onions, parsley, celery, bay leaf, salt, pepper, and tomatoes. Bring to a boil, cover loosely, and cook over low heat 3 hours. Remove the feet; cut the meat in small pieces, discarding the bones. Add the wine to the stock; cook over high heat 20 minutes. Return the meat; cook 10 minutes. Discard the parsley bundle. Beat the egg yolks in a bowl; gradually add the hot mixture, stirring steadily to prevent curdling. Serve in deep bowls, with garlic toast.

Serves 6–8.

Note: You can also make a form of headcheese. Omit the egg yolks. Pour the mixture into a pie plate and arrange 2 sliced hard-cooked eggs in it; chill until jellied. Serve as an appetizer, cut in wedges.

Game

The term "game" applies to all wild animals and birds which are hunted and eaten.

Wild game was the first and only meat available from the earliest days of man. Domesticated birds and animals have since replaced game as a source of meat, but the products of the shoot or hunt still offer a great treat to the sophisticated palate.

There are three types of game: (1) small birds, not larger than the quail; (2) game proper, which is subdivided into "winged" game—partridge, pheasant, etc.—and "ground" game—hare and rabbit; and (3) large game (wild boar and animals of the deer family).

Small game birds are usually eaten fresh and undrawn, "while the gun is still smoking," we are told. They are as digestible as poultry.

Larger birds are prepared on spits, in casseroles, as roasts or stews, similar to the methods one uses for cooking turkeys, ducks, and chickens.

The meat of all kinds of deer—elk, moose, reindeer, antelope, caribou, etc.—is called venison in the United States and roebuck in Europe and Asia. The fawn is a deer not more than six months old, the stag is between five and six years or more. The cuts of these animals are the same as those of beef, and they vary in tenderness in the same manner.

If you've bagged the game yourself, ask your butcher to hang the animal for you, as controlled temperature is important for the proper aging of meat. Venison is usually hung from five days to about a month, depending on the age and condition of the animal. If you buy your venison in a butcher shop, check to see that it has been well hung.

Unless you are very familiar with butchery, it is advisable to have the butcher dress and cut the animal for you. The meat of the young is delicate and need not be marinated before cooking; with cuts of older animals, however, marinating helps to tenderize them and imparts a flavor too.

I once spent a month in Africa, in the foothills of Mount Kilimanjaro. Here an animal hanging in a tree to age was a common sight. Venison and birds were abundant—in fact, the only meat available—and I cooked them in every conceivable fashion. Everyone agreed this wild fare tasted wonderful, even as a steady diet.

Rehrücken

ROAST SADDLE OF VENISON

1 saddle of venison	1 teaspoon thyme
1 quart dry red wine	2 cups chopped celery
1 quart vinegar	3 cloves garlic, cut in
1 quart water	slivers
1 tablespoon salt	4 strips salt pork
10 peppercorns	½ cup flour
3 bay leaves	2 cups port
1 teaspoon allspice	
1 tablespoon chopped parsley	

Place the saddle in a container large enough to hold it. In a saucepan, combine the red wine, vinegar, water, salt, peppercorns, bay leaves, allspice, parsley, thyme, and celery. Pour over the venison. Let marinate in the refrigerator 24 hours, turning it a few times. Drain, reserving 2 cups of the marinade.

Make some thin slits in the meat and insert the slivers of garlic, then arrange the salt pork over it. Dip the meat in the flour. Place in a shallow roasting pan. Roast in a 450° oven 20 minutes; reduce the heat to 325°, add the port and marinade, and continue roasting a total of 15 minutes a pound, basting frequently.

Place the saddle on a hot platter. Strain the gravy and thicken if necessary with a little flour mixed with water.

Serves 8–10.

Stekt Rensdyrrygg

NORWEGIAN ROAST VENISON

6-pound venison rib roast
2½ cups packaged bread
stuffing
1 cup canned whole
cranberries, drained

2 teaspoons salt
½ teaspoon freshly ground
black pepper
6 slices bacon

Have the rib roast boned and pounded flat. Mix together the bread stuffing and cranberries; spread on the meat, then roll up like a jelly roll. Tie the roll in several places with string or fasten with skewers. Rub the meat with the salt and pepper. Place the roll in a shallow roasting pan, and put the bacon strips over it. Roast in a 325° oven about 25 minutes a pound, basting frequently with the drippings. Let it stand at room temperature for 20 minutes before carving.

Serves 8–10.

Dyrestek

NORWEGIAN ROAST LEG OF VENISON

6-pound leg of venison
2 tablespoons salt
2 tablespoons freshly
ground black pepper

2 tablespoons minced garlic
¼ cup flour

Pierce the venison with a fork in several places. Rub the leg with a mixture of the salt, pepper, and garlic. Sprinkle the top with the flour. Place the leg in a roasting pan. Roast in a 475° oven 45 minutes, then reduce the heat to 325° and roast 1 hour longer. Serve in very thin slices with lingonberries or cranberries.

Serves 8–12.

Dyrestek

SWEDISH ROAST VENISON

4-pound rolled venison roast	1 cup orange juice
2 teaspoons salt	½ cup port
½ teaspoon freshly ground black pepper	2 tablespoons grated orange rind
2 slices salt pork	½ teaspoon thyme
2 cloves	3 tablespoons melted butter
2 small onions	1 tablespoon Worcestershire sauce
1 cup apple juice	

Rub the meat with the salt and pepper. Put the venison in a Dutch oven and place the salt pork on top. Stick a clove in each onion and place on top. Roast in a 400° oven 20 minutes. Mix together the apple juice, orange juice, port, rind, and thyme; pour over the meat. Roast in a 350° oven 1½ hours, basting frequently. Remove the salt pork and brush the meat with a mixture of the butter and Worcestershire sauce. Roast 10 minutes longer, or until meat is tender.

Transfer the roast to a heated serving dish. If the gravy is too thin, thicken it with a little arrowroot or cornstarch.

Serves 6–8.

Renstek

SWEDISH ROAST LEG OF VENISON

6-pound leg of venison	1 bay leaf
4 cups dry red wine	4 peppercorns
1 large onion, sliced	3 juniper berries
1 clove garlic, minced	6 slices bacon

The bone of the leg may be removed if you like. Mix together the wine, onion, garlic, bay leaf, peppercorns, and juniper berries. Add the leg and let marinate in the refrigerator for 24 hours, basting and turning occasionally.

Drain the meat; strain and reserve the marinade. Tie the meat with white string to hold its shape, and arrange the bacon on top. Place the meat on a rack in a shallow roasting pan.

Roast in a 450° oven 20 minutes. Reduce the heat to 325°, add the marinade, and roast 18 minutes per pound for rare (140° on a meat thermometer), 22 minutes for medium (150°), basting frequently with the marinade. Serve with red cabbage and puréed chestnuts.

Serves 10–12.

Potrawka z Jelenia

POLISH BRAISED VENISON

4-pound rump of venison	¾ teaspoon thyme
3 cups water	2 slices bacon, diced
2 cups wine vinegar	1 cup sliced onions
20 peppercorns	1 cup dry red wine
10 juniper berries	20 prunes
6 whole allspice	1 apple, peeled and diced
1 bay leaf	½ cup coarsely crushed
½ cup chopped onions	walnuts
½ cup sliced carrots	2 tablespoons pumpernickel
2 teaspoons salt	crumbs
¾ teaspoon freshly ground	
black pepper	

Wash and dry the venison. In a saucepan combine the water, vinegar, peppercorns, juniper berries, allspice, bay leaf, chopped onions, and carrots. Bring to a boil and cook over low heat 20 minutes. Cool. Put the venison in a glass or pottery bowl; pour the marinade over it. Cover and let marinate in the refrigerator 48 hours, basting and turning the meat several times.

Drain and dry the meat, reserving ¼ cup of the marinade. Rub the meat with the salt, pepper, and thyme.

Brown the bacon lightly in a Dutch oven. Pour off half the fat.

Add the venison and sliced onions; cook until the meat is browned on all sides. Add the wine, prunes, apple, walnuts, pumpernickel crumbs, and reserved marinade. Cover and cook over low heat 2 hours, or until the meat is tender. Serve with noodles.
Serves 8–10.

Poronkäristys

FINNISH BRAISED VENISON STEAK

2-pound venison steak	1 teaspoon salt
½ pound sliced bacon	¼ teaspoon freshly ground
¼ cup boiling water	black pepper

Cut the venison into thin slices. Brown the bacon in a deep skillet. Remove the bacon. Pour off half the fat. In the fat remaining brown the meat. Return the bacon and add the water, salt, and pepper. Cover and cook over low heat 20 minutes, or until the meat is tender.
Serves 6–8.

Broiled Venison Steak, Kenya Style

2 1-pound venison steaks	½ teaspoon sage
1 teaspoon salt	4 tablespoons melted butter
½ teaspoon freshly ground	2 tablespoons Worcestershire
black pepper	sauce

Rub the steaks with a mixture of the salt, pepper, and sage. Place on a greased pan. Broil about 8 minutes on each side or to desired degree of rareness. Brush with a mixture of the butter and Worcestershire sauce several times.
Serves 4.

Stekte Hjortekoteletter

NORWEGIAN FRIED VENISON CUTLET

4 venison cutlets, about 2
pounds
½ cup olive oil
½ cup lemon juice
1 teaspoon salt
½ teaspoon freshly ground
black pepper

½ cup flour
1 egg, beaten
¾ cup dry bread crumbs
4 tablespoons butter
4 tablespoons currant jelly
Watercress sprigs

Marinate the cutlets in a mixture of the olive oil and lemon juice for 2 hours, turning the meat several times. Drain the meat thoroughly; season with the salt and pepper and dip in the flour. Dip the cutlets in the beaten egg, then in the bread crumbs.

Melt the butter in a skillet and sauté the cutlets 6 minutes on each side, or until browned and tender. Transfer the cutlets to a heated serving dish. Stir the currant jelly into the skillet and bring to a boil, scraping the bottom of browned particles. Pour the melted jelly sauce over the cutlets. Garnish with the watercress. *Serves 4.*

Dyrestek a la Lapskaus

NORWEGIAN VENISON GOULASH

3 pounds venison
½ cup flour
4 tablespoons butter
1 cup chopped onions
2 cloves garlic, minced
2 teaspoons salt

1 tablespoon paprika
1 cup dry red wine
1 8-ounce can tomato sauce
1½ cups beef broth
1 cup sour cream

Pound the meat lightly, sprinkle with the flour, and pound it in. Cut the meat into 1½-inch cubes.

Melt the butter in a Dutch oven or heavy saucepan; sauté the onions and garlic 10 minutes. Add the meat and brown well. Mix in the salt, paprika, wine, tomato sauce, and broth. Cover and cook over low heat 2½ hours or until the meat is tender. Stir in the sour cream just before serving. *Serves 6–8.*

Hjorte Boller

NORWEGIAN VENISON PATTIES

1 pound ground venison	½ cup beef broth
½ pound ground lean pork	3 tablespoons butter
1 egg, beaten	½ cup sour cream
1½ teaspoons salt	¼ cup crumbled Norwegian
½ teaspoon freshly ground	goat cheese (gjetost)
black pepper	1 tablespoon water

Mix together the venison, pork, egg, salt, pepper, and broth. Shape the mixture into 6 patties. Melt the butter in a skillet; sauté the patties 10 minutes on each side. Transfer to a hot serving dish and keep warm. Add the sour cream and cheese to the skillet. Bring to a boil, stirring steadily, then add 1 tablespoon cold water. Pour over the patties. *Serves 4–6.*

Venaison Sausisses à la Créole

VENISON PATTIES, CREOLE STYLE

2 pounds ground venison	¼ teaspoon marjoram
½ pound ground pork	½ teaspoon powdered bay
½ pound ground veal	leaf
¼ cup flour	¼ teaspoon allspice
2 teaspoons salt	½ teaspoon nutmeg
½ teaspoon freshly ground	¾ cup chopped onions
black pepper	2 cloves garlic
Dash cayenne pepper	¼ cup vegetable oil
¼ teaspoon thyme	

Mix well together all the ingredients but the oil. Put the mixture through the fine blade of a food chopper. Shape into 16 patties. Heat the oil in a skillet and cook the patties in it over low heat, 10 minutes on each side. Serve with currant jelly.

Serves 8.

Civet de Venaison Française

DEER RAGOUT

4 pounds venison	**2 teaspoons salt**
2 cups dry red wine	**½ teaspoon freshly ground**
½ cup lemon juice	**black pepper**
1 onion, sliced	**6 tablespoons butter**
1 carrot, sliced	**¼ pound mushrooms, sliced**
1 clove garlic, minced	**12 small white onions**
2 bay leaves	**½ pound chicken livers,**
¼ teaspoon thyme	**coarsely chopped**
½ teaspoon tarragon	

Cut the venison into 2-inch cubes. In a glass or pottery bowl, mix together the wine, lemon juice, sliced onion, carrot, garlic, bay leaves, thyme, tarragon, salt, and pepper. Add the meat and let marinate in the refrigerator for 3 days, basting occasionally. Drain well and strain the marinade.

Melt 4 tablespoons of the butter in a Dutch oven or deep skillet; brown the meat in it. Add the mushrooms and onions; sauté 5 minutes. Pour off the fat and add 1 cup of the marinade. Cover and cook over low heat 1½ hours or until tender. Add a little more marinade if necessary from time to time.

Melt the remaining butter in a skillet; sauté the livers 5 minutes. Add to the venison. Cook 10 minutes longer. Taste for seasoning.

Serves 8–10.

Filet d'Ours Piqué à la Broches

ROAST FILLET OF BEAR

1 whole fillet of bear
3 strips salt pork
2 green peppers, cut in
strips
½ cup wine vinegar
2 cups dry white wine
¾ cup sliced onions
1 clove garlic, minced
1 carrot, sliced
1½ cups chopped celery
and leaves

2 teaspoons salt
½ teaspoon freshly ground
black pepper
1 bay leaf
½ teaspoon tarragon
½ cup melted butter
2 tablespoons butter
12 pitted black olives
Lemon slices
Wine or currant jelly

Have the butcher prepare the fillet for you by pulling out the veins and nerves. Pull strips of salt pork through it crosswise, then insert the green pepper.

In a saucepan, combine the vinegar, wine, onions, garlic, carrot, celery, salt, pepper, bay leaf, and tarragon. Bring to a boil and cook over high heat 3 minutes. Cool. Place the meat in a glass or pottery bowl and pour the marinade over it. Let marinate in the refrigerator for 3 days, basting and turning occasionally.

Drain the meat and place on a spit or in a roasting pan. Roast in a 450° oven 20 minutes. Brush with some melted butter, reduce the heat to 350°, and roast a total of 12 minutes a pound, basting frequently with melted butter.

Melt the 2 tablespoons of butter and sauté the olives in it 2 minutes.

Transfer the meat to a hot platter and garnish with the olives, sliced lemon, and wine or currant jelly. Serve with Sauce Poivrade* or Sauce Robert* (also available in bottles).
Serves 6–8.

Capretto

ITALIAN ROAST KID

1 young kid, about 8 pounds	2 lemons, quartered
6 cloves garlic, slivered	2 tablespoons olive oil
1 tablespoon salt	4 tablespoons butter
¾ teaspoon freshly ground black pepper	2 onions
¾ teaspoon thyme	2 cloves
	2 cups dry white wine

Have the kid dressed, cleaned, and scraped. Wash and dry it. Make small slits all over the surface of the kid and insert the garlic slivers. Rub the kid with a mixture of the salt, pepper, and thyme. Put the quartered lemons in the cavity.

Heat the oil and butter in a roasting pan. Put the kid and the onions stuck with the cloves into it. Roast in a 375° oven 15 minutes a pound. Add the wine after 1 hour and baste frequently thereafter. Transfer the kid to a hot platter and discard the lemons. Skim the fat from the pan juices.

Serves 6–8.

La Gibelotte

FRENCH RABBIT STEW

1 rabbit, disjointed	¼ cup beef broth
3 tablespoons butter	½ cup dry white wine
1½ teaspoons salt	4 slices bacon, diced
½ teaspoon freshly ground black pepper	12 small white onions
2 tablespoons flour	1 clove garlic, minced
	½ pound mushrooms, sliced

Clean, wash, and dry the rabbit. Melt the butter in a Dutch oven. Brown the rabbit in it. Sprinkle with the salt, pepper, and flour, stirring until the flour browns. Add the broth and wine; bring to a boil, cover, and cook over low heat 45 minutes.

While the rabbit is cooking, brown the bacon lightly in a skillet; pour off half the fat. Add the onions; sauté until golden. Add the garlic and mushrooms; sauté 3 minutes. Add this mixture to the rabbit; cook 15 minutes longer or until the rabbit is tender. Skim the fat.

Serves 4.

Hasenpfeffer I

GERMAN HARE RAGOUT

1 young hare	1½ cups sliced onions
½ cup wine vinegar	1 tablespoon flour
2 cloves garlic, sliced	1 bottle dry red wine
1 bay leaf	1 tablespoon grated
2 teaspoons salt	unsweetened chocolate
½ teaspoon freshly ground	24 small white onions
black pepper	Sliced sautéed French or
6 tablespoons olive oil	Italian bread
2 slices bacon, diced	

Have the hare disjointed and cleaned. Pour boiling water over it, scrape, rinse, and dry.

In a glass or pottery bowl combine the vinegar, garlic, bay leaf, salt, pepper, and 4 tablespoons of the oil. Add the hare and marinate in the refrigerator for 48 hours. Drain.

Put the bacon in a Dutch oven, and cook until lightly browned. Add the sliced onions, and cook until golden. Blend in the flour, and add the hare. Cook 10 minutes, turning the pieces several times. Add the wine, bring to a boil, and stir in the chocolate. Cover and cook over low heat 2 hours, or until tender; add salt and pepper to taste after 1 hour.

While the hare is cooking, sauté the white onions in the remaining oil until golden. Arrange the hare on a hot platter with the sautéed onions and bread around it. Serve with noodles.

Serves 4–6.

Hasenpfeffer II

BRAISED MARINATED RABBIT

2 2-pound rabbits
1½ cups dry red wine
¾ cup cider vinegar
2 teaspoons salt
½ teaspoon freshly ground
black pepper
1 bay leaf
½ cup chopped onions

1 tablespoon mixed pickling
spice
½ cup flour
4 tablespoons butter
1 cup thinly sliced onions
2 tablespoons sugar
½ cup sour cream

Cut the rabbit in serving-sized pieces. Wash, scrape, and soak in salted cold water 1 hour. Drain and dry.

In a glass or pottery bowl mix together the wine, vinegar, salt, pepper, bay leaf, chopped onions, and pickling spice. Add the rabbit, and let marinate in the refrigerator for 3–4 days. Turn the pieces occasionally. Drain the rabbit; strain and reserve the marinade. Dry the rabbit with paper towels and roll in the flour.

Melt the butter in a Dutch oven or deep heavy skillet; brown the rabbit and sliced onions in it. Pour off the fat and add the sugar and 1½ cups marinade. Cover and cook over low heat 1½ hours or until the rabbit is tender. Turn the pieces occasionally and add more marinade if needed. Taste for seasoning. Mix the sour cream into the gravy just before serving.

Serves 4–6.

Stuffed Vegetables

Almost every cuisine has a stuffed pepper recipe, but many other vegetables—with the possible exception of tomatoes—are neglected, particularly in American cooking. The Middle East is particularly fond of stuffed eggplant; the Italians like eggplant, zucchini, and artichokes; and the Chinese lean to cucumbers. Middle European countries favor cabbage; sometimes the leaf is rolled up and sometimes the whole head is scooped out and the cabbage "bowl" stuffed. In Spain and South America cooks use the pepper as a case for delectable combinations of meat, herbs, spices, and sometimes raisins and nuts. Grape leaves, although not a vegetable, are used for stuffing cases throughout Greece, Turkey, and the Middle East—the *dolma* is the best example of this tasteful dish.

Although the preparation of stuffed vegetables takes a little time, it simplifies the balance of the cooking, as no other vegetable is required.

Carciofi Ripieni
STUFFED ARTICHOKES

8 large artichokes	**¼ cup chopped parsley**
¼ pound ground beef	**½ teaspoon salt**
½ cup fresh bread crumbs	**½ teaspoon freshly ground**
½ cup grated Parmesan	**black pepper**
cheese	**1 clove garlic, minced**
¼ cup chopped capers	**¾ cup olive oil**

Remove the stems of the artichokes and with scissors trim the pointed ends of the leaves. Cook in boiling salted water 10 minutes; drain and press the leaves open on a solid surface. Remove the chokes (fuzzy centers) with a sharp knife or spoon.

Mix together the meat, bread crumbs, cheese, capers, parsley, salt, pepper, and garlic. Put some of the mixture in the centers and between the leaves of the artichokes. Arrange in an upright position in a heavy saucepan. Pour 2 tablespoons oil over each, then add water to a depth of ½ inch. Cover the pot and cook over low heat 40 minutes. Serve hot or cold. *Serves 8.*

Kaalikaaryleet

FINNISH CABBAGE ROLLS

1 head cabbage	2 teaspoons salt
½ cup raw rice	½ teaspoon freshly ground
½ cup boiling water	black pepper
½ cup milk	2 tablespoons butter
¼ pound ground beef	2 tablespoons brown sugar
¼ pound ground pork	1½ cups beef broth
¼ cup chopped onions	1 tablespoon flour
1 egg	½ cup light cream
¼ cup heavy cream	

Wash the cabbage, cover with water, bring to a boil, and cook 10 minutes. Carefully remove 16 leaves.

Cook the rice in the boiling water until the water is absorbed; add the milk and continue cooking until the milk is absorbed. Mix the ground meats and onions with the cooked rice, the egg, heavy cream, salt, and pepper. Place 1 heaping tablespoon of the meat-rice mixture on each leaf. Fold sides of leaf in, then roll up so all sides are closed. Fasten with a toothpick. You may need more cabbage leaves to use up the filling.

Melt the butter in a Dutch oven; brown the cabbage rolls in it. Add the sugar and broth. Cover and cook over low heat 1 hour, shaking the pan frequently. Mix the flour with the light cream and add to the cabbage rolls, stirring gently to the boiling point. Taste the gravy for seasoning and cook 40 minutes longer. *Serves 4–6.*

Hvidkaal Rouletter

DANISH CABBAGE ROLLS

1 head cabbage	½ teaspoon freshly ground
1 pound ground beef	black pepper
1 egg	2 tablespoons flour
½ cup minced onions	3 tablespoons vegetable oil
⅛ teaspoon ground cloves	2 cups beef broth
1 teaspoon salt	

Wash the cabbage. Cover with water, bring to a boil, and cook over low heat 10 minutes. Drain and carefully pull off 16 leaves. Mix together the beef, egg, onions, cloves, salt, pepper, and flour. Put a heaping tablespoon of meat mixture on each cabbage leaf. Fold in the opposite ends, then roll leaves up. If there is any filling left, use a few more cabbage leaves. Heat the oil in a Dutch oven or heavy skillet; lightly brown the rolls in it. Add the broth, cover, and cook over low heat 1 hour.
Serves 6–8.

Töltött Káposzta

HUNGARIAN CABBAGE ROLLS

1 large head cabbage	2½ teaspoons salt
½ cup white bread cubes	¾ teaspoon freshly ground
½ cup water	black pepper
1½ pounds ground pork	1 pound sauerkraut
½ pound ground beef	2 cups canned tomato
½ cup chopped onions	sauce
1 slice raw bacon, minced	1 cup sour cream

Wash the cabbage, cover with water, and bring to a boil. Let it stand 10 minutes. Drain, then carefully remove 24 leaves, reserving the remaining cabbage.

Soak the bread in the water, drain, and mash smooth. Mix together the bread, pork, beef, onions, bacon, 1½ teaspoons of the salt, and ½ teaspoon of the pepper. Place a heaping tablespoon of the mixture on each leaf; turn in the ends and roll up. If there is any extra meat mixture, use a few more leaves.

Spread the sauerkraut in a Dutch oven or heavy casserole. Arrange the cabbage rolls on it. Add the tomato sauce and remaining salt and pepper. Cover and bake in a 325° oven 2½ hours, removing the cover for the last 45 minutes. Mix in the sour cream, and taste for seasoning.

Serves 6–8.

Israeli Cabbage Rolls in Sweet-Sour Sauce

1 large head cabbage	1½ pounds ground beef
4 tablespoons raw rice	4 tablespoons grated onion
2 tablespoons butter	1 egg
1½ cups sliced onions	3 tablespoons cold water
1 29-ounce can tomatoes	¼ cup brown sugar
Beef bones	⅓ cup lemon juice
3 teaspoons salt	½ cup seedless raisins
½ teaspoon freshly ground black pepper	

Wash the cabbage, cover with water, bring to a boil, and cook 10 minutes. Drain. Remove 24 outer leaves. Cover the rice with boiling water and let stand while preparing the sauce.

Melt the butter in a deep, heavy saucepan; brown the sliced onions. Add the tomatoes, bones, and half of the salt and pepper. Bring to a boil and cook over low heat 30 minutes.

Mix together the beef, drained rice, grated onion, egg, water, and remaining salt and pepper. Place some of the meat mixture on each cabbage leaf. Turn in the opposite sides and roll up carefully. Arrange in the sauce. Cover and cook over low heat 1½ hours. Add the sugar, lemon juice, and raisins. Cook 30 minutes longer. Taste for seasoning.

Serves 8–12.

Verze Ripiene
ITALIAN CABBAGE ROLLS

1 large head cabbage	¼ teaspoon orégano
1 pound ground pork	2½ teaspoons salt
1 cup half-cooked rice	¾ teaspoon freshly ground
½ cup chopped onions	black pepper
¼ cup chopped parsley	3 cups canned tomato sauce
½ cup grated romano or	1 bay leaf
Parmesan cheese	

Wash the cabbage, cover with water, bring to a boil, and cook 10 minutes. Drain, let it stand until cool enough to handle, and remove 24 large leaves.

Mix together the pork, rice, onions, parsley, cheese, orégano, 1½ teaspoons of the salt, and ½ teaspoon of the pepper. Place a heaping tablespoon of the mixture on each leaf, turn the opposite ends in, and carefully roll up. If there is any meat mixture left, make more rolls or meat balls. Arrange in a greased casserole or baking dish; add the tomato sauce, the remaining salt and pepper, and the bay leaf. Cover and bake in a 350° oven 1½ hours. Taste for seasoning and discard the bay leaf.

Serves 8–10.

Mih-Shee Mal-Poof
PERSIAN CABBAGE ROLLS

½ cup split peas	2 teaspoons salt
1 large head cabbage	½ teaspoon freshly ground
1 pound ground beef	black pepper
1 cup chopped onions	1½ cups beef broth
½ cup chopped parsley	½ cup lemon juice
½ teaspoon cinnamon	¼ cup sugar

Cook the peas in boiling water 30 minutes or until tender. Drain. Wash the cabbage, cover with water, bring to a boil, and cook over low heat 15 minutes. Drain, cool slightly, and carefully remove 24 leaves. Reserve the balance of the cabbage.

Mix together the peas, beef, onions, parsley, cinnamon, 1 teaspoon of the salt, and ¼ teaspoon of the pepper. Put a heaping tablespoon of the mixture on each cabbage leaf. Fold in the opposite ends, then roll up into sausage shapes. If there is any filling left, use a few more cabbage leaves.

Line the bottom of a deep skillet with additional cabbage leaves and arrange the rolls in it in layers, placing more leaves between the layers. Add the broth and the remaining salt and pepper, then cover with cabbage leaves. Cover the skillet and cook over low heat 30 minutes. Mix in the lemon juice and sugar. Cook 30 minutes longer; taste for seasoning.
Serves 6–8.

Golubtzi

RUSSIAN CABBAGE ROLLS

1 large head cabbage	½ teaspoon freshly ground
1 pound ground pork	black pepper
½ pound ground beef	2 cups beef broth
1 cup half-cooked rice	1 8-ounce can tomato sauce
1 egg	¾ cup seedless raisins
2½ teaspoons salt	½ cup sour cream

Wash the cabbage thoroughly. Cover with water, bring to a boil, and cook over low heat 5 minutes. Drain, cool, and carefully remove 24 outer leaves.

Mix together the pork, beef, rice, egg, 1½ teaspoons of the salt, and ¼ teaspoon of the pepper. Place a heaping tablespoon of the mixture on each leaf, tuck the ends in, and roll up.

Arrange the rolls in a baking dish. Mix together the broth, tomato sauce, and remaining salt and pepper. Pour over the rolls. Cover the dish, and bake in a 300° oven 1 hour. Add the raisins; bake, uncovered, 45 minutes longer. Mix in the sour cream and taste for seasoning.
Serves 8–10.

Repollo Relleno

SPANISH STUFFED CABBAGE

4-pound head cabbage	1 cup chopped tomatoes
1 cup cooked rice	1 teaspoon salt
½ pound sausage meat	¼ teaspoon freshly ground
1 cup canned green peas	black pepper
½ cup chopped onions	4 cups beef broth
2 cloves garlic, minced	

Wash the cabbage thoroughly. Cut off the stem end, then scoop out the core and some of the cabbage, leaving a shell. Chop the scooped-out portion; mix with the rice, sausage meat, peas, onions, garlic, tomatoes, salt, and pepper. Stuff the cabbage, using all the mixture. Tie the cabbage in cheesecloth. Place in a saucepan with the broth; bring to a boil, cover, and cook over low heat 2 hours. Add a little more broth or boiling water while cooking to keep liquid almost to the top of the cabbage. Lift out, drain well, and unwrap. Cut in wedges.
Serves 4–6.

Gefüllter Kohl

VIENNESE STUFFED CABBAGE

1 large, firm cabbage	2 tablespoons butter
½ pound ground veal or	2 tablespoons flour
beef	2 cups beef broth
½ pound sausage meat	¾ cup sliced onions
1 teaspoon salt	1 carrot, cut in rounds
¼ teaspoon freshly ground	1 veal knuckle, sawed in
black pepper	2 pieces
¼ teaspoon thyme	

Wash the cabbage, cover with water, and bring to a boil; let it stand 5 minutes. Drain well. Remove the tough outer leaves and cut out center core carefully and discard.

Mix together the veal or beef, sausage meat, salt, pepper, and thyme. Put a little of this mixture between each cabbage leaf, starting from the center and working out, then stuff the center. Reshape the cabbage and tie firmly with string.

Melt the butter in a pan large and deep enough to hold the cabbage. Stir in the flour until browned. Mix in the broth, stirring to the boiling point. Carefully place the cabbage in the pan and add the onions, carrot, and veal knuckle. Cover tightly and cook over low heat 2 hours, adding more liquid if needed. Transfer the cabbage to a deep serving dish and remove the string. Strain the sauce and pour over the cabbage. Serve cut into wedges.
Serves 4.

Chinese Stuffed Cucumbers

6 large, straight cucumbers	**¼ cup diced celery**
¾ pound ground pork	**3 tablespoons soy sauce**
1 teaspoon salt	**3 tablespoons cornstarch**
½ teaspoon powdered ginger	**3 tablespoons vegetable oil**
¼ cup chopped green onions (scallions)	**1 cup beef broth**
	½ cup water

Peel away just a very thin layer of the cucumber skins. Cut each cucumber in half lengthwise, then in thirds crosswise. Scoop out the seeds.

Mix together the pork, salt, ginger, green onions, celery, 1 tablespoon of the soy sauce, 1 tablespoon of the cornstarch, and 1 tablespoon of the oil. Stuff the cucumbers with the mixture.

Heat the remaining oil in a skillet; arrange the cucumbers in it, stuffed side up. Add the broth. Cover, bring to a boil, and cook over medium heat 35 minutes, or until no pink remains in the pork.

In a saucepan, mix together the remaining cornstarch and soy sauce with the water. Cook, stirring constantly, until thickened. Arrange the cucumbers on a serving dish and pour the sauce over them.
Serves 6–8.

Dolmas

STUFFED GRAPE LEAVES

1 can grape leaves	¼ cup lemon juice
2 cups beef broth	1 tablespoon tomato paste

Buy the grape leaves in a Near East food specialty shop. A can contains about 60 leaves. Use 40 leaves for stuffing, and the rest for lining the pan and between the layers. Drain the leaves and cover with hot water. Drain again and spread out on a flat surface. Cut off the stems. Put a tablespoon of the stuffing (given below) on each leaf. Fold the opposite ends toward the center, then roll up like a sausage. Cover the bottom of a heavy, deep skillet or Dutch oven with leaves and arrange the rolls in it in layers, separating each layer with leaves. Add a mixture of the broth, lemon juice, and tomato paste. Put a plate on top of the top layer to weight it down, and cover the pan. Cook over low heat 1¼ hours, or until tender. Serve hot with yogurt, or cold with lemon wedges.

Stuffing I:

1 pound ground beef	½ teaspoon cinnamon
1 cup half-cooked rice	½ cup chopped green
1½ teaspoons salt	onions (scallions)
½ teaspoon freshly ground	½ cup chopped parsley
black pepper	2 tablespoons melted butter

Stuffing II:

1 pound ground lamb	½ cup pine nuts or
1½ teaspoons salt	slivered, blanched almonds
½ teaspoon freshly ground	½ cup chopped sautéed
black pepper	onions
¼ teaspoon crushed dried	
mint	

Mix all the ingredients together lightly, and stuff the leaves. *Serves 8–10.*

Dolmeh Bademjan

ARABIAN STUFFED EGGPLANT

2 medium-sized eggplants	½ teaspoon cinnamon
3 teaspoons salt	½ cup half-cooked rice
2 tablespoons vegetable oil	½ cup chopped parsley
¾ cup chopped onions	2 cups beef broth
1 pound ground lamb	⅓ cup sugar
¼ teaspoon freshly ground	½ cup cider vinegar
black pepper	1 teaspoon saffron

Wash the eggplants, remove the stems, and cut in half length-wise. Scoop out the pulp and chop it. Sprinkle the shells with 2 teaspoons of the salt and let stand 20 minutes. Rinse and dry.

Heat the oil in a skillet; sauté the onions and chopped eggplant 10 minutes. Mix together the sautéed mixture, lamb, pepper, cinnamon, rice, parsley, and remaining salt. Stuff the eggplant shells. Arrange in a Dutch oven or deep large skillet; add the broth. Cover and cook over low heat 20 minutes. Add a mixture of the sugar, vinegar, and saffron; re-cover and cook 30 minutes longer, basting occasionally. *Serves 4.*

Eierpflanze

AUSTRIAN STUFFED EGGPLANT

2 medium eggplants	¾ teaspoon orégano
2½ teaspoons salt	1 cup cooked egg barley
2 tablespoons vegetable oil	¾ cup grated Parmesan
¾ cup chopped onions	cheese
1¼ pounds ground beef	1 29-ounce can tomatoes,
2 cloves garlic, minced	drained and chopped
½ teaspoon freshly ground	
black pepper	

Wash the eggplants and place in a baking pan. Add water to a depth of ¼ inch. Bake in a 400° oven 20 minutes. Cool slightly, discard stems, and cut each in half lengthwise. Scoop out the pulp and chop; sprinkle the cavities with 1 teaspoon of the salt.

Heat the oil in a skillet; sauté the onions 5 minutes. Add the meat; cook over high heat 5 minutes, stirring almost steadily. Mix in the garlic, pepper, orégano, chopped eggplant, and remaining salt; cook over low heat 10 minutes. Mix half the meat mixture with the egg barley, ¼ cup of the cheese, and ¾ cup of the tomatoes. Taste for seasoning. Turn the eggplant halves upside down to drain for 5 minutes, then stuff with the egg barley mixture. Spread the remaining tomatoes and meat mixture in a greased baking dish. Arrange the eggplant halves over it and sprinkle with the remaining cheese. Bake in a 400° oven 20 minutes.

Serves 4.

Gefüllte Kohlrabi

STUFFED KOHLRABI, MUNICH STYLE

8 large kohlrabies	1 hard-cooked egg, chopped
2 tablespoons butter	¼ teaspoon freshly ground
½ cup chopped onions	black pepper
½ pound ground beef	⅛ teaspoon thyme
¼ cup fresh bread crumbs	2 tablespoons olive oil
1 egg, beaten	

Peel the kohlrabies and cook in boiling salted water 15 minutes, or until barely tender. Drain. Scoop out the centers and chop fine.

Melt the butter in a skillet; add the onions and beef. Cook over high heat 3 minutes, mixing almost steadily.

Soak the bread crumbs in water for 5 minutes. Drain well; add to the meat with the beaten egg, chopped egg, pepper, and thyme. Mix well and taste for seasoning. Stuff the kohlrabies with the mixture. This will use up about half the amount. Spread the remaining meat mixture on the bottom of a greased pie plate. Arrange the kohlrabies over it and brush with the oil. Bake in a preheated 425° oven 15 minutes, basting once or twice with the pan drippings. Serve as an accompaniment to meat dishes.

Serves 4–8.

Oignons Farcis

MEAT-STUFFED ONIONS

¼ pound sausage meat	2 tablespoons dry sherry
¼ pound ground beef	1 teaspoon salt
6 large onions	¼ teaspoon freshly ground
2 tablespoons butter	black pepper
2 tablespoons flour	
1 cup beef or chicken broth	

Lightly brown the sausage meat, stirring to keep lumps from forming. Drain, cool, and mix with the beef.

Peel the onions, scoop out the centers, chop, and reserve. Stuff the onions with the beef-sausage mixture. Melt the butter in a skillet; sauté the chopped onions 5 minutes. Blend in the flour; mix in the broth, sherry, salt, and pepper, stirring to the boiling point. Arrange the onions in a greased casserole; pour the sauce over them and bake in a 350° oven 1 hour, basting occasionally. *Serves 6.*

Pimientos Rellenos

BOLIVIAN STUFFED PEPPERS

8 large green peppers	2 eggs, beaten
2 tablespoons olive oil	1 cup canned corn kernels
½ cup chopped onions	¼ cup chopped green olives
1 pound ground ham	2 cups canned tomato sauce
3 teaspoons salt	⅛ teaspoon dried ground
¼ teaspoon freshly ground black pepper	chili peppers

Cut a 1-inch piece from the top (stem end) of each of the peppers; scoop out the seeds and fibers. Chop 4 of the tops. Heat the oil in a skillet; sauté the onions and chopped peppers for 5 minutes. Remove from the heat and mix in the ham, 1½ teaspoons of the salt, the black pepper, and the eggs. Add the corn and olives. Stuff the peppers and arrange in a baking dish. Add the tomato sauce, chili peppers, and remaining salt. Cover and bake in a 350° oven 1¼ hours, or until the peppers are tender. Remove the cover for the last 15 minutes of baking time.

Serves 8.

Stuffed Peppers, Creole Style

16 green peppers	1 20-ounce can tomatoes
1 teaspoon sugar	2 cups soda cracker crumbs
¼ pound butter	2 eggs, beaten
1½ cups chopped onions	2 teaspoons salt
2 cloves garlic, minced	½ teaspoon freshly ground
1¼ pounds cooked ham,	black pepper
chopped	¼ cup dry bread crumbs
1 cup tomato juice	4 tablespoons melted butter

Buy uniform-sized large peppers. Cut off the tops (stem ends) of 12 peppers and remove seeds. Cover with water and add the sugar. Bring to a boil and cook 10 minutes. Drain and cool. Chop the 4 remaining peppers.

Melt the butter in a skillet; sauté the chopped peppers, onions, and garlic for 10 minutes. Add the ham, tomato juice, and tomatoes; cook over low heat until all the liquid is absorbed. Stir in the cracker crumbs, eggs, salt, and pepper. Taste for seasoning and stuff the peppers. Arrange in a buttered baking dish and sprinkle with the bread crumbs and melted butter. Bake in a 350° oven 30 minutes.

Makes 12 peppers.

Israeli Stuffed Peppers

6 large green peppers
1 pound ground beef
½ cup grated onions
3 tablespoons raw rice
1 egg, beaten
2 tablespoons cold water
2½ teaspoons salt

½ teaspoon freshly ground black pepper
2 tablespoons vegetable oil
1 cup chopped onions
1 29-ounce can tomatoes, drained
3 tablespoons lemon juice
3 tablespoons sugar

Wash the peppers. Cut a 1-inch piece from the tops (stem ends), and reserve. Scoop out the seeds and fibers.

Mix together the meat, grated onions, rice, egg, water, 1½ teaspoons of the salt, and ¼ teaspoon of the pepper. Stuff the peppers and replace the tops.

Heat the oil in a heavy saucepan; sauté the chopped onions 10 minutes. Mix in the tomatoes and the remaining salt and pepper. Arrange the peppers in an upright position. Cover and cook over low heat 45 minutes. Add the lemon juice and sugar; cover and cook 30 minutes longer, or until peppers are tender, basting frequently. Taste for seasoning—the gravy should be sweet and sour.
Serves 6.

Chiles Rellenos

MEXICAN STUFFED PEPPERS

¼ cup olive oil
¾ pound ground beef
2 cloves garlic, minced
3 tablespoons tomato paste
3 tablespoons ground peanuts
2 teaspoons chili powder

1 teaspoon salt
6 large green peppers
¼ cup flour
2 eggs, beaten
1 cup dry bread crumbs
Vegetable oil for deep frying

Heat the oil in a skillet; sauté the beef, garlic, tomato paste, peanuts, chili powder, and salt over low heat for 5 minutes, stirring constantly. Taste for seasoning.

Cut a ½-inch piece off the tops (stem ends) of the peppers and scoop out the seeds and fibers. Put the peppers in a saucepan, cover with water, and bring to a boil. Drain immediately and cool 5 minutes. Stuff the peppers with the meat mixture. Sprinkle the tops with the flour. Brush each pepper thoroughly with beaten egg, dip in the bread crumbs, then in beaten egg and again in bread crumbs. Heat the oil to 375° and fry 1 or 2 peppers at a time until browned. Drain and serve hot.

Serves 6.

Stuffed Peppers, Southern Style

½ pound sliced bacon
6 large green peppers
3 tablespoons butter
½ cup chopped onions
1 cup chopped celery
½ pound mushrooms,
  chopped

1½ cups cooked rice
¾ teaspoon salt
¼ teaspoon freshly ground
  black pepper
2 tablespoons vegetable oil
6 tablespoons grated
  Parmesan cheese

Fry the bacon until crisp, drain, and crumble.

Wash the peppers, cut a 1-inch piece from the top (stem end), and scoop out the seeds and fibers. Plunge the peppers into boiling water for 5 minutes, then drain thoroughly.

Melt the butter in a skillet; sauté the onions and celery 5 minutes. Add the mushrooms and sauté 5 minutes. Mix in the rice, salt, pepper, and bacon. Taste for seasoning. Stuff the peppers. Brush a baking dish with the oil and stand the peppers in it in an upright position; sprinkle each pepper with a tablespoon of cheese. Bake in a 350° oven 45 minutes or until the peppers are tender.

Serves 6.

Chiles Rellenos con Puerco

SPANISH PORK-STUFFED PEPPERS

1½ pounds boneless pork	¼ cup seedless raisins
1 cup chopped onions	12 green peppers
2 cloves garlic, minced	1½ cups flour
1½ teaspoons salt	4 eggs
¼ teaspoon freshly ground black pepper	Vegetable oil for deep frying
1 cup water	

Cut the pork in small pieces and combine in a saucepan with the onions, garlic, salt, pepper, and water; bring to a boil and cook over low heat for 30 minutes. Chop or grind the undrained mixture. Soak the raisins in hot water for 10 minutes. Drain and add to the pork mixture.

Wash the peppers; cover with water, bring to a boil, and cook over low heat 10 minutes. Drain, cool, and cut the peppers in half lengthwise. Scoop out the seeds and fibers. Stuff the peppers with the pork mixture and roll in the flour. Separate the eggs; beat the egg whites until stiff, then beat in the egg yolks. Dip the peppers in the eggs, coating them well.

Heat the oil to 365°; fry 2 pepper halves at a time until delicately browned. Drain and keep warm while preparing the balance. *Serves 6.*

Gefüllte Kartoffeln

SAUSAGE-STUFFED POTATOES, HAMBURG STYLE

6 Idaho potatoes	2 tablespoons chopped parsley
2 tablespoons butter	½ teaspoon salt
½ cup minced onions	¼ teaspoon freshly ground black pepper
¼ pound sausage meat	

Peel the raw potatoes and cut in half lengthwise. Scoop out a large piece from each half, leaving an unbroken shell. Cook the scooped-out portion of the potatoes in boiling salted water until tender. Drain and mash. Mix in the butter, onions, sausage meat, parsley, salt, and pepper. Stuff the potato shells with the mixture. Arrange in a buttered baking dish and bake in a 350° oven 1 hour. Serve as an accompaniment to meat dishes.
Serves 12.

Pimientos Rellenos con Ternera

VENEZUELAN STUFFED PEPPERS WITH VEAL

6 sweet red peppers	**¼ teaspoon saffron**
½ pound ground veal	**½ teaspoon ground cumin**
¼ pound ham, chopped	**1¾ teaspoons salt**
¼ pound mushrooms,	**½ teaspoon freshly ground**
sautéed and chopped	**black pepper**
2 egg yolks	**4 tablespoons butter**
2 tablespoons dry sherry	**1 cup chicken broth**
1 tablespoon lemon juice	**2 cups chopped tomatoes**

Wash the peppers, cut in half lengthwise, and scoop out the seeds and fibers. Cover with water, bring to a boil, and cook 2 minutes. Drain, cool, and dry.

Mix together the veal, ham, mushrooms, egg yolks, sherry, lemon juice, saffron, cumin, ¾ teaspoon of the salt, and ¼ teaspoon of the pepper. Stuff the pepper halves with the mixture. Melt the butter in a casserole or deep skillet. Arrange the peppers in it in a single layer. Add a mixture of the broth, tomatoes, and the remaining salt and pepper. Cover and cook over low heat 30 minutes. Arrange the peppers on a serving dish and pour the sauce over them. (If the sauce is too thin, cook over high heat a few minutes.)
Serves 6.

Pomodori Ripieni

ITALIAN STUFFED TOMATOES

8 large, firm tomatoes
⅓ cup olive oil
½ cup chopped onions
½ pound ground beef
2 tablespoons raw rice

2 teaspoons salt
¼ teaspoon freshly ground
 black pepper
¼ teaspoon basil

Buy even-sized tomatoes. Cut a 1-inch piece off the stem end of the tomatoes. Scoop out the pulp and reserve.

Heat 2 tablespoons of the oil in a skillet; sauté the onions 5 minutes. Mix in the meat and rice; cook 5 minutes, stirring frequently. Add the tomato pulp, salt, pepper, and basil. Cook over low heat 5 minutes. Cool and stir in 2 tablespoons of the oil. Stuff the tomatoes with the mixture; arrange in an oiled baking dish; sprinkle with the remaining oil. Cover and bake in a 350° oven 30 minutes, removing the cover for the last 10 minutes. Serve hot or cold. *Serves 8.*

Banadoora Mihshee

MIDDLE EAST STUFFED TOMATOES

12 large, firm tomatoes
2½ teaspoons salt
¾ teaspoon freshly ground
 black pepper
¾ cup olive oil
1 cup chopped onions
1 pound ground lamb
¾ cup raw rice
2 tablespoons currants or
 seedless raisins

1½ cups beef broth
2 tablespoons minced
 parsley
1 teaspoon cinnamon
¼ cup pine nuts or sliced
 almonds
½ cup dry bread crumbs

Wash and dry the tomatoes; cut a ½-inch piece off the stem ends and reserve the tops. Scoop out as much of the pulp as possible.

Sprinkle the insides of the tomatoes with half the salt and pepper; chop the pulp.

Heat ½ cup of the oil in a saucepan; brown the onions and lamb in it. Add the rice; cook 5 minutes, stirring frequently. Mix in the tomato pulp, currants, and remaining salt and pepper. Add the broth; cover and cook over low heat 10 minutes. Mix in the parsley, cinnamon, and nuts; taste for seasoning. Stuff the tomatoes loosely; replace the tops. Arrange in an oiled baking dish. Brush with the remaining oil and sprinkle with the bread crumbs. Bake in a 350° oven 45 minutes. Serve hot or cold, as a main or first course. *Serves 6–12.*

Tomates Farcies Provençale
PROVENÇAL STUFFED TOMATOES

8 large, firm tomatoes	¼ cup soft bread crumbs
2 tablespoons olive oil	2 anchovies, finely
½ cup chopped onions	chopped
1 clove garlic, minced	1 tablespoon minced
½ pound ground beef	parsley
½ teaspoon salt	2 tablespoons butter
¼ teaspoon freshly ground	
black pepper	

Wash and dry the tomatoes. Cut them in half crosswise. Scoop out the pulp and reserve. Heat the oil in a skillet; sauté the onions and garlic 5 minutes. Add the meat; cook 5 minutes, stirring frequently. Add the tomato pulp, salt, and pepper; cook over low heat 5 minutes. Stir in the bread crumbs, anchovies, and parsley. Stuff the tomatoes; arrange in a greased baking pan and dot with the butter. Bake in a 350° oven 30 minutes. Serve hot or cold.
   Serves 4–8.

Dolmehs

IRANIAN STUFFED VEGETABLES

4 large green peppers
4 large, firm tomatoes
1 pound ground beef
¾ cup half-cooked rice
½ cup peeled, chopped
   tomatoes
¾ cup chopped green
   onions (scallions)
2 tablespoons chopped dill

3 tablespoons chopped
   parsley
1 teaspoon crushed
   coriander
2½ teaspoons salt
¾ teaspoon freshly ground
   black pepper
1 8-ounce can tomato sauce
½ cup water
2 tablespoons olive oil

Wash and dry the peppers and tomatoes. Cut a 1-inch piece off the stem ends and scoop out the seeds of the peppers and the pulp of the tomatoes. Reserve the pulp.

Mix together the beef, rice, chopped tomatoes, onions, dill, parsley, coriander, 1½ teaspoons of the salt, and ½ teaspoon of the pepper. Stuff the vegetables; arrange upright in a baking dish. Mix together the tomato sauce, water, tomato pulp, oil, and remaining salt and pepper. Pour over the peppers. Cover and cook over low heat 1¼ hours; baste frequently. *Serves 4–8.*

Zucchini Ripieni

ITALIAN STUFFED ZUCCHINI

3 medium-sized zucchini
⅓ cup olive oil
½ cup minced onions
1 pound ground beef
2 teaspoons salt

½ teaspoon freshly ground
   black pepper
¼ teaspoon orégano
½ cup canned tomato sauce

Select straight zucchini. Wash, scrub dry, and remove the stems of the zucchini; cut in half lengthwise. Scoop out the pulp, leaving an unbroken shell; chop the scooped-out portion.

Heat 2 tablespoons oil in a skillet; sauté the onions 5 minutes. Mix in the chopped zucchini; sauté 5 minutes. Add the beef; cook until no pink remains, stirring frequently to prevent lumps from forming. Mix in the salt, pepper, and orégano. Stuff the shells and arrange them in an oiled baking dish. Sprinkle with the remaining oil and cover with the tomato sauce. Bake in a 350° oven 40 minutes. Taste the sauce for seasoning.

Serves 6.

Zucchini Ripieni alla Siciliana

SICILIAN STUFFED ZUCCHINI

4 medium-sized zucchini	**2 tablespoons minced**
½ cup olive oil	**parsley**
¾ cup chopped onions	**2 tablespoons chopped**
¾ pound ground beef	**capers**
1 clove garlic, minced	**4 anchovies, chopped**
¾ cup peeled, chopped	**1 teaspoon salt**
tomatoes	**½ teaspoon freshly ground**
½ cup chopped mushrooms	**black pepper**
2 tablespoons fine dry	**¼ teaspoon basil**
bread crumbs	

Wash and scrub the unpeeled zucchini; cover with water, bring to a boil, and cook over low heat 3 minutes. Drain, cool, and cut in half lengthwise. Scoop out and dice the pulp. Reserve the shells.

Heat ¼ cup of the oil in a skillet; sauté the onions 5 minutes. Add the meat; cook 5 minutes, stirring frequently. Add the diced pulp and garlic; sauté 3 minutes. Mix in the tomatoes and mushrooms; cook 5 minutes. Remove from the heat and mix in the bread crumbs, parsley, capers, anchovies, salt, pepper, and basil. Stuff the shells and arrange in an oiled baking dish. Sprinkle with the remaining oil. Bake in a 350° oven 30 minutes. Serve hot or cold.

Serves 4 as a main course or 8 as a first course.

Soups

As the Mock Turtle said in Lewis Carroll's *Alice's Adventures in Wonderland:*

> Beautiful soup so rich and green
> Waiting in a hot tureen!
> Who for such dainties would not stoop?
> Soup of the evening, beautiful Soup!

Now that's the kind of reaction you want from your constituents around the dinner table.

Years ago, our grandmothers always had a "soup pot" simmering on the back of the stove, to which they added scraps of meat and vegetables from time to time. Thus, plenty of good wholesome fare was ready whenever needed. Today, however, we no longer accumulate the soup base in that fashion. We start out with fresh greens and vegetables, but if they are not available, there are any number of equally nourishing dried and frozen ingredients from which to choose.

In meat soups, beef is usually the base, although the Chinese use pork, and there is the well-known Scotch broth with its lamb content. The Italians have a creamed meat soup made with veal, and a very unusual soup from Poland has beef or calf liver as its flavorful ingredient.

Meaty soups, such as *pot au feu* and boiled beef, with hot French or Italian bread and a green salad, make a simple and easily prepared lunch or supper.

For a change of pace, try making your soups as many Europeans do, that is, in an earthenware casserole and serve it from either the pot in which it is cooked or in individual casseroles which may be placed in the oven to heat just before serving.

Beef Soup

4 pounds brisket or plate flank	Soup greens
Beef bones	1 bay leaf
3½ quarts water	¼ teaspoon white pepper
1 onion	1 tablespoon salt

Combine the beef, bones, and water in a deep saucepan. Bring to a boil. Add the onion, soup greens, bay leaf, and pepper. Cover loosely and cook over low heat 2 hours, or until the meat is tender. Add the salt; cook 10 minutes longer. Remove the beef and bones and strain the soup. Skim the fat. Serve the beef with horseradish.

Serves 8–10.

Rinderbrust

GERMAN BOILED BEEF

4 pounds brisket of beef	1 parsnip, cut in quarters
2 quarts water	1 turnip, cut in quarters
1 onion	1 tablespoon salt
4 peppercorns	1 bay leaf
½ teaspoon thyme	4 sprigs parsley
2 carrots, cut in quarters	

Rinse and dry the meat. Bring the water to a boil; add the meat, onion, peppercorns, and thyme. Bring to a boil again, cover, and cook over low heat 1½ hours. Add the carrots, parsnip, turnip, salt, bay leaf, and parsley. Re-cover and cook 1½ hours longer or until meat is tender. Slice the meat and serve with horseradish or horseradish sauce. Serve the soup with noodles or dumplings.

Serves 8–10.

Pepparrotskött

SWEDISH BOILED BEEF

2 quarts water
3 pounds brisket of beef
1½ cups sliced carrots, chopped
1 turnip, cut in quarters
3 stalks celery, sliced
2 cups sliced onions
3 sprigs parsley

2½ teaspoons salt
½ teaspoon white pepper
1 clove
1 bay leaf
¼ cup freshly grated horseradish
¾ cup sour cream

Bring the water to a boil and add the meat. Bring to a boil again and skim the top. Add the carrots, turnip, celery, onions, parsley, salt, pepper, clove, and bay leaf. Cover, and cook over low heat for 2½ hours or until the meat is tender. Serve the vegetables in the soup.

Drain the meat and place on a hot platter. Mix the horseradish and sour cream; heat but do not let boil. Slice the beef and serve with the sauce.

Serves 6.

Pot-au-Feu

FRENCH BEEF-VEGETABLE SOUP

2 pounds rump or chuck of beef
1 pound oxtail, cut in 2-inch pieces
1 marrowbone
4 quarts water
2 cloves
1 onion
3 carrots, sliced
6 leeks, sliced
2 stalks celery, sliced

1 turnip, diced
3 peppercorns
1 bay leaf
½ teaspoon thyme
2 tablespoons minced parsley
1½ tablespoons salt
1 2-pound head cabbage
2 tablespoons butter
French bread slices

In a deep saucepan combine the beef, oxtail, bone, and water. Bring to a boil, skim the top, and cook over low heat 2 hours. Stick the cloves in the onion and add with the carrots, leeks, celery, turnip, peppercorns, bay leaf, thyme, parsley, and salt. Cook 30 minutes.

Cut the cabbage in eighths and sauté in the butter for 5 minutes. Add to the soup. Cook 1 hour longer. Skim the fat and taste for seasoning. Dry the slices of bread in the oven.

Serve the soup from a tureen—the meat should be sliced and served in it or on a separate platter. Place a slice of dried bread in each soup plate and pour the soup and vegetables over it. Parmesan cheese may be sprinkled on top.

Serves 10–12.

Bollito Misto

ITALIAN BOILED MIXED MEATS

4-pound smoked beef
   tongue
2 whole onions
2 carrots
2 stalks celery
4 sprigs parsley
2 pounds eye round of
   beef

2 pounds loin of pork
8 Italian-style pork sausages
½ teaspoon freshly ground
   black pepper
3-pound head of cabbage,
   cut in eighths
6 potatoes, peeled and
   halved

Cover the tongue with water in a very large kettle, bring to a boil and drain. Add fresh boiling water to cover, and add the onions, carrots, celery, and parsley. Bring to a boil and cook over low heat 1 hour. Skim the top. Add the beef and pork, cook 1 hour. Skim the top. Add the sausages and pepper. Cook 45 minutes. Add the cabbage and potatoes; cook 30 minutes longer. Slice the meats and arrange on a serving dish with the vegetables, and a bowl of mustard or *vinaigrette* sauce. Serve the strained broth in deep plates at the same time.

Serves 8–10.

Zuppa alla Cacciatora

ITALIAN CREAMED MEAT SOUP

4 dried mushrooms, washed	2 quarts beef broth
3 tablespoons butter	¼ teaspoon freshly ground black pepper
1 cup chopped onions	3 egg yolks
1 pound ground veal	½ cup light cream

Cover the mushrooms with water and let soak 15 minutes. Drain and chop. Melt the butter in a saucepan; sauté the onions 5 minutes. Mix in the veal; cook over medium heat 10 minutes, stirring frequently. Add the broth, mushrooms, and pepper; cook over low heat 1½ hours. Strain the mixture thoroughly. Taste for seasoning. Just before serving, bring the soup to a boil. Beat the egg yolks and cream in a tureen or bowl; gradually add the soup, stirring steadily to prevent curdling. Serve immediately with croutons.

Serves 6–8.

Barley-Bean Soup

1½ cups dried lima beans	1 tablespoon salt
2 pounds soup meat	½ teaspoon freshly ground black pepper
2½ quarts water	
½ cup pearl barley	2 tablespoons chopped parsley
1 cup chopped onions	

Wash the beans, cover with water, bring to a boil, cook 2 minutes, remove from the heat, and let soak 1 hour. Drain. Or soak the beans in water to cover overnight. Drain. In a large saucepan, combine the beans, meat, water, barley, and onions. Bring to a boil, cover loosely, and cook over low heat 1½ hours. Add the salt and pepper. Cook 1 hour longer or until the meat and beans are tender. Sprinkle with the parsley and serve the meat cut up in small pieces as a garnish if desired.

Serves 8–10.

Chinese Pork-Noodle Soup

½ pound fine egg noodles
6 cups beef broth
1½ cups julienne-cut roast pork
1 teaspoon sesame seed or vegetable oil

3 hard-cooked eggs, cut in quarters
⅓ cup chopped green onions (scallions)

Cook the noodles 1 minute less than the package directs. Drain and rinse under cold running water.

Bring the broth to a boil; stir in the noodles, pork, and oil. Serve in deep bowls, with 2 quarters of egg in each, and a tablespoon of green onions sprinkled on top. *Serves 6.*

Polévka s Knedlíčky

CZECHOSLOVAKIAN SOUP STEW WITH LIVER DUMPLINGS

3 pounds breast of beef
1 marrowbone
2 tablespoons vegetable oil
2 cups sliced onions
4 stalks celery and leaves, sliced
1½ quarts boiling water
2 tomatoes, peeled and chopped
3 carrots, sliced

½ cup minced parsley
4 teaspoons salt
¾ teaspoon freshly ground black pepper
½ pound calf's liver
2 eggs, beaten
3 tablespoons flour
Dash nutmeg
¾ cup fresh bread crumbs

Wash the meat and bone. Heat the oil in a large kettle. Brown the meat together with the onions. Pour off the fat. Add the celery, water, and bone. Bring to a boil and skim the top. Cook over low heat 1½ hours. Add the tomatoes, carrots, ¼ cup of the parsley, 3½ teaspoons of the salt, and ½ teaspoon of the pepper. Cover loosely and cook 1 hour. While the soup is cooking, prepare the dumplings.

Grind or chop the raw liver very fine. Mix in the eggs, flour, nutmeg, and remaining salt, pepper, and parsley. Add just enough of the bread crumbs to make a stiff batter. Chill 1 hour. If mixture isn't firm enough to shape at this point, add a little more bread crumbs. Shape into walnut-sized balls.

Cut the meat into bite-sized pieces. Return the meat to the soup and bring to a rolling boil. Drop the dumplings into the soup, cover, and cook over medium heat 10 minutes. Serve in bowls. *Serves 4–6.*

Zupa Watrobiana

POLISH LIVER SOUP

1 pound calf's or beef liver	1 celery root, diced
2 slices bacon, diced	3 sprigs parsley
2 tablespoons butter	6 cups beef broth
1 carrot, sliced	2 egg yolks
1 stalk celery, sliced	Salt
1 leek, sliced	

Wash the liver and cut it in narrow strips. Put the bacon in a skillet and brown it lightly. Pour off the fat. Add the butter to the skillet and when melted add the liver, carrot, celery, leek, celery root, and parsley. Cover the skillet and cook over low heat 30 minutes. Watch carefully and add a little broth if necessary to keep from burning.

Put the mixture through the fine blade of a food chopper or purée in an electric blender with a little broth. Add the purée to all the broth, bring to a boil, and cook over low heat 10 minutes. Beat the egg yolks in a bowl; gradually add a little of the soup, stirring steadily to prevent curdling. Return to the balance of the soup. Taste for seasoning, adding salt if necessary. Heat but do not let boil. *Serves 6–8.*

Leber Knoedel

LIVER DUMPLINGS

3 tablespoons minced
onions
2 teaspoons melted chicken
fat or butter
½ pound calf's liver
1 teaspoon salt

⅛ teaspoon freshly ground
black pepper
¼ cup flour
1 tablespoon minced parsley
1 egg yolk
1 egg white, stiffly beaten

Sauté the onions in the fat or butter 5 minutes. Chop or grind the raw liver with the sautéed onion. Stir in the salt, pepper, flour, parsley, and egg yolk. Fold in the egg white.

Drop the batter by the teaspoon into boiling soup or salted water. (Test one—if the mixture doesn't hold together, add a little more flour.) Cook 15 minutes or until they rise to the surface. Serve in the soup or, if cooked in water, drain and serve in soup, or with melted butter, as an accompaniment to meat dishes. *Serves 8–10.*

Pancit Molo

PHILIPPINE MEAT-DUMPLING STEW

1 cup flour
1¾ teaspoons salt
2 egg yolks
1 tablespoon water
1 pound ground pork
½ pound ground ham
1 teaspoon anchovy paste
½ teaspoon freshly ground
black pepper

½ cup chopped green
onions (scallions)
4 cloves garlic, minced
½ cup chopped water
chestnuts
3 tablespoons oil
1 cup chopped onions
6 cups beef broth

Sift the flour and ¼ teaspoon of the salt into a bowl; work in the egg yolks and water with the fingers. Knead until smooth and elastic. Cover with a bowl and let stand 30 minutes.

Mix together the pork, ham, anchovy paste, pepper, green onions, garlic, water chestnuts, and remaining salt. Roll out the dough paper-thin, and cut in 3-inch squares. Place a heaping teaspoon of the mixture on each and fold over the dough into a triangle, sealing the edges with a little egg yolk or water.

Heat the oil in a saucepan; sauté the onions 5 minutes. Add the remaining pork mixture and sauté 5 minutes. Stir in the broth and bring to a boil. Carefully drop the dumplings into it. Cover and cook over low heat 15 minutes. Taste for seasoning and serve in deep bowls.

Serves 6–8.

Gulyasleves

HUNGARIAN GOULASH SOUP

3 tablespoons butter
1 pound pork or veal, cut in ½-inch cubes
1 pound beef, cut in ½-inch cubes
3 cups chopped onions
2 tablespoons paprika
1½ cups diced green peppers

1 cup canned tomatoes
6 cups boiling water
1½ teaspoons salt
½ teaspoon freshly ground black pepper
2 cups cubed potatoes
½ pound smoked sausages, sliced

Melt the butter in a saucepan; add the pork or veal, beef, and onions. Cook over medium heat until browned. Stir in the paprika. Add the green peppers, tomatoes, water, salt, and pepper. Bring to a boil, cover, and cook over low heat 1½ hours. Add the potatoes; cook 20 minutes.

Cover the sausages with water. Bring to a boil and cook 10 minutes. Drain and add to the soup. Taste for seasoning.

Serves 6–8.

Lentil Soup

2 cups lentils	1 tablespoon salt
2½ quarts water	¼ teaspoon freshly ground
2 onions, diced	black pepper
2 tablespoons fat	1 bay leaf
2 carrots, diced	4 frankfurters, sliced

Wash and drain the lentils. Combine with the water; bring to a boil and cook over medium heat 1 hour.

Brown the onions in the fat and add to the lentils with the carrots, salt, pepper, and bay leaf. Cook over low heat 2 hours. Discard the bay leaf and rub the mixture through a food mill. Return to the saucepan. Add the frankfurters and cook over low heat 10 minutes. *Serves 6–8.*

Oxtail Soup

2 small oxtails	½ cup grated carrots
¼ cup flour	½ cup diced celery
2 teaspoons salt	¼ teaspoon thyme
½ teaspoon freshly ground	3 sprigs parsley
black pepper	1 bay leaf
1 tablespoon oil	4 cups beef broth
½ cup chopped onions	2 quarts water

Have the oxtails cut in ½-inch pieces. Wash, cover with boiling water, drain, and dry with paper towels. Roll the oxtails in a mixture of the flour, salt, and pepper.

Heat the oil in a saucepan; brown the oxtails in it. Pour off the fat. Add the onions, carrots, celery, thyme, parsley, bay leaf, broth, and water. Bring to a boil, cover, and cook over low heat 3 hours. Discard the parsley and bay leaf, taste for seasoning and serve.

Serves 6–8.

Philadelphia Pepper Pot

¾ pound fresh tripe, finely
  cubed
2 pounds veal knuckles
3 quarts cold water
1½ cups chopped green
  peppers

2 cups chopped onions
3 tablespoons butter
1½ teaspoons salt
⅓ cup raw rice
1½ cups canned tomatoes

Combine and bring to a boil the tripe, veal knuckles, and
water; skim thoroughly, cover, and cook over low heat 3 hours.
Sauté the vegetables in the butter until lightly browned; add to
the tripe with the salt and rice and cook, covered, 30 minutes.
Add the tomatoes and cook 15 minutes longer. Remove knuckles
and cool; skim and reheat before serving.
Serves 8–10.

Trinidad Pepper Pot

1 pound boneless stewing
  beef, cut in 1-inch cubes
1 pound corned beef,
  cubed
1 pound boneless pork,
  cubed
1 pound smoked ham,
  cubed
7 cups water
1 clove garlic, minced

1½ cups sliced onions
2 tablespoons dark brown
  sugar
2 tablespoons Worcestershire
  sauce
½ teaspoon dried ground
  chili peppers
½ teaspoon thyme
½ teaspoon freshly ground
  black pepper

Combine the beef, corned beef, pork, ham, and water in a
saucepan; bring to a boil, cover, and cook over medium heat
2 hours. Add the garlic, onions, sugar, Worcestershire sauce,
chili peppers, thyme, and pepper. Cover and cook over low heat
1 hour, or until the meats are tender. Taste for seasoning. Serve
in deep bowls with rice.
Serves 6–8.

Polish Beet Borscht

3 quarts water
2 pounds brisket of beef
Beef bones
8 beets, grated
2 onions, diced

2 cloves garlic, minced
1 tablespoon salt
3 tablespoons brown sugar
⅓ cup lemon juice
2 eggs, beaten

Combine the water, meat, and bones in a deep saucepan. Bring to a boil and skim. Add the beets, onions, garlic, and salt. Cover and cook over medium heat 2 hours. Add the brown sugar and lemon juice. Cook 30 minutes. Taste to correct seasoning.

Beat the eggs in a bowl. Gradually add a little hot soup, beating steadily to prevent curdling. Return to saucepan but do not boil. Serve with pieces of meat as garnish.

Serves 8–10.

Russian Cabbage Borscht

3 pounds brisket or plate
   flank of beef
Beef bones
6 cups water
1½ cups diced onions
2 29-ounce cans tomatoes
3 pounds cabbage, coarsely
   shredded

1 apple, peeled and diced
2 teaspoons salt
½ teaspoon freshly ground
   black pepper
⅓ cup lemon juice
4 tablespoons sugar

Combine the meat, bones, and water in a deep saucepan. Bring to a boil and skim the top. Add the onions and tomatoes. Cover and cook over low heat 1 hour. Add the cabbage, apple, salt, and pepper. Cook 1 hour. Stir in the lemon juice and sugar. Cook 20 minutes. Taste for seasoning. Serve the meat cut up in the soup or as a separate course. *Serves 8–10.*

Schchi

RUSSIAN SAUERKRAUT SOUP

2 pounds short ribs of beef
Beef bones
2 quarts water
1 cup chopped onions
2 cloves garlic, minced
1 20-ounce can tomatoes
2 pounds cabbage, shredded

1 tablespoon salt
½ teaspoon freshly ground
  black pepper
2 tablespoons lemon juice
¼ cup sugar
1½ pounds sauerkraut
Sour cream

Combine the meat, bones, and water in a large saucepan. Bring to a boil and skim the top. Add the onions, garlic, tomatoes, cabbage, salt, and pepper. Cover loosely and cook over low heat 1½ hours. Add the lemon juice, sugar, and sauerkraut. Cook 1 hour longer. Taste for seasoning. Remove the meat and serve separately with boiled potatoes if desired. Serve the soup with a spoon of sour cream. *Serves 8–10.*

Scotch Broth

½ cup large barley
3 pounds breast or flank
  of lamb
3 quarts water
1 tablespoon butter
½ cup chopped onions
½ cup sliced celery

½ cup diced carrots
½ cup diced turnips
2½ teaspoons salt
½ teaspoon freshly ground
  black pepper
2 tablespoons minced
  parsley

Soak the barley in warm water for 2 hours. Drain. Cut the meat in small pieces (if the breast is used, cut in individual ribs). Combine the meat in a saucepan with the water. Bring to a boil and add the barley. Cover and cook over low heat 1½ hours.

Melt the butter in a skillet; sauté the onions, celery, carrots, and turnips 10 minutes, stirring frequently. Add to the soup with the salt and pepper. Re-cover and cook 1 hour longer. Skim the fat, and cut the meat from the bones. Return the meat to the soup. Stir in the parsley and taste for seasoning.

Serves 8–10.

Split Pea Soup

3 quarts water	1 tablespoon salt
2 cups split peas, washed and drained	½ teaspoon freshly ground black pepper
2 pounds plate flank	2 carrots, grated
Beef bones	2 onions, diced

Combine the water and peas in a saucepan. Bring to a boil and cook over low heat 1 hour. Add the flank, bones, salt, pepper, carrots, and onions. Cover and cook over low heat 2 hours or until the meat is tender. Remove the meat and bones.

Rub the soup through a sieve. Serve the soup with pieces of meat as garnish. Makes about 2 quarts of soup.

Serves 8–10.

Sausages

Of the smoked sausages, in the United States at least, the frankfurter is far and away the most sought after. Although it originated in Frankfurt, Germany, in America today it vies with the hamburger in national popularity. Even in Paris now, one can get *"le hot dog."*

The word "sausage" is applied to chopped meat, pork or beef or a combination of the two, in a casing, and although fresh pork sausage is sometimes made at home, the smoked variety is usually bought already prepared.

A big brother to the frankfurter is the knockwurst, which is very appealing on a cold day with sauerkraut or baked beans.

Chorizos are highly-spiced sausages. The best ones come from Spain, but there are varieties imported here from Latin America. *Chorizos* are usually sliced or diced and combined with other meats and rice or vegetables. And no really good Spanish *paella* (a seafood-chicken-rice dish) can be made without them.

Italian sausages, either hot or sweet, and spicy Polish sausage, add a flavorful note to peppers and onions or the stew pot.

Fresh pork sausages, usually in casings but sometimes made into flat sausage meat cakes, are generally browned in the skillet. Dry on paper towels to get rid of the excess fat. These sausages are wonderful with scrambled eggs, pancakes, or as a part of a mixed grill.

There are many varieties of sausages, but they are all variations of the above. The Vienna sausage, for instance, is the same as the frankfurter. Vienna sausage, however, often comes in small links, which can be grilled and added to the cocktail buffet.

Choucroute à l'Alsacienne

ALSATIAN PORK CHOPS, FRANKFURTERS, AND SAUERKRAUT

6 pork chops, cut 1-inch thick
4 slices salt pork
2 cloves
1 onion
2 pounds sauerkraut
2 cloves garlic, minced
½ teaspoon freshly ground black pepper
3 cups dry white wine
1½ teaspoons salt
6 knockwursts (thick frankfurters)

Trim the fat from the chops.
Cook the salt pork in boiling water 10 minutes. Drain well and dry. Place the salt pork on the bottom of a Dutch oven or casserole. Stick the cloves in the onion and add to the pan with the sauerkraut, garlic, pepper, and wine. Cover and cook over low heat 2 hours. Brown the pork chops in a skillet; season with the salt and add to the sauerkraut. Re-cover and cook 1 hour. Add the knockwursts; cook 15 minutes longer.
Serves 6.

Salsiccia alla Mozzarella

ITALIAN SAUSAGES IN CHEESE SAUCE

2 pounds Italian sweet or hot sausages
3 tablespoons olive oil
1 cup thinly sliced onions
1 cup chopped green peppers
¼ cup beef broth
1 cup grated mozzarella cheese

Prick the sausages and brown them lightly in a skillet; drain and arrange them in a baking dish. Pour off the sausage fat from the skillet; heat the olive oil in the same skillet and sauté the onions and peppers 5 minutes, stirring frequently. Spread over the sausages. Pour the broth over all, then sprinkle the cheese on top. Cover and bake in a 325° oven 30 minutes, removing the cover for the last 5 minutes. *Serves 6–8.*

Cazuela a la Catalana

CATALONIAN BEEF AND SAUSAGES

¼ cup olive oil
2 pounds top round of
   beef, cut in 1-inch cubes
1½ cups chopped onions
1 cup chopped green
   peppers
1 cup chopped tomatoes

1 tablespoon flour
1½ teaspoons salt
½ teaspoon freshly ground
   black pepper
1 cup beef broth
½ pound *chorizos* (Spanish
   sausages), sliced

Heat the oil in a Dutch oven or deep skillet. Brown the meat in it on all sides. Remove the meat. In the oil remaining in the pan sauté the onions 5 minutes. Add the green peppers and tomatoes; cook 5 minutes, stirring frequently. Blend in the flour, salt, and pepper; cook 2 minutes. Return the meat and mix in the broth. Cover and bake in a 350° oven 1 hour. Remove the cover and arrange the sausage slices around the edge. Bake 15 minutes longer.
Serves 6–8.

Martinique Pork Sausage Cakes

2 pounds boneless fat pork,
   ground twice
1½ teaspoons salt
½ teaspoon freshly ground
   black pepper

¼ teaspoon cayenne pepper
¾ teaspoon thyme
1 teaspoon sage
⅛ teaspoon ground allspice

When buying the pork, be sure it is untrimmed of fat. Mix the ground pork with the seasonings and let stand in the refrigerator several hours or overnight before using. Shape the mixture into flat cakes and fry until browned and cooked through. Any unused portion may be shaped into cakes and frozen for future use.
Makes about 18 2-inch sausage cakes.

Chorizos

SPANISH HOMEMADE SAUSAGES

2½ pounds boneless fat
   pork
2 cloves garlic, minced
¾ cup chopped onions
2 teaspoons salt
¾ teaspoon freshly ground
   black pepper

2 teaspoons Spanish paprika
½ teaspoon dried ground
   chili peppers
1 teaspoon ground cumin
Sausage casings

Buy pork with a good layer of fat and have it ground once by the butcher, then grind all the ingredients together in a food chopper. Fill the sausage casings with the mixture. If you don't have the casings, form into firm sausage shapes. Wrap the sausages and store in the coldest portion of the refrigerator. When ready to use, cook the sausages over very low heat until cooked through.

Carne de Puerco con Chorizos

PHILIPPINE PORK AND SAUSAGES

½ pound spicy sausages
6 pork chops, cut 1-inch
   thick
1½ teaspoons salt
½ teaspoon freshly ground
   black pepper

1 cup thinly sliced onions
1 cup diced green peppers
1 tablespoon flour
1½ cups dry white wine
1 bay leaf

Cut the sausages in 2-inch slices, and brown them lightly in a skillet. Drain and reserve.

Rub the pork chops with the salt and pepper. Brown the chops in the skillet and remove. To the skillet add the onions and green peppers; sauté 5 minutes. Arrange the chops in the pan, sprinkle with the flour, and add the wine and bay leaf; cover and cook over low heat 45 minutes. Add the sausages, re-cover, and cook 30 minutes longer or until the pork is tender. Skim the fat. *Serves 6.*

Sosiski à la Sierzputowski

POLISH KNOCKWURSTS IN MUSTARD SAUCE

12 knockwursts or frankfurters	1 cup dry red wine
2 tablespoons butter	2½ teaspoons dry mustard
2 tablespoons flour	1 teaspoon meat extract

Cook the knockwursts or frankfurters in boiling water; drain and keep over low heat until skin browns lightly. While the knockwursts are cooking, melt the butter in a small saucepan. Blend in the flour until it begins to brown. Add the wine, stirring steadily to the boiling point. Stir in the mustard and meat extract; cook over low heat 5 minutes.

Arrange the knockwursts on a hot platter and pour the sauce over them.

Serves 6.

Creole Sausage Stew

1 pound pork sausages	2 cups cooked or canned whole-kernel corn
1 cup chopped onions	
½ cup chopped green peppers	1 bay leaf
	½ teaspoon thyme
2 tablespoons flour	1¼ teaspoons salt
1 29-ounce can tomatoes	Dash Tabasco

Cut each sausage crosswise into 4 pieces; cook until browned in a large skillet. Remove the sausages. Drain all but 2 tablespoons of fat. To the fat remaining add the onions and green peppers; sauté 5 minutes. Blend in the flour. Add the tomatoes, corn, bay leaf, thyme, salt, and Tabasco. Cook over low heat 20 minutes. Return the sausages and cook 5 minutes longer.

Serves 6.

Bigos

POLISH PEASANT STEW

2 tablespoons butter
1 cup chopped onions
2 pounds boneless pork,
cut in 1-inch cubes
1 pound Polish or other
spicy sausage, cubed
3 cups shredded cabbage
1 pound sauerkraut
½ pound mushrooms, sliced
2 cooking apples, peeled
and sliced

3 tablespoons apricot jam
1 8-ounce can tomato
sauce
1 cup beef broth
¾ cup dry red wine
2 teaspoons salt
½ teaspoon freshly ground
black pepper
1 clove garlic, minced
1 bay leaf

Melt the butter in a Dutch oven or casserole. Add the onions and pork; cook over medium heat until browned. Add all the remaining ingredients; mix well, cover, and bake in a 325° oven 2½ hours. Taste for seasoning. *Serves 6–8.*

Koru Ragu

SWEDISH SAUSAGE STEW

1½ pounds pork sausages
3 tablespoons butter
½ cup chopped onions
1 tablespoon flour
1 cup beef broth
1 pound potatoes, peeled
and cubed

2 cups sliced carrots
1 teaspoon salt
½ teaspoon freshly ground
black pepper
1 bay leaf

Lightly brown the sausages in a heavy saucepan. Remove and reserve. Pour off the fat. Melt the butter in the saucepan; sauté the onions 5 minutes. Blend in the flour, then stir in the broth until the mixture boils. Add the sausages, potatoes, carrots, salt, pepper, and bay leaf. Bring to a boil, cover, and cook over low heat 20 minutes. *Serves 6–8.*

Fire Pot Cookery

The Chinese, Japanese, and Koreans all use a form of this style of cooking. The utensil used consists of a metal container, with a charcoal burner supplying the source of heat for cooking. Usually the cooking unit is round, with a hole in the middle, similar to a tube pan, which permits the heat to rise, and is placed on a stand. A chafing dish or a deep electric skillet can also be used. Boiling broth is usually the liquid used for cooking. The important factor is to use a container that can be put on the table, so that each person can cook his own food or help himself to the ingredients with chopsticks or long-handled forks.

The Swiss too have a form of fire pot cookery, the delicious *Fondue Bourguignonne**; and the charcoal brazier is always a part of the *luau* of Hawaii, as typical of the islands as the hula girl and the grass skirt.

Chinese Fire Kettle

1 cup vermicelli	1 pound fillet of beef, sliced paper thin
6 dried Chinese mushrooms	
½ cup chopped green onions (scallions)	1 pound boned pork loin, sliced paper thin
¼ cup grated gingerroot	3 bamboo shoots, thinly sliced
½ pound raw shrimp, shelled and deveined	1 teaspoon salt
4 cups shredded Chinese or green cabbage	¼ cup dry sherry
	10 cups beef broth

Cover the vermicelli with boiling water, let stand 5 minutes, and drain. Wash the mushrooms and soak in warm water for 10 minutes. Drain and cut in half.

This dish may be cooked on a range before being brought to the table. In the selected utensil, spread the green onions, ginger, and shrimp. Cover with the cabbage. Arrange the beef and pork over it, then the mushrooms, bamboo shoots, and vermicelli. Sprinkle with the salt and sherry, then add the broth. Cover, bring to a boil, and cook 25 minutes. Do not stir. If the dish was not cooked at the table, place it on a heating unit in the center of the table. Provide deep bowls, spoons, and chopsticks or long-handled forks for each person. Each person helps himself to the various ingredients and the broth.

Serves 6–8.

Fondue Bourguignonne

3 pounds fillet or sirloin of beef	**Chutney**
1 quart vegetable oil (about)	**Pickled onions**
	Pickles
Béarnaise Sauce*	**Salt**
White Horseradish Sauce*	**Pepper**
Spicy tomato sauce	**Paprika**
Prepared hot and mild mustard	

There is special equipment available for the preparation of the *fondue,* consisting of a deep earthenware or metal pan set over an alcohol burner, but a chafing dish or electric skillet may be used. The dish is prepared at the table, each person cooking his own meat.

Cut the meat into ¾-inch cubes and divide it among 6–8 plates. Put 2 long-handled forks on each plate containing the meat. Provide an extra plate for each person. Place the cooking unit in the center of the table, and pour in enough oil to half fill it. Heat the oil. Arrange the sauces and condiments on the table, including salt, pepper mills, and paprika.

Put a small cube of bread in the oil (this keeps it from spattering) and bring the oil to a boil. Each person spears a piece of meat with 1 fork and places it in the oil until it is cooked the way he likes it. The meat is transferred to the extra fork, dipped in the sauces and condiments, put on the extra plates, and then the next piece is cooked. *Serves 6–8.*

Sinsun-Lo

KOREAN STEAMED MEAT

This is a somewhat complicated dish to prepare, but the results make it worth while. All of the five different sections, marked **A** to **E,** must be prepared and reserved until finally assembled, as described in the last paragraph.

A. *Beef Mixture*

½ pound fillet of beef
2 tablespoons soy sauce
2 tablespoons minced green onions (scallions)
2 teaspoons minced garlic
2 teaspoons ground sesame seeds

⅛ teaspoon freshly ground black pepper
1 tablespoon sesame or vegetable oil

Cut the meat into paper-thin narrow strips and toss with all the remaining ingredients.

B. *Pork and Liver Mixture*

¼ pound boneless pork
¼ pound calf's or beef liver
½ teaspoon salt
⅛ teaspoon white pepper

3 tablespoons flour
1 egg, beaten
3 tablespoons sesame or vegetable oil

Cut the pork and liver in paper-thin narrow strips. Dip the strips in a mixture of the salt, pepper, and flour, then in the egg. Fry in hot oil until cooked through. Drain.

C. *Meat Ball Mixture*

½ pound ground beef
2 tablespoons soy sauce
2 tablespoons minced green
onions (scallions)
2 teaspoons minced garlic
2 teaspoons ground sesame
seeds

⅛ teaspoon freshly ground
black pepper
4 tablespoons sesame or
vegetable oil
¼ cup flour
1 egg, beaten

Mix together the beef, soy sauce, green onions, garlic, sesame seeds, pepper, and 1 tablespoon of the oil. Shape into walnut-sized balls, and roll in the flour, then in the egg. Fry in the remaining hot oil until browned. Drain and reserve.

D. *Omelet Mixture*

6 eggs
2 tablespoons water
½ cup shredded cooked
ham

2 tablespoons sesame or
vegetable oil

Beat the eggs and water; mix in the ham. Make small thin omelets in the oil. Cut into strips.

E. *Vegetable Mixture*

6 dried Chinese mushrooms
8 bamboo shoots
2 bunches watercress
1 cup blanched walnuts

2 cups thinly sliced onions
4 carrots, cut julienne
3 cups beef broth

Wash the mushrooms, cover with warm water, and let stand 10 minutes. Drain and cut in narrow strips. Cut the bamboo shoots in narrow strips. Remove the stems of the watercress.

To cook and serve, arrange the meat in **A** on the bottom of the selected utensil, with the onions over it. Then arrange all

the other ingredients except the broth in layers. When ingredients begin to sizzle, add the broth and cook 10 minutes. Place the utensil in the center of the table and plates in front of each person so that he can help himself to the different ingredients.
Serves 6–8.

Chabu-Chabu

JAPANESE STEAMED BEEF

1½ pounds fillet of beef, sliced paper thin
1 pound fresh spinach
12 green onions (scallions)
12 mushroom caps
2 bunches watercress
4 cups boiling beef broth
1 cup soy sauce
3 tablespoons vinegar
¼ teaspoon Tabasco
2 tablespoons grated gingerroot
Salt
Pepper
Monosodium glutamate
½ pound medium noodles, cooked and drained

Arrange the sliced beef on a platter. Discard the stems of the spinach, wash thoroughly, drain well, and dry. Heap in a bowl. Clean the green onions and arrange in a bunch on the meat platter. Trim, wash, and dry the mushrooms and watercress. Put on the meat platter.

Put the boiling beef broth in the selected utensil. Mix the soy sauce, vinegar, Tabasco, and ginger. Divide among 6 small dishes. Also, have dishes of salt, pepper, and monosodium glutamate. Put the noodles on a serving dish.

Provide each person with a plate and chopsticks or a long-handled fork. To cook, each person picks up a slice of meat and dips it into the broth, holding it there until the meat turns a light pink color. Do not overcook it. The meat is then dipped in the soy sauce mixture, or the salt, pepper, and monosodium glutamate, and eaten. The vegetables are cooked in the same manner, but only after all the meat is eaten. The noodles are then put into the broth to heat, and eaten last.
Serves 6.

Sauces

Sauces are said to be the mark of a good cook. Although most of the dishes in this book are cooked in their own special gravies or sauces, the sauces that follow are classic with meat dishes. A steak, broiled lamb chop, roast beef, or any plain meat dish can be enhanced with one of the sauces in this section. Sauces using meat, which can be served with rice or *pasta,* are also included.

Most of the classic sauces are of French origin, although the Italians must be credited with a few. Brown stock is the traditional liquid for brown sauces. Although the time of preparation for brown stock is long, little supervision is required and large quantities can be made and frozen for future use. For a quick brown stock, use canned beef broth, but decrease the amount of salt specified in the recipe.

Brown sauce is the basic sauce for meats. It is also the basis of a variety of other sauces. Among its many derivative sauces are *espagnole, Madère, financière, poivrade,* and a host of others.

Your sauce will be as good as the ingredients you use and the care with which you make it. If you always use high quality butter, milk, cream, and wine, and if you always give your sauce your undivided attention when adding the last final touches, you will have a smooth, delicious accompaniment for that *pièce de résistance* with which to delight your family and guests.

When a sauce includes another sauce as an ingredient, that ingredient is marked with an asterisk to indicate that the recipe for it appears in this section.

Brown Stock

3 pounds beef and veal
  bones
1 pound short ribs of beef
1 cup sliced onions
½ cup sliced carrots
5 quarts water

2 teaspoons salt
4 peppercorns
2 sprigs parsley
1 bay leaf
½ teaspoon thyme

Spread the bones, meat, onions, and carrots in a shallow pan.
Bake in a 375° oven until very brown. Drain the fat. Transfer the
bones, meat, and vegetables to a deep kettle and add the water,
salt, peppercorns, parsley, bay leaf, and thyme. Bring to a boil;
cover and cook over low heat 4 hours. Strain, cool, and remove
all the fat. Pour into jars, cover tightly, and refrigerate or freeze.
Makes about 3 quarts.

Glace de Viande

MEAT GLAZE

Glace de viande is used for enriching brown sauces or any meat
gravy. Cook 3 cups completely skimmed Brown Stock* over low
heat until very thick and syrupy and reduced to about 1 cup.
Stir frequently. Pour into a clean jar, cover tightly, and keep in
the refrigerator. Use a tablespoon or two in stews, pot roast, or
other brown sauces.

Note: *Glace de viande* is available in jars in some specialty food
shops.

Brown Sauce

½ cup beef fat	1 bay leaf
1 carrot, sliced	2 sprigs parsley
1½ cups diced onions	¼ teaspoon thyme
⅓ cup flour	3 tablespoons canned
2 quarts Brown Stock*	tomato sauce
or beef broth	

Melt the fat in a heavy saucepan; sauté the carrot and onions until browned. Sprinkle with the flour and stir until dark brown. Slowly add the brown stock or broth, stirring constantly to the boiling point. Add the bay leaf, parsley, and thyme; cook over low heat 2 hours. Mix in the tomato sauce and cook 1 hour longer. Strain and season to taste. Use as a base for other sauces or serve with beef dishes.

Makes about 5 cups.

VARIATIONS:

Sauce Espagnole

2 tablespoons butter	2 cups Brown Sauce*
¾ cup chopped mushrooms	1 tablespoon Glace de
¼ cup dry sherry	Viande*

Melt the butter in a saucepan; sauté the mushrooms 5 minutes. Add the sherry and cook over medium heat until the liquid is reduced to half. Mix in the brown sauce and *glace de viande*. Cook over low heat 15 minutes. Serve with beef, ham, or game.

Makes about 2 cups.

Sauce au Madère

¾ cup Madeira or dry	1 cup Brown Sauce*
sherry	1 tablespoon cognac
1 tablespoon Glace de	2 tablespoons butter
Viande*	

Cook the wine until reduced to half; stir in the *glace de viande* and brown sauce. Cook over low heat 5 minutes, then add the cognac. Stir in the butter only until dissolved. Serve with *escalope* of veal, filet mignon, or other beef dishes.

Makes about 1½ cups.

Sauce Périgueux

To *Sauce au Madère** add 3 tablespoons chopped truffles. Serve with broiled or roast beef.

Makes about 1½ cups.

Sauce Financière

To *Sauce Périgueux,** add 1 cup diced sautéed sweetbreads and ½ cup diced sautéed chicken livers. Serve with broiled or roast fillet of beef.

Makes about 2¼ cups.

Sauce Poivrade

2 tablespoons olive oil	¼ cup wine vinegar
⅓ cup minced onions	2 cups Brown Sauce*
¼ cup grated carrots	Dash ground cloves
3 tablespoons minced parsley	¼ teaspoon freshly ground black pepper
½ cup dry red wine	

Heat the oil in a saucepan; sauté the onions, carrots, and parsley for 5 minutes. Add the wine and vinegar, cooking until reduced to half. Add the brown sauce; cook over low heat 30 minutes. Strain the sauce and return to a clean saucepan; stir in the cloves and the pepper. Cook over low heat for 5 minutes. Serve with game.

Makes about 2¼ cups.

Sauce Venaison

2 cups Sauce Poivrade*
1 teaspoon lemon juice
3 tablespoons currant jelly
3 tablespoons heavy cream

Combine all the ingredients in a saucepan. Heat. Serve with venison.
Makes about 2¾ cups.

Sauce Romaine

½ cup seedless raisins
1 cup boiling water
⅓ cup tarragon vinegar
¼ cup sugar
2 cups Brown Sauce*

Soak the raisins 10 minutes in the water. Drain. Cook the vinegar and sugar until caramelized. Mix in the brown sauce and raisins and cook over low heat 10 minutes. Serve with game, tongue, or ham.
Makes about 2¼ cups.

Sauce Chasseur

2 tablespoons olive oil
½ pound mushrooms, sliced
4 tablespoons minced
   shallots or onions
½ cup dry white wine
2 tablespoons tomato paste
1½ cups Brown Sauce*
¼ teaspoon freshly ground
   black pepper
1 tablespoon butter
1 tablespoon minced
parsley

Heat the oil in a saucepan; sauté the mushrooms 5 minutes. Add the shallots or onions, and sauté 2 minutes. Mix in the wine and cook over low heat until reduced to half. Stir in the tomato paste, brown sauce, and pepper. Cook 5 minutes. Blend in the butter and parsley. Serve with veal.
Makes about 1½ cups.

Sauce Diable

1 tablespoon butter	1 cup Brown Sauce*
3 tablespoons minced shallots or onions	1 teaspoon Worcestershire sauce
¼ cup cognac	⅛ teaspoon cayenne pepper

Melt the butter in a saucepan; sauté the shallots or onions 5 minutes. Add the cognac and cook until reduced to half. Mix in the brown sauce, Worcestershire sauce, and cayenne. Cook over low heat 5 minutes. Strain. Serve with beef dishes.
Makes about 1 cup.

Sauce Robert

2 tablespoons butter	1 teaspoon prepared mustard
3 tablespoons minced onions	¼ cup chopped gherkins
¼ cup wine vinegar	2 teaspoons minced parsley
1 cup Brown Sauce*	

Melt the butter in a saucepan; sauté the onions 5 minutes. Stir in the vinegar and cook until reduced to half. Mix in the brown sauce and cook over low heat 15 minutes; stir in the mustard, gherkins, and parsley just before serving. For pork or ham.
Makes about 1⅓ cups.

Sauce Portugaise

2 tablespoons butter	1 tablespoon tomato paste
2 tablespoons minced shallots or onions	½ cup peeled, diced tomatoes
½ cup dry red wine	1 cup Brown Sauce*

Melt the butter in a saucepan, sauté the shallots or onions 5 minutes. Add the wine and cook until reduced to half. Mix in the tomato paste, tomatoes, and brown sauce and cook over low heat 15 minutes. Correct the seasoning. Serve with broiled or roast beef.
Makes about 1½ cups.

Béarnaise Sauce

3 tablespoons tarragon
vinegar
¾ cup dry white wine
2 peppercorns
1 tablespoon finely chopped
shallots or onion
1 tablespoon finely chopped
fresh tarragon or 1
teaspoon dried

1 tablespoon finely chopped
fresh chervil or 1
teaspoon dried
3 egg yolks
½ teaspoon salt
1 cup melted butter
2 teaspoons minced
parsley
Dash cayenne pepper

Combine the vinegar, wine, peppercorns, shallots, tarragon, and chervil in a saucepan; cook over low heat until reduced to half. Beat the egg yolks and salt in a bowl; gradually add the wine mixture, beating steadily to prevent curdling. Gradually add the butter, beating steadily until the mixture is the consistency of very thick cream. Place over hot water and beat for a minute. Strain and add the parsley and cayenne pepper. If fresh herbs are used, add 1 teaspoon of each before serving. Serve with steak, fillet, or any broiled meat.
Makes about 1½ cups.

Raisin Sauce

2 tablespoons butter
½ cup chopped onions
½ cup brown sugar
¼ cup cider vinegar
½ teaspoon salt

1¼ cups beef broth
4 gingersnaps, crushed
¼ cup seedless raisins
1 lemon, thinly sliced

Melt the butter in a saucepan; sauté the onions 5 minutes. Mix in the brown sugar, vinegar, salt, and broth; bring to a boil and cook over low heat 5 minutes. Stir in the gingersnaps until dissolved. Add the raisins and lemon; cook 5 minutes. Serve with tongue or ham.
Makes about 2 cups.

Raisin-Almond Sauce

To the recipe for Raisin Sauce* add ¼ cup blanched, sliced almonds with the raisins.

Steak-Basting Sauce

½ cup olive oil
½ cup dry red wine
1 tablespoon A.1. Sauce
½ teaspoon freshly ground
  black pepper
¼ teaspoon thyme

Beat all the ingredients together. Brush the steak with the sauce several times during the broiling time.
Makes 1 cup.

Brown Horseradish Sauce

¼ cup butter
¼ cup minced onions
2 tablespoons flour
2 cups beef broth
½ cup cider vinegar
2 tablespoons sugar
½ cup prepared horseradish

Melt the butter in a saucepan; sauté the onions 5 minutes. Blend in the flour. Gradually add the broth, stirring steadily to the boiling point. Mix in the vinegar, sugar, and horseradish; cook over low heat 10 minutes. Taste for seasoning. Serve with boiled beef or tongue.
Makes about 2¼ cups.

White Horseradish Sauce

1 tablespoon cornstarch
1½ cups milk
½ cup freshly grated
  horseradish
2 tablespoons butter
1 teaspoon salt
⅛ teaspoon white pepper
1 teaspoon lemon juice

Mix the cornstarch and milk until smooth. Cook over low heat, stirring constantly to the boiling point, then cook over low heat 10 minutes longer. Add the horseradish, butter, salt, pepper, and lemon juice, stirring until butter melts. Serve with boiled beef.
Makes about 1¼ cups.

Salsa Salsiccia alla Calabria

SAUSAGE SAUCE, CALABRIA STYLE

1 pound sweet or hot Italian sausages	1 16-ounce can Italian-style tomatoes
2 tablespoons water	2 8-ounce cans tomato sauce
1 cup chopped onions	2 bay leaves
½ cup finely chopped celery	
1 tablespoon chopped parsley	

You may use a combination of sweet and hot sausages. Slice them and place the sausages and water in a skillet; cook until the sausages begin to fry. Add the onions, celery, and parsley; cook until the sausages brown, stirring frequently. Add the tomatoes, tomato sauce, and bay leaves; cover and cook over low heat for 1 hour, stirring occasionally. Uncover and cook 10 minutes longer. Discard the bay leaves, and taste for seasoning. Serve with any *pasta*.
Makes about 5 cups.

Salsa di Polpette
MEAT BALL SAUCE

2 slices white bread
1 cup water
½ pound ground beef
½ pound ground pork
½ cup grated Parmesan
  cheese
2½ teaspoons salt
1 teaspoon freshly ground
  black pepper

¼ teaspoon basil
2 cloves garlic, minced
2 tablespoons olive oil
½ cup chopped onions
1 29-ounce can Italian-style
  tomatoes
1 cup water
¼ teaspoon crushed dried
  chili peppers

Soak the bread in the water. Mash smooth and press dry. Mix together the bread, beef, pork, cheese, 1 teaspoon of the salt, pepper, basil, and 1 clove of the garlic. Shape into walnut-sized balls.

Heat the oil in a skillet; brown the meat balls in it. Add the onions, tomatoes, water, chili peppers, the remaining salt and garlic. Bring to a boil and cook over low heat 1½ hours. Taste for seasoning. Serve on any *pasta*.

Makes about 5 cups.

Ragù
BOLOGNESE SAUCE

2 tablespoons butter
¼ pound ham, cut julienne
¾ cup chopped onions
¼ cup chopped celery
½ cup grated carrots
¾ pound ground beef
½ pound calf's liver, diced
1½ tablespoons tomato
  paste

1¼ cups dry white wine
1 cup water
1 teaspoon salt
½ teaspoon freshly ground
  black pepper
⅛ teaspoon nutmeg
1 cup heavy cream

Melt the butter in a saucepan; sauté the ham, onions, celery, and carrots 10 minutes, stirring frequently. Add the beef; cook over medium heat, stirring almost constantly, until browned. Stir in the liver; cook 2 minutes. Blend in the tomato paste, then stir in the wine, water, salt, pepper, and nutmeg. Cover and cook over low heat 45 minutes, stirring frequently. Stir in the cream and taste for seasoning. Serve with *pasta* or use as a sauce for broiled or roast meat.

Makes about 3 cups.

Salsa Genovese

MEAT SAUCE, GENOA STYLE

3 dried mushrooms	2 cups peeled, chopped
3 tablespoons butter	tomatoes
¾ cup chopped onions	1½ teaspoons salt
¼ cup grated carrots	½ teaspoon freshly ground
¼ cup chopped celery	black pepper
½ cup ground veal	1 cup dry white wine
2 tablespoons flour	1¼ cups chicken broth

Wash the mushrooms, cover with warm water, and let soak 15 minutes. Drain, and slice fine.

Melt the butter in a saucepan; sauté the onions, carrots, and celery 5 minutes. Add the veal and mushrooms; cook over medium heat until browned, stirring almost constantly. Blend in the flour, then the tomatoes; cook 3 minutes. Stir in the salt, pepper, wine, and broth. Cover and cook over low heat 45 minutes. Taste for seasoning. Serve with veal dishes or *pasta*.

Makes about 3 cups.

Salsa di Carne

MEAT SAUCE

2 tablespoons olive oil
½ pound ground beef
½ pound ground pork
¾ cup chopped onions
1 clove garlic, minced
1 29-ounce can tomatoes
1 6-ounce can tomato paste
2 bay leaves

1 teaspoon basil
1½ teaspoons salt
¼ teaspoon dried ground
    chili peppers
2 tablespoons chopped
    parsley
2 tablespoons melted butter

Heat the olive oil in a saucepan. Mix in the beef, pork, onions, and garlic. Cook over high heat, stirring constantly, until the meat browns. Add the tomatoes, tomato paste, bay leaves, basil, salt, and chili peppers.

Cover and cook over low heat 1½ hours, adding water if the sauce becomes too thick. Taste for seasoning. Stir in the parsley and melted butter. Serve with any *pasta*.

Makes about 4 cups.

Barbecue Sauce

4 cups ketchup
½ cup prepared mustard
½ cup cider vinegar
½ cup Worcestershire sauce
2 tablespoons Tabasco
½ cup prepared horseradish
2 teaspoons salt

1 teaspoon freshly ground
    black pepper
1 tablespoon sugar
1 tablespoon garlic powder
1 teaspoon sage

Combine all the ingredients in a saucepan; bring to a boil. Use for basting spareribs, pork, or hamburgers.

Makes about 5 cups.

Index